EVOLVING CITIZENS

Exposing the Hidden Content

Michael B. Medland

BARCROFT Publishing

Publisher's Cataloging-in-Publication Data

Michael B. Medland
    Evolving citizens: Exposing the hidden content.
    by Michael B. Medland

    Includes index
    ISBN: 978-0-96-330091-1
    1. Early Childhood Education   2. Child Development
    3. Citizenship.   4. Learning
    I. Evolving citizens   II. Exposing the hidden content

Library of Congress Catalog Card Number: 2022946575
ISBN: 978-0-96-330091-1

First Published in 2022
Barcroft Publishing, Seaside, CA 93955
Printed in the United States of America
Printing: 10 9 8 7 6 5 4 3 2 1

Epigrams

At the margins of precision, the universe wavers.
Max Black
The Margins of Precision

No, Jim, we are the final frontier.
Mr. Spock
Reply to Cpt. James T. Kirk's edict

Dedication

To the children who will inherit planet Earth.
To the teachers who will teach them to manage it.

Acknowledgements

Thanks go to Nicholas Gardner for his superb editorial assistance. He challenged me at every turn to be consistent, grammatical, and logically correct, as well as "Get this thing done!" encouragement.

Preface

Evolving Citizens focuses on what children need to become participating and contributing citizens. This is not a new focus; these citizen attributes have been discussed for a long time—at least since the Age of Enlightenment. However, given our world's social and environmental problems, this text assumes that our social structures—those large and small—do not function as systems. They do not have the methods to work together to solve problems; we see this behavior on the nightly news.

Now, several other assumptions are needed. First, the method to build or repair systems is by fixing its members, so that they interact as a system. Second, for members to work together requires that they have repertoires (as complex behavior) that allows them to communicate and interact. Third, to modify our social systems, so that the forms of war are not the standard, requires evolving its members. Fourth, the "best way" to modify members is to evolve them from young children, so that they have the "repertoires of working together" from an early point.

Evolving Citizens focuses on the evolution of these repertoires within the classroom. The classroom is the place where nearly all children go to be "socialized" by the social structures in which they live. Answers are provided for three questions: 1) what are these content areas—these repertoires of behavior, 2) how do these repertoires interact, and 3) what do we, as their teachers, need to know about children and the classroom that will make it possible to teach them to become our future citizens?

Children gain a picture of themselves as part of a social system. The goal is to "instill" the content and interaction methods so children can take them into the adult world. Evolving Citizens does not argue for any particular approach within a particular discipline—it takes something from all of them. There is literally nothing new. There is just a reorganization of what has existed.

Evolving Citizens takes the educational system of classrooms and schools as they stand in most nations. These systems are already teaching the content—they just don't see the content pieces and their relationships for the same reason I did not: there is no systems picture of the content for instilling citizenship. Without it, the world's teachers will not be able teach these complex repertoires, so that children can solve the complex problems we are handing them. We must give children more than we have.

Because we are dealing with classrooms, I wrote the book as if talking to elementary school teachers. They stand between families and the rest of our children's education and how they handle their futures.

Apologia & Apology

This book touches on disciplines from genetics to sociology. As the book developed, many problems were encountered.

The first problem was in trying to integrate the terminologies of these disparate disciplines. The only solution found was to rename and redefine many terms, so that communication across chapters and readers remained consistent.

The next was finding a way to integrate these disciplines' content, so that the whole ball of wax fit together as a system that could represent the classroom as a practical problem-solving model. This model had to be capable of representing both the underlying behavioral and social mechanisms governing classroom interactions, as well as outlining a few operations based on these mechanisms, so that teachers would have a way to proceed and the content presented "made sense." This is the "logic" presented in Part 1.

The third was referencing all the background work done by these disciplines. Since this book says little if anything that is new, my approach was to reference the background work using only a few sources like Wikipedia and PubMed. This gives the reader easy access to the book's background by way of the links provided, which are functional in the PDF version. Only philosophy proved difficult. Here I had to cite a few original sources, which expose my leaning toward scientific and pragmatic methods to solve real-world problems.

The fourth was how to make this book readable. The logic of Part 1 and the content of Part 2 are so interdependent that the book will literally have to be reread to put the pieces of the classroom-members puzzle into clear, readable form. Please accept my apologies for inflicting a challenging read on all those interested in evolving citizens.

TAblE of CONTENTS

1

Introduction
Becoming Citizens

We live in a complex, evolving world. We seek to teach our children to handle this complexity. We want them to be cognitively, socially, and physically adaptive to complexity and its ever increasing nature. To solve this problem, we have established educational systems that seek, at least in the ideal, to give children the behaviors needed to handle the complexity that we are handing them. However, much appears to be amiss. This text takes the position that we have taken the right direction, but one that is not much more than a path: We have yet to "realize" or "sense" the content and their relationships that will make our educational systems consistently effective across the vast range of children who enter it.

This text began as a question about ensuring that young children were adaptive. But it soon became: Can we teach young children to be aware, rational, civil (ARC) citizens? The answer, in the end, depended on four types of knowledge. The first identifies what behaviors compose our aware, rational, civil young citizens. The second clarifies the interactions between these behaviors within groups of children in the classroom. These first two types fit together to form a system of behavior, one that allows children to handle the cognitive, social, and physical levels of complexity they will face. The third type of knowledge identifies the ways humans learn, both individually and socially. The fourth focuses on decisions about the content sequence and teaching methods to ensure that aware, rational, and civil citizens evolve within their classrooms.

This text focuses on content and the ways that humans learn. It presents answers to the first two types of knowledge (the content elements and their relationship). The third type, the ways humans learn, helps in discovering some of the teaching methods (operations) needed to ensure that our ARC citizens emerge. These first three types of knowledge help us organize the content into what most educators call a curriculum—our fourth type of knowledge. Although this text is not about teaching or organizing content, it is impossible to fully separate content from methodology. However, by exposing the mechanisms of individual and social learning, we are guided in finding the teaching operations (methods) needed for curriculum development.

1

Assumptions

This text makes many assumptions, but for now, here are six. First, communities want their children to be ARC-like citizens. Second, classrooms have a *moral-value purpose*; they exist to "foster" children to become citizens within some community context. Third, by starting early, the community has the best chance to *instill* children with ARC content, rather than be *authorities over them*. Fourth, to move forward, we need to unpack the content that makes up such citizens. Fifth, this unpacking needs to be organized into a model that represents 1) our future citizens, 2) the classroom environment in which children and teachers are emersed, and 3) a few problem-solving tools about individual and social learning that guide teachers in fostering ARC citizens. Only then will it be possible to rationally explore the teaching methods and organization of content that will increase the probability of children becoming ARC-like citizens. Finally, teachers need to gradually evolve the classroom into an ARC project.

As a classroom project, children gradually learn to investigate their own individual and social repertoires (ARC content) and learn to control them to meet the *valued purposes* that underpin all classroom activities, which are usually called their *learning objectives*. Building and implementing such a classroom is an engineering project, first undertaken by the teacher and later by its members, our children. All members become both the independent and dependent variables, the experimenter and experimentee, and the builder and buildee in a *complex adaptive system* called the classroom. They learn to "bootstrap" themselves into new forms of behavior. This system replicates the organization of the larger social system in which it is embedded. Over years, children engage in gathering knowledge, designing plans, and supervising themselves across the ever-widening range of classroom subsystems called *activities*. They ask questions and evaluate the answers by way of past and emerging evidence (rationality). They learn to manipulate the *means to achieve* its valued purpose ends in a group context. Hidden in all this doing is another assumption: Teachers are teaching both the individual and the group. Not one or the other, but both simultaneously.

Children are learning *with others* and, as a result, they must behave in ways that allow activities to begin, continue, and end. "Working with others" to achieve an activity's value-purpose (e.g., its learning objective) is their "civilness." They learn to see themselves as the subject matter of their project and to place themselves in objectivity's impersonal frame-of-reference (awareness). They become ARC in the only way possible: *in the context of others*.

Starting Point

Infants enter the world without aware, rational or civil (ARC) behaviors. They react toward others with behaviors that are built into their biology—

they cry, suckle, squirm, giggle, react to caregiver touch, listen to their speech, and observe and respond to their surrounding world with their pre-language repertoires. In return, their caregivers "nurture" them with food, water, touch, movement, speech, and objects. This is the very beginning of infants' civil (social interactive) behavior. They are learning how to interact *with* others, but they have no awareness or language about what they or others need or want. This reciprocal-interaction pattern between caregivers and infants gradually builds their initial social relationships—the methods they use to control each other to complete activities, be it "cooperating" enough to get their diaper changed, getting fed, learning to walk, opening a door, gaining hugs and kisses, or—if they are fortunate—learning to read or play music.

When these children enter the classroom, their tactics to control themselves and others are still those of neophytes. They still lack a language with which to talk about their civil (social) behavior; as a result, they can analyze or manipulate it, either their own or others. It is this language-practice combination that opens their eyes to the means and ends that surround them and their contributions in a wide variety of activity contexts. This combination gradually gives them an *awareness of themselves in the world of others*. They gain a language that allows them to talk about *who is doing what to or for whom*. Over years, this language of awareness expands as their knowledge of rational and civil behavior expands.

Today, we witness eye-opening events from various social movements that call for all types of political, social, and economic reforms. Should we wait until children are adults faced with the need for drastic reforms before they learn to observe parities and disparities in these practices and can talk about them with a clear and precise language? Should we wait until this later point before we allow them to engage in methods that control these practices? Or should we teach them from these early beginnings to observe and apply methods to solve the social problems that confront them? Could they, by the end of elementary school, have enough language about and practice at building social interactions that will guide them in solving the complex problems that we are leaving them?

Being to Becoming Citizens

Children, as neophyte citizens, enter the classroom to be taught and to practice—at least in an idealist sense—at becoming contributing citizens. However, children have already been influenced by the interaction of their first two nations of residence: their genetic endowment and their family history. Given their diverse backgrounds and the open-system complexity of the classroom, how can elementary teachers ensure children will become ARC citizens? The first step is understanding the content.

Rationality

Rationality has many specialized meanings across the range of human disciplines.[1] Rational thought and action are usually associated with such attributes as consistent reasoning; well-confirmed, evidence-based beliefs; and an ability to predict and, maybe, control the course of events in the world.[2, 3] These are "purpose-based" (goal-oriented) concerns. However, when we focus on ourselves with rational thought and action, we move outside the "comfort zone" of goal-orientation that has allowed humans to control nature and invent things, be they social structures or a host of mechanical and biological devices.

Rational citizens, for the purposes here, are those, who can think about and operate on the world around them, including themselves, through the use of unbiased evidence and the logical tools with which evidence is manipulated.

Acts of reasoning, in general, are defined as methods that build arguments that combine premises that lead to a conclusion. Here, conclusions emerge from the premises with which the discipline's members agree.[4, 5, 6] Yes, at the margins of knowledge the universe of disciplines have doubts and may well be wrong. But if members see the knowledge as "right enough," they should be able to move ahead. If not, they should be patient enough to wait for the evidence that deals with their doubts. No matter what path they take they must be prepared for both the rightness or wrongness exposed by the experience of gathering evidence.

Types of Reasoning

The types of reasoning have emerged through a long history of human activity. Out of this slow evolution, three types have emerged and been carefully studied.

Deductive reasoning was the first type of reasoning to be investigated. It deals with the structure (form) of an argument. Its elements—premises and conclusion—must be joined in specific ways. Deductive arguments are *valid* if they have an "accepted" form and invalid if it does not. Validity is only concerned with the relationships between the premises and conclusions.[7] The "trueness" or "reasonableness" of the premises and conclusions are not the focus. For example: All living thing are mortal & Ants are living things; Therefore, ants are mortal.

[1] https://en.wikipedia.org/wiki/Rationality

[2] von Wright, G. H. (1993). *The tree of knowledge and other essays.* p. 172-173. @ https://vdoc.pub/download/the-tree-of-knowledge-and-other-essays-1fd2d2c45ruo

[3] https://en.wikipedia.org/wiki/Rationality

[4] https://en.wikipedia.org/wiki/Reason_(argument)

[5] https://en.wikipedia.org/wiki/Logical_reasoning

[6] https://en.wikipedia.org/wiki/Propositional_calculus

[7] https://en.wikipedia.org/wiki/Deductive_reasoning

Inductive reasoning deals with the *support* that premises give to a conclusion, often called a hypothesis. If the premises' evidence strongly support (are reasonable) then the argument's conclusion is said to be strong. If not, it is weak.[8] There is no single form to these, but the premises may be "wrongly" assembled.[9]

Abductive reasoning deals with finding premises that appear to support some desired (i.e., believed) conclusion, and uses evidence to evaluate the conclusion and the premises as well. Relative to inductive reasoning, it involves the building of two predictive arguments. The first is a *planning prediction* that may or may not be supported by acquired knowledge and methods. The second is an *evaluative prediction* based on the evidence observed during and after implementation. The evaluative prediction more or less "confirms" or "challenges" the planning prediction to some degree. The evidence from the plan's means or its ends may confirm or challenge the planning prediction. Ideally, all human plans have a purpose and are clear enough to be evaluated against that the plan's stated means and ends.

Abduction is the only type of reasoning that appears to allow 1) for new ideas to be brought forward and 2) provides for the possibility, with repeated adjustments, to *converge toward* the truth.[10] The truth we seek here is the convergence toward a *social value* by way of these arguments.[11] A great deal of science, engineering, and art proceeds in this way. *The criterion for acceptance is success.* However, success has many facets. It can be related, in general, to the plan's means or ends or both. The classroom's first *value purpose* is the *learning objective* selected by the community—something they want children to learn. If all children learn, then teachers can move forward. If some don't learn, then teachers adjust the means to get to the intended end, at least ideally.

In human planning, we know what we want to answer—there is a purpose that we value. It is here called the *valued purpose* of an activity, something to achieve. Educating children has a great many *valued purposes* that span the curricula, but it also has a *moral values* component: we want children to "work with others" within the community's social-interactive structures. We want to live together without extensive conflict. It is this moral component that is one of the problems that must be solved to achieve ARC citizens. But we have to find the way to get there. There are means and ends, but there are also many unknowns. Additionally, there are resource restrictions (facts, materials, and theories). Yet, plans are still built to achieve the *moral-valued purpose* regardless of known and unknown risks. It is the implementation that exposes the extent to which a plan achieves its valued

[8] https://en.wikipedia.org/wiki/Inductive_reasoning
[9] https://en.wikipedia.org/wiki/Informal_fallacy
[10] Black, Max. (1970). *Margins of precision.* Ithaca, NY: Cornell University Press. Page 81-82.
[11] https://en.wikipedia.org/wiki/Abductive_reasoning

purpose and its moral-valued purpose. Both planning and its implementation expose the extent to which children are evolving into ARC citizens. But just what does it expose? When we can answer this question, we will know, at least approximately, what being an ARC citizen entails.

Truth

In abductive reasoning, the *truth-of-an-argument* is compared against its valued purpose. The comparison tells us the extent of the argument's effectiveness. This is just another way of saying "with some degree of success." We seek an evidence-based planning argument that appears "sufficient" or "satisficing" for achieving a valued purpose. Yet, we are always bound by our limited rationality.[12] We have a qualified truth or something that is *true enough* for now [13] that moves us forward.

Every entity designed, modified, or built by humans—from classrooms to governments, from wheels to space vehicles, from hypotheses to theories—began as an argument, or a question that spurred forming an argument. We evaluate these arguments during the design, evaluation, and long-term follow up phases of planning—one of the main tools for developing rational behavior based on evidence. When our belief in a plan appears true enough, we begin to implement it or start to build a prototype.

Civilness

At the most abstract level, civilness refers to a humanistic attitude, stance, or perspective toward life in the context of others with whom we live.[14] When this "perspective" becomes behavior (action), we are talking about human moral values.

> *Moral values are rule statements about how*
> *we "relate," "treat," or "interact" with others.*

If we strip away the political, religious, and cultural elements that surround the history of moral discussions, they all refer to how we interact with each other. To say that someone is civil is to evaluate (judge) their interactions with others against this set of moral-value statements.[15] Thus, one is to some degree either civil or uncivil toward others against these moral rule statements.

The *moral statements* are designed by the social environment. When individuals establish a government, they design constitutions that specify what citizens can and can't do. These documents are *moral-value statements*. Being able to speak out, assemble, or seek justice are moral values, as are not assaulting, injuring, or murdering.

---

[12] https://en.wikipedia.org/wiki/Bounded_rationality
[13] Elgin, Catherine Z. (2017). *True enough*. Cambridge, MA: The MIT Press.
@ https://vdoc.pub/download/true-enough-3mji8fkfkuog

[14] https://en.wikipedia.org/wiki/Humanism
[15] https://en.wikipedia.org/wiki/Morality

With instantaneous worldwide communication, newscasts provide evidence that the problems of humanity are caused by the way humans interact across the globe. Yes, problems can arise out of ignorance about the "impact" our behavior has on the social and natural environments. But often these problems arise because some citizens have moral values that sanction events like fraud, murder, sex trafficking, and terrorism.

The exact form of these moral-value statements depends on two factors: 1) the social structures that are established and 2) the founders' civil (moral) perspective toward other members. These statements are often vague and ambiguous about the morals outlined. As a consequence, conflicts often arise and are exaggerated as time passes and social complexity increases.

However, our social environment of interest is the elementary classroom. The valued purposes of classroom activities require children to interact. This interacting requires *moral values* just as they do in the larger social system. As a *set of statements*, moral values indicate how children *should* interact, so that their activities can begin, continue, and end as planned.[16, 17] As *moral citizens*, they are or are not civil toward themselves or others. Classrooms, like all social structures, have "laws" or "rules of conduct" specifying behaviors that allow activities to begin, continue, and end. When *what-should-have-been-done* between children has been done, it is called *civil behavior*. When it is not, it is called *uncivil*.

Our civilness focuses on two types of interactive behaviors. *Civil behavior* denotes interactions (social relationships) with others, be they an individual, a group, or the world. It is often associated with 1) "polite" behavior towards others and 2) the *rights* they have within a structure. *Civic behavior* denotes social behavior within a structure that focuses on one kind of interactions: *duties*,[18] which are often called responsibilities or obligations, depending on the context.[19] Thus, governments, at all levels including the classroom, give us *rights* in various spheres of human activity (biological, social, political, cultural, economic, environmental) and *duties* in these same spheres. Our civilness can be seen as a harmony or tension between rights and duties.

When we define our civil or civic behavior—as through a constitution and its laws—we are talking about our *moral values*. *Civil* and *civic* are two words that represent the two sides of our *moral-value statements: rights* and *duties*. The question, when working out these rights and duties for the classroom, focuses on "demarcating" the relationship between the two. Does either one take precedence over the other, or are they reciprocally weighted?

---

[16] https://en.wikipedia.org/wiki/Morality
[17] https://en.wikipedia.org/wiki/Value_theory
[18] https://connected.socialstudies.org/blogs/cynthia-resor/2019/01/20/civic-behavior-and-civil-behavior-whats-the-differ
[19] https://en.wikipedia.org/wiki/Moral_responsibility

For every *right* allowed does someone have a *duty* to help achieve and maintain it? For every *duty* undertaken does someone gain a *right*? Chapter 9 examines this issue.

Face-to-Face Interactions

Children's problems emerge with other parts of the system. In the classroom, this involves *face-to-face interactions* with other children and their teacher. It is at this interaction point that rational and civil (moral) behavior breaks down. This failure goes well beyond that of just our children. We observe this failure between adults, corporations, states, and nations on a daily basis. At times, these failures are called law breaking, corporate fraud and deceit, high crimes and misdemeanors, and crimes against humanity. Should we prepare children for the future by giving them methods to observe, promote, and correct their interactions in the classroom? If so prepared, could problems like those of human suffering to environmental pollution be solvable as well?

Rational and moral behavior occurs in nearly every human activity —even in the play of children. In families, classrooms, organizations, and governments, rational and civil (moral) behavior *can become* an *aware, intentional* behavior. But only if we know what to be aware about.

Given the advances in science and technology, rational behavior is not the problem. But it is not enough to create adaptive social structures. The problem is in the ways that children are taught to interact. They have yet to learn *the moral use of rational behavior for some value-purpose like educating children or saving the planet*. Can we make rational and moral behavior overt and, thus, teachable? If we can, then the behaviors can be observed, evaluated, and changed to achieve not only our value-purposes but our moral values as well. If want to make rational and moral behavior a part of children's repertoires, we must answer the following question. Do we want our activities to be moral in the sense of achieving equality or enslaving others? Or something else?

The *qualities* of aware, rational, and civil behavior expand throughout life. Communities across the world set up *social-technical development systems* like education to do this work. Do we want to give children the means (social-technical behaviors) and ends (social-evaluation behaviors) to adapt to their future needs? Simultaneously, do we want to ensure that they do not become slaves to the social system or some subsystem? Do we want their social-technical behaviors powerful enough, so that when the world is theirs, they can adapt it into something that they find beautiful and inspiring?

Rationality and civilness are not separate when we study ourselves *in the world*. Both involve aware and, then, intentional actions of citizens. Our civilness can be rationally evaluated against evidence if both the *moral-value statements* and the *behavior toward others* are clear and unambiguous. Both the means to achieve ends and the ends achieved within an activity requires behaviors toward others where everyone seeks their rights and undertakes their duties. When considering ourselves as citizens in any cultural plan—like schooling children—we are performing an "experiment" on ourselves. Do we want our educational structures to be "right enough" to give children a brighter future? We will only know through rational planning, which is achieved through abductive reasoning practices.

Repertoires of Human Behavior

The model of an aware, rational, civil citizen contains four inclusive repertoires of behavior—moral values, awareness, management, and technical—as well as their relationship. The technical repertoires are seen as a long and winding road from the domain of language arts to those of the sciences, arts, and humanities. At some point, moral values, awareness, and management are also technical because they, like classical technical repertoires, need to be directly taught. However, moral value, awareness, and management repertoires guide the use of the classical technical repertoires in order to achieve the value purposes within and, eventually, outside the classroom. These four repertoires are introduced here.

Technical Repertoires

Today, we talk about two technical repertoire (curriculum) areas. The first includes Science, Technology, Engineering, and Mathematics (STEM).[20] The second is the Humanities, Arts, and Social Sciences (HASS).[21] Closely related to HASS is SHAPE, which refers to Social Science, Humanities, and Arts for People and the Economy.[22] STEM has been given a degree of curriculum clarity and the others are following suit. Their value-purpose is to give children systems of thought and action to observe and solve problems. The problem may be to invent a theory, build an artifact like a baby bottle, clean the oceans of plastics, or induce an emotional state through a work of art.

These technical behaviors are usually the *value-purpose objectives* of classroom activities. They represent a fine-grained valued purpose within the educational system. Some technical behavior is involved in every human activity. When children learn to talk, eat, use the potty, and walk, they are learning technical repertoires that support future repertoire learning. When children enter a classroom, the first four technical repertoires that they learn are called listening, speaking, reading, and writing in the context of others.

---

[20] https://en.wikipedia.org/wiki/Science,_technology,_engineering,_and_mathematics
[21] https://en.wikipedia.org/wiki/Humanities,_arts,_and_social_sciences
[22] https://en.wikipedia.org/wiki/Social_Sciences,_Humanities_and_the_Arts_for_People_and_the_Economy

With these, they have a chance to learn other technical repertoires that are members of the sciences, humanities, and arts.

Technical repertoires are seen by most nations of the world as critical to later success, cultural survival, and continued understanding of our rapidly changing world.[23] All but five sovereign nations of the world have, thus, made education compulsory.[24] But these technical repertoires do not stand alone, nor do those like listening, speaking, read, and writing. Even play and relaxation activities require some technical behaviors. *However, this text says nothing about the content and methods related to any of these "standard" or "classical" technical repertoires.* They are known, even if the opportunities to learn them varies greatly across classrooms, schools, and nations.

It is the other three repertoires—moral values, awareness, and management—on which the classical technical repertoires move forward. However, these have remained hidden.

The goal is to analyze these three repertoires, so that we know what needs to be taught, as well as to show how they support the classic technical ones.

Management Repertoire

The *management repertoire* guides our technical repertoires, so that they are performed efficiently and effectively. Management is as technical as STEM or SHAPE repertoires. It is based on a human history of exploration like what has advanced all other technical domain repertoires. Like them, management has gradually winnowed out (discarded) management practices that do not work; there is no magic or mysticism involved. This does not mean that what has been discarded has been discarded by all; witness how long it took for doctors to start washing their hands and stop letting blood once the objective evidence was found and disseminated. The classic technical repertoires have been in gradual development for about four centuries. But the management of social-technical systems has only been in development for about seventy-five years; yet much has been learned. But as of yet little has been disseminated—it is not yet cultural lore like the Earth is round, is the third planet in the solar system, and circles the sun. This text steps towards making management common knowledge lore.

Herbert Simon points out that the management repertoire is composed of a host of behaviors that are situation specific.

---

[23] National Research Council. 2012. *A Framework for K-12 Science Education: Practices, Crosscutting Concepts, and Core Ideas.* Washington, DC: The NAP. https://doi.org/10.17226/13165.

[24] https://en.wikipedia.org/wiki/Compulsory_education

Behaving like a manager means having command of a whole range of management skills and applying them whenever they become appropriate.[25]

Mario Bunge identified management behavior in terms of its function within a situation (i.e., activity).

The management of an organization is the regulation, in particular the coordination, of the social behaviors of its members in view of the efficient performance of the tasks of the organization.[26]

The management repertoire presented is a system that consists of a set of sub-repertoires that are called *strategies*—Simon's "management skills." Each is applied relative to a "context of need" within an activity. This need may or may not be planned. The strategies represent the social behavior used to guide the beginning, continuing, or ending of the technical behavior of an activity—Bunge's efficient coordination of tasks (i.e., activities). The value purpose of a classroom activity is usually called the *technical behavior* being taught or practiced—the *objective* of the activity. The technical behavior may

SCIENCE FRAMEWORK

Science and Engineering Practices

1. Asking Questions/Defining Problems
2. Designing & Using Models
3. Plan & Carryout Investigations
4. Analyzing & Interpreting Data
5. Using Mathematics & Computational Thinking
6. Constructing explanation & Designing Solutions
7. Building Arguments from Evidence
8. Obtaining, Evaluating, & Communicating Information

Crosscutting Concepts

1. Patterns
2. Cause & Effect / Mechanism & Explanation
3. Scale, Proportion, & Quantity
4. Systems & System Models
5. Energy & Matter / Flows, Cycles, & Conservation
6. Structure & Function
7. Stability & Change

BOX 1.1: NRC's Framework for K-12 Science Education: Practices, Crosscutting Concepts, and Core Ideas.

---

[25] Simon, Herbert. (1997). *Administrative behavior, 4th edition.* New York: Simon & Schuster. p. 139. (First edition was published in 1948).

[26] Bunge, Mario. (1989). *Treatise of Basic Philosophy, Volume 8. Ethics: The good and the right.* Boston, MA: D. Reidel Publishing. p. 349.

be reading a book, solving a math problem, determining why one can't see in the dark, or inventing a method to capture and recycle ocean-bound plastics. At the advanced stages, the lines between classic technical disciplines and the management strategies blurs. This blurring occurs because all four repertoires to some degree, at some point in time, require the practices and concepts involved in solving problems related to human social behavior. The National Research Council identifies these scientific and engineering practices and concepts (Box 1.1). They are used to solve and bring about any complex activity, be it in a classroom, operating room, or laboratory.

Management is a social technology or sociotechnology like logic, mathematics, science, and government. All of these are designed by us for us—for our purposes, moral or otherwise. They help us create, discover, and work together—or they do not.[27, 28] The management strategies do so, in part, because they are, first, a set of *verbal-behavior guides* that promote observing, communicating, and evaluating the methods of managing our social interactions to achieve the moral and valued purposes of an activity. If carried out as designed, each instance of a management behavior is an instance of the *civil (moral) behavior* that keeps the flow of an activity moving forward.

When management behavior is clear and observable, it can be evaluated against the moral values of the classroom. Thus, it can be taught, changed, and strengthened like any technical behavior found in the arts and sciences. We see the context, select a management strategy, implement it, evaluate the outcomes, and redesign it if the evidence suggests doing so. This is exactly what scientists and artists do to invent and create changes in the world.

Managing as a Set of Strategies

Seven strategies make up the management repertoire. Each strategy is a sub-repertoire like the sub-routines of a dance or gymnastic routine. They are classified as strategies because: 1) each consists of behavioral steps (small operations); 2) they can be applied to all human activities as needed; 3) they strongly ensure that the activities undertaken will be completed successfully; and 4) they *can* contribute to the harmonious relations between activity members.

Graphic 1.1 identifies management's sub-repertoires, the strategies. Each consists of five steps (subclasses of a strategy). Each of these steps is made up of a number of action and decision elements (lower subclasses of behavior). These are not shown but detailed in Section 2 of this text. Together, the steps and decisions guide children in applying the strategies

---

[27] https://en.wikipedia.org/wiki/Social_technology
[28] Bunge, Mario. (1985). *Treatise of basic philosophy, volume 7—Epistemology & methodology III. Part II: Life science, social science, and technology*. Hingham, MA: Kluwer Academic. p. 274-278. ISBN: 90-277-1913-6.

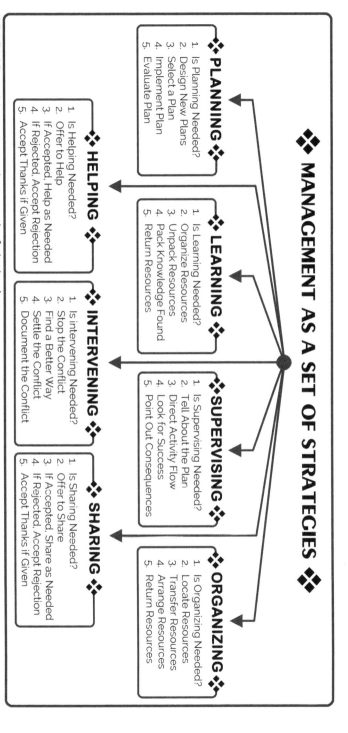

❖❖ **MANAGEMENT AS A SET OF STRATEGIES** ❖❖

❖ **PLANNING** ❖
1. Is Planning Needed?
2. Design New Plans
3. Select a Plan
4. Implement Plan
5. Evaluate Plan

❖ **HELPING** ❖
1. Is Helping Needed?
2. Offer to Help
3. If Accepted, Help as Needed
4. If Rejected, Accept Rejection
5. Accept Thanks if Given

❖ **LEARNING** ❖
1. Is Learning Needed?
2. Organize Resources
3. Unpack Resources
4. Pack Knowledge Found
5. Return Resources

❖ **INTERVENING** ❖
1. Is Intervening Needed?
2. Stop the Conflict
3. Find a Better Way
4. Settle the Conflict
5. Document the Conflict

❖ **SUPERVISING** ❖
1. Is Supervising Needed?
2. Tell About the Plan
3. Direct Activity Flow
4. Look for Success
5. Point Out Consequences

❖ **SHARING** ❖
1. Is Sharing Needed?
2. Offer to Share
3. If Accepted, Share as Needed
4. If Rejected, Accept Rejection
5. Accept Thanks if Given

❖ **ORGANIZING** ❖
1. Is Organizing Needed?
2. Locate Resources
3. Transfer Resources
4. Arrange Resources
5. Return Resources

GRAPHIC 1.1: Management as a set of strategies

effectively. The set of strategies are learned over years to ensure proficiency. Like any social technology, these strategies can undergo change as our knowledge changes. But the consistent use of the *language of management*, as outlined in Graphic 1.1 and detailed in Section 2 of this book, is critical. Socio-technologies only cleanly emerge when a consistent and unambiguous language of content and methods exist, as the STEM and SHAPE repertoires illustrate. We need to establish a language of management, so that we talk unambiguously about human behavior when trying to design and develop *social structures*, so that all citizens can operate within them.

Initially, each strategy is set in motion with a discrimination query like "Is organizing needed?" or "Is planning needed?" If answered in the affirmative, the strategy is set in motion. When activities become complex, each step of each strategy can be expanded with additional sub-step discrimination queries that help ensure that the strategy remains successful. Chapters 11-17 analyze these steps and their sub-step discriminations.

The terms and operations identified in Graphic 1.1 were selected because they can be easily demonstrated to young children through direct instruction techniques that can involve children in modeling strategy use. The classroom offers them numerous activities in which to observe and practice them *with others*. However, the language used to model each strategy and the sets of examples that define the range and limits of each step must be clear, as well as consistently and persistently used.

The sooner children can read, the easier both the teaching and learning of the strategies becomes. Each strategy is brought out into the open (made overt) as a wall posting and gradually expanded to include the additional sub-step discrimination queries. Displaying the strategies both prompts strategy usage and gives children a chance to reflect on when and how they are using them. This reduces the chance of *non-functional management behavior* slowing or stopping an activity from achieving its valued purpose.

MANAGEMENT AS A SYSTEM OF STRATEGIES

Graphic 1.2 illustrates how the strategies form a system: they work together to begin, continue, and complete any activity. Children move from planning, to organizing, to supervising. If they can't complete the plan for whatever reason, they turn to the learning strategy. When they think the plan can be followed, they begin organizing and supervising as the plan indicates. As the plan's implementation progresses, they help, share, and resolve conflicts as needed.

After an activity has been completed, they return to planning to evaluate success and re-plan if the activity outcomes were not those desired or to try an activity in a new way. However, we don't begin with the system, but with organizing. It is required of every human activity—resources must be in the right place at the right time.

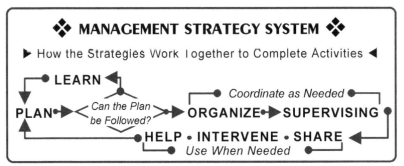

GRAPHIC 1.2: Management as a system of strategies.

The *management system cycle* (Graphic 1.2) never ends, but for most activities much remains the same and only small changes are required. The possibility of small changes is key to teaching the more complex strategies, especially planning and intervening. For example, once children have been taught and have practiced strategies like organizing, helping, and sharing, they can plan other ways to perform them within one or more of their existing activities. Thus, complex strategies are introduced through micro-problems. They operate on a part, not the whole activity.

In general, once a strategy is learned, practiced, and successfully performed, children can attend to both the teaching and their learning as the activity unfolds. Reciprocity emerges between teaching and learning as the management and moral repertoires are expanded.

MANAGEMENT & TECHNICAL REPERTOIRE RELATIONSHIPS

Both the technical and management repertoires are *moral-value neutral*. We have used them to design and build the good, the bad, or the ugly. We can use technical expertise in nuclear energy to build weapons of mass destruction or highly safe fourth-generation reactors that generate electricity, hydrogen, or clean water. We can use management strategies to foster chaos or harmony, or to build democracies or tyrannies. If those involved don't know much about the technical or the managerial, then there is a good chance that chaos will prevail. As the 2020 Covid-19 pandemic glued everyone to newscasts, we witnessed the abuses to citizen groups and the dysfunctional behavior of Earth's governments. What children need to avoid such behavior are languages about and methods to proceed with rational and civil awareness. With these, they can learn to 1) observe if their or others' behavior does or does not fit the moral values and purposes behind their human activities and 2) do something about both the behavioral fits and misfits.

Learning technical repertoires like STEM or HASS have a *valued purpose*. However, they are not related to moral values. They are repertoires that allow us to invent, design, and do things in the world. It is the management repertoire that makes it possible to evaluate children's (and our own) congruence between the *moral values* and *management behavior* in an ongoing activity,[29, 30] both in terms of the activity's means and ends. This evaluation is made possible because:

> *Every instance of management behavior represents either a fit or nonfit with a moral value statement.*

Both the management repertoire and moral-value statements focus on the relationship between members—their interactions during an activity. If children learn to perform the management behavior, then they take the first step toward observing and evaluating their fit (congruence) with the classroom's moral value statements. However, this observing and evaluating requires two more clearly defined repertoires: moral values and awareness.

Moral-Values Repertoire

A *moral-values repertoire is a verbal (language-based) repertoire* that takes the form of statements (speech, text, graphics) that express *what relationships should exist between citizens.* They are *rule statements* that guide managing ourselves. Within the classroom, the "should" can more accurately be replaced with "needs to" because without this set of behaviors, the valued purpose of an activity could not be achieved. This view of values focuses only on *moral values.*[31] We are not concerned with valuing vegetables over grains, sports over reading, card playing over chess, or handshakes over bowing. A moral values repertoire is a *social technology* invented by humans, so that we can relate to each other in ways that ensure activity behaviors (as means) achieve their ends. The question is, what do we want to promote? Is it human wellbeing and becoming, or something else?

All science-based disciplines have a moral code that involves how discipline members must behave towards themselves, others in the profession, and subjects involved in research. These are moral values that involve standards like unbiased objectivity, replication, and the accurate representation of data; the second with sharing and full disclosure; and the third with the relationships between researchers and their subjects.

These moral value statements go by several descriptions that include code-of-conduct,[32] pro-social behaviors,[33] and in the present case "classroom duties." The focus is on *who-is-doing-what-to-or-for-whom*, which requires an awareness of the *moral-management fit or nonfit* that is taking place *in-the-moment*. In the classroom, duties (classroom rules) represent the moral values required to keep the social structure moving harmoniously forward

---

[29] Bunge, Mario. (1989). *Treatise of modern philosophy, Volume 8. Ethics: The good and the right.* Boston, MA: Reidel. Chapter 8, especially pgs. 264-270.
[30] https://en.wikipedia.org/wiki/Research#Research_ethics
[31] https://en.wikipedia.org/wiki/Morality
[32] https://en.wikipedia.org/wiki/Code_of_conduct
[33] https://en.wikipedia.org/wiki/Prosocial_behavior

toward its valued purpose. To instill children with a "sense of moral values" requires 1) a clear classroom (social) structure, 2) direct teaching of the management behavior needed to begin, continue, and end activities, 3) linking management behavior with the moral value statements (classroom duties), and 4) ensuring that the technical behavior of the activity is learned.

Moral value statements—like any known (believed) fact—control our individual or social behavior. At all levels of government, including the classroom, these moral value statements are almost always vague, ambiguous, or negatively expressed. Often, they are never clearly evaluated by the evidence from our implemented plans. As a result, we *discipline* children. We do not teach them to *discipline themselves*, which involves teaching them to observe, evaluate, and, if needed, correct their own interactions. This amounts to teaching them a *system of justice* as we teach them the value purpose of an activity. Thus, a system of justice is embedded in our *system of education*. From another perspective, we are always teaching the group, as well as individuals.

We have all observed managerial behavior that is not civil. We see the modern version of non-civil abuse in the insidious schemers, cyber scammers, those who use children for purposes of cheap production, and the scientists who abuse human subjects or build weapons of mass destruction. Often, all of them have strong technical repertoires and they may even have strong a management repertoire, but the consequences of their behavior abuses others (i.e., it is non-civil).

> *Being given a technical repertoire does not ensure civility.*
> *Being given a managerial repertoire does not ensure civility.*

Civilness does not, with any assuredness, arise with trained technical or managerial behavior. Our civility, especially in a complex society, arises only by being instilled though directly exposing the relationships and consequences between moral values, management, and technical repertoires across a range of activities. This exposure brings about an *awareness* of the interactions of these three repertoires of behavior across all members.

AWARENESS REPERTOIRE

Awareness is a *meta-language repertoire* that describes a field of investigation.[34] The most common example of a meta-language is English grammar. It describes English utterances (e.g., parts of speech and syntactic relationships), evaluates an utterance's correctness to the grammatical standard, acknowledges the well-formed statements, and helps correct any of the nonstandard utterances within the range of allowed grammatical options.

---

[34] https://en.wikipedia.org/wiki/Metalanguage

Awareness has nothing to do with acting on the world. Here, awareness is a "cognitive," "thinking," "verbal," or "communicative" repertoire used to observe, describe, and evaluate the behavioral congruence between members management behavior and the moral values of a group who pursue an activity's valued purpose. Essentially, the management repertoire directs the means and the technical repertoires represents an activity's ends, either of which may be congruent or not (roughly). Awareness encompasses both the means used and the ends obtained.

Children's management behavior, no matter what its evaluation, has varying degrees of control over other children. The main synonyms for control include induce, influence, direct, persuade, socialize, govern, regulate, manipulate, and indoctrinate. When we talk about methods to alter others, we switch our view from an *awareness repertoire perspective* to *being a manager* acting on other members. However, awareness is the "lead" repertoire because it sets other management behavior in motion. Once a congruence or non-congruence between the two repertoires is evaluated, then the needed management behavior can be employed.

Since the technical and management repertoires are moral-value neutral, we must have a way to describe, compare, and evaluate if there is either congruence or not between a management behavior and moral value statements. This is one's *awareness repertoire.* The members can evaluate the degree of congruence with moral values, their fit, and move forward with the needed management behavior. The members' management behaviors are classified either *cohesive* (congruent) or *coercive* (non-congruent) relative to the classroom's moral values statements. The former supports the moral values of the activity and the latter does not. Both management and technical repertoires, as said, can be used to bring about the good, the bad, and the ugly. However:

Only management needs to be directly connected to moral values.

This statement is supported by two facts about relationships. First, management behavior controls the use of technical behavior; it both selects what technical behavior to perform and consequents it (Chapter 3). Second, if children fail to learn the technical behavior being taught, it is a problem for teachers and the social, scientific, and technical communities in which teachers are embedded and trained.

Observing the *moral-management relationships* represents the first step toward evaluating anyone's management behavior as cohesive (congruent) or coercive (non-congruent) toward others.

Because we are interested in young child, there is no need to try to unpack the labyrinth of social influence theory and its experiments involving agents and their agency.[35, 36, 37, 38] They focus on "adults" and have not defined content structures for either agents or their agency. Here we talk about managers and their management repertoire. We are concerned with children *becoming aware, rational, civil (moral) citizens*. We are, thus, concerned with specifying and providing a history of experiences that evolve children into becoming such citizens. Only with clear content, can we begin to find methods to achieve our ends even if they are different from what was the case for us and our forebears.

Awareness requires *situational awareness*—the observation of the extent to which management behavior occurs *in-the-moment* as an activity proceeds. Only *in-the-moment awareness* can help children evaluate and do something about moral-management congruence or non-congruence. When such awareness can be performed, then the *awareness evaluation* can be used to plan activities that avoid or promote the management and technical behavior required for activity success in terms of both its means (everyone behaves in ways that helps it begin, continue, or end) and achieving its ends (everyone learns the behavior being taught).

A good chunk of awareness, as a *linking repertoire* between the management and moral value, answers the question: *Who is doing what to or for whom in the moment*? The "doing what" can be classified on a continuum from cohesive to coercive management. There are degrees of congruence between management behavior and moral values. Human laws define and evaluate all sorts of non-congruence, but seldom evaluates *congruence* with anything like the same voracity.

Promoting, evaluating and acknowledging the congruent is critical to instilling moral values and fostering cohesive groups.

Only by exposing and exploring the breadth of what should and could be done will children know what to do and can become aware of the consequent events that occur through the means used and the ends obtained. *Non-congruence only exposes what should not be done.* Achieving cohesive management behavior is the end game if the educational system has the long-range purpose of *children becoming aware, rational, and civil (ARC) citizens.*

INSEPARABLE RELATIONSHIPS

The morals, awareness, management, and technical repertoires are inseparable. Essentially, moral values and management, if clear and unambiguous repertoires, allow us to observe, evaluate, and change either behavior. Yet, this can only happen if an awareness repertoire is based on

---

[35] https://en.wikipedia.org/wiki/Social_influence
[36] https://en.wikipedia.org/wiki/French_and_Raven%27s_bases_of_power#/Coercive_power
[37] https://www.sciencedirect.com/topics/social-sciences/social-influence/pdf
[38] https://en.wikipedia.org/wiki/Psychological_manipulation

the criterion of unbiased (impersonal) objectivity toward evidence (as what is observed) and the use of rational management methods to untangle who is doing what to whom.

Children can become *the managers of their own becoming*, but to do so they must be taught to observe behavior in-the-moment and evaluate it (awareness) and, then, do something about it (management repertoire). This most assuredly requires that they know *what to do*—how one manages oneself during an interaction with others to promote congruence and correct its absence. However, we have never directly taught children moral, management, or awareness repertoires. Most certainly we have not directly taught their relationship. Teaching the relationships helps ensure that the repertoires are instilled in children.

However, even if well taught, these three repertoires are not sufficient for citizens to become ARC citizens. They need advanced technical repertoires for something to be done in the world. For example, most environmental issues that confront us are solvable with advanced technologies, but it is the lack of instilled values, awareness, and management repertoire relationships that keep us from moving toward solutions. It is by teaching all four repertoires (moral, management, awareness, and advanced technical repertoires) and, especially, their relationships that instill ARC behavior.

Humanity is now—with instantaneous world-wide communications—beginning to gain a *world-level awareness*. Today, much of this awareness is not pretty. To allow children the chance to move from where we are now to where *they* want to be, we will have to give them all four repertoires. They will need to be clear and unambiguous, taught, and related. Only then will children have a chance to solve the problems that we are handing them. How we teach and coordinate values, management, and awareness will determine if their science- to art-based repertoires will help them survive and solve the problems we are leaving them.

What we observe worldwide is a *me/my perspective*. Those who are controlling are often called *agents*. They are the "powerful"—no matter how they got that way. Often, they are out to protect their own or their groups' wealth, to control over human activities, or to keep things as they are without regard to social and technological advances. The local *we/us perspective* of the classroom, where it exists, has not managed to become a regional- or world-level reality, which has been recently referred to as the *intergenerational we/us perspective* (Chapter 19).

Presently, we see this tug-of-war between the me/my and the we/us perspectives in social activities like the Covid-19 vaccine distribution methods; voting, abortion, and weapon access; invasions of sovereign nations; and cleaning and protecting the environment. Such world-level problems will be inherited by our children. All of these issues are *face-to-face conflicts* involving individual and groups. Without moral values as a *social-*

quality-to-be-achieved and our awareness *as observing, describing, evaluating moral-management fitness,* our wellbeing may well be left, as it has been, to the pirates of freedom and equality. Do the world's children need to think that the future should be as insidiously one-sided as it has been throughout history? Should they be taught to observe the insidiousness and, at the same time, be given the means to do something about it?

Somehow, humanity started down a trajectory of warring entities. The winners became the masters and the losers the slaves. Has much changed? In most cases, we have just renamed the winners and losers and failed to clearly redefine slavery as it exists in our age. Again, does what-has-been-the-case have to be the case? Can our children be given repertoires that give them an alternate trajectory?

It can be asked, who has the right to dictate values? The answer is all of us. The answer is related to the purpose of our activities, in the sense that *"what is evidence for one is evidence for all."* [39,40,41] This is the application of the *criterion of objectivity* to evidence. An awareness repertoire requires the criterion of objectivity. All technical disciplines require this criterion. It is set out by the discipline's members and held before them as the "social criteria" for working within the discipline; thus, it is disseminatable knowledge—the We/Us perspective for the discipline. Notice, however, that members only learn it as adults, not as children. Today's world illustrates that this late start is too late.

Every classroom is a social structure, and, like all social structures, the classroom requires moral values to be successful. These morals are encapsulated in the rules of the classroom, as its members' duties and rights. They "sum up" what is socially required from all members (duties), so that activities can begin, continue, and end harmoniously (rights). But we see through school "discipline" procedures, truancy behavior, and dropout rates that much is amiss. Something is not being directly taught. That something is the morals-management-awareness content and their relationship to classical technical repertoires.

The Four-Repertoire System

The four repertoires represent a *system of human behavior* that are required for the emergence of ARC citizens. However, if *any* of these repertoires are weak, missing, or not "congruent" or "aligned," the chance of the emergence of a rational, civil world may not occur in the short or long term.

---

[39] Rescher, Nicholas. (1997). *Objectivity: The obligations of impersonal reason.* Notre Dame, IN: University of Notre Dame Press. Chapter 1.
[40] https://plato.stanford.edu/entries/scientific-objectivity/
[41] https://en.wikipedia.org/wiki/Objectivity_(science)

The complex, interaction between management and technical repertoires has contributed to keeping the curriculum of management hidden. It has only emerged over the last 75 or so years with the rise of quality engineering and systems design technologies.[42,43] Values and awareness have remained hidden for different reasons, ones related to obscure and ambiguous talk regarding our biological and social selves—remembering that we had thousands of years of *belief* before the Enlightenment and the rise of "objective investigation" to analyze and guide beliefs, and to correct "common knowledge." We now know that the Earth is round.

Humans are at least partially *artifacts*, a product of their social interactions in a given society. Change homes and societies, and different human beings emerge and develop. This is why, humans need an explicit recognition of their moral and legal rights and duties.[44,45] Today, we witness the work by the United Nations and international non-governmental organizations who are attempting to make our moral and legal rights and duties explicit and acceptable across the world (Chapter 19).

Given what all of us can observe about the world's present ills, it appears that we have not done much to date. We plead and work for human rights and a better world, but we continue to produce and sell weapons of destruction that sow discord between groups and states. All societies, up to now, have a split personality: they are simultaneously a Dr. Jekyll and a Mr. Hyde. The last number of years can be seen as dipping toward the Hydian on all social, economic, cultural, and political fronts. Our Dr. Jekyll selves may have failed to see two basic rules of systems engineering: 1) *Quality springs from clear evaluation data and repeated replanning*, and 2) *there is no perfect plan because our world and our notion of quality constantly evolve.*

There is no way to design, implement, and evaluate our activities in terms of moral values, awareness, and management as we apply technical repertoires without stating positives clearly through multiple examples (Chapters 3 and 4). All evaluations are based on the moral values to be achieved as expressions of what we think *should* be done (the positives). We may value a well-built home, know how to build it, and evaluate the "well builtness" during each step (means) that adds to its completion (end). But with human behavior, we may value human relationships, even loving relationships, but we have no idea how to observe, describe, construct, or evaluate "well-built" human relationships as they "unfold" step-by-step toward some valued purpose (end) in everyday life and work. Within the

---

[42] https://en.wikipedia.org/wiki/Quality_management

[43] https://en.wikipedia.org/wiki/TRIZ

[44] Bunge, Mario. (1989). *Treatise of modern philosophy, Volume 8. Ethics: The good and the right.* Boston, MA: Reidel. Pgs. 96-97.

[45] https://en.wikipedia.org/wiki/Declaration_of_Human_Duties_and_Responsibilities

classroom, well-built human relationships focus on avoiding conflicts, as well as carrying out activities successfully.

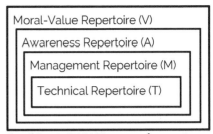

Graphic 1.3: VAM-T system of repertoires.

The four repertoires that make up our activity behavior are illustrated in Graphic 1.3. All our behavior, in the classroom and beyond, can be seen as fitting into this system, even if there are times when it is hard to classify or evaluate a specific instance of behavior. These four repertoires are called:

The VAM-T System of Repertoires

The methods to link the VAM-T repertoires to any activity require direct instruction that supports inquiry into the relationships of group members. Teaching methods are used to link VAM-T behaviors consistently and continuously across activities and years of schooling. As a result, children will learn to 1) observe their evolution, 2) identify their moral values, 3) identify the behavior that make it so, 4) recognize their and others' contributions to it, and 5) identify the consequences that result. But before teaching methods can be engineered, the content must be made as explicit as possible. That is the value purpose of this text.

VAM-T, as a system, requires more than content. It is necessary but not adequate. If we really want to engineer teaching methods that have a high degree of quality control, we must be able to observe the patterns of behavior during its evolution and expose their interactions. Without putting patterns in plain view, we will have little chance to evolve aware, rational, and civil citizens with high reliability. That is, if the reader "believes" what the history of science has taught us about observing patterns, so that all members see them. When the content is clear and observable and the mechanisms known, we have the best chance to create quality-engineered teaching methods. Part 1 of this text outlines the patterns, models, and mechanisms of the system.[46]

Relative to VAM-T content, Graphic 1.3 indicates we start with the moral values shell and work inward (Chapter 9). The VAM-T system applies to the classroom. As children move out into the world, VAM-T becomes the "VAMT-?". This movement requires that students engage in real-world problem solving where the T becomes part of the plan to solve the "?". If we can't leave the next generations a "good life," can we at least instill in them the repertoires that they will need to face their complex world? Doing so would empower them to confront the challenges of the imploding world that we are handing them.

---

[46] https://en.wikipedia.org/wiki/Scientific_modeling

PART 1

Background Knowledge

Part 1 presents the "underlying" knowledge about human behavior that makes the teaching of the VAM-T repertoires possible. It is based on two foundational assumptions of modern science.

1. Nothing surges up out of nothing without having antecedents that existed before.
2. Everything is in a perpetual state of transformation, motion, and change.

These assumptions spring from philosopher scientists David Bohm and Mario Bunge.[1, 2] They see these two concerns as the difference between *being* (1) and *becoming* (2). These two guide the exploration of classrooms.

Chapters 1 identified the basic repertoire elements and their relationships and called it the VAM-T system of behavior. In Part 1, Chapter 2 provides a language to talk and observe these repertoires. Chapter 3 provides a functional model of the classroom's interactions. Together, Chapters 1 through 3 explore the elements and relationships within the context of the classroom. They deal with *being*— as the way the classroom exists as a system across the world.

Chapter 4 examines the mechanisms that promote individual learning. Chapter 5 examines the mechanisms that promote social learning. Based on these two levels of mechanisms, Chapters 6, 7, and 8 provide some initial teaching operations to promote VAM-T repertoires that are based on the mechanisms of which they are a function. Together, Chapters 4 through 8 deal with the *becoming* of citizens who can build a social system that has a high probability of functioning and surviving.

The problem is that the classroom is a two tired system—one that consists of individuals and groups. Very roughly, individuals function to "optimize" the group and the group functions to "optimize" the individual. The end game is "unity" between the two. Ideally, both the individual and the group survive "optimally."

Part 2, returns to the content of the repertoires, but does so from the perspective of young children *evolving into* VAM-T endowed citizens.

---

[1] Bohm, David. (1957). Causality and chance in modern physics. NY, USA. D. Van Nostrand. @ https://vdoc.pub. See https://en.wikipedia.org/wiki/David_Bohm.

[2] Bunge, Mario. (1979). *Causality and modern science, third edition*. MA, USA, Harvard University Press. (First published in 1959 as *Causality: The place of the causal principle in modern science*.) @ https://vdoc.pub. See https://en.wikipedia.org/wiki/Mario_Bunge.

2

OUR BEHAVIOR

Chapter 1 identified four repertoires of human behavior—moral values (V), awareness (A), Management (M), and Technical (T)—that fit together as a system. The system components were named VAM-T. They were presented as a knowledge base for teaching elementary-aged children to become aware, rational, and civil (ARC) citizens. This chapter sets out the basic terminology, examples, and perspectives to help with observing and talking about these repertoires, as they occur in the classroom.

Teachers are trained to examine children's behavior from several perspectives—biological, psychological, sociological, and cultural. However, this knowledge base is seldom integrated into a system to help direct their teaching. With an integrated model, they would have a clearer picture of human behavior and how to design teaching and solve the problems they face. We see such models throughout science—as, for example, the periodic table of elements in chemistry or taxonomies of plant and animal life in biology. Without such an "integrating model," teachers do not have the language behavior needed to analyze and simultaneously evolve VAM-T repertoires and their linkages. This chapter sets out the basic terminology to classify human behavior. It is our starting point.

BEHAVIOR

The term *behavior* is used as a global identifier that refers to anything that humans do, think, or feel. It can be classified from many levels. As a first cut, it can be viewed physiologically as involuntary or voluntary.

INVOLUNTARY BEHAVIOR

The involuntary behavior includes what is often called an "autonomic response" like a heartbeat, eye blink, startle, salivation, or a private emotional/feeling event. It may also be a "brain event" like dreaming and reacting in ways that today are classified as a PTSD reaction. Some of these behaviors are governed by the *autonomic nervous system* that controls homeostasis. The *parasympathetic* branch of the autonomic nervous system governs the body-at-rest events. The *sympathetic* branch of the autonomic nervous system governs the flight-fight-freeze responses to a perceived threat or to a sudden event that makes us duck, blink, or jerk.

Voluntary Behavior

On the voluntary side, the behavior can be a "private behavior" like remembering and thinking. It can also be an "overt behavior" like speaking, questioning, baking a cake, reading a book aloud, or solving an arithmetic problem.

Both the public and private behaviors of children often occur simultaneously. Even if we read a book aloud or do a math problem, some of the behaviors are private. At times, a private event like a sudden remembering of a past event, starts behavior that is not compatible with that required for a classroom activity. From the positive side, the evoking event may "bring about" helpful behaviors as when children remember a forgotten procedure while working on a math problem or spot a grammatical error while writing a story.

Our focus is on how involuntary behavior is associated with voluntary behavior. The question is, what events relax, focus, or engender a flight-fight-freeze behavior when working with others during activities? These involuntary behaviors are treated as the "emotional" or "feeling" component of the voluntary behaviors of interest. The change in emotional behaviors is usually caused (induced or influenced) by other classroom members. We call the buildup or occurrence of bad emotions as "stress" or "fear," and we call the buildup or occurrence of good emotional states as "joy," "wellbeing," and "happiness." When children are induced by others to emit a voluntary behavior, the first effect is often emotional. Within psychology, involuntary behavior is called respondent and voluntary is called operant. The first is elicited and the second is emitted. We will study their operation during respondent and operant conditioning.

Behavior of Young Children

There is always an associated *emotional-feeling-physiological* component to operant (emitted) behavior. We are always in an emotional state. The first question is, how can we "wrap" children's learning in "positive emotional states" day-in-and-day-out? The second question is, how can we eliminate or radically reduce "negative emotional states? When a "history of teaching" is "sufficient," it builds "positive" emotional states along with the voluntary behavior being taught—morals values, awareness, management, and technical behaviors (VAM-T).

When children enter Kindergarten, most of them have already had about five years of teaching and learning. This history may support or impede classroom activities. The emotions brought into the classroom context may be incompatible with teaching the social and technical behavior to all students. Additionally, the emotional consequences of teaching and learning may be "stressful" or "fear invoking" because of this history. It is often hard to separate cause and effect.

The goal of ARC teaching is to have children's new, developing brains, the *cerebral cortex*, become the controlling "home" or "seat" from which aware, rational, civil behavior emerges and "stays in charge." Said another way, we want the new brain to gain sway over the old brain, the *limbic system*, whose operation governs children's initial, untrained, often involuntary, behavior toward others and the events around them. Hopefully, inappropriate emotional, verbal, and physical behaviors will be replaced with those like helping, sharing, and caring.

Just how do we train the new brain to overcome or manage the aggressive or frightened sides of the old brain and promote aware, rational, civil behavior? The answer is related to what, when, where, and how children are taught. Chapter 1 outlined the rough approximation of what and when of VAM-T teaching.

Classes of Behavior

Behavior can also be examined in terms of classes of voluntary behavior. All classes of behavior involve two components. These are called *discriminations* and *operations*. Children may know how to walk, but can't discriminate when to walk, so someone holds their hand, especially in dangerous situations. Children may know how to eat, but don't know when, so they are called.

When children ride a bike, the child must discriminate when to perform each of the operations of turning, braking, pedaling, or shifting gears. When classes are connected, the finishing of one operation may even be the *discrimination event* for the next operations: when we finish bushing, we rinse; when we finish eating, we clean up.

The terms *discrimination* or *discriminating* are technical terms. They have a long, useful history in psychology. When the terms are used in their social sense, as *discriminating against* or having a *bias toward* a group, it will be evident by the context. The point is that all classes of behavior require a careful analysis of the discriminations and operations that play a part in their successful performance. This analysis is the first step to efficient and reliable teaching.

Instances & Classes of Behavior

The observation of classes of behavior begins by recognizing that we observe only single occurrences of an individual or group's behavior. These single occurrences are called *instances*. Each instance is bound to a particular time and place. Consider the following examples with the *instance of behavior* in CAPITALS.

1.   Zelda HELPED Jose during reading today
2.   The Electric Reader Group will ORGANIZE their questions prior to the teacher's presentation

3. Sidney SHARED his drawing supplies during art

Each of these example statements identify one instance of behavior and its occurrence in a context. Examples 1 and 3 talk about past behavior, helping and organizing. Example 2 talks about future behavior. Instances, because they are fleeting, ephemeral events, make behavior difficult to talk about accurately, as well as study and evolve. Of course, a science and technology researcher knows this fact, but applying it to children's behavior in-the-moment is another story.

When we talk about behavior in terms of *classes* something different happens. This time, we are talking as if the behavior were a permanent thing—it is almost something we can grasp, expect, and consider as a permanent part of the individual or group's repertoire. When a behavior is referenced in this way, the talk is about a *class of behavior*. Consider the following talk about classes that is congruent with the above examples of instances.

1. Zelda is a HELPFUL individual
2. The Electric Reader Group is very ORGANIZED
3. Sidney is a SHARER

Zelda is a helper, the Group is organized, and Sidney is a sharer. All are spoken of as if they were "real parts" of a person or group across contexts. They are likened to permanent qualities or properties not much different from the color of a cup or the size of a box. These classes of behavior are what we expect to remain the same over time, as much as we expect a person's eye color to remain so. This talk about classes radically departs from talking about the momentary, fleeting instances of behavior. Yet, it is the first step towards making the study of our behavior technical enough to begin to establish repertoires like management, awareness, and moral values. In general, we desire to build qualities into our behavior that make them resilient and adaptive classes (Chapter 6).

Instance & Class Relationships

Both ways of referencing behavior are closely tied because our knowledge of the instances of behavior controls our referencing (denoting) classes of behavior. Instances are the *evidence* for referencing behavior as a class. Here is what the instance evidence for the above classes might look like.

1. Zelda has been HELPFUL every day for three months without an instance of not being helpful.
2. The Electric Reader Group members ORGANIZED their activity resources all but one day during the first semester.
3. Sidney has never failed to SHARE his supplies with other students during art.

Each example indicates that multiple instances have been observed before the class name was applied (in CAPITALS). Yet, we must be cautious because some classes of behavior require only one instance before we apply a class name. Terrorism and murder are the first two that come to mind. In the school and classroom, verbal and physical "assaults" are common. Thus, it behooves teachers to be aware of behaviors that can precede the occurrence of such "negative," "unwanted," or "coercive" classes. Often these *pre-behaviors* are witnessed in body language, emotional displays, verbal silences or outbursts, or their combination.

The dependence on the observation of multiple instances in referencing a class becomes apparent when the class applied to a person or group undergoes evolution.

1. Zelda used to be HELPFUL, but now she is an UNCOOPERATIVE student
2. The Electric Readers were DISORGANIZED, but now they are ORGANIZED
3. Sidney has always SHARED his supplies

Examples 1 and 2 concern a change in the class of behavior which describes the individual or group. But example 3 concerns the consistency or maintenance of behavior over time. To make these *class statements* about individual or group behavior, the speaker must have observed a number of instances over an extended time period. Notice that there is no talk about how to evolve or maintain (teach) behavior. The concern is for identifying and analyzing behavior, not evolving it at this point. As with all science, we need content before methods, at least initially.

To help children reach mastery of our classes of interest and their relationships—the moral value (V), awareness (A), and management (M) repertoires—we need to 1) clearly define them, 2) accurately observe them across a range of activities, 3) see their interactions, and 4) master their performance ourselves. As with STEM or SHAPE disciplines, we can't teach without knowledge about the system of behavior being taught—VAM-T in this case. The deeper our knowledge of any system—our movement from its description to its control—the greater the probability of successful teaching, and the better the chance of solving problems through communicating with others (Chapters 6 - 8).

Complex Behavior

Voluntary behavior can also be examined as classes that are made up of many subclasses. When it is, it is classified as complex behavior. We speak of complex classes in several ways.

Complex behaviors are learned by children through play, observation, direct instruction, or their combination. All of these methods can be employed in evolving aware, rational, civil behavior. By learning these complex behaviors, we hand them a heavy-duty method to control their own behavior. However, these behaviors must be practiced repeatedly until they are used in the right context at the right time—an *in-the-moment* application. This takes years.

Procedures and Strategies

Many complex behaviors are called *procedures* or *strategies*. Procedures are often performed in a fixed order, as in solving a long-division problem, repairing a bicycle tire, or brushing one's teeth. Strategy behaviors usually have a degree of performance flexibility. In Chapter 1, for example, the strategy called *organizing* was described as composed of the five *sub-class steps*. These steps were *is organizing needed, locating resources, transferring resources, arranging resources,* and *returning resources.* When the strategy's *selection step*—"Is organizing needed?"—is answered in the affirmative, the strategy is set into motion. Only in the context of very simple activities are these five steps of organizing performed in a strictly fixed order.

As activities become more complex, each of these steps require additional *thinking events* (discriminations) that direct how each step's *overt behavior* is performed. These thinking behaviors govern the when, where, and how the step's overt behavior is performed.

For the organizing strategy, the thinking sub-steps for *locating resources* requires two *discrimination queries*. These are expressed as questions: 1) *How can they be located?* 2) *Where are they located?* When these two questions are answered, the organizer can perform the step with a greater probability of success. The next step, *transferring resources*, requires three decisions: 1) *Where are they needed?* 2) *When are they needed?* and 3) *How can they be transferred?* Each discrimination makes the steps as unambiguous as possible. But for very young children these discrimination queries are not needed because teachers' model, prompt, and reinforce them within a set of relatively simple activities. When children can read, the complex strategies with their discrimination queries can be displayed to remind children of what to do or to reinforce them when they read it to see if they did or did not remember to perform the sub-steps needed to successfully use the strategy.

Repertoires

A *repertoire* is a set of strategies or procedures that fit together into a "family" of related behaviors that can be performed, often, in various orders. For example, consider dance, gymnastics, and debate repertoires. The dance repertoire may include dance sub-repertoires called the tango, foxtrot, samba, lindy, and waltz. A gymnastics repertoire may include the backflip, forward summersault, round off, cartwheel, aerial cartwheel, and handspring. A debate repertoire may include tactics formulation, argument rebuttal, case making, fallacy spotting, gestures, as well as aspects of voice control and posture. When using these repertoires, their sub-repertoires (as complex classes) can be used in many manners, orders, and for various durations depending on the activity context for which they are employed. This is especially obvious in a dance repertoire were the sub-repertoires used depend on the type of music, the size of the dance floor, and the number of dancers who inhabit that floor.

In Chapter 1, the *repertoires* of moral values, awareness, management, and technical behaviors (VAM-T) were defined as a system of repertoires. These are the large *parent class* of repertoires. Out of these, aware, rational, civil behavior emerges. Management (M), for example, consisted of the seven *child-repertoires*, called strategies. These included planning, learning, organizing, supervising, helping, sharing, and intervening. This decomposition, as a type of analysis, is one of the first steps in solving any behavioral problem that in the present case relates to the purpose of evolving (controlling over time) the development of young children's behavior.

Management, awareness, and moral values are three interrelated repertoires of behavior. Their relationship is complex; thus, they must be brought out into the open in much the same way they were for the organizing strategy illustrated above. By "pointing out" the matches or mismatches between moral values (V)—as a set of statements—and children's management behavior (M), children learn to be aware (A) if others behavior is appropriate or inappropriate. This classification, if inappropriate, is the discrimination that sets in motion the use of the intervening management strategy (conflict resolution) or the planning strategy. If the behavior is classified as appropriate (cohesive), what should be said and done?

HEURISTICS

There will come a point in the evolution of the advanced repertoires, management strategies included, when even its *discrimination queries* may not be enough. The more complex the activity the more there becomes a need for guidelines to keep the strategy behavior moving forward. They give its user a wider perspective on its application. These guidelines are called *heuristics*.[1] For example, during organizing or planning, the heuristic "Change any resource and others change as well" can help ensure that the right resources are identified even if an activity has an element of newness or involves different individuals. Heuristics, learnable and useful to children, are discussed for several of the management strategies in Part 2. We have already seen two powerful heuristics that keep us focused on being and becoming:

1. Nothing surges up out of nothing without having antecedents that existed before.

---

[1] https://en.wikipedia.org/wiki/Heuristic_(psychology)

2. Everything is in a perpetual state of transformation, motion, and change.

Complex Behavior, Language, & Teaching

The decomposition and synthesis of all complex behavior requires *verbal behavior* (speaking, writing, and graphic components usually called language) for gaining a grasp and the eventual control over the transmission of behavior at any level of complexity. Without verbal behavior, teaching and learning are inhibited, if not stopped. One may get through basic behaviors like walking or holding a spoon. However, complex behavior is impossible to teach without language. Try teaching dance, debate, management, or any STEM discipline without verbal behavior. Without it, there is no way to consistently and efficiently teach or coordinate complex behavior among learners.

With increased subject matter knowledge, children acquire *verbal views* of reality and use those views to observe and operate on the world differently than in the past. Once changed, there is often no turning back.

They have been _qualitatively_ changed.

It is their use of verbal behavior, at least initially, that gives children control over the external world, learning activities, and themselves. Their verbal behavior links reasoning and doing—it establishes a *representation* between the two. However, when our actions fail to change reality, we search for new ways to change our behaviors, and we often "go exploring" to finding ways to change the way we talk relative to the area of failure—our ignorance undergoes modification. (Of course, curiosity also leads to invention that simultaneously gives us new language components.) There is a constant *interaction cycle* between language and behavior that allows for solving problems. This means that neither has primacy. However, once learning is well underway, the prime mover in knowledge transmission and acquisition is verbal behavior—it becomes our guide, as we explore reality, within or outside ourselves or the classroom.

This primacy is true for all classical technical disciplines, as it is with the moral values (V), awareness (A), and management (M) repertoires on which this text focuses. All these repertoires are human *socio-technical systems* invented and built by humans for humans. These systems have the valued purpose of helping us communicate about and operate on reality, including ourselves.[2] Such systems can become the prime controller over our emotional and overt behavior. The problem is to make sure that children see this relationship across activities and learn to control it. This requires direct teaching, just like any of the scientific or technical disciplines.

---

[2] https://en.wikipedia.org/wiki/Sociotechnical_system

The helpfulness of these verbal repertoires (organized, precise knowledge) can't be overestimated. It is the method that helps us control our built-in biological, automatic reactions—our flight-fight-freeze reactions—to events that confront all of us on a day-to-day basis. If we are walking in the woods and see a snake, we may run, scream, or freeze. However, if we know about snakes and can classify the one seen as non-poisonous, we just walk around it. If our vehicle gets a flat tire and we know how to change it, we just change it. If we wade through a swamp and find leaches on our legs, we do not panic if we know that sprinkling a little salt on them will make them fall off. If salt was forgotten, we verbalize to ourselves about being "forgetful." We don't react against the leaches or panic in the same way that knowledgeless adventurers do. These potential problem situations become *activity tasks* and nothing more. All such thinking behavior is rational. *"Knowing" pushes behavior forward before our old-brain takes us down a primitive, reactive road.* We must, as Andrew Huberman intones, master our autonomic nervous system.[3] Our rational self can gain control over our reactive, automatic, primitive self.

If a group or multiple groups (classrooms, schools, societies, states, nations) have a storehouse of knowledge-based repertoires, then there is a higher probability of rational behavior.[4] If a set of clear moral values are intertwined and strongly associated with rational behavior, then civility will have a higher probability of governing the rational. As a result, we may be able to build a rational, civil world—one where, for example, our talk and behavior about achieving "equality" need not be preceded by words like social, political, economic, racial, gender, and religious. The preventative approach starts by *instilling* young children with the repertoires of survival, which Chapter 1 described as VAM-T.

At present, the police-legal-prison system is not preventative nor a remediation mechanism to solve our inappropriate (non-moral) behavior problems. It is too, too late. Prevention comes—if we believe various philosophers—less from our human laws, than from the people themselves, as expressed in their interactions with other members. The laws and the legal mechanisms of their enforcement can't distribute "fairness" on a case-by-case basis or "switch" it to cohesive management while the inappropriate is in its infancy. Fairness appears to need instilling early on, at the local level. Thus,

A _system of justice_ is a subsystem of a _system of education_

---

[3] https://www.youtube.com/watch?v=xbYOONg_JvY (Huberman's podcasts on mastering the adult self through knowledge.) Here, part of our objective is about instilling this control in young children.

[4] https://en.wikipedia.org/wiki/Social_and_behavior_change_communication

Classroom Activities: The Physical Context

We are always behaving and all behaviors are performed in some context. Here, the physical context is a set of events called *activities*. In the elementary classroom, these activities are usually defined by the curriculum subjects, along with the social-interactive components needed to engage in the activities successfully (to learn a technical behavior, -T). There are four common types of activities: *regular, project, special,* and *emergency*.

Regular Activities

These activities include those that repeat themselves, often on a daily basis. Reading, writing, mathematics, and science are the big four of regular activities in elementary classrooms.

Project Activities

Regular activities often generate *project activities* that deal with individuals or groups learning about, practicing, or applying acquired knowledge to accomplish some end—often to decompose or build something be it a poem, a story, an electric motor, or a miniature ecosystem. All introduce the language of and behaviors that make up the *technical repertoire space*. If teachers give children the right language model and practice for a discipline, they will use the model to invent, build, and solve problems.

Special Activities

These are designed to keep the classroom running smoothly. They include behaviors that will allow children to keep the "appropriate behavior" for a regular or project activity moving forward smoothly. These mini-activities are social structures that include, for example, 1) procedures to get help, 2) use the restroom, 3) sharpen a pencil, or 4) what to do when one finishes early.

Of these, the most problematic is getting help. All children have different levels of mastery relative to their various repertoires. To get help in-the-moment often requires others to give that help. Who can be recruited to give it? Can the helper be someone besides the teacher? Can it be another child from inside or outside a particular classroom? Can it be a simple answer sheet or a computer interface?

Emergency Activities

These are undertaken in case of fire, storm. or any event that has extreme consequences, no matter how unlikely their occurrence. These are "security activities" or "risk reduction activities." Today, attacks on schools are the latest form of a school-level emergency activity. We have stopped teaching children to hide under desks in case of a nuclear attack, now they may need much the same behavior for terrorist attacks.

Establishing all four types of activities is the starting point for effective, efficient, low-risk classrooms. Classically, designing and implementing these activities is called the "management of the classrooms" (by teachers). The analysis and design of classroom activities provides the initial physical context in which to promote appropriate social (management) behavior, the precursor to advancing young children's ARC behavior. It is the structural side of our problem in socializing citizens. Essentially, you can't function without structuring the context in which behavior takes place, and the "behavioral patterns" for activities are the social structures required. Learning in a chaotic world is impossible. It just needs to be remembered that teachers are not the lone arranger. Everyone in the classroom and beyond contributes.

Successful Teaching

Even though Chapter 1 and the above gives the "gist" of what an ARC citizen entails, we need clarity to make such citizens "come alive" in society. A clear plan *within the classroom* embraces four components that make it possible to evolve (induce, influence, socialize) such citizens.

1. Clearly define the behavioral repertoires, through definition and examples that are part of ARC behavior.
2. Identify workable, effective, and satisfying methods to teach (1).
3. Lay out a clear timeline or timelines for teaching the content with the methods identified in (2).
4. Provide support materials that ensure that the repertoires are learned and practiced in such a way as not to impact an already filled teaching schedule that exists in our schools.

This text only focuses on the first and fourth, and only suggests the second and third. All of these components are necessary for the successful teaching of any curriculum—without considering the larger system that provides the resources and funding for teaching. If any of these four are poorly designed, implemented, or evaluated, the quest for raising ARC citizens is jeopardized. Chapters 3 through 8 expand on this chapter's analysis of behavior by presenting a model of behavior and the mechanisms that underlie their operation in the classroom. This background allows us to talk clearly and consistently about human behavior and human relationships. The chapters of Part 2 present a detailed analysis of the moral values (V), awareness (A), and management (M) repertoires. These chapters include an introduction to the support materials and their location.

As said, a management repertoire is as technical as any of the STEM repertoires. Only with a detailed analysis of the management and the moral values repertoires makes it possible to evaluate our moral value and management behavior relationship as *matches* or *mismatches* during activities (Chapters 9-17). This is because of one fact:

Every instance of an awareness evaluation represents a relationship between moral values and one or more steps of a management strategy.

This evaluative evidence *sets-the-occasion* to reward matches, correct nonmatches, and describe or query children about their linkage (Chapters 6, 7 and 8). These steps illustrate the need to understand not only the content of moral values and management, but the use of verbal behavior, so that complex repertoires can be evolved and linked (shaped) bit-by-bit across time.

But these matching and mismatching occasions must be observed and actions taken almost automatically, much as chess masters see the game board and almost instantly move according to a "plan of moves." However, chess (as rules of the game, general strategies, and momentary tactics) is a *closed system.*

The languages for moral value (V), awareness (A), management (M), and technical (T) repertoires exist in *open systems* that are always changing and expanding. Thus, VAM-T, as a system, is open and evolving. Presently, knowledge of the "rules of ARC citizenship" and the strategies and tactics to achieve classroom-citizenship success are to a great extent unclear. Repertoires in *open social-technical systems* allow for outside forces to intervene across members. Success, as opposed to chaos, will prevail only if children learn both the "game" and something about the outside forces (variables) that are constantly shaping them in ways that can only be partially predicted. Teachers and, eventually, children must in-the-moment spot who is doing what to whom and have behaviors that support or correct the doing.

Final Note: This chapter has talked about behavior from a narrow perspective. A much better picture of how human behavior is both similar to and different from other animals can be seen from an ethnologist's perspective.[5] This view can help put the contents of Chapters 3 through 8 in a wider, more revealing perspective. What is essentially found is that human language, not just animal communication behavior, allows human's to constantly expand on their "knowledge base of behavior" so they can continue to adapt across environments that were not their original habitat. We will talk about this as a form of recursion—a process of changing ourselves and our language through continual reapplication, with each instance gradually adding to the change.

---

[5] Wyatt, Tristan D. (2017). *Animal behavior: A very short introduction.* Oxford, UK: Oxford University Press. ISBN: 978-0-19-871215-2.

3

A Model of Behavior

Chapter 1 provided a gross analysis of the repertoires of interest—what is to be taught to children—based on the moral-valued purpose of modern education. It was a structural and relational picture of these behaviors. Chapter 2 dug deeper into the composition of behavior, so that we had a way to talk about and observe human behavior in terms of the instances, classes, and repertoires composed of operation and discrimination components.

It is within the context of classroom activities where the teaching and learning of the repertoires takes place. The argument was that the VAM-T (moral values, awareness, management, and technical) repertoires were the component behaviors that control the beginning, continuing, and ending of these classroom activities. The extent to which these repertoires are directly taught and related determines if and when children start becoming aware, rational, and civil (ARC) citizens.

This chapter presents a model of the classroom as a system of activities that makes it possible to meet its valued purposes (T), which is the moral-value purpose to engender ARC citizens. This model is called the *activity contingency system*. It provides a *representation* of activities within a classroom structure that allows teachers to analyze, design, and teach activities to achieve their valued purpose (T) *and* evolve ARC enabled children (VAM).

Why a System Model?

A classroom activity, like any scientific or technological investigation, has a valued purpose (Chapter 1)—to find out how to make things happen and to figure out why they happen. The valued purpose is the question the investigators, as teachers in the present case, seek to answer. It is assumed that investigators only seek answers to that which is valued. This has been the case from the foundational beginnings of science and technology. Copernicus asked, how do the earth and heavens move? Kepler asked, can we accurately describe how these bodies move? Newton asked, what are the *mechanisms of operation* (underlying mechanisms) of how bodies like those in the Keplerian model are moved (controlled). Guttenberg asked and answered the question about how to build a machine—a set of mechanisms that work together—to quickly disseminate such knowledge. With these events, the rise of modern science was established, even if many did not believe in the observation-experimental approach or the knowledge found.[1]

Teaching essentially performs the same technical behavior. First, we are aware of what we want to do (the valued purposes of the classroom contingency system). Second, we plan activities to meet these purposes. Third, we implement our plans. Fourth, we gather evidence about how the plan is working or worked. Fifth, we evaluate the extent to which the valued purpose is being or was achieved. Sixth, we redesign for more effective results. This is the "generic" scientific approach of "reality finding" that emerges from the success or failure of one's implemented *belief* (as a held value within one's present knowledge base). To be successful, we need to put these methods together to ensure that teaching becomes an "established science-based engineering profession guided by moral values." Chapter 1 called the process abductive reasoning. With the addition of moral values, we enter the age of Enlightenment.

However, finding a model to guide us (as Copernicus did), improving the model (as Kepler did), seeing its mechanisms of operation (as Newton did), and applying it to classrooms (as engineers do as they design the range of human artifacts) has to deal with three facts.

First, the model needs to represent an entire system.[2] In this case, that includes all its members (teachers and children) in a context (the classroom) in which activities take place. In a sense, all members are both experimenter and experimentee, designer and designee, practitioner and practitionee. This makes it a complex (interactive) adaptive system. Second, all members are in various states of operational effectiveness relative to the social (VAM) and the technical (T) repertoires that allow members to begin, continue, and end the wide range of classroom activities (Chapter 2). Third, much is unknown about human behavior individually or in groups. The model guides, but with caution.

However, we do not begin in the dark—we know what a model of human behavior should do. First, the model should fit with science and engineering methods in general—we humans are part of the universe of things. Second, it helps with the decomposition of problems (i.e., to find efficient means or sufficient ends) relative to the experimenters' valued purposes (i.e., scientific method view) and the development of solutions (i.e., teaching-engineering methods used within a context). Third, it seeks to find the *mechanisms of operation* at the classroom level—explanations (i.e., as hypotheses) that "guide" us in designing and controlling the system, so that children become ARC citizens. In the end, teachers will 1) understand the controlling variables, 2) discover who-is-controlling-whom, 3) how to

---

[1] https://en.wikipedia.org/wiki/Printing_press. (See the sections on the model for printing press, its refinement, and it spread across Europe.)
[2] https://en.wikipedia.org/wiki/Scientific_modelling

control the development of the interactions required to achieve the classroom's two value purposes (T and VAM), and 4) how to fix problems when they arise.

The Valued Purpose of Teaching

Teaching socializes children. Socialize, in this context, means something like "to cause to accept or behave in accordance with social norms or expectations." [3] It is also a word that has many synonyms like evolve, influence, train, foster, and educate. One may use any of these words. but all of them are just "beautifications" for what we are trying to do: *control children's evolution.* In the present case, we want them to become ARC citizens (VAM) with enough knowledge of the technical world to solve the problems we are leaving them ("VAMT-?", Chapter 1). This is simultaneously a moral value statement and the present text's moral-value purpose.

The word *control* is a technical term. No matter what beautifications one wants to apply to the activity of changing children. Yet, one point is critical:

Content is the problem.

We could use the same controlling methods (e.g., teaching) to evolve individuals with narrow "xenophobic" or "fanatic" or "terrorist" repertoires as we would for aware, rational, and civil repertoires. For example, we can engender negative emotions toward certain groups, teach children to shoot weapons, and, then, reward and rereward them for shooting at a target representing specific political, cultural, or social groups. However, we can use much the same methods to evolve repertoires that allow children to rationally and civilly solve the problems that they will face when the world is theirs. For example, we can reward children to recognize their and other's negative emotions during negotiations, teach them "calming techniques" and how to "negotiate" under such conditions. When such behavior is repeatedly practiced, expanded, refined, and rewarded for seeking and achieving compromises that resolve their differences, then children will do so in the future.

However, we have some cultural norms (behavior specified in the law or just "common knowledge") that indicate that we can't use punishing (inappropriate) management methods. The "modeling" (demonstrations) of such human relationships—presented intentionally or not—between all caregiver-child interactions—would conflict with our methods. We, as a culture, now see more clearly: we want to provide children with content repertoires that allow them to work with others with appropriate management behavior. Some may say we have moved beyond Machiavellian

---

[3] https://www.thefreedictionary.com/Socialize

or power-politic techniques, as some did during the Age of Enlightenment.[4,5] Yet, our teaching methods are often unclear, resources scarce, and content statements may not have a focus on building strong, lasting human relationships—a moral value, V, of the VAM-T repertoires. We want to give children a system of thought and behavior, not just bits and pieces, that make them adaptive to the complex open-system in which they are living and will live. We want to combine both the Scientific Revolution and the Age of Enlightenment, so that children can light up their own way.

Whether intentional or not, these methods (both those with which we investigate and those that we use to teach) define the *qualities* of our future citizens. They will imitate because that is what children do and, perhaps, because it is, at their young ages, all they have observed or know about the world.

So far, there seems to be a failure in raising children who are VAM enabled. They are often not aware (A) of how their management behavior (M) controls the relationships with others (V). Often such non-endowed children seem to magically appear well after their schooling. They use inappropriate (violent or self-serving) management methods. They have no language with which to talk and direct their moral-management behavior. They have "agentship in the world" without an aware repertoire to help them control themselves and others. In the end, the neighbors and friends of these non-VAM enabled people are surprised or shocked at the events perpetrated by these "hidden" coercive members of society. Their moral and management behaviors were taken for granted.

A Contingency-Based Model

Every human activity—this includes all technical undertakings—can be represented and expressed as an *If-then contingency*, which expresses a relationship between events—some *dependency* links two or more events. Within the classroom, the dependency has some degree of probability or uncertainty. Within the classroom, the *teacher's activity plan* represents a contingency. It can be represented as follows:

$$[X: M \rightarrow T \leftarrow M]$$

This contingency expression can be briefly expressed as follows: Given an activity context (physical and social structures) indicated by brackets ([ ]), and an entering emotional/physiological state (X) of members, the teacher's management behavior (M) helps children learn the technical behavior (T) of the activity by inducing and consequenting (M) it. This view leaves out important components and interactions that are taking place between teachers and children, and children and children. More accurately,

---

[4] https://en.wikipedia.org/wiki/Niccol%C3%B2_Machiavelli
[5] https://en.wikipedia.org/wiki/Age_of_Enlightenment

both teachers and other children are involved in the management and technical behavior of an activity. Classically, the [X: M → T ← M] contingency representation is the "teaching individuals" view of the classroom contingency plan. But if we consider "who is doing what for whom," we find that the contingency representation needs to be modified.

[X: Mi → (M or T) ← Mc]

Here, two things are being taught, M and T. Additionally, management has been divided into two types, Mi and Mc. The first is the "inducing" side of management (Mi) and the other its "consequent" side (Mc). Inducing behavior controls setting other behavior in motion." Consequenting behavior controls its reoccurrence in the future—it is more likely to happen again. Here is a walk through to contingency model:

1. Children enter the classroom in some physiological-emotional state, some degree of M, and some degree of T.
2. Mi inducing events by the teacher or other members can change these three entering states.
3. Mi inducing events can change the Mi or Mc behavior of others.
4. Mi inducing events can change the T of others.
5. Mc consequent events can change the future Mi or Mc events of others.
6. Mc consequent events can change the future T events of others.

This is mostly standard behavioral stuff, but what we can warrant from these points is the fact or belief that:

Teachers and others are always teaching the individual and the group.

Just what are these inducing and consequenting events? They are the subject of Chapters 4 through 8. For now, let's see a few examples of each.

1. Teachers and members happily greet each other as they enter the classroom (Mi induces X, the good feeling in members).
2. Seeing others prepare for the first activity, these members start to prepare (members induce others management, Mi).
3. As children are preparing for this activity to start, the teacher acknowledges the children's management behavior (teachers management as Mc for children).
4. As teaching proceeds, children see others attending to the demonstration, so they attend (Mi though imitating others).
5. The Mi of everyone is consequented when they learn the T (T as Mc for management).
6. The teacher presents a positive consequent event for learning T (Mc for T from teacher).

The contingency system model has rectified two of the three problems of the first contingency representation. Now, all members of the classroom contribute to the teacher's contingency plan and what is taught is not just M, but M and T. However, the Mi and Mc is just part of the VAM social repertoire.

Because children are VAM neophytes, they may or may not facilitate the teacher's contingency plan. Essentially, each activity member enters the classroom in a *contingency state* that contributes to the activity's evolution or not. The children's behaviors can be cohesive with or in conflict with the teacher's *activity contingency plan* that has an activity objective (T in VAM-T), its valued purpose. Now, the teacher's activity plan and the children can be looked at from the same perspective, except that the children need to *become VAM-T enabled* before all members can contribute to the same contingency plan with the needed awareness (Chapter 10).

Although, the model represents the relationships between its overt components (X, M, T), it fails to describe these relationships in terms of the four behavioral content areas of interest—the VAM-T repertoires. This requires three clarifications.

First, moral values (V) are not included in the model's representation because they are statements about what social (management) interactions *should occur* between members in order for an activity to begin, continue, and end within some time frame.

Second, awareness (A), as a meta-language, is not included in the model because it represents the conclusion to an argument about the relationship between moral value (V) statements and management behavior (M). *Awareness evaluation statements* (A) are inductive inferences about the relationship between the moral-management repertoires and the management-technical repertoires. If there is congruence, then the conclusion is that the member's management behavior is cohesive behavior (facilitating to the plan). If there is no congruence, then the conclusion is that the member's management behavior represents a conflict (non-facilitating to the plan). All management behavior, in a sense, tips the contingency plan toward children learning or not learning T and M. A "truer" representation.

To proceed with VAM teaching, moral (V) and management (M) repertoires must be clear and unambiguous. When they are clear, justified consequent effects can be exposed and used to gradually evolve VAM repertoires. However, if either of the two repertoires are "ambiguous" or "vague," then a strong conclusion (awareness) about the fit between them has a high probability of bringing about "unjust" consequence effects. With accurate evaluations (Chapters 15 and 16), the *system of education* incorporates a *system of justice*.

Third, the model indicates that technical behavior (T) interacts with management behavior (M). If T is learned, then the management behavior used (as Mi and Mc) will come to support learning T. Put negatively, if children are not successfully taught T, then M, as a social repertoire, will not be learned or used to support T. This situation is like asking for someone to shop for food, but there is no food in the stores. Soon, shopping stops. There is no contingency (dependency) between the two behaviors. The whole point of the VAM repertoires, as "social repertoires," is to increase the probability that members put themselves on the same "contingency page." They work toward the same ends using cohesive means to achieve them. By including the ARC repertoires, the teacher is teaching both the individuals and the group.

When a contingency plan is implemented, many possible effects may arise because all members are on different emotional and behavioral pages. Yet, we have to deal with the fact that causes and effects in a complex open system with multiple members are not nearly as clear as they are in a small closed system like the psychologists' experimental chamber. Imagine 20 to 30 rats in a single experimental chamber where each rat controls some set of events like food and shock delivery, grooming behavior, or exploring the environment. Would many psychologists have a clue as to how to represent or control behavior within such a chamber? The teacher deals with such a chamber each day across many hours. The difference is in the mechanisms that support humans in the classroom—they are not quite the same as for non-humans (Chapters 4 and 5).

We have four repertoires. If the technical (T) is learned, then strong consequent effects (Mc) can be delivered to both management and technical behavior (M or T). If only some learn T, then the consequent effects differ across children. This imbalance leads to potential conflicts between the learners and non-learners of T (Chapter 16). This is the first place that the activity contingency plan must be strong. It becomes so by structuring activities, which is the "context," so that children always have ways to get help, so that they can stay appropriate and, thus, avoid conflicts (Chapter 2).

The main concern at this point is to realize that 1) each activity member is different and 2) each enters an activity in a slightly different contingency state. All have different emotional/physiological states (X), different levels of management (M) and technical (T) behaviors, and react differently to consequent effects (Mc) delivered by members. These varying differences provide a rough picture of the open-system complexity of the classroom.

Teachers can learn to handle this complexity for three reasons. First, this text lays out the content of moral values (V), awareness (A), and management (M) repertoires and their relationships, as well as their relationship to technical (T) behavior. Second, by knowing the mechanisms of which all classroom behavior is a function, as outlined in Chapters 4 and 5, they gain a method to analyze problems and synthesize solutions (i.e., methods to teach). Third, it does not take but a handful of teaching methods (operations, tactics) to control the mechanisms of which X, M, and T are a function. Chapters 6, 7, and 8 begin this exploration. (The principles and tactics of direct instruction go much further, but the present concern is with identifying repertoire content, their relationships, and the general mechanism and operations that support content evolution.) These make it possible to gain greater control over the evolution of ARC behavior across the range of classroom activities. However, these three reasons depend on the above realization that the first thing that makes for activity success is that all children learn T. If children don't, they would ask the primary contingent question, "If I am not learning the objective (T, the value-purpose end), then why should I be emotionally and managerially positive?" Of course, they could say pretty much the same thing if the means to ends are made into "drudgery."

Logic of Contingencies

The above sections described the contingency model. But we still need to understand the logic of contingencies—how the parts relate within the context of a classroom activity. This amounts to a *path of thinking* to remedy not obtaining M and T, to continuing to obtain M and T, or finding even better ways to obtain M and T that makes X positive.

Following this path is an example of rationality.

We need clarity to meet the valued purpose of the classroom, especially when we want to teach both the VAM and the T repertoires. This logic, which represents children's "first foundation of rationality," can be expressed as a set of contingency-based queries:

1. What methods can be used to control X, so that M is facilitated? ($X \rightarrow$ [Mi or Mc])
2. What methods can be used for M, so that M has control over X? ($X \leftarrow$ [Mi or Mc])
3. What methods can promote X and Mi, so that they work together to induce T? ([X + Mi] $\rightarrow$ T)
4. What methods can be used to expose consequences (Mc), so that they increase the probability that Mi and T continue to evolve? ([Mi and T] $\leftarrow$ Mc)

These are the main questions that all members—teachers and children—have to ask and answer as they contribute to achieving the classroom contingency plan. They are also the "schematic" of awareness.

Without these thought-promoting queries, members remain unaware and without intent. Teachers do all the above. Here is an example of each.

1. ($X \rightarrow M$): Access to school breakfast can replace one X with another.
2. ($X \leftarrow M$): If children appear tired, a little exercise can wake them up or a nap can do much the same.
3. ([X + M] $\rightarrow$ T): If a positive emotional state meets a clear activity statement, by the teacher or others, children are more

likely to observe the teacher's demonstration of T and then engage in performing T as they manage each other to do so.

4. ([M + T] ← Mc): The teacher asks, "Who feels they learned T today?" Followed by: "What makes you feel good about it?" Or even given a future orientation, "Who helped you learn T yesterday? How did they help you today? Do you think they will do so again tomorrow?" ·

Although children do not have such moral values (V), awareness (A), or management (M) behavior to do the same, teachers can get them there. First, by using direct instruction of VAM as well as T. Second, by modeling what they teach in their own behavior—morals, awareness, and management. Third, by giving children opportunities to do the same. In combination with the fact that children are always behaving and have some level of M and T, teachers should realize that:

A teacher is not the "Lone Arranger" in the classroom.

Eventually, teachers recruit members and members eventually recruit themselves to help manage the classroom. Additionally, teachers can use the member's existing repertoires to help achieve success. (Classically, this is just *children-helping-children*, which was absolutely needed in the one-room school in which grades K-12 were housed, but then most of the T was reading, writing, and math.) Most children can help with changing a poor X into a good one. Many can help with M because they have the level needed. Some can help with practicing or learning T, because they already know T as demonstrated through their practice.

Awareness involves being able to verbalize the activity's contingency element relationships, especially that between morals and management. When members can, they are taking the first steps toward becoming ARC citizens. The answers, as discriminations, guide their management behavior, which in turn guides the use of their technical behaviors. The actions may be "wrong" or "off-base," but the use of the management strategies— especially planning and intervening—allows these off-base behaviors to be improved (changed). This potential improvement alters the probability of achieving T or finding a better way to manage themselves to do so.

This is the same as when engineers alter their product or services: they do so by gathering data, develop evidence (see the pattern in the data), and use the evidence to evaluate and redesign the artifact under investigation. Managers don't "discipline" engineers for not getting the "perfect artifact." They set them on a course to improve the product. Often, they don't have to do that because engineers like all human beings are *inferential creatures* (Part 1, Chapters 4 and 5). As soon as they use the product, they will see better ways to achieve the same end or change the end, even if it works okay. In the classroom, this activity always involves a change in process, either as redesigned teaching methods, a change in the classroom's structure (context), adjusting the repertoires, or some combination of these.

However, a change in a service or product first requires that managers change themselves, so that they can observe, talk clearly about, and perform the new human behavior process. This change is based on evidence. Only with a model can teachers (or any other engineering profession) reliably rip apart contingencies and remake them to better achieve valued purposes, and to do so morally.

CONTINGENCIES IN THE CLASSROOM

When all children in a group, classroom, or school can observe and use the same contingency logic and work toward the same T (by way of VAM repertoires), they illustrate awareness and begin to establish *compatible contingencies*. Such establishment marks the beginning of civility that is founded on rational thought, management, and moral values. Everyone is working within the classroom's moral values, to manage themselves to achieve the same valued purposes. The real problem is to observe *in-the-moment* what the self and others are doing managerially that keeps or establishes compatible contingencies in-the-moment.

As all of us know, there are inappropriate members in most classrooms. They do not contribute to the X, M, and T components of the activity. If all other children are modeling X, M, and T, then these "surrounding contingency models" can be an inducing event for another member's behaviors—X, M, and T. However, most of the time when young children "subvert" engendering T, they do so without awareness, usually because they do not have the needed M or the prerequisite T to help engender T for themselves or others. This requires that classrooms have a structure and social methods that allow any child at any time can get "help" to continue to behave appropriately (Chapter 2). This helping, as a management behavior, just makes it easier to fulfill the valued purpose of the activity, its T.

When children use management methods that subvert their own or others T, they establish *incompatible contingencies,* which is just a way of describing inappropriate behavior that does not fit the activity's master contingency plan. The strongest controlling hand, at such a point, is the application of the management repertoire's intervention strategy. It focuses on identifying the interaction of involved members that was coercive to the activity's value purpose, finding a "better way," and practicing it, so that the future will be different from the past. Teachers model intervening behavior, but children very gradually take over the strategy. Teachers are always adjusting to the following:

1.   On any day or moment children's background, X, is unknown (for some more than others).

2. There is a limited consistency of M because each child has different levels of the management repertoire on any day.

3. The component behaviors—those that make up the T being taught—are often unknown because some children do not have the prerequisite behaviors.

Thankfully, children are reflexive and adaptive learners; they come into the world ready to learn.[6] Young children are like goats; they munch on everything before their eyes. However, this munching may include the "right" as well as the "wrong."

TEACHERS' CONTROL OF CONTINGENCIES

As Chapter 2 indicated, the first step in controlling contingencies is to structure activities, so that children have opportunities to 1) stay appropriate, 2) get help, or 3) deal with an emergency at any time. From here, teachers deal directly with the contingency components for each activity (X, M, T). As children's behaviors unfold during activities, teachers' methods focus and evolve these activity behaviors. This "communication," as a contingency expression, has four basic functions:

1. It *induces or consequents* children's behavior at any moment,

2. It *points out inducer* and *consequent events* (as behaviors) that are taking place, about to take place, or may take place,

3. It *queries children to describe or predict* what was modeled in (2), but under slightly altered conditions, and

4. It *links together the repertoires* that are being performed during an activity.

When children can also "communicate" about how they *and* others are contributing to the activity contingency, they have acquired an *awareness repertoire*. If the communication fits the "reality" of the activity, they are *rationally aware managers*; they are following the evidence. If their management behaviors fit the activity, so that it can begin, continue, and end, they are *civil (moral) managers*.

We can look at classroom contingencies as a 1000-piece puzzle. If only a few non-functional pieces are added, the puzzle will never come together to produce children that we would describe as "on the road to becoming ARC citizens." Some may make it but some may not. How many irrational-noncivil citizens does it take to "beak the back" of the classroom, school, community, state, or nation? Not many it appears. Witness the changes, to our rights *and* duties since the 9/11 terrorist attack. These often take the form of armed and cyber security activities. These security changes have

---

[6] Shonkoff, J. P., Phillips, D. A. (Eds.), & National Research Council (U.S.). (2000). From neurons to neighborhoods: The science of early child development. Washington, D. C: National Academy Press. https://doi.org/10.17226/9824.

social, economic, and political costs (consequent events). The 2020 global pandemic and concurrent climate events have shown us the need for a rational, civil world government that can take on duties. What 2020 brought us was a daily view of the entire world. What most of us can now see is that every nation state appears to have the same, similar, or overlapping problems—resource allocation and distribution; diseases and climate events; and social justice issues. Our physical and social ills can only occur if we "band-aid" ourselves together and work from the bottom up and the top down (Chapter 18). Perhaps we need our present level of security because we have no clear idea about the moral duties of citizens or how to manage ourselves; thus, we have no clear idea regarding our awareness in the world. Is our reptilian brain still in control?

Contingency Viewpoints

Our first view is called the teacher's *activity contingency system* view. The teacher (or any caregiver) is attempting to control contingency events of an activity to bring about new, functional behavior in children. This contingency view goes like the following.

Teachers' control activity contingencies,
so that children learn to control their own contingencies.

This is a moral value statement. Teachers, all of us, seek control—to change children's behavior—so that they evolve more complex repertoires that are often given the names social, emotional, and academic learning. What the above statement does not reflect is the *communication interaction* between teachers and children. This communication exposes what has been hidden from clear view: the VAM-T content and their relationships.

Teachers and children are simultaneously both the "changers" and the "changed." In other words, human behavior in the classroom—as in the rest of life—is not one sided. There is some degree of reciprocity between members. There is a moment-by-moment *communication loop* (some may say feedback loop) that can be stated as follows:

All behavior—as X, M, or T—impacts other's behavior.

This interactive control between members is not equal relative to efficient means and satisfactory ends. Moreover, the impact of cohesive and coercive control can "accumulate" over time with each "instance" of behavior by members. Awareness, as a meta-language, describes or evaluates the relationship between management and moral-value behaviors. In the classroom, these moral values are for the most part duties required of members that acknowledge what members must do, so that everyone can experience activity success.

Historically, teachers have been considered the strong controller, the expert. However, teachers are controlled by children as much as mothers are controlled by their infants. This impact can focus on any contingency component—X, M, T. Children differ in their degree of control and methods (practices) to alter *contingencies* (Chapter 4). Some have more control or methods to control others or themselves. However, a management repertoire that unifies members can be a counter weight to unequal control. It is analogous to a manager being confronted by a "union of managers." The union can control the manager. That union of control is an element of the management repertoire (Part 2).

Our entire educational system—starting from infancy through graduate school—seeks to move children from those who originally could only suckle, cry, wiggle about, and act reflexively into those who can control the world around them, including themselves and others. When children gain such control, the system has been successful relative to its valued purposes as long as their management fits within the range of acceptable (moral) behaviors.

Children can be taught to observe their and other's management, awareness, and moral values that support their technical behavior. With all four repertoires in place, children facilitate the completion and success (achieve the value purpose) of their activities. These children have doubt; they see the risks, can be persuaded or challenged by rational argument, and can undergo an alteration in various VAM-T repertoires. They are *not locked into* traditions, texts, or various 250 year after-the-fact interpretations of them. If they are locked into anything, it is in the need for evidence to evaluate the activities they and others undertake. If they can learn to do so, then their futures can be radically different from what has been the case for human relationships throughout history. They learn that this evidence helps them evaluate their activity plans, the extent to which their moral value and management repertoires have helped them move forward in the context of others, and what consequent events are produced.

To accomplish changing the standard classroom or school control procedures requires answers to two questions.

1. How can planning and intervention strategy practices be evolved at the classroom, school, and district levels?
2. What are the criteria that allow children to enter into each level of (1), as well as helping others directly?

These two planning questions can be answered in many ways through the use of the planning strategy (Chapter 15). The answers, which are not independent, will determine when children can begin to participate in these management activities. The answers have almost nothing to do with age or grade level, but on their behavior towards themselves and others as controllers and controllees.

The answers can, for example, focus on rites-of-passage into these major parts of *school-taught citizenship*. However, success can only be achieved if the system redesigns their contingencies, so that children are given enough activities with sufficient levels of practice to gain proficiency in the management, awareness, and moral value repertoires. These are what they will take with them as they move from the classroom to the outside world. This taking will determine, in the long run, the "style" of the world they will create when it is their turn to govern. If we want the probability of ARC citizens to move beyond chance or happenstance, we will have to change ourselves by first learning about the model, its mechanisms, and the repertoire content that is to be taught (Part 2 of this text), as well as designing, implementing, and evaluating strong teaching methods.

System of Behavior

We are all artifacts built, in part, by the interaction with our genetic, natural, and social environments. This can be seen by examining the thousands of languages and social structures that populate the world. Each slowly evolved in separate and often very different physical contexts. As a result, these languages sound very different, are written in a wide variety of ways, and are often not translatable one to the other word-for-word or even phrase-for-phrase. Social structures are just as diverse.

Those, who live in the same context, speak a common language. Look at the scientists, engineers, and technologists with their common languages—they put landers on Mars and manufacture solar panels, as well as having invented and built weapons of mass destruction. However, they can communicate, they can work together, they can control events (their X, M, T contingency components) relative to their valued purpose. Context— both social and environmental—appears to be the defining difference between groups. The first three chapters of this book can be summarized as a *system of behavior*. This system does not mean we will all become the same—we are all different but we have commonalities. It is the commonalities that will allow us to communicate with each other more effectively and, perhaps, even form harmonious, lasting human relationships. We just have to tap into these commonalities, these mechanisms of human behavior.

Broad View of the System

There are three broad interdependent levels that contribute to the "development" of ourselves, individually and relationally. They are highly complex, with much that is unknown. The three levels include our:

1. genetic endowment,
2. past history, and
3. current circumstances.

Genetic Endowment: Level 1

Genetic Endowment, from one perspective, provides our children with all the basic life processes, such as their heart beat, breathing, seeing, hearing, movement, and much more. From another perspective, it provides the neurological mechanisms that make behaviors like language, remembering, learning, thinking, imagining, and emotions possible—these may be called our "dispositions" toward such behaviors. As parents and teachers, there is not much we can do about a child's genetic endowment once birth has occurred. Yet, all of these basic life and dispositional neurological processes are influenced by what, how, and when we interact with our children, which includes prenatal interactions.

We all know to be on the lookout for emotional-physiological states (X) in children that indicate social events that negatively affect learning (poor nutrition, lack of sleep, stress, and abuse) and neurological states that affect social relationships and learning (autism, ADHD, Rett Syndrome). All of these can stop or inhibit learning whether in an individual or social context. We also know that there are powerful genetic-based mechanisms that control children who exhibit prodigy talents in music, math, science, language, and art. How these "gifts" develop is dependent, at least in part, on social mechanisms and associated environmental events.

Past History: Level 2

Past history refers to children's genetic development after birth in combination with the physical and social environments in which development occurs. These two interact. Essentially, the development of the genetic givens all require a social environment to see expression, to develop. For example, if children are fed a diet deficient in protein, their physical and intellectual development will be curtailed. Our goal as caregivers is to develop these environmental events to the fullest extent possible—within the scope of existing knowledge and resources. If this development is done efficiently and effectively, many future health and neurological problems can be prevented. These last two sentences represent the fundamental moral tone and perspective of this text.

If the physical and social environments are not presenting optimal events, then problems can ensue. To make matters difficult:

1. Genetic abnormalities often appear after birth, in infancy or early childhood, that lead to or cause behavioral abnormalities.
2. Genetic and physical environment factors can interact, setting off behavioral abnormalities.
3. Physical environment factors can set off behavioral abnormalities, irrespective of genetics.
4. Social factors can set off behavioral abnormalities, irrespective of genetics or an exemplary physical environment.

The word "abnormality" represents a continuum from those who have disorders that "inhibit" their learning and those, like prodigies, who have some "gift" for learning. A behavioral abnormality, no matter what the cause, can restrict a child, prodigy or not, from fully participating in any number of activities. The above four types of abnormalities are often hard to separate. Again, there is not much we, as teachers, can do about the first, except to be aware of and look for the genetic-based behavioral manifestations of these abnormalities. We now have some genetic tests that provide identification and a few methods are being developed that allow for a small degree of control over a few of them. We can, in conjunction with health care professionals, carefully monitor the second and third, thus reducing the probability of preventing some inhibiting factors and curing others. It is the fourth level of behavior abnormalities that we can do something about presently.

Current Circumstances: Level 3

The third level, *current circumstances*, refer to the more or less immediate time frame. It is part of the X in the contingency model. It is the period over which we can overcome some "weak" genetics that predispose children to abnormalities that restrict their participation in life's activities, as well as some "poor" social and environmental histories. Think in terms of vaccinations as preventions and remedial reading programs as cures. The first protects a child's immune system (a genetic given) against disease and the second can remediate reading deficiencies, depending on when the program is initiated or if genetics are involved. The present focus is on *prevention* within the limits that the educational system allows.

Controlling Contingencies

Children's repertoires are originally controlled by their genetic endowment, which quickly begins to interact with their social history and current circumstances. As they interact with the social environment, the control that they have over themselves changes. They will try to control activity contingencies in ways that engender *their* purposes. If there is no "learning" purpose, the behaviors are called things like play or aggression.

Most certainly, the VAM-T repertoires are controlled to an extent by the interaction of genetics, past history, and current circumstances. But the greater our children's knowledge, most of which is verbal, the less their future is left to happenstance and their old "reactive" brain. Some would say they have "free will." It seems more accurate to say that they gain the repertoires to control themselves and others within the bounds of physical, biological, psychological, sociological, and anthropological laws (those known and unknown).

By directly teaching the underlying repertoires of management, awareness, and moral value, the greater the control we can turn over to children. If these repertoires are clearly defined—the main point of this book—and taught, the greater the likelihood (less happenstance or chance) that our children will develop into aware, rational, civil citizens. Will they, eventually, populate and build a more rational, civil, and safe world? The eventual answer will be up to us as adults. By directly teaching these repertoires, we take a step towards ensuring what some would call the "quality control" of our world's citizens. This quality can't be legislated. We must instill it in our children, beginning at an early age. Graphic 3.1 outlines one perspective of the VAM-T repertoires relative to ARC endowed citizens. From another, we could say that the children are being given the social, emotional, and academic (technical) learning that are seen as important to the socialization process.

The figure indicates that the four sub-repertoires (arrowed repertoires) of our behavior are interrelated (center circle). Together, they foster the emergence of aware, rational, civil citizens. However, we must be aware of the open-system influences that our genetic endowment and social past history (families, community, and cultures—dashed circles), as well as their interactions. Often these "outside the school" events are in conflict and, thus have an overall impact on the development of children's ARC behavior. Many of these community clashes revolve around access to educational resources and very specific curriculum elements like the views that surround the teaching of history and evolution. The VAM-T repertoires emerge out of the social behaviors required to engage in schooling, not from either of the above elements. However, these stakeholders can't be ignored.

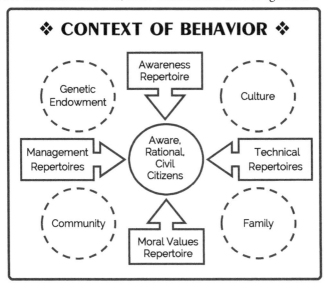

GRAPHIC 3.1: VAM-T in fuller perspective.

It can't be said too strongly: All four repertoires are learned by way of the social environment—children's families, schools, and communities. If parents started this teaching with knowledge and intent, they could inoculate their children against many of the negative social forces that occur in children's later history that often block their awareness of their moral-manage development.

Our past laissez-faire approach to socializing children has most certainly played a part in fostering our present non-rational, non-civil world. As our educational technologies emerge, we are beginning to see their place in the world and their duties therein. Yet, a tension still exists between the we/us and the me/my group perspectives. This tension will remain until we take a stance and instill in our children the VAM-T behaviors that comprise aware, rational, civil citizens worldwide. This statement is, of course, a moral value.

SUMMARY

We can summarize this chapter with the contingency model.

$$[X: Mi \rightarrow (M \text{ or } T) \leftarrow Mc]$$

Mi is management that induces (sets in motion) M or T. Mc is management behavior that consequents M or T. From the management side, for example, Zen offers Zena a pencil (Mi) and Zena says, "thanks," which is a consequence (Mc) for Zen's management behavior that allows Zen to keep working. From the technical side, Xen asks Xan if her worksheet answer is correct (Mi), and Xan replies, "yes," which is a consequence (Mc) for Xen's technical behavior (worksheet answer) and for asking (Mi). The aim of this representation is to illustrate the extent of the complexity of our *adaptive open system* with multiple members.

Second, the contingency model can be re-represented as done in Graphic 3.2. The three big circles in Graphic 3.2 represents members ongoing VAM-T repertoires and that each interacts with all other members (thick double arrowed arrows). X has some degree of control over M and T, as when a member is happy or depressed, hungry or sated, rested or tired. M represents the management repertoire that induces T (Mi) or delivers consequent event (Mc) for T or both. The teacher or other members can induce this M of the activity. T (center circles of big circles) represents the technical behavior, the activity objective. M induces T, as indicated by the arrow from M to T.

Awareness, A, and moral values, V, are verbal repertoires. Awareness is the verbal classification of management, M, as fitting or not fitting the moral values, V. This classification is based on the linkage of V and M (as the double arrow between V and M). The double arrow between M and V, indicates that both M and V must be known before awareness evaluation statements can be uttered. If M fits the V, then M is cohesive (fitting) behavior, otherwise it is coercive (misfitting).

The valued purpose, T, and the moral values, V, may or may not be congruent or compatible. Other members, as indicated by the box in Graphic 3.2, illustrate that all members contribute to each other in the same

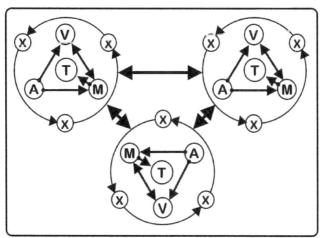

GRAPHIC 3.2: Multiple members interacting with VAM-T Repertoires.

way, even if the contributions are not equally weighted—some children and teachers have more control than others. This differential control is called "power" to many social scientists (Chapter 10).

For the most part, children come into the classroom without awareness of their values or much in the way of management repertoires. However, they may become aware gradually. For example, if children greet each other with positive statements (Mi), then they are inducing (engendering) a positive emotional state (X). If children congratulate one another for getting problems correct (T) or working together (M), then they are cohesively consequenting T and M repertoires (Mc).

Gradually, these nascent repertoires are evolved. Children learn to manage themselves, as well as thinking about their management as the way they "treat" others and others "treat" them—their moral repertoire begins to control their management repertoire. They are taught to verbalize about these interactions (awareness). They use management strategies (operations, methods, tactics) to control 1) what they do for or to others and 2) what others do to or for them. When they can perform all the needed behavior within the context of their moral values, they are classified as aware, rational, civil citizens. Now, look at Graphic 3.2 and multiply this three-person complexity by the number of members in the classroom, and divide by 3. This results in a view of a classroom's open-system complexity (even if one can't define "social complexity" with any real rigor).

4

Contingencies:
Behavioral Mechanisms

Chapter 3 modeled classroom activities from a contingency perspective. It was diagramed as:

$$[X: Mi \rightarrow (M \text{ or } T) \leftarrow Mc]$$

From the teacher's perspective, this contingency model represents the activity contingency plan. It identifies the processes to achieve the valued purpose of the activity, its technical behavior (T). As Chapter 3 indicated, each member of the classroom enters in their own contingency state. They are in some emotional-physiological state (X) and have various amounts of management (M) behavior with which to work with others and technical (T) behavior to learn what is being taught. Thus, each child adds or subtracts from achieving the activity contingency plan.

What is missing are the *mechanisms that make learning possible*. What is it about children that allows them to learn? These mechanisms can be examined from the internal or external side of children. Knowing these mechanisms allows teachers to develop operations (methods) that increase the probability of controlling the classroom's open-system complexity. The qualifying caveat is that group success begins with learning the T of the activity. Without this learning, it will not matter what classroom management or teaching methods are used to initiate learning. For children, it would be like getting excited about eating (X), walking to the store (M), and finding no food on the selves (-T).

There are three parent classes of mechanisms: *genetic-physiological*, *behavioral*, and *social*. What we skip over is the genetics and neuroscience, although Chapter 3 briefly touches on them. The behavioral deals with the qualities that help humans learn. The social deals with the qualities that allow humans to form functional groups that can achieve a variety of value purposes.

Behavioral Mechanisms

Behavioral mechanisms are *qualities* of the individual that makes learning possible. The introduction to Part 1 grouped these mechanisms into the quality of *inference*. However, two mechanisms make us inferential creatures. The first of these processes is association between behaviors. We originally studied association with *respondent conditioning* (also called Pavlovian or classical conditioning). The second of these processes is the effect of consequences on behavior. These consequences follow behavior. We study effects with *operant conditioning* (also called instrumental conditioning). Most teachers know about these two types of learning processes. However, these processes 1) interact and 2) are dependent on a prior history, which at any moment may be different for all classroom members. The objective is to observe and control these events within the classroom context. The greater the control of these, the greater the probability to achieve the activity's valued purpose across all members.

Respondent Mechanism

Children come into the world with a wealth of *autonomic-based behavior*. They suckle, cry, or giggle under conditions ranging from hunger and pain to being touched and hugged. Respondent conditioning makes "neutral" events effective at producing these physiologically-based behaviors. Moreover, once a neutral event is effective at producing a change in behavior, other neutral events can be associated with it. In the long run, across a life, *layers of associations* can be built up—each being effective at producing some change.

By the time children enter the classroom, such layers of association may have already been built up. Children may at this point be startled, cry, freeze, or relax in the context of various surrounding behaviors just like Pavlov's dog salivated in the context of a bell after it was paired with food. These autonomic-based behaviors are often called *reflexive behavior*, which is part of X behavior in the contingency model (Chapter 3). After they are "paired" they are called *conditioned reflexive behavior*.

When the neutral event—like a bell, a bright light, or a human being—becomes conditioned to the unconditioned behavior like a startle, cry, or nausea, it is followed by the unconditioned behavior. The new, once-neutral event is now said to *elicit* the old, physiologically-based autonomic behavior. For example, access to the classroom, as a new event, may set off such unconditioned behavior because that is what new, strange situations often do. We need to realize that any of these physiologically-based behaviors, as part of X, may well be incompatible with the desired behavior M or T. Children can't learn as well or at all in such states. The autonomic state that we wish to promote usually have names like calm, relaxation, attention, and focus.

In such situations, the purpose is to get children into such a calm-attention-focus state and then associate that state with the learning process. In the long run, when teaching is underway, children go into such states and stay that way throughout the teaching activity. If children are already in such a calm-attention-focus, then the teaching activity should try to keep them in that state. One way to do that is use operant conditioning methods.

Instrumental Mechanism

Operant conditioning evolves behavior that is said to be *emitted* by the learner in particular contexts. The presentation of consequences delivered contingent on the emitted behavior will alter future behavior in some way. It may alter old classes of behavior or develop new classes of behavior. In both cases, we are altering their *becoming*. Thus, this altering or development is a moral-value undertaking. Often, we talk about the *shaping of behavior* to bring about change—the step-by-step process of changing behavior, which is based on differential consequences needed to build complex behavior. Thus, we need to ask about 1) the types of consequent events and 2) what effects do they bring about in members.

Four Classes of Consequent Events

Four classes of operant consequences provide various patterns of control over instrumental (operant) behavior. These patterns illustrate how behavior changes when the consequences that come after the behavior are altered in various ways. Historically, the focus of the manipulation of consequences has been on T behavior in the experimental chamber under the control by an experimenter. However, in a social context, consequences are delivered through the management behavior (Mi or Mc) of all other members. But until the next chapter, we will set the social aside.

Each cell of Graphic 4.1 gives the name of the contingency class (center cells) and the arrows indicate what happens to behavior (think M or T) when additive or subtractive consequences are presented or removed, contingently. What happens to behavior depends on a history of presentations or removals. It often takes a long history of either to instill either type.

Each presentation represents an *example*, which is an *instance* of a class of behavior (Chapter 2). For each of the four contingency classes, children develop a pattern of behavior consistent with the *set-of-examples* presented. Yet, over time, many interesting changes to the patterns develop depending on what types consequences (1-4) are operational. Yes, more than one is often operational across activity members, and they are often in *behavior change conflict*—are in conflict with each other relative to whether they increase or decrease the likelihood of cohesive behavior needed for an activity contingency plan to work.

In all four cases, the consequence—think Mc—promotes some sort of effect on other behavior. We know this because it does so—yes, this is a circular statement. But if Mc works again and again across behaviors, children, and contexts, the circularity is rendered irrelevant within the system, at least in terms of its control if not its explanation. Repeated successes across individuals, behaviors, and contexts are *replications*, a

❖ Four Classes of Consequences ❖

	Subtractive Event	Additive Event
Remove Event ①	Subtractive Reinforcement (↓ Behavior)	Subtractive Punishment (↓ Behavior) ②
Present Event	Additive Punishment (↓ Behavior)	Additive Reinforcement (↑ Behavior)
③		④

GRAPHIC 4.1: Four types of contingency consequences.

pivotal science and engineering methodology. It is the pattern of behavior that emerge from each of the consequence classes that are important.

Subtractive Reinforcement (Cell 1)

Subtractive Reinforcement (Cell 1) is the *removal* of a *subtractive consequence* contingent on behavior (M or T). The subtractive event is also thought of as a painful event. It increases the behavior that turns off the subtractive consequent event. The behavior that turns off (removes, eliminates) the subtractive consequence increases. Subtractive reinforcement was originally called *negative reinforcement*. Notice that *the behavior learned is not the T of VAM-T*, but something else like being quiet, or keeping one's head down.

Subtractive Punishment (Cell 2)

Subtractive Punishment (Cell 2) is the removal of an *additive consequence* contingent on behavior (M or T). This action like subtractive reinforcement causes a decrease in M or T, at least in the short term. With subtractive punishment, we are taking away what children have "earned" in the past or what they could have earned. Additive events like a chance to learn interesting things, or interacting with peers are in jeopardy.

Again, what is not learned is T.

In the classroom learning T is its value purpose. What is learned is, again, some behavior that stops the loss of something valued like talking with friends during the day or playing with them at recess.

Additive Punishment (Cell 3)

Additive Punishment (Cell 3) is the presentation of a *subtractive event* (think Mc) contingent on behavior. A subtractive event decreases behaviors and is classified as a "painful" event. As Graphic 4.1 indicates, a subtractive event delivered contingent on behavior may decrease the behavior.

Again, what is not learned is T.

Children, all of us, will generally try to *avoid* this subtractive event or *escape* it altogether. The avoidance behavior may be to "run silent and deep" by keeping quiet, siting in the back of the room and not volunteering to answer anything. The escape behavior may be to become sick as often as possible or become a truant. When escaping and avoidance do not work, children may *counter control* against the punishing system, as represented by teachers or the school.

Additive Reinforcement (Cell 4)

Additive Reinforcement—Cell 4—is the presentation of an *additive behavior consequence*, contingent (dependent) on behavior M or T. This arrangement increases the probability of these behaviors in the future. *Additive* refers to that which most of us find to be positive, pleasant, approachable events. We return to the same behavior because it has an emotional-physiological basis—it is part of our inferential biology.

Relationship Between Consequent Events

As indicated above, cells 1 through 3 have a common outcome:

What is learned is NOT the valued purpose (T) being taught.

Subtractive reinforcement. is usually something—some person or context—that exists as children set foot in the door. It may be the presence of a bully or just a history of painful events like a failure to learn some technical behavior (T) being taught. *Subtractive punishment* is often called "timeout," were the possibility of engaging in learning and social interaction is eliminated during the timeout. *Additive Punishment* is a painful event delivered contingent on some behavior that is not part of the activity contingency plan. So, what do children learn from these three types of events?

They learn to escape, avoid, or counter-control from the context.

Children still adapt but they do so by escaping, avoiding, or counter controlling a manager or managers that brings about these three classes of coercive effects. Thus, only *additive reinforcement (Cell 4)* can be used to evolve or engender the X, M, or T of an activity, and learn other VAM repertoire components.

Effects Produced by Consequent Events

Consequences are changes that follow from other behavior. These changes may occur after an inducing or a consequent event—our two types of *causes of change*. The terms *consequences* and *consequent events* are two different things. Think of their differences this way:

Inducing events (Mi) cause consequences.
Consequent events (Mc) cause consequences.

Each type of event—as our own or the other's behavior—may or may not have the *power* to change another's behavior—the change is probabilistic. These consequences can occur contingently or by accident (unplanned or unintended consequent events). The first is *planned* and the second *just happens*. We witness the latter when a rung on a jungle gym breaks, a child falls, and an ankle is broken. We witness the latter when the child is seldom selected to be part of a group and gives up trying. Accidents are everywhere, physical and social.

The consequences of inducing or consequent events come in three basic flavors: *emotional, access,* and *restructuring*. All three can occur from a single instance of inducing- or consequent-event behavior by others. It is learning to observe the interactions of behavior as inducing or consequenting events that effect (control) others. What we want to do is to observe the inducer or consequent events and identify consequences produced by Mi or Mc. However, we want ourselves and our children to observe these contingencies *in-the-moment* or as they occur—a somewhat difficult observation to imagine, at this point, without repertoire content knowledge (V, A, M, T).

The most difficult consequences to observe are the emotional and those that take place well into future. This makes *in-the-moment* observation of the interactions and their resulting consequences from behaviors very difficult. The distant effects are what often make up the *unintended consequent events*, something we see emerge as individuals or societies plan for the future. At times, the near-term consequences interfere with "believing" in the long-term consequences. The near-term has some powerful, immediate cohesive consequences. These must be brought out into the open during teaching, as should the potential coercive consequences.

Emotional Changes in Behavior

Emotional changes can be represented as the changes in the brain and associated physiology that result from some behavioral event (Chapter 3). In a gross sense, these can be described at one extreme as a "stressed" state and at the other as "joyous." These changes are the body's, often, immediate reaction to our own or others' behavior. Some are brought about directly within the body as "reactions" to various internal physiological states produced by all sorts of events like hormonal imbalances or a particular organ dysfunction or sleep deprivation. However, some are produced because of 1) one's "thinking behavior" that produces an embarrassed flush because a statement is immediately recognized as inappropriate, 2) "ruminating" that brings about a depressed state, or 3) when a "behavioral event" is remembered. These examples indicate that one repertoire of our behavior changes another repertoire. The biological, psychological, and social variables interact to bring about or restrict behavior.

Also, other classroom members bring about emotional behavior. It may be an emotion from a sudden hug, a verbal put down from classmates, or a "thank you" by someone helped. At the extreme, such behavioral events are often called "significant emotional events." If they are repeated or violent enough in and of themselves, they produce an emotional state called PTSD. Our talk about emotions is approximate at best.[1]

Yet, we all understand the "wow" from doing a backflip, the "exhilaration" of solving a problem, the "high" or "rush" from exercise, the "pride" from building a home, the "rush" and "relaxation" of a new relationship, and the "contentment" from reflecting on work that is placed in the "fine day's work" category. In Chapter 7, music, song, and dance will be used to cause an "emotional state" designed to unify the classroom members. These positive emotional states get repertoires going and evolving. But the same can be said for the behavior of a group that performs such feats as ensuring that all community members have food on the table, clean drinking water, heat for their domiciles, and a ride to their voting location.

We also understand the punishing emotions brought about by our own or others' behavior that is associated with (contingent or non-contingent) consequent events. These include the pain from a back-flip done wrong; the frustration from a problem not solved; the child hit by a drunken driver; the girl, who's bicycle gets a flat tire, falls and breaks an arm; the nausea from witnessing a dangerous situation; and the stress that comes from a day of excessive work. These are the painful punishers of behavior that often occur in the context of others or by others.

Access Changes to Behavior

Access changes make other behavior possible; access is given or gained. These may be contingent on behavior or accidental. After children learn to read, they can read to themselves and talk to others about what they have read. Once a door is opened, one can enter as well as have their previous sensory or emotional state altered. Once the home is complete, it can be lived in. A new baby gives access to a very different life. On the negative side, a gunshot wound engenders medical care, as does a broken bone. Some behavior has caused access for the self or others.

Restructuring Changes in Behavior

Restructured behavior is a physical or repertoire change caused by interacting with the social or environmental. Again, the change can be contingent or non-contingent on behavior. Teaching reading changes children into readers. Building activities may produce a home. Making love can conceive a child. An accident can cause injury. Writing may bring into existence a poem. Some part of the world within ourselves or external to

---

[1] https://en.wikipedia.org/wiki/Emotion

ourselves has been changed by some behavior, either our own or others. Some of these changes support the activity contingency plan (as any behavior that keeps VAM-T evolving) and some distract from the plan (as any behavior that slows or stops VAM-T evolution).

Often the most powerful *restructuring consequent events* occur in the far distant future, as when we do not exercise, eat a healthy diet, take legal or illicit drugs, or fail to alter our gas-guzzling transportation methods. Also, they occur in near time, as with a gunshot wound or a bone-breaking fall. We begin to be aware and prepare for these consequences because we gain knowledge through experience, direct instruction, or research, as we have relative to the use of fossil fuels, asbestos, chemical cleaning agents, and plastics. Should we give young children a graphically real taste of the long-term consequences that occur because of such long-term behaviors? When and how become important if the answer is in the affirmative.

Relationship of the Three Types of Effects

Most often, these three types of consequent events, contingent or accidental, occur closely in time and space, and are caused by the same instance or instances of behavior—by the self or others. For young children, the three classes of consequences often follow 1, 2, 3, but not always. Each contributes to the control of behavior. For example, getting dressed changes those dressed, as it allows them access to places that require clothes and can make them feel good. Making love provides a rush and exhilaration, can conceive a child, and may provide access to conversation, further intimacy, sleep, or worry.

Yet, at times, the three classes may be delayed well into the future. As an extreme example, did Henry Ford realize that by the last half of the 20th century that his product type would be a significant contributor to local and global pollution that harms others? Did the public realize that individual transit exacerbates pollution more than mass transit? It is doubtful, since the "science of pollution" was not yet born. This new type of transporting most certainly caused immediate positive emotional, access, and restructuring consequences. But the long-term consequences are now in front of all of us and it only took about a century of human history for such to come about.

Without a knowledge of consequences, they remain invisible—consider our initial ignorance not only of using fossil fuels, but of smoking cigarettes, breathing asbestos, or failure to eat a balanced diet. Often, this ignorance is based on unfounded or wrong *beliefs* that get in the way. Today, we challenge these beliefs through evidence. Doctors no longer let blood or invade bodies with dirty hands because of the evidence and their impersonal objectivity toward it. However, many are still resistant to evidence. For example, many still refuse to take vaccines, even though billions of inoculated people have shown their effectiveness in protecting health across a wide range of microscopic life forms that cause bodily harm. If children understood consequences from a social perspective—as who is doing what to whom—would we continue to behave in the same ways? It may all depend on what moral values exhibited within the social structure in which we live and our overt awareness of them. Often, these moral values are hidden deep within our belief systems about what a human being represents and signifies.

DIRECTION of CONSEQUENCES

The direction of consequences was implied during the analysis of the types. The direction of consequent events refers to the emotional, access, and restructuring consequences an individual's or group's behavior provides not only for themselves but for others as well. This direction needs to be clearly represented.

On the positive side, when children take their first steps (walking behavior), they emit giggles (emotional expression), locate themselves across the room (restructuring), and play with the toys that the walking has brought them to (access). At the same time, parents, because of their child's new behavior, have many emotional, access, and restructuring consequences as well. The walking behavior gives direction to both the child and caregivers' lives for a long time.

On the subtractive or punishing side, the same can be said for the child who gets injured or becomes sick. This behavior causes extensive and long-term emotional, access, and restructuring consequences for parents and other family members as well. The same holds for classrooms. At minimum, it was suggested that we need processes to keep emotions positive. We want to give children access to ways to "make up work" or "find better ways", so that absent behavior is soon present or conflict behavior is replaced with cohesive behavior. These are restructuring consequences produced by either inducing or consequent events.

If children learn to observe the direction toward which the three types of consequences take, will it affect behavior toward themselves and others? Will it help them learn the VAM-T repertoires? If children learn to observe what they have control over and what has control over them—that they are controller and controllee at the same time—will their behavior be changed by this knowledge? Is knowledge a consequence, do the consequences create knowledge, or both?

COMMONALITY of CONSEQUENCES

Consequences do not have the same effectiveness (power) for all classroom members. They are often relative to various children because of their genetic, past histories, and current circumstances (Chapter 3). However, there are consequences that work for nearly everyone. This *commonality* across members is built into our humanity. We are gregariousness creatures. Here, the expression, *hugs, kisses, caresses, smiles, laughs, and kind words* sum up this common thread of positive consequences that cause a change in behavior. At the same time, we have a commonality relative to punishing consequences. We all avoid pain of various sorts; when extreme, we establish contingencies that help us avoid risks.

Although we focus on commonality, relativity is also important. Because all members are different (a foundational assumption of this text), consequent events work differently, we have a variety of individuals from accountants to zoologists, who take joy in what they do and often give joy to anyone for whom they do it.

Yet, we know that some individuals can't easily learn. Still others have "dispositions" or "aptitudes" towards a repertoire that allow them in various ways to easily learn one repertoire over others. Notice the music, math, or language prodigy, polymath, or savant who sees and then does, or just does. Is it the teacher's duty to help sort out these members, so they can become what they are capable of becoming? Whatever direction is taken, it is based on moral values—as how we interact with others—and the available resources.

Compatibility of Consequences

Compatibility occurs when all activity members' behavior act as events for other's behavior related to beginning, continuing, or ending an activity's contingency. They are all attempting with inducing or consequent event behaviors to support the activity contingency plan. When all members' management behavior contributes to the activity plan, *the group is classified as compatible.* When all members use management behavior that does not contribute to the activity plan, it may still be compatible, but we call it rebellion or revolution. Will creating compatibility toward the activity contingency plan add to evolving ARC children? We will find an answer only if we can find teaching operations that can expose and build positive compatibility.

In the classroom, members often cause a variety of behaviors, only some of which are compatible with the activity's contingency plan. These are seen as "competing" behavioral events. Often, they set the stage for conflict. The result may well lead to emotional, access, and restructuring chaos. The achievement of compatibility across all group members may be a necessary step towards building a consistent and effective learning environment—one where the children walk in the door ready and eager to learn.

Compatibility is a <u>quality</u> of the group.

Just how it is achieved depends on the way classrooms are structured, what children know about VAM-T repertoires, and what operations the teacher uses to make the classroom one filled with compatible operations between members. The teaching operations (methods) begin with additive reinforcement that has demonstrated that a great deal of learning can occur when the appropriate arrangement of contingency elements exists. The use of an additive consequent event or events, as the primary method of management, appears to engender positive, let's continue, emotional states, which is just another bit of learned behavior associated with other social and environmental events that foster the direct learning of T in a contingency arrangement. If done "sufficiently right," will children want to continue learning, seek out further learning, and be prepared to solve problems whose solution process was not directly taught? Can they become their own managers for change in a world that is now far from compatible?

WHAT HAS BEEN LEFT OUT

This chapter has left out at least three important elements. First, the associations that are set up by both respondent and operant mechanisms. These induce behavior. Children escape, avoid, or counter control the managers delivering punishing events (Cells 1-3 in Graphic 4.1). Children approach a context (of structures or members) when managers have consistently used positive consequences like learning T (Cell 4 of Graphic 4.1). Here the teachers, like the experimenter, control events before and/or during activities. This requires that contingency mechanisms need to be concerned with antecedent events (operations) prior to or during sessions. This concern is dealt with in the next chapter.

Second, the shaping of complex behavior has been ignored. This is because the steps in shaping a class of behavior is for the most part embedded in the curricula and its teaching methods. Shaping, as the moment-by-moment adjustments to contingencies, uses cohesive consequences (Cell 4 of Graphic 4.1). Shaping techniques—be they applied to discriminations, operations, or both—are a very important part of any teaching (Chapter 2). They involve the use of a combination of models, prompts, tests, and consequent events to bring a class of behavior to life and make it a permanent part of children's repertoires. The curricula content is covered for VAM in Part 2, Chapters 9-17.

Third, details of inductive behavior have been left out. All *complex adaptive systems* have one key attribute: emergence.[1] It is the performance of behaviors not directly taught. With discrimination learning, we know, for example, that we stop on red and go forward on green. But what happens when we set up complex contingencies? Remembering that we have a classroom of members each establishing congruent or noncongruent contingencies. Said another way, what will emerge that was not directly taught? Humans often wonder why conflicts or heroics occur. Here is a single example that may point the way.

It is called *emergent relationship learning.*[2, 3] As illustrated in Table 4.1, this occurs when selected pairings of different X-Y item sets of "things" are learned with additive reinforcement.

Learning these sets leads to *emergent relations.* For example, given that children can **identity match** three sets of 20 items each (e.g., match spoken with spoken words, match printed words with printed words, and pictures with pictures), they meet the basic requirement for proceeding with training: identity matching establishes that children can both see, hear, and speak within the learning context.

The spoken words-pictures set and the spoken words-printed words are parallel but separately trained. The spoken word set includes words like "cat," "tree," and "house." Correspondingly, the picture and printed word sets includes corresponding sets with that of cat, tree, and house.

Next, the children were trained on the following X-Y and X-Z relationships indicated in **Rows 1 and 2** of Table 4.1. They are leaning to **match-to-sample** through positive reinforcement. **Row 1** trains the children to match pictures to words spoken to them. **Row 2** trains them to match printed words to the words spoken to them.

The above two relationship training sets resulted in four **emergent relationships** (behavior that comes about without training). Emergent behaviors are usually matched to their new relationship on the first trial of these new sample relationships. **Row 3** is picture comprehension. **Row 4** is word reading. These two rows illustrate the emergence of symmetry between the trained sets,(e.g., if X, then Y, therefore if Y then X for Row 1). Row 5 is picture-word comprehension. **Row 6** is word-picture comprehension. these two Rows illustrate both symmetry and transitivity [(if $X \leftrightarrow Y$) and $X \leftrightarrow Z$), then $(Y \leftrightarrow Z)$].

TABLE 4.1 Emergent Relationships	
Trainer	**Child**
1. (X-Spoken) ➜	(Y-Pictures)
2. (X-Spoken) ➜	(Z-Printed)
Then These Relations Emerge	
3. (Y-Pictures) ➜	(X-Spoken)
4. (Z-Printed) ➜	(X-Spoken)
5. (Y-Pictures) ➜	(Z-Printed)
6. (Z-Printed) ➜	(Y-Pictures)

This example illustrates a naturally occurring inductive process that is important in learning. It appears to be "facilitated" by one of the first technical behaviors humans learn: language. But it is just the tip of the language learning or language assisted iceberg. For example, by adding to the above training

---

[2] This naming convention does not follow that used in Behavior Analysis, Positive Behavioral Support, or Relational Frame Theory. Our context is different. We are not doing stimulus equivalence experiments or single-subject therapy sessions. We are taking an evolutionary and social perspective toward a system of human repertoires within a system called the classroom.

[3] Sidman, M. & Cresson, O., Jr. (1973). Reading and transfer of crossmodal stimulus equivalances in severe retardation. *American Journal of Mental Retardation*, 77, 515-523.

process with phonemic and morphemic analysis methods, one could potentially move from a whole-word teaching approach like that used above, to an approach that greatly increases reading vocabulary and word comprehension at a far faster pace. Notice that this complex training process was discovered by humans for humans. If we can learn to use these emergent relationships within an instructional program, we will supply teachers with a powerful tool for teaching.

Emergent relationships could be applied to all subject areas, and can be used to explain a great range of single-trial learning where no "shaping" or "systematic" step-by-step evolution of the behavior is required. The above example is only one possible example of emergent relationships that can arise as the behavior of individuals in a group are changed. Humans have not explored these emergent relationships within STEM or "literacy" teaching methods. But, if such untrained behavior can emerge without direct instruction, then a form of direct instruction could essentially "pre-load" teaching by following the biological-based "logic" of emergent relationships. Children don't have to "discover" the logic, they are given it. If we want to teach them to see the "pattern-of-logic" give it to them—they will extend it. What is important is that they can see the pattern or lack of it across a variety of activities. You can't teach them to see patterns across a variety of subject matters. You just want them to see them in complex situations in some domain of inquiry. Children's inferential underpinnings will try to solve new problems with its use.

From a rational behavior perspective, this logic is just part of sphere of behavior called making an "inductive inference" (Chapter 2). We make inductive inferences—with or without awareness. With awareness, we may be able to make our inductions (projections about the future) more accurate.[4] Should we not "catch the wind and waves" of our biology to help learning along, especially in this age of complexity with all its dangers? There is a good chance that understanding and using equivalence methods may promote faster "content" learning.

Then, there are the VAM-T repertoires. If we think in terms of equivalent relations, we can find easy ways, which could "interlock" and "strengthen" our four repertoires of interest. Sidman says that equivalence relations are an elusive kind of stimulus generalization where we come to match stimuli that share no physical properties that have never been paired, and are not directly related to each other.[5] With the Sidman and Casson study, we pivoted on auditory language and made two connections and got

---

[4] See Nelson Goodman's *Problems and Projects*. Indianapolis: Bobbs-Merrill (1972). He saw that we make projections (inductive inferences) and our goal is to figure out how to make better ones (ones that are "warranted" by "evidence"), See section VIII.

[5] Sidman, M. (2009). Equivalence relations and behavior: An introductory Tutorial. *The Analysis of Verbal Behavior*, 25, 5-17, p. 5.
https://www.ncbi.nlm.nih.gov/pmc/articles/PMC2779070/

four "for free." What is or are the pivot points—that which has to be taught—relative to the VAM-T repertoires? One of them will have to be awareness. It is a meta-language and can verbally be related to the others with relative ease (Chapter 10). With the advent of modern imaging techniques, the neuropsychologists are also been exploring transitive relationships.[6]

The methods of additive reinforcement demonstrate that a great deal of learning can occur with the appropriate arrangement of multiple contingency elements. The use of additive reinforcement as the primary method of teaching appears to engender an additive (cohesive) emotional state, which is just another bit of learned behavior associated with other social and environmental events that foster the direct learning of M or T in a contingency arrangement. If done "sufficiently right," children will want to continue learning, seek out further learning on their own, and be prepared to solve problems that were not taught to them, as all scientists and engineers do. They can become their own cohesive managers for change.

SUMMARY

We are primarily concerned with both the behavioral and social mechanisms of which classroom behavior is a function. This chapter focused on the behavioral mechanisms of respondent and operant conditioning. Only the management indicated by Cell 4 of Graphic 4.1, additive reinforcement, can be used to cause complex, positive, value-based repertoires to evolve. It directly identifies the behavior to be performed relative to the activity contingency plan. Cells 1, 2, and 3 are also consequent events, but they support escape and avoidance from the value purpose of an activity. At the extreme, Cell 1, 2, and 3 lead negative behavior including counter control against the prevailing managers who establish such contingencies. From here on, *cohesive* will be used to indicate the types of consequences called additive reinforcement that engender learning. The term *coercive* will be used to indicate the other three classes of consequences—subtractive reinforcement, additive punishment, subtractive punishment—that inhibit or prevent learning VAM-T.

---

[6] Merritt, D. J., & Terrace, H. S. (2011). Mechanisms of inferential order judgements in humans (Homo Sapiens) and rhesus monkeys (Macaca Mulatta). *Journal of Comparative Psychology*, 125 (2), 227-238. https://pubmed.ncbi.nlm.nih.gov/21341909/.

5

Contingencies: Social Mechanisms

The members of the social environment shapes or evolves members to fit within the social structure. Chapter 3 modeled classroom activities from a contingency perspective. It was diagrammed as:

$$[X: Mi \rightarrow (T \text{ or } M) \leftarrow Mc]$$

From the *teacher's perspective*, this contingency model represents the *activity contingency plan*. It identifies the process to achieve the valued purpose of the activity, some technical behavior (T). Chapter 3 indicated each member of the classroom enters in their own contingency state. They are in some emotional-physiological state (X) and have various amounts of management (M) and technical (T) behavior available with which to work with others and continue to learn the technical behavior being taught.

Chapter 4 outlined the behavioral mechanisms of which learning is a function: respondent (classical) and operant (instrumental) conditioning. It was indicated that these mechanisms both induce (result in) or consequent (follow) behavior. The first pushes behavior forward and the second pulls it forward, roughly speaking. This implies that two causal mechanisms are at play. First, we have the classical billiard-ball notion of cause where the cause always precedes the effect. We induce something. Second, we have the notion that an effect that follows behavior can change behavior. We consequent behavior. Both notions of cause arise because we are dealing with *inferentially endowed living things* (Chapter 4). They are capable of adapting because they are capable of learning through 1) antecedent (inducing) events and 2) post-behavior consequent events. Both "causes" are possible because we, as living things "remember" the past and make inferences about the future given past experiences. These sub-qualities endow living things with the quality of being able to "adapt" to events. Researchers have primarily studied organisms like mammals and birds, who are so endowed.

With humans the quality of adaptation is given a *qualitative attribute boost* with language. Now, we have an entirely new level of complexity, one where the cognitive and physical qualities that have helped adaptation are now passed on to succeeding generations.

Knowing the mechanisms of social behavior allows teachers to further design and gain control over the evolution of children's behavior, as well as their interactions. By knowing these, teachers 1) increase the probability of controlling the vast open-system complexity that occurs within activities, so that all repertoires (X, M, V, A, T) are learned by group members and 2) evolve children, so that they can control this open-system complexity through their awareness and their repertoires. Shaping a group's V, A, M, and T repertoires simultaneously is a challenge, but doable.

Social Mechanisms

When we move from the isolated context of the behavioral experiment into an interactive social environment, other mechanisms are added. Social mechanisms are built on our inferential quality. They involve interactions between members of a group, who at any moment, promote or impede contingency-appropriate behaviors. These mechanisms change the emotional (X), management (M), and technical (T) behavior in-the-moment. Essentially, the social controls (shapes, develops, and evolves) members, so they fit within the social structure. This social control is at best probabilistic[1,2] but still within determinism where nothing can arise out of nothing and everything is in a perpetual state of becoming (Part 1: Introduction).[3,4]

To deal with this social environment, a different perspective is needed. Instead of a "micro view" of behavior that establishes the patterns of various contingency arrangements controlled by a single experimenter (Chapter 4), we must take a "macro view" of behavior where multiple members are at work simultaneously. The methods of multiple members in the same activity go beyond experimenter-controlled events.

When we step away from the psychological and move into the social, all members induce or consequent each other. Each is doing what the experimenter did to control respondent or operant behavior:

1. *Induce* (Mi) any activity behavior, or
2. *Consequent* (Mc) any activity behavior.

They can do either of these at any moment, contingent on other's behavior or not. Both the *inducing* and *consequent events by members* can

---

[1] https://en.wikipedia.org/wiki/Probability_theory
[2] https://en.wikipedia.org/wiki/Stochastic_process
[3] Bunge, Mario. (1959). *Causality and modern science*. MA, USA: Harvard University Press. @ https://vdoc.pub/documents/causality-and-modern-science-third-revised-edition-1t97jptr55q8 and see https://en.wikipedia.org/wiki/Mario_Bunge
[4] Bohm, David. (1957). *Causality and chance in modern physics*. NY, USA: D. Van Nostrand. @ https://vdoc.pub/documents/causality-and-chance-in-modern-physics-7t7of8kqt640 and see https://en.wikipedia.org/wiki/David_Bohm

promote or *inhibit* some behaviors needed within a teacher's *activity contingency plan*. However, we can take the following as fact:

Young children are unaware members.
They can't talk about, observe, or control their behaviors.

Yet, they are controlling even if they have no "awareness," to say nothing about "intension"—which is required by some to be classified as controlling members (called agents to some).[5] [6] Pointing out this fact leads to another emergent fact:

Unaware members are rational and civil only by accident.

In other words, their instances of behavior *may* or *may not fit* within the "boundaries" or "limits" of the activity plan. In general, such non-fitting instances are classified as "inappropriate" or "off-task" behavior that are here classified as "coercive" toward others and the activity contingency plan to varying degrees. Coercive control refers to either antecedent or consequent behavioral events that are not compatible with the activity plan. It can apply to emotional, management, or technical behavior. In sociology, coercive control refers to unequal "power dynamic" in a relationship. We return to the nature of power in Chapter 7.

However, we are starting with the very young, who for the most part have control without awareness or intension. We see the unaware control in a newborn's behavior that controls parents. There is nothing like an "awareness" or "intension" involved on the part of the infant. Children in the classroom are no different. They just have the beginnings of social awareness. They are curious about others.

How do teachers shape (evolve, develop, assemble) the VAM-T components that engender aware, rational, and civil children? Given that teachers know 1) the content components of the needed repertoires and 2) how they fit together (as specified in a curricula document), can they find operations that use the social mechanisms as their first guides in the shaping process. There are three social mechanisms.

1. Humans *imitate* modelers (who are usually other humans),
2. Humans *seek unity* with others, and
3. Humans *seek verbal interaction* with others.

Of course, other animals, especially other mammals and birds, have such social mechanisms. But with humans these three are highly sophisticated and interdependent. These "sit atop" the mechanisms of learning and make it possible to learn without controlling the antecedent events with deprivation or shock, or consequent events like food reinforcement or shock avoidance (Chapter 4).

---

[5] https://en.wikipedia.org/wiki/Agency_(philosophy)#In_other_sciences
[6] https://en.wikipedia.org/wiki/Social_influence

Humans Imitate Modelers

The humans imitated are called *modelers*. Within the classroom, modelers minimally induce some class of activity behavior. Maximally, they can model the details of an entire activity contingency. However, imitators may imitate cohesive or coercive behavior of modelers. There does not need to be awareness on the part of imitators and modelers need not be aware of or intentional about their modeling. Just being in the "sensory vicinity" of possible imitators is all that is required for behavior to be called modeling. The models may demonstrate emotional, management, or technical behaviors. The modelers, be they children or adults, can model respondent or operant behaviors. From a social psychology perspective, this is called *social proof* by some: Humans often do what others are doing, especially if they don't know what to do.[7] What others are doing is the evidence for what to do.

Modelers can be 1) an individual, 2) all activity members, or 3) any nearby group that can be observed. The *cause of imitating* is usually given names like *liking, authority,* or *expertise*—as someone, like a teacher or friend, who is *trusted* or *consistent* in some way. These modelers *induce* behavior by doing and that doing is *imitated* by other members. Outside of the fact that there are neurological processes involved, we do not really know precisely why someone imitates, but with all but a few exceptions individuals do imitate from shortly after birth.[8] The origins are biological, but require interacting with the social environment. The origins are not really important, the behavior exists across humanity. It is a qualitative attribute of human beings.

More importantly, terms like *liking, authority,* or *expertise,* along with *trust* and *consistency* are just the potential emotional-physiological states (private events) that *push* us to imitate. These terms represent naming the attributes of others that cause us to make an *inference* to imitate. However, what needs to be done by the *intentional modeler*—like the teacher—is to ensure that learning T is occurring. Children will imitate if they are learning, especially if the emotional-physiological state that results during imitative learning is a "wow," "my gosh," "that's interesting," or "I did it."

When modelers and imitators have a language repertoire, modeling can take a verbal form. The modeler can now be a book, wallchart, or what others say, especially when it cues members to stop or start some instance of behavior needed in-the-moment during a complex activity. Such modeling's can "tighten" the boundary of the behavior that fits within the *activity contingency plan*. The modelers *induce a class of behavior to some context*.

---

[7] https://en.wikipedia.org/wiki/Social_influence. (See section on Robert Cialdini.)
[8] https://en.wikipedia.org/wiki/Imitation

The probability of the induced behavior increases, even if we don't know to what extent.

For example, a teacher may say, "Zelda, I know you can do these. Please, give them your best effort." Here, the teacher has induced behavior without directly modeling a behavior. The inferred model was Zelda's past performance on similar material. Yet, any classroom member may induce behavior in almost the exact same way, "Zelda, you always get math. Can you check my work when you are done?" In both cases, Zelda's behavior has been more or less induced. For some children, the teacher's request may have more control and for others it may be the members. We have no certainty here. All we really need to know is that the events are compatible with those of others, and with the valued purpose and moral values of the activity contingency plan.

Humans Seek Unity

We have come to know that unity—some would call it fraternity—is important, as experiments dealing with social isolation have shown. These started in the late 1940s and 50s when arguments about what young children need relative to social interactions with others were of concern. This eye-opening research was established in the 1950s by Harry Harlow and other researchers.[9] Recently, most of us felt the consequences of a lack of social interactions during the 2020 pandemic. It was given the name "lockdown fatigue." Harlow's monkeys showed "depressed states" that were roughly equivalent to what both children and adults experienced during the pandemic.

When activity members have worked together successfully, a unity (or "bond") usually forms—as that between mothers and their infants. This unity is our second social mechanism. When we think of such groups, terms like "family," "collaboration," and "cooperation" are applied. We can use this mechanism by designing operations that employ it. Essentially,

By being and acting together members can form a unity or bond.[10]

Everything from building governments to landing on the moon requires group unity. The members "influence" (control to some extent) each other. Why they do so at any moment can only be hypothesized. In the classroom, it is seen as an attempt to achieve the activity's valued purpose. This unity can be called a *reciprocal interaction mechanism*, so to speak. Everyone induces and consequents an *evolving equilibrium* (toward a purpose) within and across activity members. Just put children in a group and unity will emerge if everyone is learning T. Learning T can be considered the "first

---

[9] https://en.wikipedia.org/wiki/Harry_Harlow#Partial_and_total_isolation_of_infant_monkeys

[10] Cialdini, Robert. (2015). *Pre-suasion: a revolutionary way to influence and persuade.* New York, USA: Simon & Schuster. Chapters 11 and 12.

consequent event" for children managing themselves with others in a group. This first level of success starts children on the road to unity. But it is an unaware start. For unity to emerge fully formed, more is required.

Even though, unity is "in our biology," it has and is evolved through the social environment. If members do not have congruent management behaviors, unity will not emerge. Witness the governments of the world. Today, they are called "gridlocked" organizations. There are no *cohesive managers* to "unify" the group. They don't know how to induce or consequent behaviors. In the classroom, knowledge of the need for social unity can be used to foster learning through inducing or consequent events that build social unity. Cohesive members are building unity across members. When all members are cohesive members, the group is classified as unified. They are exhibiting compatible contingency elements.

Unity is a _quality_ of a group.

When unity is achieved another quality emerges: The qualities of individual members can become a quality of the group. Members are all different, so that each brings various repertoires or attributes to the "activity table". It may be expertise in math or language, or it may be a sensory attribute like fine-grained color vision or perfect pitch. With unity, all of these qualities are available to the group during its activities.

Unity, as a social mechanism, applies to nearly all children (and adults).[11] It can help develop and implement an activity plan. For example, think in terms of children getting problems right on a worksheet. Without thinking about unity, the teacher may collect then and eventually hand them back, with or without comments. With *unity thinking*, the teacher establishes groups of two. They self check each other's work as they move through the problem set. Everyone sees and feels correctness *in-the-moment*. It is a correctness embedded in their interaction with others. They are *simultaneously being and doing with others* with the "first consequent event" (success with T) firmly in place.

Together, they succeeded emotionally and academically. Unity has been promoted. If done numerously and consistently, the probability of unity will increase in likelihood over time, from activity to activity. Such activity unifying structures incorporate modeling, each member models and imitates from problem to problem. Now, expand the idea of unity into groups of 3 to 6 and examine how being and doing together can promote unity. Who is inducing what to whom, who is consequenting for whom, and how often does it happen during an activity? This is a complex question that needs to be asked and answered during activity planning. These questions lead to the third social mechanism.

---

[11] Cialdini, Robert. (2015). *Pre-suasion: a revolutionary way to influence and persuade.* New York, USA: Simon & Schuster. Ch. 11 & 12.

Humans Seek Verbal Interaction

Seeking verbal interaction is an extension of seeking unity with others—their being and doing together. It exposes and builds unity through statements and questions about a contingency's beginning, continuing, and ending. That is what verbal behavior does.

Verbal behavior represents fragmentary or complete contingencies.

However, the contingency expressed may not be a "true enough representation." Humans get things wrong and getting them wrong is often hard to correct—witness the emergence and advance of science and technology. Their evolution has been filled with bumps in the road, as when past modeling that was taken as "sacred." But science and technology use methods to challenge any statement that is taken for *the truth, the whole truth, and nothing but the truth.* We no longer use bloodletting as a cure or operate on the body with dirty hands,[12, 13] but it took a very long time to wean ourselves away from these practices. Today, such knowledge has entered the domain of "common knowledge," which has been extremely enriched with the findings of a "scientific approach" to problem solving.

A member's social (verbal) communications may be coercive relative to the value purpose of the activity. Often these interactions lead to conflicts that truncate the beginning, continuing, or ending of activities. Everyone may lose their *right* to learn new behaviors if no one takes on a duty to build cohesive, unifying behavior. It only takes one member to "realign" the group towards its value purpose. It only takes one to "misalign" the group. This verbal mechanism can be stated positively as:

What humans come to do or continue to do
is cemented together through social communications.

As a social mechanism, verbal behavior is a "representation" of the social relationships (interactions) that surround us.[14] Historically, these social interactions have evolved with the social environment and are based on common knowledge. And such knowledge is at the heart of the problem of fostering ARC citizens. Only after the content of being aware, rational, and civil has been acknowledged, can *verbal interactions* be used to expose the ongoing *social interactions* of classroom members. Children are shown a representation of that they themselves have, are, or will create. Awareness begins here. With the addition of moral and management repertoires, children will have the social tools to change themselves and, thus, control the direction of their future. The learning strategy (Chapter 17) brings this

---

[12] https://en.wikipedia.org/wiki/Bloodletting
[13] https://en.wikipedia.org/wiki/Ignaz_Semmelweis
[14] https://en.wikipedia.org/wiki/Social_relation

control out into the open, so all children have a language with which to talk about and tackle the things that they want to learn about.

To become aware of these interactions and eventually gaining control over them, children must be directly taught to see the effects their own or another's management behavior—what are its antecedents and consequent effects. This interaction exposing mechanism can be put into operation in the classroom in two ways. The first is pointing out how members are interacting in-the-moment during activities. Essentially, these verbal interactions piece together who is doing what for whom and the consequences that emerge from these interactions. The second is to slow the process down and undertake exposing or re-exposing the interactions. This method is used during the planning or intervening strategies (Chapter 15 and 16). To use these methods effectively requires content knowledge of moral values, awareness, and management (VAM) and their relationships.

If these methods are used over and over, the exposing will 1) unite what is directly taught and 2) engender aware and unbiased objective observations and evaluations in-the-moment. Left on their own, children do not "discover" how their interactions effect what others are doing to others, or what others are doing to them. If they eventually do, it may well be too late to repair the damage done to any possibility of unity. They may "feel" that something is right or wrong, but they do not have the language tools to observe and evaluate it, nor the management repertoire to change it—both of which can employ verbal means to an end.

These verbal teaching methods, like the management repertoire, are of recent origin. It is a social teaching technology based on the social mechanism of our "disposition" for communicating about what is happening around us. In western history, the first stage of being socially aware in the context of our moral values was called the Age of Enlightenment.[15] Can we give young children such an enlightenment?

Teachers are usually taught to give children *knowledge of results* or *feedback* about children's management or technical behavior. These are usually considered consequent events that cause a change in behavior. As said, verbalizing about social interactions can function as an inducing or a consequent event, or both. The teacher can use this talk to expose these from a personal perspective or from the perspective of what others are doing to each other. With either one, the talk (the verbals) models two behaviors: 1) how to talk about social interactions and 2) pointing out social interactions that are ongoing. Thus, both perspectives use verbal social interaction. Eventually, children will imitate this way of talking to varying degrees.

However, expressing social interactions—called *social communications* from this point—are not restricted to the linearity of cause and effect. They can represent the past, present, and future contingency relationships (as

---

[15] https://en.wikipedia.org/wiki/Age_of_Enlightenment

behavioral events) that expose members to the *evolution of their behavior in the context of others.* Modeling these *social communications* (verbally representing contingencies) through time and space, connects members' behavior in a cascade of possible contingency relationships. This cascade can represent the multiple and at times simultaneous behaviors that control others' behavior. Thus, some children may *induce* the needed activity behavior and others may *consequent* it at any moment. When everyone's behavior is cohesive to everyone else's, *compatible contingencies* have emerged.

From Establishing to Abolishing Events

The above was idyllic. It focused on using the three social mechanisms to cause (induce, establish, or shape) cohesive behavior. However, abolishing events in a group context usually decreases various behaviors or decreases the control of various consequent events. If a group has unity, they will usually 1) work to decrease control of coercive behaviors that induces inappropriate behavior and 2) decrease control of coercive behavior that consequents inappropriate behavior. When unity is not being achieved, the abolishing and establishing events are in conflict relative to the management and technical behavior required for an activity to begin, continue, and end successfully.

We know that the world, as a group, does not exhibit unity. There is a lack of *compatibility* among group members and groups about when, where, and how to engender or cause what behavior. Usually, there are both methodological (means) and valued purposes (ends) differences. If all members held the same activity-based moral values toward means ends, they would only have to compromise 1) on means to their ends and 2) on which ends to work on in what order. Such a situation does not sound like the struggles about hunger, healthcare, economic stability, abortion, gun control, voting, war, and the environment that are at the forefront of civilization's discontents.

Fortunately, as said earlier, we are not beginning with adults already raised with a Me/My perspective about the world (Chapter 1). We are working with young children who have not yet been socialized as we were. They are not yet the non-compromising, biased members who, at the extreme, are the selfish, egoists, ideologs, plutocrats, or terrorists that inhabit the world. Young children remain teachable and adaptable members who may just learn to manage themselves and use their technical repertoires, so that their world will survive the crises we are giving them.

In the classroom, the abolishing events by comparison to the above discontents are mild at best. But they are there. If these coercive events, even if done without awareness, are handled at this point, children may have a chance to unify and flourish. To make it so, we operationalize the same social mechanisms. We just pattern their use in a slightly different manner. What we would see, if successful, are groups that become "glued" to the context and to each other's behavior. As soon as they enter the classroom, they will have "directed attention" and "focus" (a needed X state). Not only will they imitate and give social communication comments, but they will, as a unit, induce and consequent value-purpose behaviors, M or T. Here, we must remember that all valued purposes are usually, at some point in time, moral values—they will have impact on the lives of others.

Many abolishing events happen by accident or ignorance. For example, the teacher may say, "Mary, I am not sure that you can do these problems. They are very hard." Or a child member may say, "Mary, you are a math dummy. I don't want you in my math group." Again, all of this "pushes" behavior—X, V, A, M, or T—and is part of the "accumulation" of the child's past performances. These actions may well abolish cohesive behavior or make the classroom a coercive place that distorts management and moral values (as verbal descriptions and evaluations about themselves and others).

To ensure cohesive activities, the logic of contingencies applies (Chapter 3).

1. What methods can be used to control X, so that Mi is facilitated? $(X \rightarrow M)$
2. What methods can be used for M, so that M has control over X? $(X \leftarrow Mi$ and/or $Mc)$
3. What methods can promote X and M, so that they work together to induce T? $([X + (Mi$ and/or $Mc)] \rightarrow T)$
4. What methods can be used to expose consequent events (Mc), so that they increase the probability that Mi and T continue to evolve? $([M$ and/or $T] \leftarrow Mc)$

However, for members to exhibit this logic requires direct instruction and the use of social communication methods (Chapter 8). Modeling these relationships requires inducing and consequenting events that have been consistently and persistently repeated across activity behaviors. Eventually, the context and others induce or consequent behavior just as it does for a *discriminated operant contingency* (Chapter 4). If the group induces, it will also require cohesive consequent events for any technical (T) behavior being taught. Children must first learn activity's technical (T) behavior. Then, the associated X and M behaviors will be positively altered—if awareness is promoted by social communication.

However, some coercive management behaviors require that group members not only stop them but must replace them immediately with appropriate behavior that is practiced. This is the intent of the intervention strategy outlined in Chapter 16. It uses group unity, social communications (as verbal behavior, spoken or written), and imitation mechanisms simultaneously to engender change.

Summary: Behavioral & Social Mechanisms

All children and teachers are controllers and controlees. They are controlling and controlled by the contingencies they produce within some structure, which is the classroom and the X states in which all members enter it. The mechanisms of which all this behavior is a function are at two levels.

1. The behavioral—as respondent and operant conditioning— make it possible for humans to learn.
2. The social—as imitation, unity, and verbal interaction—makes it possible for humans to observe and control their own becoming, to make of themselves what they will.

Throughout this chapter, the examples used to illustrate the mechanisms were operations in the world, both within and outside the classroom. Realizing that humans have moved from mechanisms, as an abstract representation, to real world operations that afford control over the phenomena of interest, makes it possible to re-represent our contingency model. Graphic 5.1 does so.

The operations we perform do one or both of two things. They push behavior into the future in the sense of getting it going. These are the *inducing operations.* Those that pull behavior into the future are what keep behavior going. These are the *consequent operations* [16,17]. Circle 1 of Graphic 5.1 indicates that consequent operations, if powerful enough, will in the long run induce a context that members want to enter and behave with others. Circle 2 of Graphic 5.1 indicates that the behavior pushed into the future must have consequent events to be repeated or further evolved. Inducing is not enough. These consequent events need to be contingent on behavior T, if the classroom is to become a place that is enthusiastically entered: They must learn something, which is T, the value purpose of the activity. M does not help because it is only a means to the end T. If we manage ourselves without T, the ends of the activity will not be achieved. The logic—by way of

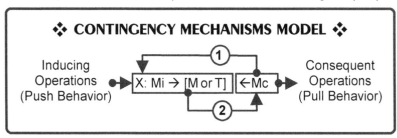

❖ CONTINGENCY MECHANISMS MODEL ❖

Inducing Operations (Push Behavior) ➡️ ① X: Mi → [M or T] [←Mc] ② Consequent Operations (Pull Behavior)

GRAPHIC 5.1: Contingency mechanisms model of classroom activities.

---

[16] I have made no attempt to integrate the details of what behavioral psychologists have called "motivational operations." See https://en.wikipedia.org/wiki/Motivating_operation.

[17] Cooper, John, O. et al. Applied behavior analysis. Available from: VitalSource Bookshelf, (3rd Edition). Pearson Education (US), 2019. Chapter 16.

the behavioral mechanisms—is simple; we do not continue that which does not produce *consequences that are in tune with our biology.* Such biology-based consequent events were called *cohesive* in ⊠hapter 4.

We can build a cohesive activity environment only with the use of cohesive contingencies. When the classroom is successful relative to its value-purposes, teachers and children use their repertoires to:

1. Induce emotional-physiological behavior, X, that is compatible with M or T,
2. Induce M and T related behaviors that are compatible with the activity's valued purpose, T, or,
3. Induce an activity's effects with consequences, Mc.

What must be discovered are the operations (methods) that bring about members' compatible behaviors. All of these are based on the mechanisms identified in this and the last chapter. Chapters 6 and 7 consider general inducing and consequent operations. Chapter 8 outlines *social communication operations,* so that children learn to see themselves as both controllers and controllees. Part 3 lays out ⊠ AMT content areas to be used by them. What remains are the specific teaching methods and time line that makes VAMT a curriculum.

Once members can give answers to the above three points, they can use their management strategies to change themselves or others. This is the power of what most describe as "influence" or "persuasion,"[18, 19] which are two closely related and often confused terms. We eventually persuade or influence ourselves as much as others do to us. We talk and think to ourselves. That is what we do with language. We don't have to "justify" this doing, it is just a fact. ⊠ hat teachers want to give children are flexible management discriminations and operations, so that efficient means to ends and productive ends are achieved with cohesive methods.

Most teachers would want to neutralize the probability of incompatible (coercive) behavior. Part of solving such problems is to, first, recognize the problem—to observe and classify it. What has been done so far is put the contingency model in place and identify the behavioral and social mechanisms of which behavior is a primary function. Thus, teachers can induce or consequent the behaviors dependent on what they observe and their evaluation of it relative to the moral values of the activity. If children gain control of themselves in a group, we often call such doing *cooperative behavior*—it's evolution requires linking the VAM-T repertoires with social communication (Chapter 8).

The above three steps are important to all teachers. But without knowledge of the operations (methods, tactics) to induce or consequent

---

[18] https://en.wikipedia.org/wiki/Persuasion
[19] https://en.wikipedia.org/wiki/Social_influence

behavior within a classroom or school context, as with *social communications*, all possibility of educating children to be ARC citizens will still be left to "happenstance." The result is that children are "disciplined," not taught to be "self-disciplined among themselves." All this begins by establishing appropriate emotional states. In doing so, we may just create cohesive members who can unite enough to spur adaptation and change when the world is theirs. One important question is:

> *Can we change ourselves and our communities enough,*
> *so that all of us want to make it so for our children?*

The answer and the effort put toward it will determine our children's survival and wellbeing.

6

Contingencies: Inducing Operations

Chapter 4 and 5 divided the mechanisms of human evolution at work in the classroom into two levels:

1. The behavioral makes it possible for individuals to adapt and learn.
2. The social makes it possible for the group to control learning, so that both the individual and the group can evolve in the directions selected.

The group changes individuals and, eventually, the individuals change the group. Within the classroom context, individuals and groups have reciprocal control, if uneven control, which divides into inducing and consequent operations. Both operations are causal, even if there is no awareness or intent. As we move from mechanisms (used to describe and explain the subject matter) to operations (used to control the mechanisms) the graphic from Chapter 5 changes only slightly. The word "mechanisms" is replaced by that of "operations" in Graphic 6.1.

This chapter examines three operations (methods) that teachers can use as inducing events for any class of behavior. First, it illustrates how to unify children through music, song, and dance. Second, it illustrates how working in groups can contribute to unifying children. Third, it illustrates how children can be used as models to directly teach specific moral values, awareness, and management repertoires. All three operations are designed to cause cohesive behaviors between children. However, like all contingencies designed for humans by humans, there is no strict, causal

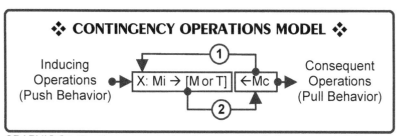

GRAPHIC 6.1: Contingency mechanisms model of classroom activities.

dependency. They may or may not cause the behavior on any particular day, but over the long run they will do so. Thus, the dependency is probabilistic.

These three operations are—in the ongoing stream of classroom behavior—almost inseparable. All of these push children into the future—something like a morning wakeup call. And like a wakeup call, their effect is usually short-term. But they serve the purpose of getting members going toward learning T.

Toward Unity Through Unifying

Of the three social mechanisms, imitation and unity are built into our biology; perhaps, right down to one's DNA. Roughly, we can't live well without others or learn complex repertories without imitating them.

Social communication—as verbal interactions between members—is a very different story. It is like an epigenetic mechanism [1], though not in the biological sense of gene expression that occurs without altering DNA. It has similarity to the field of social development that talks about how the environment and culture influence each of us. Often such developmentalists take a Hebbian approach when they say, "Cells that fire together, stay together." [2] Here, that statement is translated as: Repertoires that are linked together. stay together. Essentially, aware, rational, civil (ARC) citizens result from an on-going exposure to the multidirectional interaction of X, V, M, A, and T repertoires that are employed by all activity members—children and teachers.

Specifically, this epigenetic mechanism refers to "extra growth" that has resulted from the expansion of human knowledge about ourselves, and how we operate among others. The Renaissance [3] may be considered as the germination point of this extra growth. The Age of Enlightenment [4] may be considered the flowing point at which we turned the corner of seeing ourselves in control of our own evolution and began to think and talk about what that evolution should look like. Today, the image of our group-self can be summed up in the 18th century phrase:

To form a more perfect union.

At present, the achievement of a more perfect union is corrupted by social groups still operating using incompatible coercive control operations. Such control has slowed the unified social growth between group members and between groups. We may have only a "cloudy idea" of what a unified world of humans would entail, but we have a much clearer idea within the classroom:

---

1 https://en.wikipedia.org/wiki/Epigenetics
[2] https://en.wikipedia.org/wiki/Epigenetics#Developmental_psychology
3 https://en.wikipedia.org/wiki/Renaissance
4 https://en.wikipedia.org/wiki/Age_of_Enlightenment

An activity group is unified if its members use compatible means that achieve their ends.

If the means are cohesive and the ends are achieved, unity is "true enough," at least in the present. This unity can only happen with direct instruction and the teacher's social communication repertoire that links in-the-moment the interactions between morals, management, awareness, and other technical repertoires. This verbal communication repertoire opens children's observational eye to the causes and effects that they create for all classroom members. The heart of this repertoire is dealt with in Chapter 8.

However, there are other teacher operations that can help build unifying links. These operations employ the children's own behavior to build and demonstrate strong cohesive group relationships. It is here that the children learn to use their social communication behavior about their relationships and by controlling one of the very things that unity provides: joyful, positive, compatible emotional states—the X state—among members. Children do so by being together and doing together in special activities that expand on the ones specified in Chapter 2. Although, these operations are designed to cause cohesive behavior, they can be employed as coercive methods relative to interactions with outside groups.

Unifying Operations

Although inducing and consequent operations are almost inseparable, there are operations that are primarily inducing activities (events) that push behavior into the future—get it going. These inducing events seek to "bond" children with similar thought, speech, and emotional state.

Unity is a double-edged sword. First, there is the emotional support each member gives to others. This support is needed as much as food, water, and shelter. The latest pandemic taught nearly everyone this fact. When we lack a group with which to interact, we become "stressed" and "depressed." Our emotional state, thinking, and performance are degraded. This is a fact. The variation within this fact is the degree to which any individual needs to be in a group for emotional support. Some need almost continual group interaction; some only need occasional interaction. For these two extremes, we often name the first "clinging" and the other "independent."

Second, our group changes us by inducing and consequent events that keep us going. The members induce by modeling behavior and through social communications. The members' consequent behavior primarily deals with verbal behavior that expose interactions and the consequences produced. However, if our group is xenophobic, we will most likely be so. If our group is close knit, we will most likely help and share with other members. We need a group, but the "sum" of group member behavior may or may not be of benefit relative to an activity's means or valued-purpose ends. Such a situation induces conflicts.

In the classroom, unifying can be a group process that "aligns" emotional states so members enter activities focused on the activities before them. How can the members of a group join together to establish cohesive emotional and management behaviors that facilitate an activity to move forward smoothly?

There are three primary teaching operations to do so: 1) control X with music, dance, and song; 2) group children, so that they observe and feel—initially with guidance—their control over their behavior; and 3) use children as the models during the teaching of any behavior related to children interacting with each other with the appropriate management behavior. Gradually, awareness—as a language-based repertoire that discriminates and evaluates cohesive from coercive management behavior—will be added to the content mix to ensure that members become ARC citizens with the in-the-moment language-based awareness that lets them talk about who is doing what to whom, and then doing something about it.

Controlling X Behaviors

Just how do we put or attempt to put all members on the same emotional page, the "I-love-it-here" page? They walk in the door and from there it is up to us and them to work together, so that all VAM-T behaviors are shaped (evolved) and cemented together. To induce the same emotional page, teachers can use at least four operations: Using music. Using song. Using dance. Using pledges. Connect all of these when possible. Teachers back these up with consequent events like presenting badges of achievement or prizes for excellence that everyone can earn by demonstrating the repertoires of interest.

There is nothing new here. These operations have been used by groups—be they religious or secular, tyrannical or liberal, rich or poor—since the dawn of human history. When a Me/My group uses them, we call it indoctrination—witness Hitler's youth camps and their activities, or a terrorist group's "child soldiers." When a We/Us group uses them, we often call it "team building." And today, we have "social cohesion"[5] and intergenerational projects[6] that are We/Us groups with long-term moral-valued purposes, not just valued purposes.

The problem with unifying events with young children, relates to the level of abstraction and the amount of doing-together involved. For example, the Pledge of Allegiance is in abstract language that includes words like allegiance, republic, and country, with very little in the way of doing. Instead, bring the unifying event close to children's "realm of knowledge" and, as some would say, involve their right brain, their artistic, creative side.

---

[5] https://en.wikipedia.org/wiki/Intentional_community.
[6] Bjornerud, M. (2018). *Timelessness: How to think like a geologist and help save the world.* Princeton and Oxford: Princeton University Press. Chapter 6, especially pages 167-169.

For example, hold hands, sing the words, and move or dance to the music. Use music like "We are the World" that helps create an emotional state.[7] The words could be something like"

> "We do our duties. We work together. We help each other. We love to learn with everyone. Yes, we do. Yes, we do. We help others. We seek help. We love to be happy. Yes, we do. Yes, we do. Doda. Doda."

> "We say these words. We do. We do. We are a world. We are family, friends, all of us. A world within worlds. A world for all. Where we smile. Where we do duties. Where we learn. Where all enjoy. Enjoy. Enjoy. Doda. Doda"

Add strong choruses and a bridge and have a fun minute to start a class or a day. Why use such words to induce the emotional tone? Because they can represent the rules of the classroom—the behavior needed here, now, and in the activities that follow. They see that classroom rules are just the "first expressions" of duties that all members have to perform for learning in a group to be successful (Chapter 1 and 2). Such interactions as the above, do two things: 1) they express the We/Us group behavior required to succeed within a group and 2) connect this language of we/us to a strong, positive emotional state.

This is just the first stage of linking that establishes unity. We can do more with songs that represent each management strategy, as well as awareness. As cognitive psychologists might say, with each song we have given children a "cognitive-emotional map" to follow. This is similar to the verbal strategies taught to children to control impulses and behave appropriately in groups (Chapter 4).[8]

Who makes all this up? Teachers do, but only at first. By the second grade, children should be deeply involved in modifying the wording, designing the dance, and changing the wording. Each moment of doing these things strengthens the cognitive map (as a verbal representation), as well as each child's observation, thinking, and verbal interactions. At the elementary school level, it is necessary to maintain the "song activity" for some period of time, so when the whole school sings and dances it, they know what to do. A school is a government, and some level of sameness is needed to unify members. As we see today, policies and practices take time to implement, time to be revised, and time to see bits of success—as evidence—that leads to maintaining or changing activities.

The possible variations are endless—why not let a classroom or subgroup give their renditions before, during, or after a school event. Many

---

[7] For example, see Clarksville Elementary School, Clarksville, IL on YouTube @ https://www.youtube.com/watch?v=J7711tVOzJQ&ab_channel=WRTVIndianapolis

[8] Meichenbaum, D. H., & Goodman, J. (1971). Training impulsive children to talk to themselves: A means of developing self-control. *Journal of Abnormal Psychology, 77*(2), 115–126. https://doi.org/10.1037/h0030773

creative changes will emerge—even consistency evolves, although each generation may not recognize it. When inappropriate X states emerge and conflict arises during an activity, we turn to the intervening strategy that children will eventually redesign (Chapter 16).

Generally, we think of inducing an activity to get things going. However, after the activities, at the end of the day, do a rendition of the morning. Now, the words can be changed towards what has been done to link the today's achievements that sends them home with a positive emotional state. They have unified, let them feel and see it, so that they will do it tomorrow. Bring this doing out into the open with music, song, and dance, or a bit of poetry.

Grouping Members[9]

Unity, as being together, already exists within every classroom and its activities. However, the first problem is that in a large group—let's say 25 or so children—teachers do the directing (or try to). Teachers show children how (modeling) and they imitate. Historically, most of this modeling focused on technical behavior, the objective of the activity. But more is required if VAM repertoires are to be integrated with the classical technical repertoires. Children have not learned to be modelers, imitators, or use social communication that unifies themselves, so that they become an independent functional group. Without learning about VAM, as well as the T, unity-as-a-feature-in-their-group may never emerge with any assuredness. Unity, as doing together successfully, is required. Besides inducing an appropriate X state, grouping children makes it possible for children to learn about and practice VAM behaviors. Three basic variables control the success of grouping.

Sizing Groups

The first important operation in grouping involves the size of the groups. Usually, this ranges from pairs to groups with 5 or 6 members. These group sizes have two advantages:

1. It gives members a better opportunity to observe who-is-doing-what-for-whom, as well as experience the consequent events of their interactions (emotional, access, restructuring).
2. Teachers can model, prompt, correct, and link interactions between members of these small groups with accuracy and consistency.

---

[9] Much that is said about groups can be found in books like: (1) Kagan, S & Kagan, M (2009) *Kagan Cooperative Learning*. San Clemente, CA: Kagan Publishing. (2) Mandel. S. M. (2003). *Cooperative work groups: Preparing students for the real world*. Thousand Oaks, CA: Corwin Press. (3) Jacobs, G. M. & Power, N. A. (2016). *Teacher's Sourcebook for Cooperative learning: Practical techniques, basic principles, and frequently asked questions*. Thousand Oaks, CA: Corwin Press.

It takes time to learn to do the second. The most difficult part is becoming proficient in knowing and talking with children about the social interactions categories of behavior and what the categories entail. This is precisely why Part 4, Chapter 9 through 17, covers moral values, awareness, and management content knowledge. They supply the language repertoire to talk about what is observed, evaluated, and the type of interactions to focus on when cohesive or coercive behavior occurs. When it is not, the intervention strategy (Chapter 16) is often used in one of several ways. The latter stops and resolves conflicts, so that children quickly move away from conflict towards appropriate, cohesive behavior.

FORMING GROUPS

The second important operation is to know the in-and-outs of forming groups. This is a four-part story.

The first is knowing the basic structures of groups. For example, they can be heterogeneous, homogeneous, children-determined, or some combination. Each has distinct advantages. As a longer-term objective, we want heterogeneous groups working well enough together, so that the feature-of-unity emerges. This is a moral value call: do we want children to be able to work with any sentient being without putting them in some class of evil beings because of their shape, size, color, sexual orientation, or beliefs about the universe?

If this question is answered in the positive, the best way to accomplish this is to vary group placement and ensure that all children perform the various elements of the activity management behavior required to reach the activity purpose. Over time, this teaches children to observe unbiasedly that their success at T was based on the management behavior of all members, no matter what their group job entails—think of these management variations in terms of supervisor and supervisee, organizer and organized, and helper and helpee.

The second operation of grouping is placing children within a group. First, think in terms of the probability with which any child will stabilize or destabilize a group's X, M, or T behavior. Generally, we place more stabilizers in a group than destabilizers, and stronger stabilizers with strong destabilizers. A stabilizer is anyone who, in general, behaves in appropriate ways most often. A destabilizer is anyone who behaves inappropriately more often than others. Usually, there are only one or two strong destabilizers in a classroom. There is no bias in this distinction; especially, considering that the classroom has been set up, so that children always have a way to "exit" at any moment to a "getting-help activity" (Chapter 2). We are just trying to use members with a higher probability of appropriate behaviors to model, prompt, and socially communicate with those who need such support for some period of time.

Eventually, teachers can test to see if these destabilizers can work with other groups or work together effectively as a group—this testing is just part of the model-prompt-test-retest-consequent method of teaching. If group failure occurs, we can always fallback on the intervention strategy that resolves conflicts and replaces it with appropriate behavior between members (Chapter 16). Look at language use, past learning, and, for the very young, their "separation anxiety" on the first days of class. Teachers, most certainly, find out about various children's emotional state, management, and technical behaviors in the first week or so of class.

The third element of grouping is knowing the specific VAM that is the present focus while children learn, demonstrate, or practice a T. This focuses on the manner in which they interact within their group. For example, in pairs, they may work individually and then interact during an evaluation of their work. Or they may each work a problem, evaluate it against some master sheet, and, then figure out how to correct it, get help when they can't, and if correct, give themselves a high-five, fist-bump, or smile. Each group activity type needs to be modeled and prompted for some time. Most of the management behavior children use to achieve the value purpose of the activity is new to them. But, notice the difference in the ways the two pairs work together. The first involves one social interaction, the second gives as many as there are items to work—they build up the instances of working together over time. This increased interaction, if successful, becomes their armor against failure in the future. The teacher's social communication is a key ingredient to teaching children to see their behavior in-the-moment.

When moving to larger groups, a careful analysis of interactions is required. For example, if one other child is added to the above pairs, the activity is essentially new. Adding this one member requires new management behaviors. Perhaps the third person is now the "arbitrator" or "evaluator" of the work done by the pair who are now working together to solve each problem. Perhaps all three work each problem separately, evaluate the answers as a group, and then compare their selected answer against a guide. When planning these group activities, will children do independent bits of work and then combine them, or do they cycle through group members, so that they must work "cooperatively together" to determine the content of each bit and then put all bits together? The first promotes a single group event; the second, continuous group interactions, which involves children inducing and consequenting other member's behavior.

The fourth element is knowing where the direct teaching will be done. Direct instruction can be done before and at times during small group activities. The more the former, the greater the management load on the children. The more of the latter and children may miss out on unifying as a feature of their groups—they are in the teacher's activity group, not theirs. However, it is often not one or the other, but some before and some during.

This is the difference between modeling and prompting children's learning during the slow process of shaping complex repertoires.

As VAM behaviors become more sophisticated, eventually a group will teach other groups. This already happens within many STEM-type activities as children approach upper elementary grades. One group may learn about weather; another about bugs. Then, each group teaches the other. As further unifying, they may, as a larger group, identify the weather and ecosystems the bugs live in. With group "self-teaching," teachers can spend time observing and evaluating VAM behavior that make the T-to-be-taught-to-others or learned together possible. However, such group teaching is most likely a few years into the future.

Rotating Group Members

The third operation of group formation involves assigning various management positions on a rotational basis. The goal is for all children to experience both sides of all the management strategies—as controllers and controllees. One day a child may be a supervisor and the next the supervised. The supervisor becomes the planner and the planner becomes the supervisor. The organizer becomes the intervener and the intervener becomes the organizer. This rotational operation will make the most sense after children start learning the management strategies (Chapters 11 through 17). The manipulation of positions within and across activities, helps to resolve the classical problem that has befuddled philosophers and educators for centuries: Who is going to control the controller?

The answer rests in experiencing both sides of controller/controllee fence (manager-managed). With two-sided experience, all members observe that cohesive groups require that all members need to use cohesive means and achieve activity ends, no matter what managerial part they play in the activity. They may make this inference, but it will facilitate learning if social communication describes it in the moment, across a number of activities. Testing their observational inference at a later point only requires querying them (Chapter 8). When they can observe and evaluate this dependency between members, the probability of a member becoming a coercive controller will be radically reduced and the classical controller problem becomes false because the problem was "invented" from the perspective of adults and not from the evolution cohesive citizens. What has been the case does not have to be the case when members are "instilled" with the interdependent VAM-T repertoires. This is, of course, a prediction about the direction that interrelated VAM-T repertoires will take group members.

Use Children as Modelers of Behavior

All teaching uses models to demonstrate things and action—from naming things, to adding numbers, to forming groups, to walking to the lunchroom. The first two are academic; the latter management. In these cases, examples (models, demonstrations) are used to represent what something is or is not, or how to do something or not do it. The words that represent the classes of behavior, the examples (as models) represent the range and limits of the instances that fit the classes. The same situation exists in biological taxonomies.

Yet, if the objective is to unify groups from the earliest point, start by using children as modelers of the needed management behaviors like working in a small group, getting help, or walking to the lunchroom. The modelers of these behaviors are illustrating instances of being unified (examples) or not (non-examples). By observing these child modelers, others will infer that they can do it like their peer modelers—they will at least attempt to imitate.

The strategies of organizing, helping, and sharing are about equal in language use and steps to remember as walking to the lunchroom or eating lunch. Each is an operation (process) that has only five major steps and a few decision points (discriminations—Chapter 2), but with each step having some degree of latitude. They can be modeled by classroom members. Two examples illustrate this point. One deals with naming things and the other with naming moral behavior.

We use examples to teach children to 1) discriminate (classify) between the abstract classes of "vehicle" and "not a vehicle"; and the abstract class "working together" and "not working together." In the first case, children can't be the modelers, but in "working together" some set of persons is required. The teaching process begins with gathering attention to the modeling demonstration. Since all but those children who are classified as learning-impaired have their attention and focus on other human beings, this first step of teaching is not generally problematic—attention and focus on others literally shows itself shortly after birth. However, in the classroom, it does require some inducing event to shift young children's attention and focus to the demonstrating person or persons. This is only hard to achieve if children's emotional-physiological state (X) is interfering, for whatever reason. Thus, teaching begins at the point of gaining children's focus.

A teaching demonstration (modeling) treats the above two abstractions—vehicle and working together—exactly the same.

The difference is in the content, not the teaching method.

In the first case, "What is a vehicle?" we could see the following interaction (communication) between teacher and children.

1. The teacher manipulates multiple models, giving each a name as "vehicle" or "not vehicle," the goal of the example set is to model the range and the limits of what is considered a vehicle for the children in question.

2. This is followed by a test set with some new examples that fit the range and limits of the first set.
3. During the test, children answer the query, "Vehicle or not a vehicle?"
4. If the children are wrong, the answer is given and the examples shuffled or started over again, or replaced by new ones.
5. The success of their answers—vehicle or not a vehicle— determines if the teaching of the abstract class "vehicles" has been learned (imitated) within the example set's limits.

The second case starts with "What is working together?"

1. The teacher manipulates multiple models to show the range and limits of what entails "working together," giving each a name as "working together" or "not working together."
2. This is followed by a test set with some new examples that fit the range and limits of the first set.
3. During the test, the children answer the question "Working together or not working together?"
4. If the children are wrong, the answer is given and the examples started over again or replaced with new ones.
5. The success of their answers—working together and not working together—determines if the abstraction "working together" has been learned (imitated) within the example set limits.

There are a few qualifications to the above example sets. In the first case, the children were most likely taught lower-level abstractions like "bus," "car," "train," and "bike" to help make the transition to the more abstract class. In the second case, the children may have been taught to discriminate "working" from "nonworking" and "together" from "not together." Also, the teacher may have to do some "gathering of group attention," perhaps by asking something like "Who knows what a vehicle is? or "Who knows what working together is?" Once the children have given their variations, the teacher may follow it by saying, "Let me show you some examples. Let's see if it helps you think. First example…." Hopefully, three points emerge from the two example sets.

1. Teaching moral values is no different than any other teaching. The examples of "not working together" represent the non-moral behavior involved in the set of examples modeled.
2. The difference is in sorting out the content. The content is related to the limits of what is or is not a particular class of moral behavior, as a member of the "duties of the classroom."
3. The Teaching-learning communication is guided by very short social interactions (communications) between teachers and children. Both teachers and children are altered by it.

In the above example sets of vehicles and working together, the teacher's verbal interaction is intertwined with physical reality. The modeling illustrates the contingency of interest: "if this, then that" across a set of examples that show the range and limits applicable to the children in question. Young children need not classify all the things that are "vehicles" in the world, nor do they have to classify all the various ways groups "work together." When children answer the example set questions, teachers communicate by, at least, moving (give access) to the next example. If children are correct or wrong about any example, teachers communicate with a consequent event. If the children give a "we are terribly wrong" communication, teacher's go back to redoing the example set. Additionally, teachers may even add a verbal interaction during or after the set of examples. It may be something like saying, "You got the first two right let's continue" or "You got all the examples correct the first time. Great work. Can we do it again tomorrow?" These social communications express the details of the contingency of the teaching-learning interaction. They can both induce and consequent behavior. We explore these interactions in Chapter 8. We can sense the power of social communication behavior with a slight modification of an old adage as it would apply to young children.

> *Sticks and stones can break my bones,*
> *but words can make or break my spirit.*

The abstract class of "vehicles" is easy to sort out—just ask most six-year-olds. But human history has shown us that sorting out moral members from non-moral ones has not been so simple. Moral members are a three-part harmony of morals, awareness, and management repertoires. Such members "know" the morals (as statements and what they entail), the management strategies, and can evaluate their fit (awareness). The evaluation is then followed by using their management repertoire to do something about it. At times this doing requires an entire strategy like planning or intervening, but usually—especially in the case of cohesive behavior—it amounts to nothing more than thanking an individual or group with a description of the cohesive behavior and the consequent events (as other children's behavior) entailed.

> [Child in a group] Thanks for helping me supervise. We worked together. I think we all feel good about our project. Now, we can present it to the class.

> [Child being helped] You have shown me how to do this. That allows me to keep working on my assignment. You sure did help.

However, until the three interdependent social repertoires are learned, classroom "duties" like "working together" represent the entry point to directly teaching moral values, awareness, and management repertoires, and their interrelationship (Chapters 9-17). Later, when known, if not mastered, they will interact with more specificity than the above two examples illustrate.

Children's behavior is being "shaped" or "evolved" through their underlying inferential process that does not need to be explained. It just is. Children will interpolate within and extrapolate beyond (discriminate more and generalize further) than the examples given. This is just what inferential beings do. This inferential behavior ensures that the discrimination or operation being taught continues during activities outside of the "example set teaching arrangement."

Summary

This chapter illustrated inducing operations that teachers can use to unify a classroom, so that activities can begin, continue, and end. The first operation involved using music, song, and dance that is attuned to the children's language level, so that they have at least an emotional-physiological state (X) that is cohesive with learning. These can be extended to representing the steps of the management strategies.

The second was how to use groups members to promote unity, so that teaching and learning have a higher probability of success. This involves the size and forming of groups, so that "destabilizing" children, as those who do not exhibit the needed management behavior, are controlled by children around them, mostly through the use of verbal behavior. Within activities, children take on different management functions, usually called "roles", so that they can experience management strategies from those who are the controllers and those who are controllees.

The third operation involved using children as modelers of the VAM behaviors. This use of modelers first involved directly teaching some VAM behavior through the use of example sets that employed children as modelers. The second use involved children to verbally model a management behavior during an ongoing activity. All three uses involved setting up events that used the mechanism of social communications to unify children, so that learning occurs. It was a very brief glimpse at the use of social communication in the classroom. Chapter 7 will slightly expand on this glimpse into the context of consequent operations that follow behavior and create changes in behavior. Chapter 8 presents how to verbally represent the interactions between teachers and children, and children and children.

7

Contingencies:
Consequent Operations

Both inducing and consequent events affect (produce changes in behavior) that in turn are causes for yet other behaviors. Who-does-what-for-whom can be very difficult to disentangle. We are lucky, we are dealing with children not yet fully formed. They are truly becoming because we build the "complexity for success" into them. If we do so efficiently and effectively, they will become ARC citizens. But to do so requires that we "imagine" ways to control the mechanism through operations implemented in the classroom.

Chapters 4 and 5 represented the behavioral and social mechanisms of which our behavior is a function. The behavioral mechanisms—respondent and operant conditioning—are those that make us adaptable to and able to learn from the environment because of our "inferential disposition." The social mechanisms—imitation, unity, and verbal behavior—are those that give us control over the behavioral mechanisms to change ourselves in the directions we chose—to alter our own becoming. What we do with our expanding knowledge of these mechanisms and how they are used to change ourselves is a hypothesis.

What we do know is that both types of mechanisms are buried deep in humanities history—propelled at least in part by our DNA. At present, we are just beginning understand these, to understand ourselves. As our knowledge expands, we will develop operations (methods, procedures, tactics) to, hopefully, enhance our becoming—both as individuals and groups. This view of mechanisms was summarized in Chapter 5. When moving from mechanism to classroom operations, we seek to discover operations that "support" or "work with" these mechanisms. Thus, Graphic 7.1, first presented in Chapter 6, only changes the word mechanisms to that of operations. This change means that abductive reasoning—along with the "imaginings" that language brings to our inferential behavior—is required to discover these operations.

In the social world of the classroom, consequent operations play as critical a role as in the isolated experimental chamber. However, they take on very different forms. However, unlike the psychologist's experimental chamber, children can't be deprived of food or water before they enter the

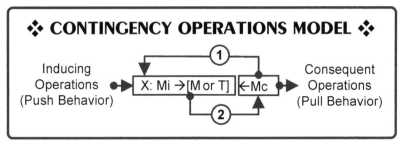

GRAPHIC 7.1: Contingency operations model of classroom activities.

classroom or shocked while in it. As a result, teachers are faced with two questions. First, what operations can create cohesive consequent events that induce VAM-T behaviors? Second, how can consequent events be used to help shape (evolve) VAM-T repertoires? The answers are not separate. Besides direct instruction, there is only one way to consequent any behavior that induces or consequents behavior by classroom members. It involves the using social communication operations to 1) expose who is doing what to or for whom and, then, 2) gradually turn over the exposing to the children themselves, and then 3) allowing them to use their management behavior to change themselves, individually or as a group. Since social communication exposes both inducing and consequent events it is taken up in Chapter 8. This chapter delves into observation of behavior in the classroom and the qualities of behavior that indicate how behavior has changed. Both facilitate the use of social communication operations.

Observing Behavior

From a classroom perspective, the origin of any behavior may be hard to explain because it is the product of the interaction of biological, psychological, and social mechanisms (events) as discussed in Chapter 3. Children behave and how they continue to do so depends on how members induce and consequent each other's behavior. All of these affect others. Hopefully, by the end of this chapter, just enough was said, so that there exists a "general knowledge-belief state" about what we can and cannot control through the manipulation of contingencies designed to promote the emotional, social, and academic learning—our value purposes. We turn now to just what can be observed to determine if children are heading toward aware, rational, and civil behavior.

Qualities of Behavior

Chapter 2 examined behavior in terms of observing and naming instances of classes. In the long run, children learn the classes of VAM-T only by way of instances that define the range of the classes. At this point, the specifics of what these instances of the VAM-T repertoires entail have not been analyzed; they will be in Chapters 9 through 17. Even though we have not analyzed them, we have a final question to ask; What do we observe, in practical terms, so that "awareness" can be taught and evaluated? The answer is that we observe the *qualities of behavior* that tell us about the "extent" of our success at teaching any repertoire of behavior. But this general awareness is just the beginning. From here, we observe the interactions of children during any activity contingency. This requires a "contingency awareness" of children's behavior—to see who is doing what to or for whom.

Clear, reliable measurement of M and T repertoires gives everyone the power to alter knowledge and our control over these two repertoires. If we have no idea what we are doing or talking about, we are behaving irrationality. Without measurement (as gathering a set of reliable data points) and the resulting evidence (as the pattern in the data points), the argument that we are achieving or have achieved VAM-T enabled children would be impossible. Only with observable measures at the level of detail of repertoire design can we achieve success—remember that designing a classroom and its needed repertoires are "social inventions," not "natural phenomenon." We may improve or totally redesign our classroom contingency system.

VAM-T classes, like all classes and subclasses of human behavior—as with all things in the universe—have qualities that vary across disciplines. They are often called properties, attributes, or features. There are those like size, shape, color, elasticity, hardness, viscosity, and many thousands more. All of these can be observed and measured. But first these qualities have to be found, shown to be useful, and related. Eventually, the knowledge gained becomes a system and then a discipline. Next, the discipline keeps drilling down to gain further knowledge and control.

So, what qualities describe any class of human behavior, any repertoire, so we can see it change in performance. (Some would say, along its unmotivated-to-motivated continuum.) Here, we ask, what qualities of children's behavior would help describe it as being effective within and across activities? Uncovering these is the first step towards observing behavior, so that it can be evaluated (judged) as existing and the extent of its existence.

The Qualities of Members' Behavior

All classes of individual and social behavior can be seen in terms of six qualities. These qualities include exhibiting one or more of the following.

1. **Willingness** to perform the class of behavior when asked.
2. **Quickness** with which instances of a class start from the asking or an opportunity to perform the behavior presents itself (often called the *latency* of behavior).
3. **Accuracy** of a class of behavior increases over time.

4. **Efficiency** with which class instances are performed. (Performs the behavior more quickly than in the past).
5. **Persistence** at performing the class as the extent to which it keeps occurring across time.
6. **Preference** for performing the class (one chooses to do it instead of doing other classes of behavior when opportunities knock).

Children, when asked to read, do so (1 above), start to engage in it without delay each day (2), over time their reading accuracy increases (3), and along with it they become more "efficient" at reading smoothly, expressively, and/or with greater speed (4) depending on the specifics of the objective. Next, they persist at it until done or time is up (5). Finally, given choices, they choose to read—perhaps during free time or while at home where they have a choice between of reading, gaming, or some other activity (6). Only three (3) and four (4) have multiple components. One can read for accuracy by decoding words correctly or by answering comprehension questions correctly. Efficiency in reading can involve fluency, comprehension, or decoding new words with ever faster performances.

Understanding and observing these qualities is our first step in teaching that produces VAM-T linked repertoires. Of course, biological and outside social factors may limit our ability to evolve such qualities. We already observe these differences, we just needed a bit of language to help unpack them, so that we can observe the components of children's behavior that guides teaching.

Observing and Measuring Qualities

The above six qualities are used relative to various VAM-T. Evaluating them is relatively easy. When *willingness* (1) appears, many would describe children as "following directions." By the time they reach *quickness* (2) nearly everyone would call them "disciplined." Children see when to do it and do it without much delay. When the other qualities appear, children are often called "eager," "engaged," "reliant," "motivated," and many other positive terms. All of these are related to the inexactness with which humans talk about social and academic behavior.

Persistence and *preference* are things that we would all like to see across the VAM-T repertoires. But no one will persist at and prefer everything. Thus, a willingness, quickness, and improved *accuracy* and efficiency are what we often look for in many repertoires. With just these four, most would proclaim that children are in a positive emotional state; the children are often called focused, engaged, and upbeat. Perhaps, if asked, they would say "happy."

Usually, the reverse is the case when these qualities are absent. At present neurobiologists are trying to figure out the interactions between affective (emotional) and cognitive neurological networks.[1] However, even if we knew all the neurological correlates, it is the social environment that plays the pivotal role in "connecting" these networks and bringing them to their "wired together" maturity.[2]

WHAT QUALITIES WHERE?

What are the causes that bring about these qualities of behavior? How do we teach children so all the qualities emerge in VAM-T? Most assuredly, children vacillate from day to day and their emotional (X) state for any class of behavior can only last for some length of time before a change is needed. An hour class of any of these large repertoires (M, T) is usually enough for a while. What we look for next is that the qualities reappear day-after-day. When we see this, we have no worries beyond keeping up what we are doing or improving it (because that is what humans do—with or without extensive evidence).

The qualities vary relative to the behaviors being learned. For example, if we are teaching children to plan, speed is less important than accuracy. A "workable" plan is more important under most conditions. If we are teaching children to read, we want to eventually see all six qualities emerge, but not in any fixed order. However, we first seek willingness, quickness, and a bit of persistence, and then work towards the other qualities. For many new classes of behavior, we want to see accuracy before speed. Willingness and persistence will most certainly precede preference—we are helped here by our biologically-based need for control—teachers foster this sense of control through consequent events that begin with success at T. With the six qualities we have an idea of what success entails.

For some behaviors, like doing some necessary drill-and-practice exercises, cleaning up after an activity, doing the dishes, or taking out the trash, we may never see preference emerge. But as long as there is a willingness that starts with reasonable quickness and has acceptable accuracy, all is okay.

Choice (i.e., preference) usually occurs when a class of behavior has been successful over some period of time and is more rewarding than other classes of behavior for reasons we may never fully understand. Look at how many children learn to enjoy playing a musical instrument like the piano, drums, or guitar only after struggling for a long time through undesired lessons. What turned them around? Usually, seeing a level of success, which begins with the teacher directing the learner's observation so they can

---

[1] Williamson, P. and Allman, J. (2011). *The Human illnesses: neuropsychiatric disorders and the Nature of the Human Brain*. New York, NY: Oxford University Press.

[2] Pakulak, E., Stevens, C., and Neville, H. (2018). Neuro-, cardio-, and Immunoplasticity: Effects of Early Adversity. *Annual Review of Psychology*. Volume 69, 131-156. https://www.annualreviews.org/doi/10.1146/annurev-psych-010416-044115

observe that success. The teacher gives them a language of success and provides examples. The next would be participating with others in making music. The same progression applies to the VAM-T.

Comparable Qualities

When we are talking about the qualities of any class, we often make a comparison; we indicate how a class of behavior has changed relative to something else. Yet, we must be careful to compare apples to apples. We compare qualities in terms of *frames of reference*. Relative to human behavior, we use four common frames-of-reference.

Comparable to the Past

A class of behavior can be viewed relative to its past state, as first explored in Chapter 2. We often say things like, "Zelda was the most dedicated student in school, but now she does not seem to care and is unprepared." or "Zelda is now a diligent student." In both cases, her degree of behavior has been compared to her past behavior (clearly specified or not). What is exposed here is the evolution of behavior. This is an important comparison as Chapter 8 will illustrate.

Comparable to a Standard

Second, a class of behavior can be viewed relative to some established criteria. "Zelda is at the 99th percentile in reading." "Jomer is near to bottom of his class in spelling." Zelda has been ranked high relative to a standard. Jomer on the other hand is ranked low and with a "less accurate" description than that of Zelda.

Comparable to Other Classes of Behavior

A person's qualities of behavior are often compared to his or her other classes of behavior. We often say things like, "Zelda likes math but not science" or "Zelda excels at both math and science." This comparison cuts across present but different classes of her behavior. It is useful because often children, like anyone, are proficient at some things and not at others. There are times when teachers need to expose the strengths and down play the weaknesses, but continue to work at the latter.

Comparable to Others

We speak of a person's degree of behavior relative to others as well as to themselves. We often say things like, "Jomer is less motivated to do math than Zelda, but he is much more enthusiastic about writing stories." Jomer and Zelda have different degrees of the compared classes of math and writing.

We must be careful with comparisons like the above. Because we don't often realize that we are using these frames, our talk about someone's behavior is often ambiguous, confused, or "damages" our chances at evolving their behavior. The usefulness of various comparisons all depends on which comparisons are made, under what conditions they are made, how they are made, and the evidence they are based on. Essentially, accurate, early childhood examples of our talk to or about children's behavior focuses on 1) how it is evolving over short time frames and 2) deals with the emotional-physiological, access, and restructuring it brings to their lives, through their new management behavior.

ChildREN COME REAdy TO LEARN

Children come into this world seeking to control their environment. Some call this entering the world "ready to learn," or "reflexive behavior" like the suckling and grasping of newborns, or 3) as a "biological primacy" as important as seeking food and shelter. This seeking to control, eventually and hopefully, comes under the control of the individual's aware, rational, civil behavior, not the reactive flight-fight-freeze behavior that biology gave to our untrained or unsocialized selves.

Control over the environment is a very powerful consequent in producing changes in the above qualities of children's repertoires. Watch a child move from crawling to walking, or from their first attempts to ride a bike to zooming around corners and jumping off curbs, steps, and hills. There is more than a glint in their eyes; it is in their entire biology. They willingly do it. They persist at doing it. They choose to do it. We classify them as "motivated" and the immediate and long-term consequences of achieving control made them so. Control means success in accessing or restructuring their physical and emotional selves, as well as their environment. As each new behavior is learned, it allows further emotions produced by accessing or restructuring built on prior access and restructuring that keeps up the emotional thrill that goes hand-in-hand with it. For young children everything is new and exciting. Only for some is it new and frightening.

Children are slowed or stopped in their learning from three directions. First, environmental-induced changes like malnutrition, lead poisoning, diseases and infections, brain tumors, and accidents that reduce cognitive functioning. Second, genetic disorders like Down syndrome, fragile X syndrome, and Huntington's disease do much the same. Third, the social environment contributes to their behavior either being appropriate or inappropriate. To promote value-purpose compatible behavior, only the social environment is within the scope of teachers. The first and second are in the past and largely irreversible with present biological and/or medical technology.

What constitutes control evolves (Chapter 5). Children evolve from being reinforced for controlling their basic movements like going to the bathroom and eating—no dippers to change or food to clean off the floor—to riding bikes, throwing balls, flying kites, and dancing with others. Gradually, most gain repertoires, so that they are called accountants, carpenters, lawyers, physician, and zoologists. Yes, they like all of us will eventually begin to lose control of their behavior. Bodies grow old (they become uncontrollable) and social lives decay (we can't get around as well and many friends have passed). However, keeping up the qualities of behavior often lengthens the period of control and shortens the period of instability. Of course, genetic engineering and other medical technologies are helping the body stay healthy for longer periods of time. But without the six qualities of behavior in our repertoires, living long means little.

The Child and the Adult

Why do children take to learning as fish do to swimming? They don't ask why; they just participate, and as they do, their control of the environment evolves. Adults take to learning for different reasons. They still love control over their behavior and the world, but they direct their learning. They want to discriminate and operate on the world in specific ways. Their joy of learning is "bracketed," "narrowed," or "focused" by a purpose (e.g., goal, objective, dream, or desire). It may be useful for adults to keep some of the childlike joy for learning, to learn for learning's sake. Yet, most of the advances in science and technology have come about because of a bracketed, focused kind of learning. Those "dedicated" to solving a difficult problem are just as easily called "motivated" as is any child. They often see themselves as having a "duty" to solve one type of problem or another. The social environment both protects them and prepares them through teaching-learning interactions.

Quality Learning Environments

If children are to become aware, rational, and civil, then teachers must build learning environments that "make it so" (within the limits of their knowledge of how behavior works and the methods available for evolving that behavior). Such learning environments must contain at least four interrelated components. They must foster:

1. Technical behaviors to tackle "interesting" problems that lead to successful solutions.
2. Management behaviors like planning and learning, that help children use their technical skills to solve problems in ways that produce purpose-based consequent events (Chapter 5).
3. Learning to observe and clearly express how they are controlling others or being controlled, as well as the means to do so.

4. Children design, express, and see their values as they use their repertoires to work for the good of themselves and others around them—their management practicums.

The first, provides the management and technical behaviors required of any activity. The second controls these behaviors, so that activities can begin, continue, and end with efficiency. Eventually, we achieve persistent- and preference-based children. However, given the problem that today's young citizens face, they need more.

The third addresses the "more" and begins with observing behavior and the consequent events that their behavior produces. Observing consequences lets them know they are capable of solving difficult problems using the technical, managerial, and values repertoires they possess. If we ask children, "Can you solve this problem?" their answer is, hopefully, based on past observational evidence and not on what others want to hear. The answer may be cautionary, but caution may mean they see the risk involved in all human activities.

The fourth provides them with practical experience with the repertoires that allow them to design, clearly express, and observe their values in their everyday activities. At which point, implementation and evaluation follow.

Do they want to live in a peaceful world that provides all citizens with the resources, wellness, and happiness that makes for a good life or not? The four elements are a tall order, but doable, if our generation of caregivers are willing to construct learning environments that focus on VAM-T content and evolve the repertoires through the above four components as starting guides. The hardest part is changing ourselves—the caregivers—so we can design, implement, evaluate, and redesign learning environments that bring about VAM-T endowed children. All design work requires that the designers change themselves first, so that they can see and operate differently than in the past.

SUMMARY

Contingencies are complex. This chapter focused on this complexity. It examined consequences from the perspectives outlined in Chapter 5: consequence classes (emotional, access, and restructuring), their direction (cohesive or coercive behavior), and the compatibility of the group. These perspectives can be delivered or pointed out before, during, or after an activity. When we focus on them before an activity, it is part of preventative planning. During an activity, they help keep the implementation moving forward. After the activity, they are remedial and can focus on activity replanning. The latter is where children redesign activities in order to achieve greater compatibility in the future.

The contingency components—the X, Mi, Mc, T—are often insep-arable. But even if we don't know exactly if, for example, one's verbal behavior induces, consequents, or does both, we can still move forward enough to achieve effectiveness, efficiency, or both (some might say mastery). The key words are type, direction, commonality, and compatibility. Knowing what they entail will facilitate observation. All VAM-T teaching requires reflection. The process for doing so is embedded within a number of the management strategies, especially planning, intervening, and learning. In Chapter 8, we turn to the details of talking with children, so that they learn to observe the contingencies they are generating for themselves and others.

8

CONTINGENCY OPERATIONS:
Social Communications with Children

Social communication is a social technology. It is designed to teach children to observe and evaluate the interactions taking place during an activity. Social communication is classified by a host of names. Along the way, psychology, social science, and linguistics have added much in the way of analysis and theories related to conversations, dialogues, and communications.[1, 2] To some, a "communication" is considered a process (operation, method) to "transform thoughts and words of groups of people into meaningful action."[3] Because we are raising young children, the first step provides children with a *verbal representation* that matches the reality in-the-moment. Since all verbal representations are about contingencies, we already have a model to guide our talk with children. (Graphic 8.1 repeats that model.)

The graphic indicates us that there are two primary types of talk. First, there are inducing operations (events) that gets the needed activity behavior going (X and M); it pushes behavior forward (Chapter 6). Second there are consequent events that expose what behavior was actually performed; it pulls behavior forward (Chapter 7). The numbers in the Graphic, 1 and 2, indicate that the two causes of behavior are not separate. They can be mixed and matched. However, the model fails in one sense: It does not represent the activity across time. The rule for time is this:

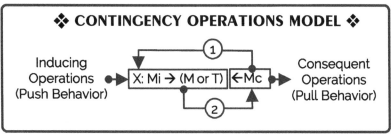

GRAPHIC 8.1: Contingency operations model of classroom activities.

[1] https://en.wikipedia.org/wiki/Social_relation
[2] https://en.wikipedia.org/wiki/Conversation
[3] https://en.wikipedia.org/wiki/Bohm_Dialogue

At any time an activity, any member can use either inducer,
consequent or combine these operations that change behavior.

The real difficulty for both teachers and children is observing
and evaluating the behavior as it happens in-the-moment. We can
only teach children to observe and evaluate the effects of their inducing or
consequent behaviors with two types of instructional operations.

The first is through *direct instruction*. This can usually be done during
the teaching of planning, intervening, or learning strategies (Chapters 15, 16,
and 17). Direct instruction is helpful because it takes behaviors (as examples
of problems or benefits of children's social interactions) and slows them
down—takes them out of the in-the-moment interaction process. There is
no need for the immediate analysis, evaluation, and action that are often
necessary to keep an *activity contingency plan* moving forward; for example,
when children adjust the means of the activity with management strategies
like organizing, helping, and sharing that facilitate its end (T of VAM-T).
Taking behaviors out-of-the-moment, allows children to develop (through
instruction and guidance) their "verbal representation of reality" that in part
or whole leads to developing in-the-moment observation and evaluation.
Once evaluated, children can take meaningful action with a management
strategy that is appropriate. Essentially, direct instruction helps ensure that
contingency (dependent) relationships can be expressed clearly and
accurately.

The second method is through *social communication* with children as
an activity unfolds in-the-moment. This is helpful because much of the
classroom, like much of life, requires observation, evaluation, and action in-
the-moment to keep an activity contingency plan moving forward or to keep
dangers at bay. However, social communication with young children is
vastly different than that between adults. It involves following three basic
steps: 1) modeling (verbally reflecting back) what is taking place in-the-
moment, 2) prompting children's contingency observations, and
3) querying children about their observations. The latter functions as a
test of what they are observing and how they are able to express it.

These three basic social communication steps are the outline, but what
the first seven chapters have exposed is the complexity of an *activity
contingency plan*. This complexity arises because each child's behavior
represents a contingency plan that is or is not "congruent" with the teacher's
activity contingency plan. The goal is to teach children to: 1) observe the
management and technical behaviors in the classroom and 2) talk about
them in terms of the meta-language of awareness (Chapter 9). If they can do
both, then they can apply a management strategy operation to keep the
activity going, improve it, or change any behavior that needs changing.
When children can do all of these, they are ARC citizens—at least within the
classroom.

Contingency Components

Chapter 3 exposed the logic of classroom contingencies. It is complex and included the following relationships.

1. What X behaviors control Mi inducing behaviors? (X ➔ Mi)
2. What Mi behaviors control X behaviors? (X ⬅ Mi)
3. What X and Mi behaviors control T? ([X or Mi] ➔ T)
4. What T behavior controls X and Mi? ([X or Mi]⬅T)
5. What Mc consequent behaviors control X, Mi, and T, so that the probability of X, Mi, and T continue to evolve? ([X or Mi or T] ⬅ Mc)

Although (4) relates primarily to the teacher's instructional behavior, children who help or share with others gain T also contribute. However, anyone who does not learn T, may often perform management behaviors that are not congruent with the teacher's activity contingency. Thus:

The first step is to ensure that all children learn T.

The remaining queries involve children as much as the teacher. Taken together, these five queries indicate two points. First, a moral repertoire (rights and duties) is required by all members to achieve a plan's end. In each query, the word "behaviors" can be replaced with the words "rights" or "duties." These word changes give "opposite" perspectives on the same interaction. Second, they indicate the "interaction relationship components" that make up any contingency. Social communication "focuses on" and "points out" these relationships.

Note that both inducing and consequent events (behaviors) can produce change. As said, change is a consequence of some other behavior, intended or not. It may seem paradoxical that both inducing and consequent events are both causes that produce change and that the change is called a "consequence." We can say the following about both inducing and consequent events. They produce various types of change that have been named *emotional*, *access*, and *restructuring* (Chapter 7). The same events work differently on different children.

Taken together, the five logic queries represent 1) rational behavior, 2) what behavior children (and the teacher) use to bring about the beginning, continuing, and ending of an activity (the change), and 3) the queries that need to be answered to indicate awareness. What remains is adding the *meta-language of awareness* (Chapter 10), the management strategies that can represent the inducing or consequent event behaviors (Chapters 11-17, and making explicit the moral repertoire (Chapter 9).

As already expressed, children do not enter the classroom with moral, management, and awareness repertoires to any extent. All three languages and their interactions are invisible to them. Direct instruction and social communications make the invisible visible. But it will take years to for these repertoires to become unified—welded together. Remembering Chapter 4, repertoires that work together stay together. When the group "stays together" they are unified. This is as close to a definition of "unity" as we will get. Some would call it "bonded together."

Social communication pivots on behavior, its evolution, and the consequences it produces. However, Chapters 4, 5, 6, and 7 illustrated that contingencies can be viewed from many perspectives. These include:

1. The behaviors that make up inducing or consequent events.
2. How these behaviors evolve across individuals and groups.
3. Emotional, access, restructuring consequences produced by (1).
4. The extent to which behaviors fit classroom morals.
5. The direction of change (toward the self or others).
6. The reciprocity between members (how they interact).
7. The compatibility across members.
8. The commonality across members.

Although everyone is different in terms of the first seven, our commonality (8)—summed up by the phrase *"hugs, kisses, caresses, smiles, laughs, and kind words"* (Chapter 4)—is the "human force," the unity that binds us together. Social communication can expose all these perspectives. By doing so, it moves well past what is usually termed *praise, descriptive feedback,* or *knowledge of results.* As (3) points out, there are only three types of consequences that our behavior causes (produces). The other perspectives add context and detail, so that observation and evaluation are as accurate as possible.

More importantly, these eight perspectives make up the content of awareness (A). They supply the above logic with content. To complete a repertoire of awareness, two components need to be added: 1) observing and evaluating the contingency relationships in-the-moment, and 2) adding the technical language of awareness that encompasses these eight perspectives (Chapter 10). The later make sure that children's awareness is "unbiased" by ensuring that "liking," "disliking," "prejudice," and "discrimination" are not the basis for an "awareness."

When members' behaviors are compatible among members (7), the group is often called "participative," "cooperative," "reciprocal," or even "prosocial." The use of these terms is based on morals, but they all ignore the complexity of the management repertoire that pinpoints what behavior causes compatibility to emerge in the context of a moral-value repertoire. The existence of "compatibility" is a *feature of the group,* not an individual. The day-by-day exposing of compatibility represent the stepping stones to unity, the social mechanism discussed in the Chapter 5. Teachers are always teaching individuals *and* the group.

The above eight perspectives take a long time to develop. But in the long run, what develops is a new, strong human quality: the ARC citizen. Once learned, there is no turning back. Children have a new *quality of being* that helps their *becoming*. Such a quality is as powerful as walking and talking. Like walking and talking, being an ARC citizen represents a *behavioral cusp*—a method of behaving that replaces one or more behaviors that are usually less effective.[4] Essentially, the new behavioral operation can't be "extinguished" or "reversed" by others or the self. ARC behavior will continue to observe, describe, evaluate, and then do something about who is doing what to whom. The "something" can be about inducing or consequent event behaviors. If they don't have the individual control to bring about change as needed, they will through group strategies like planning, intervening, and learning within groups (Chapters 15, 16, and 17).

Social Communication

Social communication techniques (operations, methods) can occur before, in-the-moment, or after an activity. Social communication exposes the components of contingencies (Chapter 3) and how the behavior that represents the components are interacting across the group. The contingency was expressed as follows:

Push →[X: Mi → (M or T) ← Mc]→ Pull

If we "unpack" this contingency representation, we discover that there are 12 two-direction interaction relations that can be expressed.

1. X that induces M or not-M.
2. X that induces T or not-T.
3. Mi that induces X or not-X.
4. Mi that induces other M or not-M (either Mi or Mc).
5. Mi that induces T or not-T.
6. Mc that consequents T or not-T.
7. Mc that consequents X or not-X.
   (Did you come here happy? Are you leaving here happy?
8. Mc that consequents Mi or not-Mi.
9. T that induces X or not-X.
10. T that consequents X or not-X.
11. T that induces M or not-M (either Mi or Mc).
12. T that consequents M or Not-M (either Mi or Mc).

The two directions represent cohesive and coercive behavioral events—those that promote the classroom activity plan and those that do not. X-behavior, as the emotional-physiological state on entering an activity, are always inducive—they push behavior toward the means and ends of an activity or they do not. Mi also pushes behavior, but it may also pull the

---

[4] https://en.wikipedia.org/wiki/Behavioral_cusp

emotional state forward or not. Mc is a pulling operation. It is T that is most interesting. Without T, future X, Mi, Mc behavior may only induce not-X, not-Mi, not-Mc. The inference is that T is needed for the possibility that the other contingency components (X, Mi, and Mc) will be part of the causal waterfall that maximizes the probability of the activity plan being successful. When all these components, from the teacher and children, are compatible (Chapter 7), then a reciprocity between members is occurring. Each is taking on their duties and receiving their rights. If one multiplies these relationships by the number of children, one begins to get a picture of the complexity within the classroom. There is some good news and bad news relative to this complexity.

The good news is in three parts. First, we can represent most of these interactions during direct instruction of various strategies, especially during the teaching of the planning and learning strategies. Second, we can teach children to see these in-the-moment with social communication operations. Third, as Chapter 4 pointed out and Chapter 10 embellishes on, only a handful of these have to be directly taught. Our inferential organism, our children, will make inferences to other relationships through what Chapter 4 called *emergence*, which can be easily evaluated through social communication queries.

The bad or hard news is that we, the children's teachers, have to change enough, so that we can see and evaluate these contingency relationships. The social communication—as verbal behavior that exposes these interactions —can either describe or query children about these 12 components.

Analysis of Communication Operations

Social communications are "packaged" into two distinct forms: statements and queries. Statements describe contingency relationships that are wanted or are observed. They begin the teaching. Queries seek out what awareness children have acquired. Queries test if children can observe, describe, or predict contingency relationships. In both forms, the communication can be about past, present, and future relationships. Through either statements and queries, social communication

1. Pivots around behavior, its evolution, and the consequences it produces.
2. These pivots can focus on an individual member's behavior or behaviors (intra-relationships), or the interactive behaviors across members.

> *It is the interactive behavior across members*
> *that is the primary concern.*

But we begin by representing each in terms of their focus on behavior(s), its evolution, and the consequences produced. For each a descriptive statement is followed by a query in parentheses. The terms used in these statements and queries will often need to be pretaught (as part of direct instruction).

Focus on Behavior

We begin with an individual behavior, move to intra-relationship behavior, and then to interactive behavior relationships. Each example includes a statement followed by a possible future query. These queries can be very narrow or globally focused. The behaviors are in **bold**.

1. Hober, please **take your turn to read**. (Hober, what do you do now?)
2. Marvel, **planning the resources** needed for your project assisted you in **finishing it early**. (Marvel, how did your planning help you?)
3. Vernice, thanks for **helping Zelda** with her **new math problems**. (Vernice, how did you assist others today?)
4. Sharon, by **letting Marlowe help you**, you **helped him help you**. (Sharon, how can you help Marlowe tomorrow?)

The first pivoted on a request for a single behavior, the second on an intra-relationship, and the third on interrelationship between Vernice and Zelda. The second will only be clear if Marvel has been taught organizing and, perhaps, planning. The fourth illustrates the complexity of all interactions. Even if Sharon is the helpee, the helpee can cause other behavior. Marlow's helping behavior was dependent on Sharon's "letting disposition" towards being helped. Nearly every interactive relationship can be flipped, so that members see it from both ends. Moral: leaders depend on how others manage themselves to be classified as such.

Focus on Behavior Change

Behavior evolves in a great many ways. For example in Chapter 7, the discussion focused on five possible evolutions: willingness, quickness, accuracy, persistence, and choice (preference). Behavior can also evolve across context (e.g., home or school, math or reading) and how often it has been performed. Now we take the above and modify them, so that consequences are pointed out.

Again, we can talk about single, multiple, and multiple interactive behaviors and their evolution. The following example proceeds like those above, but adds how the behavior has changed (evolved). When dealing with multiple behaviors, the second behavior is a consequent event that depends on the first behavior. Thus, the first is the cause of the second.

1. Hober, you have **taken your turn to read each day this week** without being asked. *This is the first week you have done so!* (Hober, what do you predict about taking you turn to read from now on?)

2. Marvel, **planning the resources** needed for your project *assisted you* in **finishing it early**. (Marvel, how does your planning make you feel?)

3. Vernice, thanks for **helping Zelda** with her **new math problems**. *You gave her access to finishing early.* (Vernice, what happens when you help others, so that they can finish their work?)

4. Sharon, by **letting Marlowe help you**, you **helped him help you**. *He now likes helping others.* (Sharon, do you now like to be helped?)

The first is a change in the persistence of behavior; it has continued for a week. The second focuses on what the first behavior helped with the second. This is a behavior change simply by the fact that without the first behavior, the second would not be possible. Thus, the second is a behavior change, at least for this one instance. The fourth example restates and, thus, emphasizes that Sharon has helped Marlowe to feel emotionally positive about helping, which may not have been so in the past. This is not a clear case of cause and effect. But by flipping the individual behaviors around, in a later interaction, it can become so: "Marlowe, do you now like to help others?" or "How does helping Sharon make you feel?" or "How does Sharon help you help her?"

Focus on Consequences

It's important to remember that when children hear statements or queries repeatedly across a range of behaviors and activities, they will make inferences as to how behaviors create consequences and most of those consequences are linked to other behavior. The above examples have already included such consequences. Now, we make these consequences explicitly linked. Here the behavior(s) are in bold and the consequences in italic.

1. Hober, you have **taken your turn to read each day this week** without being asked. *That helped your group finish the activity all week.* (Hober, how can you help your group this week?)

2. Marvel, **planning the resources** needed for your project *was the cause of* **finishing early**. (Marvel, how does your planning help you?)

3. Vernice, thanks for **helping Zelda** with her **new math problems**. *You have restructured her thinking, so that she can do them on her own.* (Vernice, what happens when you help others?)

4. Sharon, by **letting Marlowe help you**, you **helped him help you**. *You now seem emotionally positive about getting help when you need it.* (Sharon, do you now like to be helped?)

These four examples illustrate that when we deal with interactive behavior, one is always dealing with consequences. But by making them explicit, children learn to observe their interaction effects as well as talk about them with a language that helps them clearly—without vagueness or ambiguity—describe what they have observed or predict what they will observe. The first example moved from Hober taking his turn, and then illustrated how it helped his reading group. The second rephrased the previous second example from planning "assisted" to it being the "cause," which is just a stronger suggestion of the behavioral linkage. Of course, Marvel must know what a "cause" represents. The third example points to a restructuring change that resulted from Vernice's helping Zelda. The last example makes an inference about Sharon's emotional state toward helping.

Inducing Events

The above statements did not clearly separate the difference between inducing events (often call condition events) for behavior (the pushing in Graphic 8.1) and consequent events (the pulling in Graphic 8.1). The following represents some inducing events. Notice that it first makes a request. Later, such questions can query children about when to do such behavior. Here are three examples that focus on single, multiple, or interactive behaviors. The behaviors are in bold.

1. Ashley, when you **finish your math**, can you **help Tan** with his math. (Ashley, what can you do when you finish early?)
2. Class, who thinks they can **organize for reading**? [Students reply.] I think so too! Tim, what is the first step of organizing [Tim: asking if organizing is needed.] Sharon, what is the second. [Sharon responds and the teacher continues until all five steps of organizing are stated.]
3. Marlowe, can you **help** Sharon with her spelling practice?
4. Who is willing to **hand out milk** during lunch?

Each example asks for some behavior. Ashley is asked to help Tan (behavior) when she has finished her work (condition). The class was asked to organize for reading and then queries the children to see if they remember the steps of organizing. In three, Marlow is asked to help. In four, an open request is made to the class. Of course, most hands will go up. That does not matter. What all the hands indicate is a willingness. After a number of times, children may come to observe that passing out milk takes away from their lunch time and their chance to talk with classmates.

These four examples indicate that condition talk usually occurs at the start of an activity. Thus, they function as a prompt that includes support for the behavior. Most of condition talk is short and to the point. Usually, this can be in one sentence unless the students are involved in the process as when they identify the behavior and predict its future occurrence. Condition talk can become elaborate when it involves children naming the steps of complex management behavior like organizing. Here, various children can be asked to name a step of the organizing strategy.

CONSEQUENT EVENTS

Consequences focus on emotional change, access to other behavior, and the restructuring of behavior. Here are three examples that extend the above. Each focus on one type of consequent event. Behaviors are bold, consequences are in *italic*.

1. **Rhonda, this plan has clear steps.** *You should feel emotionally positive about such planning.*
2. **Marlowe, helping Sharon** *gave her a chance to finish her assignment on time.* That's a fine example of giving others access to success. (**Marlowe, what can you do to make success possible for others?**)
3. **Blanco, helping Carl with long division** *restructured his thinking. He can now do the problems himself.*

Only the first of these can be given without some preliminary direct instruction about the three types of consequent events. The second example indicates how we can define a term in context, as done with "access." As said, every time one behavior leads to another behavior, the first behavior is a cause of the second and the second is the effect that can be clearly stated as a consequence, which can 1) indicate an emotional, access, or restructuring type; 2) a quality like willingness, quickness (latency), persistence, or choice; or 3) the general frequency or duration of the behavior. These consequences are not entirely separate.

When making statements about behavior, clear, unambiguous reference is necessary. Here are three examples of unclear statements about behavior.

1. Mandel, you are a tremendous worker.
2. Fire Engines, I think that was a great reading session.
3. Marie, you did it today!

Technically "tremendous worker" could have been clearly defined. More likely, the description is an expression of teacher approval (i.e., a consequent event for the teacher), but one must ask, "To what work does it refer?" The second, also begs for a description of what is "great reading," especially to young readers. Words like tremendous, great, good, excellent, fantastic, wonderful, and so forth are not descriptions of behavior. They usually represent an emotional state, for the speaker. It is a consequence for someone.

Teachers' Interactive Social Communications

With a general idea of social communication, we can return to the inducing event that included music, song, and dance (Chapter 6). When done, what behavior has changed and what consequences occur? Of course, we may expect children to be invigorated and ready to work together. However, consider this:

[After the music, song, and dance.]
Teacher: Everyone, I feel great [smiles, raises arms]. How do you feel?
Children: Great! [some raise arms.]
[After several days of something like the above]
Teacher: How do you feel?
Children: Excellent! Great! Good! [fist bumps, raise arms, smile.]
Teacher: You make me feel like teaching. Are you ready to learn?
Children: Yes!

The purpose of the music, song, and dance activity was to induce learning. It was designed to activate compatible emotions that induce entering into the day's activities. The social communication that followed (above) exposes the consequence caused by members' music, song, and dance activity. Afterward, the teacher models a cohesive emotional state and an access consequence for children. Next, the teacher moved from a personal description to querying children about their emotional state (emotional consequence) and if they are ready to access their learning activities (access consequence). Here, social communication both models through description and queries children to see how they reply.

If the children have success learning T, much the same type of exposure can be used. When children imitate, it becomes their behavior. If children learn T, the teacher can add, "What can you do now?" or "What can you do better?" Such questions often expose restructuring consequences. The key to social communication is knowing when, where, and how to use it during activities with children.

VAM-T social communications model, expose, ask about, and test children's interactions and verbal representation of ongoing contingencies. While doing many of these, teachers may rephrase contingency relationships between members, teachers and children. This rephrasing aims to add technical vocabulary like morals, cohesion, coercive, awareness, and contingency (Chapter 10).

In very general terms, teachers begin with 1) descriptive statements about any "relationship part" of an on-going contingency, 2) prompts children to express them, 3) queries them for descriptions or predictions, and 4) tests them to observe the extent to which children can accurately describe or predict the various contingency relationships. All this takes multiple interactions across an extensive period of time. What can't be easily done for a long time is to shape (induce) children, so that they can fully describe or predict contingencies either in-the-moment or during direct instruction. The latter can take place while teaching the planning and intervening strategies as technical repertoires (M becomes the -T of VAM-T).

The following breaks down the contingency-relationship interactions into primary relationships and then combines and extends them, so that a more complete view of classroom contingencies emerges. In our talk with children, these relationships are often mixed together.

Three assumptions surround the following. First, the classroom has a few simple classroom rules that represent members rights and duties like (1) work together, (2) follow directions, (3) get or give help, and, perhaps, even, (4) make happiness. They are the moral values of the entire classroom, including the teacher. Each can be expressed as a right or duty. The second assumption is that these rules have been modeled with examples that define their range and limits. It does not matter what rule descriptions are used. What matters are the examples that define the rules as both rights and duties needed to bring about activity means and ends. Third, the children are learning the various -Ts being taught, which means the classroom is a reasonably harmonious place, so that instruction can take place.

Interactive Inducing-Behavior Relationships

We begin with the teacher modeling one relationship.

(1) Zena, thanks for working on your assignment on your own. That let me work with Zander for a while.

The statement could have focused on the entire class.

(2) By everyone working on their assignment, I was able to help Zander.

In both of these examples, the teacher was given an opportunity (access) to do other behavior. The members' behavior induces other behavior by giving access. After a few of the above, it is possible to move to questioning.

(3) Zena, how did you help me? [Zena: I did my work.] What was I able to do? [Zena: Help Zander?] You see how you helped me.

The first three examples were *teacher-children interactions*. But more important are *children-children interactions*, as in the following.

(4) Zena, you worked with Zander by showing him how to do the problems. Now he can do them.

(5) Zelda, you showed the Blue Team how to do the problems. Now, they all can do them.

A child has brought about new behavior by simply modeling how to work on some type of problem. Technically, the modeling is "teaching" but it is inducing new behavior in others (restructuring). Number 5 could have focused on a group.

(5a) Blue Team, you showed the other teams how to organize. Now all the teams can work together.

Questioning children about such interactions can soon follow.

(6) Zena, did you help Zander? [Zena: yes.] how did he change [Zena: he can now work his subtraction problems.] You see what you are doing for others and how it helps them?

(7) Zena, what happened with the Blue Team? [Zena: I showed them how to play the game *and* they can now play it according to the rules.] Excellent! You most certainly know who is doing what for whom.

In the last example, Zena has made an inference about the interaction that the teacher initiated. The teacher followed it by rephrasing Zena's statement in terms of the fundamental element of awareness: knowing who is doing what for whom. After a number of such examples, awareness could be introduced without elaboration. "You know who is doing what for whom. That makes you an aware manager."

The last interaction (7) can be expanded to illustrate that interactions are often reciprocal (bi-directional).

(8) Zena, you supervised the Blue Team. Did they do anything for you? [Zena: I don't think so.] I feel very good when I help others. Do you? [Zena: Yes.] So, they also helped you. Yes? [Zena: Yes.]

Reciprocal interactions are mutually-supporting behavior. It is also an example of compatible behaviors. The question that can be asked, "are the reciprocal interactions of the group an inducing event or a consequent event?" At times, it is impossible to know. Since the Blue Team did nothing, to promote Zena's "feeling good," it is, here, classified as an inducing event. If the group would have thanked Zena in some way, then it could be considered a consequent event, especially if Zena's "good feeling" were brought about or intensified by it. Managers have only some degree of control over others; it is never complete, at least not in the long run— remember escape, avoidance, and counter control (Chapter 4).

Interactive Behavior-Consequent Relationships

Again, we begin with the teacher modeling this relationship.

(9) Zena, I thank you for working on your assignment. Zander can now do the math he missed.

The statement has two behavior-consequent relationships for Zena. The teacher *directly* thanked her (emotional consequence) and *indirectly* indicated that her work helped Zander by giving the teacher time for working with Zander (access consequence). Now for a group consequent relationship.

(10) Everyone, thank you very much for working on your assignment. Zander can now do the math he missed.

This example is the same as the previous one by exposing interaction relationships both directly and indirectly. Notice how little the difference there is between (1 and 2) and (9 and 10). Eventually, they can be drawn together and combined. Consider the following that makes all three relationships direct.

(11) Everyone, thank you very much for working on your assignment. It allowed me to work with Zander. Now, he can do the math he missed.

The first relationship is the emotional consequent delivered by the teacher. The second is the access consequent the teacher received from the members. The third is the restructuring consequent delivered to Zander—he can now do the math.

After a few of the above (9, 10, 11), it is possible to move to questioning.

(12) Zena, how do I usually help you? [Zena: you tell me how I did and what else I helped you do.] What was I able to do? [Zena: Teach Zander something?] You see how I help you and how you gave an me time. Now, Zander can do his math. We are working together.

All the above were *teacher-children interactions*. Next are the *children-children interactions*. With a history of the above and the previous use of inducing interactions, it may be possible to skip directly to questioning.

(13) Zena, what happens when you work with Zander? [Zena: He does his problems correctly.] How does he help you? [Zena: He thanks me and often gives me a stick of hard candy.] So, you two are working together.

(14) Zelda, what happens when you show the Blue Team how to do their problems? [Zelda: They can do them on their own.] How do they help you? [Zelda: They thank me and ask if I will help them again.] That is what I call working together, as well as seeing who is doing what for whom. Good observing.

Zelda has brought about new behavior (restructuring) by modeling how to work a type of problem. The group delivered an emotional consequence by the "thanks" and the "request." If Zelda does not like the group, then the group's control is insignificant. But if Zelda continues to work with them or volunteers to do so, then we can infer that 1) the group has consequent efficacy or that 2) she just likes helping others learn. Questioning children about such interactions can soon follow.

(15) Zena, did you help Zander? [Zena: Yes. He read correctly and he thanked me for my help] Again, you see who is doing what for whom.

(16) Zena, what happened with the Blue Team? [Zena: I showed them how to play the math game and they let me join them in a game.] Excellent! You do see who is doing what for whom. You and the Blue Team are working together. You are all cohesive managers.

The last interaction can be expanded to illustrate the reciprocity (cohesive reciprocals) that often occurs in children-children interactions. The last part of the interaction introduced the relationship that "working together" is one example of "cohesiveness."

(17) Zena, you supervised the Blue Team. Who did what for whom? [Zena: I helped them learn the math game and they thanked me and let me play a game with them.} You do see both sides when working with others. You and the Blues are reciprocal.

Reciprocal indicates mutual relationships and is one side of the direction of consequent behaviors (Chapter 7). When the reciprocal behavior is not mutual, one side is being non-reciprocal. There may be coercive management involved.

Extending Relationships

In Chapters 6 and 7, the terms used for inducing events (as behavior) was push. The term used for consequent events (as behaviors) was pull. The term used when relationships were unifying was cohesive and not unifying was coercive. These terms are used because they promote the language of awareness and contingency. They can be easily used to directly teach children to observe the four relationships that define the heart of awareness: 1) some pushing helps members be cohesive, 2) some pulling helps members be cohesive, 3) some pushing inhibits (distracts) members from being cohesive (the pushers are coercive), and 4) some pulling inhibits (distracts) members from being cohesive (the pullers are coercive). A cohesive and *compatible contingency* occurs when all members push or pull toward the activity end during an activity. When all the terms are defined, they can replace the above with less elaborate queries and eventually requests like:

1. Was the pushing cohesive or coercive?
2. Was your pulling cohesive or coercive?
3. Did your behavior push or pull others toward our goal?
4. Were you moral toward others today?

5. How would you describe your behavior toward others?
6. What do you predict about your relationship toward others?
7. Was your prediction correct?

With all of these, the teacher can ask the ultimate rational question: "What evidence told/tells you so?" or simply, "How do you know?" Additionally, these queries are time savers.

Being cohesive to others when they are coercive may well require a double-edged communication. The following is an example

(18) Zena, [to Group 1] Can I play with you? [Group 1: Why would we want a bubble head like you. Go find some other bubble heads to play with.] Zena: You are a coercive group, not a cohesive team.

Zena's reply indicates that her classroom was taught the difference between working together, which was termed *cohesive*, and not working together, which was termed *coercive*. We will take up such non-reciprocal directional consequent behaviors in Chapter 16, Intervening Strategy.

Here is an example of how the terms could have been introduced during an ongoing activity. Example 18 is repeated with rephrasing.

(18a) Zena, you supervised the Blue Team. Who did what for whom? [Zena: I helped them learn the math game and they thanked me and let me play a game with them.} When members work with each other, it is called cohesive. When members work against each other, it is called coercive.

Let's reduce 18 to a query and ask for evidence.

(18b) Zena, can you describe your work with the Blue Team? [Zena: we were a cohesive team.] What is your evidence? {Zena, I pushed by showing them how and they pulled me with their thanks. They can do their work and we worked together to complete the activity. We all like the rule, be happy.]

This query-evidence relationship could have been directed at the Blue Team. Their answer should have been something parallel to Zena's. The important point is that teachers keep their part of the interaction to a minimum. What the last interaction exposes is that a "contingency perspective" is developing. When teachers ask for a prediction, it usually—if modeled—takes an "if-then" form. This is done easily during the use of the planning strategy where the plan is a prediction that can easily be expressed in an if-then form and the evidence for the "success" of the plan is acknowledged.

EffecTiveNess of VerbaL CommuNicaTioN EveNTs

Like any social technology, we must master it. This mastering involves three elements

What Must be Learned

The first step toward effectiveness is to know what to master and how to master it. Five behaviors are involved.

1. Name and identify its components,
2. Identify how its components fit together,
3. Know when to use a component or components,
4. Observe what talking content to insert at any particular time, and
5. Undertake constant practice until the first four emerge, so that our talk appears and is effortless and sincere.

Thus, our talking is like any tool, be it a word processor or a pencil. Even if we can perform the first three, but haven't performed the fourth, we have nothing to talk about or write about. Finally, like any type of writing, constant practice and editing are required to get children absorbed in the story of their learning and its impact on their and other's worlds.

Presenting Social Communications

We want our social communications to be effective without interrupting the flow of an activity plan. Following these six guidelines will help maximize the probability that talk will be effective.

1. Believe in the importance of what is said.
2. Present talk in a relaxed and positive manner.
3. Clearly identify the person or group being talking to.
4. Use a positive, varying tone of voice.
5. Keep the presentation short and clear.
6. Match the presentation to the age-level of the group.

First, the examples and the examples presented above should support our belief in the importance of clear communication. Yet, it is our use of this talk and seeing it change behavior that will heighten this belief.

Second, by building and practicing various types of statements and questions prior to their use, we take the first step toward a relaxed and positive presentation. For many, social communication, as forms of talk, often feel "unnatural" at first. Only practice and use, in the context of seeing their effects, can overcome any such feelings.

Third, clearly identify the audience by using a child's name or a group name. Add eye contact when talking. Personalizing statements and questions help gain listener attention. Without it, the communication has no power to change behavior or point out the relationships taking place.

Fourth, changing contexts require a change in voice. The context may require an exclamation, speaking softly, or a formal tone. The tone indicates that what we are saying is important and projects our respect for the listener.

Five, keep the presentation short by avoiding wandering and repetition (5). Knowing when to present what type of talk helps, but mostly the focus of statements is achieved by knowing the behaviors required of children, the resources needed, and the consequences that have or could result. Talk is required, but most of it is not focused on the relevant contingency relationships, especially when children are just entering school.

Finally, match statements to the age level of the children and carefully consider the social context. For younger children, especially those below the third grade, tenderness and enthusiasm often go hand-in-hand with clear description. Recent cultural changes have reduced the use of friendly, physical social contact, like the hug or pat in most classrooms, although an elbow or fist bump can usually be used. As a result, the appropriate use of talk moves to the forefront of human communication with younger children.

Evaluating the Immediate Impact of Your Talk

Just how do children think and feel about the content and presentation of our statements? Two practical procedures can be used to answer this question.

The first is to take a look back at the child or group to whom the statement was directed a moment or two after turning (physically) to something else. If the child's or group's facial expressions are like tasting unpleasant or unfamiliar food, the statements most likely are not effective in content and/or style of presentation. However, give them time to work.

The second is to ask the students directly about the content or presentation. Do this with individuals or a group. Here are three examples of asking about the presentation.

1. Frank, how would you tell yourself that?
2. Zelda, how would you tell Mary what I just told you?
3. Marko, would you prefer that I talk to you privately?

It is important not to overdo such statements. Also consider a student or group's need for privacy. This is especially important in the upper-elementary grades. Many other variations are possible.

Summary

This chapter has focused on the two basic relationships—children's behavior as inducing and consequent events for themselves or others—that are the parts of classroom contingencies (Chapters 3 through 7). However, there is a whole social technology of teachers' verbal behavior that is slowly developing to shape children's behavior.[5] Almost all this talk describes or asks about children's behavior—what someone has done (past), is doing (present), or is about to do (future). This talk about behavior can reference instances of behavior, a class of behavior, or the relationships various

---

[5] https://www.managingourselves.org/teaching/talking.php

behaviors enter into as parts of a contingency. When talking about instances and classes, the description can be about single or multiple behaviors. When relationships are described, multiple behaviors are always referenced, usually across members. The chapters of Part 2 will expand on social communication using the languages of morals (Chapter 9), awareness (Chapter 10), and management (Chapters 11 through 17). All are necessary for the development of the aware, rational, civil (ARC) citizen.

PART 2

CONTENT REPERTOIRES

Part 1 presented the "underlying" knowledge about human behavior that makes the teaching of the VAM-T repertoires possible. It dealt with the categories, relationships, mechanisms, and operations that make it possible for teachers to evolve children into ARC citizens.

Part 2 focuses on what it means to be an ARC citizen. Simultaneously, Part 2 explores how caregivers, teachers, and the school system have a hand in evolving children into aware, rational, and civil adults. But as Chapter 3 pointed out, nearly everyone in society who interacts with children plays a role in their evolution. The chapters do the following.

Chapter 9 analyzes moral values in the classroom. It illustrates how these must be "known" before classroom activities can function to achieve their value purpose, the objective of the activity. If there are no moral values, then there can only be a civilization, or a classroom, with discontents and anarchy.

Chapter 10 analyzes awareness. It sits as the "evaluator" between management behavior and the classroom's moral-value statements. Members ask, "Does the management observed fit the moral values of the classroom?" To answer this question, the moral value statements and management behavior need to be clear and unambiguous. Once the evaluation is made, management behavior can control what happens next given whether or not there is a congruence (fit) between the two. The evaluation induces the management repertoire to resolve conflicts that are the "misfit" between management behavior and moral value statements.

Chapters 11 through 17 analyze the seven sub-repertoires that make up management: Organizing, helping, sharing, supervising, planning, intervening, and learning. During an activity, the classroom member learns to discriminate which one is appropriate to engage in and the steps use to engage in it. In general, the evolution of any of these sub-repertoires evolves through four levels of complexity. These evolutionary levels require considerable time for children to master. However, the speed of this evolution is dependent on children's reading and comprehension behavior—it allows teachers to employ more "tools" with which to evolve their children into ARC citizens.

Part 3 will explore how the Part 2 repertoires fit together as a system of repertoires. Part 3 moves beyond the "narrow" confines of the moral values of the classroom to the "broader" concerns outside of schools as children become adults and control the world that we are leaving them.

9

Moral-Values Repertoire

Chapter 1 defined the moral-values repertoire as a set of descriptive statements, spoken or written. They are often classified as classroom rules. They specify the behaviors needed by group members in order to begin, continue, and end group activities successfully. These statements are embedded within the physical and social structures created. For activity members to carry out the means to the value-purpose ends, moral values need to be as clear and unambiguous as possible. We are gregarious, and we seek to form ourselves into groups. These are two basic facts. But without well specified moral values for the classroom, the means desired and the ends to be achieved will remain problematic. This chapter unpacks moral values, how they fit within the classroom, and the extent to which the classroom is the mirror of the larger social system.

Moral Values in Society

We have civil rights and civic duties. Rights are usually "intermingled" with terms like freedom and liberty. Duties are usually intermingled with terms like responsibility and obligation. All of these terms have proven problematic for a number of reasons. First, they are almost always poorly defined. Second, various moral value documents, like constitutions and various tomes, fail to address both rights and duties with a level of balance. Third, these documents are often seen as "cast-in-stone," which means they are not subject to rational or investigative behavior.

The "laws of the land" no matter how they get embedded into the culture, focus on how members interact. both in terms of rights and duties. For example, we have a right to use cell phones, but have a duty not to do so while driving. We have the right to cross at the crosswalk, but we must wait for the walk signal. We have the right to drive a vehicle but only after a certain age, as well as a duty to stop at stop signs and stay within the speed limit. Yet, not all right-duty relationships are created equal. For example, we have a right to vote, but no duty to do so. We have a right to be parents, but no duty to prepare ourselves for the right, as with driving. We have the right to own a weapon, but no duties to prepare us to use or not use it.

Then there are groups with various degrees of control over various activity members (Chapter 10) who impose "blockades" to events like access to voting, home ownership, or jobs. By *imposing blockades to rights* or *neglecting duties*, even if only through inaction, we create conflicts. These conflicts may arise out of our ignorance or a set of moral values that do not fit with the group that has a value purpose. In other words, various Me/My subgroups conflict with other groups.

Taking a *rights-duties interaction perspective* on what behaviors need to be performed by all activity members helps solve conflicts. It does so in terms of both the means (as micro-level management behavior) used and the ends achieved (as the macro-level short- or long-term consequent events). This perspective helps view both sides of the social interaction equation. Everyone has both rights and duties within any activity. If I have a right to learn, then someone (or many) have a duty to allow or support that learning.

Creating our ARC citizens requires work. They do not come ready-made. They are artifacts springing from a long biological history of interacting with various social environments—language makes this history "transferable." Unless we change, our children will become like us. Given the conflicts that are occurring in all the Nation States around the world, this likeness needs changing. That is if we believe what the nightly news casts tell us about what is here called coercive behavior between individuals, local communities, and Nation States. Such coercive behavior is called immoral behavior at all levels of society.

Moral Values in the Classroom

Infants enter the world surrounded by moral values in their home and community. By the time they enter school, they have "absorbed" some of these through observing relationships between others and acting in relationships with others. Thus, they enter the classroom with moral values, but they are unaware of them. They behave towards others in ways that are usually impulsive. At this point, young children have no way to observe and talk about moral values or their management behavior. These repertoires and their relationships are nonexistent. What children "sense" when management behavior does or does not fit moral values are emotions usually called pain or pleasure.

Schooling represents a culturally sanctioned moral activity about the kinds of repertoires children need in order to become functional citizens. At the turn of the 20th century, reading, writing, and doing basic math were enough. The world had but a billion or so members and the communication between groups was very slow. Today, we have far greater technological complexity and environmental risks. This situation calls for an updated version of our moral vision of education. It might be worded as follows:

> Children should be given the opportunity to evolve, so that they can invent physical, biological, and social environments to overcome old problems, avoid potential problems, and solve unforeseen ones in ways that support their future and those of their children.

This educational statement, as policy, can be classified as an *intergenerational survival-based moral value* that combines both an individual and cultural focus. Yet, it does not state the two sides of the human relationship coin required, so that progress can be observed on a day-by-day basis. These two sides, from a classroom member perspective, are:

1. How does my management help others during activities?
2. What do others do to help my management during activities?

Moral values, as said, are not about the valuing of vegetables over grains, one sports team over another, or the taste of broccoli over spinach. They are about human interactions, the relationships between ourselves. The question of concern is the relationship between the *should do* (morals) and the *doing* (management). We evaluate the relationship with the meta-language repertoire of awareness (Chapter 10).

The only way we "know" another's morals is by inference from our observation of their management behavior. What makes this "moral inference" possible—for the most part—is the combination of clear management and moral statement repertoires. This inference is often easy to reach, but at times very hard. What usually makes the inference (evaluation) hard is that the morals and management behaviors are clear or clearly related. There are also times that the evidence is just not clear. Evidence and its clarity represent one of the "plagues" of any social justice system (Chapter 16). At times, we must be patient and wait for the arrival of evidence. In general, what makes the *doings* between classroom members moral values fitting? The answer was given in Chapter 1:

> **Behaviors that foster, support, and reward the beginning,**
> **continuing, and ending of classroom activities.**

The above statement is our initial guide. Yet, this expression still does not tell us about the two sides of moral values: 1) how we behave toward others and 2) how others behave toward us? How do we bring these two sides of management behavior together to achieve our moral values? Because young children have little in the way of either morals or management repertoires, they must be taught.

Morals as Right-Duty Representations

Chapter 1 stated that 1) teachers are already teaching moral values and that 2) the "classroom rules" represent these moral values. The difficulty is representing these morals. We can begin by characterizing classroom rules as "trickling down" from more global moral value statements about educating children.

1. A community has moral values.
2. Educating children is a moral value (it seeks to change them).
3. A community has a duty to "support" learning and teaching.

4. Community caregivers have a right to educated children.
5. Teachers have a right to teaching resources.
6. Children have a right to learn (to be educated).
7. Teachers have the duty to deliver the "best" teaching.
8. Children have a right to receive the "best" teaching.
9. Teachers have a right to children who "support" teaching.
10. Children have a duty to support the "best" teaching.

This "trickle-down" of rights-duties from the higher-level moral of "educating children" indicates that at the classroom level, there exists reciprocal rights and duties for both teachers and children (6, 7, 8, 9, 10). However, the real problem is how various stakeholders' behavior interferes with whatever rules are presented and enforced at the local level.

The first interference relates to community members who do not value education (1, 2, 3). Caregivers may not instill in their children the value of getting an education (4), to say nothing of instilling an excitement for learning or the right to learn (6). As a result, children may not participate in the teaching-learning process because they don't care about the best quality of teaching (8) or do not support teaching (10). It only takes one or two such children to make teaching and learning a nightmare for the other classroom members (6, 9).

The second interference occurs when a community that does not supply teachers with the resources needed to provide the best teaching (5). There may exist a bias toward various community schools or they charge teachers with a great many duties that may interfere with teaching (7). For example, America's past "separate but equal" stance was biased. Eliminating bias, intended or not, requires that members can 1) observe who is doing what for or to whom, 2) inferring the morals that could be behind the doing, and then 3) being able to do something about it.

The third interference occurs when teachers receive an education that lacks some key practices that stop them from delivering the best teaching (7). This interference originates from the outside by those who educate teachers. These teacher educators may have biases about curricula, methods of teaching, or toward some subset of teacher candidates. However, our ignorance about how children learn and how to teach are most likely at the heart of this interference.

The fourth interference is a subset of teachers who have implicit or explicit biases toward a certain subset of children (6), so they do not teach equitably (7). With bias present, children who initially care about their schooling may eventually stop caring because the teaching does not support their learning (7), and, thus, they do not support teaching (10).

With the first and fourth interferences, a vicious cycle is perpetuated. The breakdown of the classroom or school social structure is a mirror of the breakdown occurring in society. (Such a breakdown is exacerbated by disasters like the 2020 Covid-19 pandemic.) If this happens from an early point, the social structures within and outside of education suffer because children are not prepared to be aware, rational, civil citizens—the repertoires that this text assumes are important. This text is, in part, about the content and mechanisms that can alter this vicious cycle by instilling in all children VAM, so that T can occur, thereby imparting the joy of learning to children.

Classroom Rules

Educational systems are a part of nearly all nations of the world. It is from here that these young citizens hopefully begin an explicit evolutionary journey to become aware, rational, civil citizens. Nearly every classroom includes a set of rules that can be presented as rights and duties—for every right we have a duty. These represent management behavior and the 12 interactions displayed above. If we step back about 100 years these rules can be expressed as in Table 9.1.

TABLE 9.1		
Classroom rules and management behavior relationships		
	Classroom Rules	Management Relationship
1	Follow directions	Manager➔Managed
2	Stay in your seat	Self-Managed
3	Keep hands to self	Self-Managed
4	Talk only when asked	Manager➔Managed

A hundred years ago the classroom was a very different place, usually with a "lecture-based" structure. Table 9.1 expresses a set of possible rules (as moral values) and the management relationships required to meet them. In rows 1 and 4, the teacher is the *manager* and children are *managed*. Rows 2 and 3, illustrate what is usually called self-control, self-restraint, or self-management. However, these children are never directly taught to manage themselves in activities with other children. To exhibit self-control with a teacher as the manager is not teaching them to manage themselves. "Following" as controlled by the teacher may only represent children's *compliance*. In other words, explicit, direct teaching is required for children to learn to manage themselves in the context of others. Moreover, what occurs when the 2nd and 3rd rules were not followed was often the administration of punishment by the teacher (coercive management).

Table 9.2 illustrates the rules that are needed for an interactive social structure that teaches the management strategies. Again, there is a list of four common rules (left side) followed by the management required to follow them (right side). Both represent the human relationships required to begin, continue, and end classroom activities.

TABLE 9.2	
Classroom rules and management behavior relationships	
Classroom Rules	Management Relationship
1	Follow directions	Manager→Managed
2	Work with others	Manager←→Managed
3	Get help or help	→Managed *or* Manager→
4	Make happiness	→Managed *or* Manager→

The first row indicates that following directions requires that the manager gives directions to the managed who hopefully follow them. The teacher begins as the manager but as children learn various strategies like organizing, supervising, planning, and intervening, the child can take over the manager roles. This often happens in activities that have multiple groups working on their own projects or various parts of a larger project.

The second row indicates that there are times when two members or two small groups must work together. Here the members have reciprocal control, indicated by ←→. They share the duties and rights of achieving their activity's means and ends.

The third row indicates that a member may need some resource or knowledge to continue toward an activity's conclusion. Children can also be the members who give the help or supply a needed resource. Here, the helping and sharing strategies play a role in the context of the activity structure. It allows help to be given or received. For example, children may check math problems for each another or seek a check on the way they are doing problems.

The fourth row indicates an emotional consequence that occurs because of some management or technical behavior. Children "make happiness" for themselves and others as an activity unfolds. But the making and the emotional relationship must be exposed by the teacher. It is a useful rule from several perspectives. First, management behavior causes these emotional states. Second, it is a good place to start teaching children to be aware of how they feel (emotional consequent). Third, emotional states are usually the first to undergo change as a consequence of ongoing management behavior of the self or others. Fourth, it can indicate that a change in management is needed. If children are aware of a negative emotional state (Chapter 10), then a management behavior change is needed. This may require rule three management, get help or help. If happy, they can comment to themselves about how well the work is going; another management behavior—supervising the self. Social communication connects the emotional state to the activity and what management behavior is or is not "making happiness." From here, access and restructuring consequences can be taught and pointed out by the teacher. Later, the teacher can query children about how they feel as well as what other consequences are occurring. At this point, they are getting the gist of the cause (as Mi or Mc) and the effects of various management behavior (Chapter 4).

If children follow the rules by using the management strategies needed at any point in time, their management is classified as rational and civil (moral). This eventually entails using a plan and behaving morally relative to that plan. If they have not followed the classroom's moral rules, their management behavior is less rational and civil. Often there is only a small difference between being moral or not. But if teachers deal with small differences before large ones appear, they decrease the probability that radically coercive managers will appear not only in their classrooms, but later in life. To learn such moral-management relationships requires that teachers connect the dots for our future-managers-of-change for a number of years across a range of activities.

How children manage themselves in following the rules determines if they are cohesive or coercive. The only way to know this is by observing and making an inference if management behavior observed is congruent with the moral values as the activity unfolds. The evidence is gathered during the activity's implementation. As Chapter 15 and 16 point out, this not a difficult job once one realizes that the plan identifies what the evidence is, and the intervention strategy documents a good portion of the social behavior evidence.[1] Most of the remaining evidence is bundled in the learning of T. If T is not learned by a portion of the class, then problems remain: something is wrong when the totality of stakeholders can't engender willingness, latency, accuracy, persistence, and choice in children (Chapter 7). This is a planning problem for those who establish educational policy to the children in the classroom. Along the way, parents, community members, and teachers throw in their moral values and management behavior, which may help or hinder the education of ARC citizens.[2]

Example Sets of Classroom Rules

Naming the classroom rules is only a small step towards moral development. In fact, it does not matter what names you give them (besides being positively stated). It is the initial set of examples of each rule that gives children a "picture" of what behavior can be discriminated as fitting the rule (as a right or duty). With activities being added and subtracted across classrooms, later examples will expand on this initial picture the same way

[1] There are many ways to involve children in the gathering of evidence, for example, that makes the activities an engineering project that deal with what the NGSS framework calls science practice and crosscutting concepts (Chapter 1).

[2] National Academies of Sciences, Engineering, and Medicine. (2022). *Science and Engineering in Preschool Through Elementary Grades: The Brilliance of Children and the Strengths of Educators*. Washington, DC: The National Academies Press. Page 33. https://doi.org/10.17226/26215.

that an initial set of examples of "vehicles" defines the vehicle class that eventually gets larger as related teaching continues. Thus, the rule "work together" can be called "together work," "work with others," or "harmony with others." One could use just the "Make happiness" rule. It would just take longer to present the examples of management behavior that would make one happy or not.

One of the best ways to teach these rules for any particular classroom— Kindergarten is not the same as third grade—is to slowly walk children through a few activities that need the rule or rules, and what management behavior to perform to be classified as the rule. A few non-examples will be needed. To find the activities to walk children through, teacher's need to walk through their activities and select those in which children often get some management behavior related to the rules wrong. The rule for teaching is this:

> *Very young children require more walk throughs*
> *across a larger range of activities.*

We must acknowledge that all children are different. Yet, as language and reading behaviors emerge, the "walk throughs" can be done verbally by pointing to a rule and asking for verbal examples and non-example. Some of this can be done with music, song, and movement (Chapter 6) that includes wording and actions that induce rule following.

Social Communication and Moral Values

Chapter 8 introduced social communication techniques (operations, methods) that can occur before, in-the-moment, or after an activity. They expose the components of classroom activity contingencies (Chapter 3) and how the behavior that represents its components are interacting across the group. Here we focus on the interactive descriptions or queries by illustrating how teachers can use them, so that such moral values and management behavior relate to the children. We start with the teacher.

Teachers Representing Moral Values

Teachers can 1) describe a moral-management interaction, 2) request it, 3) consequent it, or 4) query children about it. These four operations are not always separate. We begin with the above four rules (Graphic 9.2) as our moral values: 1) Follow directions, 2) work with others, 3) get help or help, and 4) make happiness. It is assumed here that the rules have been directly taught in terms of right-duty relationships. Most of the following examples are extensions or modification of those in Chapter 8. The reference to moral-management interaction is in **bold**.

1. Ashley, would you **take on the duty of helping Tan** with his math when you have finished yours?

2. Who is willing to take on the duty to hand out milk during lunch?

When a request is made, the main thing to do is either express it as a specific rule, a duty, or a right.

3. Marlowe, helping Sharon gave her a chance to finish her assignment on time. She is happy and you give her access to success. You followed the **helping and happiness rules**. Excellent!
4. Blanco, taking on the duty of helping Carl with long division, gave him his right to learn. He can now do long division on his own.

Example 4 juxtaposes both sides of a rule: rights and duties. All interactions that describe behavior after-the-fact can use this very explicit relationship form. Both examples 3 and 4, like all other after-the-fact interactions not only indicate a cohesive relationship between students but supply a consequent event from the teacher.

5. Hober, you have **taken on your duty** by taking your turn without being asked.
6. Marvel, by **doing your planning duty** for your project, **you gave yourself the right to finish early**. Without duties there are no rights.
7. Sharon, you did your duty by letting Marlowe help you. You let him do his duty of helping you.

Example 6 illustrates that a behavior that is part of a chain of steps, function as both a duty and a right. One is an inducing event and the other is a consequent event. Example 7 points out how someone can take on a duty that allows for someone else to perform a duty.

8. Zena, thanks for being dutiful by following rule 1. **Your dutiful work gave me my right to help Zander** with the work he missed.

The statement could have focused on the entire class.

9. Because everyone followed rule 1, I was able to do my duty and help Zander.

Examples 8 and 9 reverse the rights-duty perspective. Notice in 8 that a rule following event allowed a right, but in Example 9, the right was skipped over and the duty became the focus. This is an example of how a stream of behavior (chain of steps) can be mixed and matched to represent inter-actions as rights or duties.

In all of the above, teachers will usually add a "thank you" or an "excellent" to cement the idea that these statements represent cohesive relationships and, also, a cohesive event from the teacher as well.

10. Zena, how did you help me? [Zena: I did my duty.] What was I able to do? [Zena: Fulfill your duty to help Zander?] You are aware of how rights and duties work together.
11. Zena, you supervised the Blue Team. Did they do anything for you? [Zena: They helped me do my duty by doing their duty of following my supervising.] We all felt very positive about the project we worked on.

Examples 10 and 11 transition to querying children about how they see their morals as rights and duties. If the term "morals" has been connected to rules and the right-duty relationship. The above can be done in short-hand version.

12. [End of the day summary.] Let's see if you know what morals you followed today? [Calls on children.]
13. [During summary as children respond to 12] Was that doing a duty or a right? [Calls on children.]
14. [During summary as children answer 12 or 13.] What rule was that? [Calls on children.]
15. [During summary as children answer 12 thru 13.] Who can give me another example like that one? [Calls on children.]

When others can hear these, there is no need to call on more than a few students. In a small-group situation, you can move across the group asking for one or two of these bits (Examples 12-15), so that all can participate. Another way to do the interactive element is to ask one child to answer the first question and ask the other children to confirm it or to expand upon it.

Children Representing Moral Values

In the examples that follow, the speaker is describing his or her M or T behavior (the B following it), with the related moral value (Z), that may induce (Ms) or deliver consequences (Mc) for themselves or others. Where it applies, the speaker's behavior is connected with its function relative to others, which can be an inducing event (B1/S1) or a consequent (B2/C1). The clearer, more consistent, and patterned the activities, the more quickly the contingencies will be seen and become expressible by children. The following begins with a child describing an activity contingency. It begins with one of the above rules of the classroom (a moral value statement, Z).

(1) Today I followed the working-with-others rule (Z1) during reading group (S1), by organizing (B1/S2) and taking my turn (B2/S3). My management (B1/B2) helped the group continue (C1) and complete the activity on time (C2), with only one reading error (C3). We all applauded working together (C4/Z1).

This description talks about the past. Working together was the moral value (Z1) for the reading activity (S1). Two of the child's behaviors related to maintaining the conditions through organizing (B1/S2) and taking turns

(B2/S3). The first consequence was an access-to-continuing the activity (C1). The second was finishing on time (C2). The third was low reading errors (C3), which may indicate a restructuring—the members' reading accuracy may have improved. When the group applauded (C4), they are most likely expressing an emotional consequence for their activity work (T). The speaker expressed it as "working together," (Z1), but the applauding could be for the low errors, a consequence, C. This complex contingency expression (communication) has some ambiguity, especially relative to the prediction of what B1 and B2 did for the group: did it induce as indicated (S2 and S3) for others, consequent them, or both? We would have to look closer at the evidence from the other members to disambiguate what the behavior (B1 and, B2) did for others (C1 and C2) or if the applauding was for working together (C4).

If we wanted to clarify the description, we would ask the child for more evidence. Alternatively, we could ask other activity members to substantiate the statement's elements in doubt. But in reality, seldom will such happen. What will happen is that we will ask other members to express their picture of the activity contingency or we will simply add, as a form of extension or paraphrase, what the child said.

There are also consequences for the teacher. Setting up the activity and the children's working together would most likely be an emotional consequence. The success may lead to at least thinking about restructuring the activity, so that children have a greater opportunity to manage the group.

Such verbal behavior can be expressed in various syntactical arrangements. For simplicity, the following continues grammatically like example (1), but is a prediction.

> (2) Today I will follow directions (Z1), during math (S1) by listening to the teacher (B1/S2), by organizing my materials (B2/S3). and by answering when called on (B3/S4). If I do these things, I will learn the new procedure (B4/C1) and do the rest of the problems correctly (C2). I will be happy (C3) if my group can do the same to help me learn.

These first two examples are about the contingencies as they relate to the manager (speaker), as a description (1) and a prediction (2). Additionally, the focus can shift to talking about others in much the same way, as might a child who is an activity supervisor.

> (3) Being the group manager (Z1) is fun (C1). I directed their organizing by reciting its steps (B1/S1) and called on them to take their turns to read (B2/S2), by. As a consequence, our group finished early (C2). I also pointed out that they had no errors (B3/C3).

This description from the group's *manager* (speaker) sets up the conditions through the organizing strategy (B1/S1) and called on members to take their turns (B2/S2). This behavior resulted in two consequences (C2, C3) for everyone. This is how a supervisor would talk about the contingencies of the activity they manage. The description exposes "who is doing what for whom," be it coercive or cohesive in relationship to the activity plan and, thus, the classroom rules. The consequences may be reinforcing both for the supervisor and the supervisees. But the verbal expression does not delve into that element of the contingency. The next example is a prediction of a similar sort.

> (4) I will be the helper (Z1) during independent work (S1). I will supervise them by walking them through each step of at least one problem (B1/S2), have them recite the steps as they work (B2/S3), and then watch them do at least one problem on their own (B3/S4). This supervising procedure should allow them to be successful with the rest of the problems (C1).

Supervising manager (as helper) is similar to (3), but now it is a plan, as a predictive procedure, for helping others. The plan illustrates how the helping supervisor will attempt to control the acquisition of a behavior by the helpee. The consequence (C1) is most likely related to both the supervisor and the supervisees.

> (5) I helped (Z1) during independent work (S1). I supervise them as planned by walking them through each step of at least one problem (B1/S2), had them recite the steps as they worked (B2/S3), and then watched them do one problem on their own (B3/S4). This supervising procedure allowed them to be successful with the rest of their problems (C1).

Notice that the child is expressing in (5) the outcome of (4). This is the evidence, at least in part, that the supervising process was successful (C1). This helper is both planning and gathering evidence about their management, connecting it to a value purpose, and seeing their management as a supervising strategy. Perhaps this child is even seeing what this supervising is doing. It may be doing more than inducing others, but consequenting them as well. In this case each (B1-3) is also allowing the helpee to access the next step in the procedure, all of which leads to (C1).

Next, we flip the last two examples and view what the helpee might say during a reflective moment (prompted by social communication). Here the Bs are for the helpee and Ss are for Zelda, the helper, setting-the-occasion.

> (6) I followed the getting help procedure (B1). Zelda helped me with my reading passage (S1). I did not understand it (B2/S2). She walked me through the first sentences until I understood the big words (B3/S3) and the sentences (B4/S4). She then asked me to tell her what some sentences told me (B5/S5). She showed me how the difficult sentences fit together (B6/S6). I got all the remaining questions correct on my homework for the first time (C1). I think I will continue to get help when I need it (Z1). I thanked Zelda the next day for helping me (C2) and she smiled and nodded (C3). We both made happiness together.

B2 is the problem and using the helping activity (B1) inducing Zelda's helping (S1), which involves a number of behavioral steps (S2-S6) to help the reader read. B2 through B6 are the helpee's behavior relative to Zelda's helping behavior (S2-S6). The helpees and helper's behaviors are almost inseparable. They represent the interactive flow of teaching and learning (as a communication). C1 is a powerful consequent event that helped the helpee "feel" and "see" the value in getting help (X1). Notice that engaging in the getting-help procedure is a behavior but at the end can be seen also as a value (Z1). C2 and C3 are most likely positive emotional consequences for both parties. They also add to making getting help and giving it a strong value (X1) for both parties. The evidence for the helpee is the success (C1) that is connected to the value (Z1) and perhaps Zelda's smile and nod (C3). The helpee's success is most likely a positive consequence for Zelda with her smile and nod as evidence indicators. Thus, they both are happy; they satisfy the "making happiness" rule.

How do children arrive at such descriptive and predictive pictures of their reality? Only through a long history that describes the contingencies and queries children about their interactions with other members, activity to activity, and across years. Gradually, we move from expressing to prompting their descriptions and predictions with queries about activity contingencies (Chapter 8).

The Flow of VAM-T Learning

When teachers expose the above interactions (description) and, then, ask (query) children about them, five behavioral events gradually occur.

First, children observe the causal relationship between management (M of VAM-T) and academic success (T of VAM-T). Without this relationship, members would not induce or consequent management—M would have no control over T because it did not induce T (Chapters 5 and 7). Second, children begin to observe who is doing what for whom—children become aware—they are gaining an awareness repertoire. Third, children begin to imitate the teacher's modeling of social communication (as long as it leads to success with the technical behavior being taught). Fourth, the teacher reinforces this imitation; thus, increasing its probability. Fifth, as a consequence of four, teachers end the need to be the "lone arranger" in regards to children's becoming aware, rational, civil citizens; all classroom members can contribute, be it to support the cohesive behavior or begin the correction of coercive behavior (Chapter 16). When the fifth happens, teachers have achieved unity—everyone is working together. A child may not enjoy reading, science, or some other subject, but they can do their duty, so that others receive their right.

Hidden behind all this civil interaction is rational thinking—the making of inferences based on unbiased (impersonal) evidence that can be observed, potentially, by any member. And behind the rational thinking are the languages of management, morals, and their relationship.

Avoiding Group Problems

There are several reasons why members' management can go "wrong" or be in conflict with a plan and its value base: 1) activity members evolve physically and emotionally; 2) their knowledge about the world changes—a cognitive or thinking change; 3) their management behaviors, as the operational methods used during activities evolve; and 4) their surrounding social and physical environments continuously change. As a result, their moral-value system—the rights and duties of individuals and groups— undergoes evolution.

During this evolution, children will always have moments when they "lose awareness and intentionality" and, thus, behave in ways that are classified as coercive. On the positive side, as the "should" and "doing" change, they usually do so in terms of more details within the existing hierarchy of moral values. The valued purposes they undertake also become more detailed. What will hopefully be maintained is an evidence-based view of the world. But with a VAM-T background, even the "lost ones," as those children who do not seem to "get the picture" of their interactive place with others, will usually awaken to the "systems picture" and begin to strive forward. We often call them "late bloomers."

More importantly, there may be stakeholders who feel that morals should not be taught or that rights and duties are not the approach to take in managing a classroom. It only takes one or two strong stakeholders to put a "wrench in the works" of teacher and/or school planning. If such events impinge on planning, one can always say that the rules of the classroom are "learning rules" that make the classroom function effectively for all children. If one suspects or realizes such a stakeholder situation, just don't refer to teaching moral values within the classroom. In this context, we must remember that every human interaction is an instance (example) of a moral that children are witnessing. To make sure what class of moral behavior it is an example of requires direct instruction and social communication to ensure that both teachers and children know who is doing what for whom.

Summary

The moral values of classroom activities are expressed in the "rules of interaction." These rules can be seen in terms of the rights and duties of members. As the degree of members' interactivity increases, the more complex the "rules of interaction" become, as does classifying members' congruence (or fit) with corresponding moral values. The moral values for a classroom are minimalistic; they do not attempt to branch out beyond the classroom. However, by teaching a management repertoire, children are given behavior that can support managing themselves outside the classroom. With these repertoires, children are given the opportunities to build plans that attempt to solve the types of problems that exist in the world.

Implementing such plans gives them the behaviors that will allow them to transfer their VAM-T repertoires into the world.

Very young children do not know or can't express their values. Yet, their biological reactions to events may be "pointers" to moral values. Their built-in flight-fight-freeze responses (via the sympathetic nervous system) or their built-in relaxation responses (via the parasympathetic nervous system) may well be these pointers. Thus, their biology or genetic logic (so to speak) shows us some of the behaviors towards which they "naturally" avoid or approach. However, it does not take long for the social environment to influence even these biologically-based behaviors and associate them with a wide range of behavior, many of which are not civil. Can we give our children enough directional push, so that they can keep going under their own power? What direction is it to be, toward Unity or something else?

As Chapter 8 indicated, teaching values in the classroom involves social (verbal) communication that describes, relates, evaluates, and predicts moral-management relationships during activities by those involved in them. Without this social communication repertoire, teachers may never, with any degree of assurance, instill aware, rational, civil behavior in children in a way that gives them the tools to build the rational, civil world out of what they will inherit from us. Will such repertoires be enough to help them solve the problems that will confront them?

Initially, we "impose" moral values on children. This imposing starts in their homes and continues during schooling. They learn to manage themselves with others or they don't. But if we want to ensure that they can observe and follow moral values, especially in the classroom, three events are required:

1. Classroom-level moral values need to be observable and as unambiguous as possible.
2. They need to be directly taught, so that young children can discriminate the management (social) behaviors that represent examples and non-examples of them.
3. They need to be illustrated in-the-moment through the use of social (verbal) communication methods (Chapter 8).

None of these are easy. The first requires that morals be defined "upfront" before instruction begins. The second requires "defining" moral values through a set of examples and non-examples that show the range and limits of each moral as a right or a duty. The third requires that children can discriminate them during the ongoing stream of classroom behavior. None of this happens overnight.

The difference between teachers and their children is that the former may well have a past history, a frame of mind, that gets in the way of children's aware, rational, civil development. Our children can, with extensive social communication, acquire aware, rational, civil thinking that builds (shapes, evolves) a We/Us moral perspective that is embedded in the *right-duty perspective.*

10

AWARENESS REPERTOIRE

From neuroscience [1] to philosophy [2], "awareness" has a wide range of meanings. These disciplines often talk about attention, consciousness, theory of mind, and brain correlates that support self and external awareness.[3] Communications and information systems give some initial guidance. To them awareness conveys how individuals monitor and perceive the information surrounding their members and their surrounding environment. Awareness in cooperative environments—as the classroom is meant to be—involves four characteristics:

1. knowledge about the state of an environment,
2. environments are changing and, thus, awareness must be maintained,
3. individuals in the environment maintain awareness through interacting with its elements, and
4. awareness takes place during a primary activity; thus, awareness is a secondary goal within the primary activity contingency plan.[4]

Each of these characteristics of awareness within a potentially cooperative group are relevant to the classroom's social and physical setting. However, we need to define what each of the four entails. First, "knowledge" needs to be defined. Chapter 1 outlined four repertoires of knowledge: VAM-T. Awareness represents one of these four repertoires of knowledge; thus, awareness does not standalone. Second, continually updating awareness is required because learning changes all members. Awareness in the classroom is an ongoing process. Chapters 3 through 9 are congruent with this view. Third, that interactions are maintained through interactions is an extension of (2). But there is *being aware* and *becoming aware*. Here, the interactions for becoming aware have been identified as the methodologies of direct instruction and social communication. These two interactive methods evolve and maintain awareness through the long-term teaching of VAM-T. When something is "maintained," it is essentially

---

[1] https://en.wikipedia.org/wiki/Awareness#Neuroscience
[2] Rudy-Hiller, Fernando, "The Epistemic Condition for Moral Responsibility", The Stanford Encyclopedia of Philosophy (Fall 2018 Edition), Edward N. Zalta (ed.), URL = https://plato.stanford.edu/archives/fall2018/entries/moral-responsibility-epistemic/.
[3] https://en.wikipedia.org/wiki/Awareness
[4] https://en.wikipedia.org/wiki/Awareness#Communications_and_information_systems

"linked" across the VAM-T repertoires and, thus, "instilled" in the learner. Chapter 8 stated that ARC repertoires are eventually maintained because they become an integrated set of repertoires that form a "behavioral cusp" that replaces prior behavioral operations. In essence, why fight-or-flight when you know how to build cooperative activities? Fourth, awareness as being secondary (4) may or may not be relevant. What is accepted here is that both awareness and the two behavioral relationships —V-M and M-T of VAM-T—are ongoing. It may be more accurate to say that awareness is embedded in the activity plan if members want "cooperation" to occur and the activity's value purpose is to be achieved. It is assumed that cooperation requires members' management behavior to be congruent with the moral duties of the classroom.

Most certainly, the above points are helpful, but all four characteristics emerge from the study of *being* and not *becoming aware citizens*. Here, we want operations that ensure children *become aware* within the classroom's social system and beyond. To date, all "awareness training" is remedial in focus, be it with children or adults.[5] Our goal is prevention by teaching children to be aware from an early age (Chapter 1). We do it, as stated above, with two methodologies: direct instruction and social communication. Both make reality explicit, which is a fifth characteristic:

Awareness must be congruent with the reality of the activity.

With fake news, disinformation, and unsubstantiated conspiracy theories surrounding all of us, the "reality fitting" element of an awareness repertoire becomes critical. It is brought out through the planning and intervening strategy teaching (Chapters 15 and 16). Here, children learn to employ one of the most fundamental concepts of science: *impersonal objectivity*. This chapter analyzes awareness within a contingency framework and how social communication operations (Chapter 8) can illustrate awareness observations in-the-moment, so that children see examples that verbally represent interactions in terms of contingencies.

Analysis of Awareness

Without *moral-management awareness*, citizens can become despots, tyrants, dictators, or home-grown terrorists. Without *management-technical awareness*, citizens can't guide their technical behaviors, so that the ends are moral as well. Essentially, if management behavior is congruent with morals, then the technical ends would be so within the framework of moral behavior. Why? Because management behavior controls the selection and performance of technical behavior. The technical repertoire is only immoral if the "guiding light" of management planning (Chapter 15) selects value

---

[5] https://en.wikipedia.org/wiki/Large-group_awareness_training

purposes whose means or ends are non-congruent relative to a group's morals. This is where we see the wars between politicians and scientists.

Chapter 1 defined the awareness repertoire as a verbal meta-language that is used to observe, describe, and evaluate human social interactions. Relative to those who study "awareness" across the range of adult human behavior, this is most certainly a "narrow" definition. Being aware is to verbalize (talk about) the contingencies created by the self and others during an activity that either are or are not congruent with the classroom's moral statements.

The definition is concerned, first and foremost, with the degree of "congruence" between the above two relationships: 1) *moral-value statements* and the *management behavior* and 2) *management behavior* and *technical behavior consequences* that emerge in the short or long run. Management can be seen in terms of two attributes: 1) selecting the technical behavior and 2) the means to achieve that technical behavior, the activities valued purpose. Morals are considered "well-formed" verbal representations of management behavior needed for activities. If we observe management behavior during an activity, we ask, "Is it congruent with our moral rules." By seeing our two relationships as steps to an end—morals to management to technical to consequences—teachers can discern what children must be aware of over time. Aware children can see these contingency relationships. Ideally, an adult citizen with awareness observes, compares, and evaluates these relationships across a range of social, political, and economic interactions. However, we want our children to go one step further: to do something about the evaluation with their management repertoire. When they can do so, they become ARC citizens.

The problem, as with most meta-languages, is in the clarity or ambiguity of either of the two things being compared. With an awareness repertoire, the same sorts of problems exist; both moral statements and management behavior are almost always filled with vagueness, ambiguity, or both. Chapter 9 sought to clarify moral values within the classroom in terms of a set of reciprocal rights and duties that members follow to ensure that activities begin, continue, and end so the valued purpose is achieved. Chapters 11 through 17 seek to rectify the vague and ambiguous nature of the management repertoire by laying out seven management strategies and their sub-steps.[6] Management controls who does what for or to whom. Awareness induces selecting management behavior. For young children, both morals and management repertoires require the use of clear examples and non-examples (i.e., example sets), so that children get the "initial gist" of both morals and management. These sets are, of course, expanded through careful extension of existing examples, terminology, and activities.

---

[6] The seven management strategies can be considered replacements for what philosophers, psychologists, and social scientists would most likely call an agent's "agency" repertoire.

Eventually, young children will see a wide range of management behavior to help maintain moral-management and management-technical congruence.

Gaining moral-management-technical awareness has two other problems. The first is observing the fleeting momentary instances of ongoing management behavior and evaluating them in-the-moment against the moral value statements of the classroom. This evaluation may be right or wrong to some degree. To move toward "true enough" evaluations, two primary processes are used: 1) the intervention strategy and 2) social communication methods. They push and pull this evaluation into "alignment with reality." Teachers need to directly instruct students in the relationships, but only with social communication can they be assured that children are observing member relationships in-the-moment.

The second problem is that nearly all instances of management behavior involve direct interactions between other members' management. This is where the cause or the effect of a management problem becomes unclear. Often, we fail to observe the cause, the effect, and how the management of behavior problems between members escalates across a wide range of time periods, or that some unseen background condition applies. As a result, the resolution to a *moral-management conflict* may not be "fair justice." Add to this potential unfairness the biases described in the intervening strategy (Chapter 16), and we witness the type of complaints that justice systems across the globe accrue. Even young children will and can engage in escape, avoidance, or counter control tactics.

VAM-T Component Relationships

Thus far, eight points have been made about the VAM-T repertoires. These include the following:

1. Moral statements (V) guide all M and T behavior.
2. Classroom rights and duties are "representations" of morals (M).
3. When Management behavior (M) is congruent with morals, one is civil.
4. When Management behavior (M) causes cohesive X, M, or T, one is civil.
5. When Management behavior (M) causes coercive X, M, or T, one is not civil.
6. When one can accurately express the relationships between 1-5, one is demonstrating rationality (the logic of contingency relationships).
7. When one can do 6 in-the-moment, one is aware (A).
8. When one can do 7 and do something about the behavior observed, one is an ARC enabled citizen.

One through seven, represent the awareness repertoire, if not its language specifics, in the sense of expressing the awareness. Here, those specifics take the form of a contingency expression. Point eight uses seven as an "entry behavior" to selecting further management behavior. These points emerged from an analysis of the contingency expression first given in Chapter 4. If we simply the graphic from Chapter 6, 7, and 8, we get the following:

$$\text{Push} \rightarrow [X: Mi \rightarrow (M \text{ or } T) \leftarrow Mc] \rightarrow \text{Pull}$$

Chapter 8 "unpacks" this contingency representation into 12 two-direction interaction relations that can be expressed as:

1. X that induces M or not-M.
2. X induces T or not-T.
3. Mi induces X or not-X.
4. Mi induces M or not-M.
5. Mi induces T or not-T.
6. Mc consequents T or not-T.
7. Mc consequents X or not-X.
8. Mc consequents M or not-M.
9. T induces X or not-X (eventually).
10. T consequents X or not-X.
11. T induces M or not-M. (eventually)
12. T consequents M or Not-M.

The two directions represent cohesive or coercive behavioral events. X-behavior, as the emotional-physiological state on entering an activity, always induces—it pushes behavior toward the means and ends of an activity or it does not. Mi also pushes behavior, but it may also pull the emotional state forward or not. Mc is a pulling operation. To be aware of these 12 relationships separates awareness from the other repertoires—it observes and evaluates these other repertoires.

It is T that is most interesting. Without T, future X, Mi, and Mc behavior may only cause not-X, not-Mi, or not-Mc. The inference is that T is needed for the possibility that the other contingency components (X, Mi, and Mc) will be part of the causal cycle that maximizes the probability of the activity plan being successful—we would not go to the store if the shelves were always empty (coercive ends); especially if we had to walk 5 miles to get there (coercive means). When all these relationships—be they by the teacher or the children—are compatible (Chapter 7), then a reciprocity between members is occurring. Each is taking on their duties (help others learn) and receiving their rights (others get to learn) as indicated in Chapter 9. If one multiplies these relationships by the number of children, one begins to get a picture of the complexity of classroom interactions. There is some good news and bad news relative to this complexity.

The good news is in three parts. First, teachers can represent most of these interactions during direct instruction of various strategies. Second, they can teach children to observe these in-the-moment with social communication operations. Third, only a handful of these have to be directly taught. Our inferential organism, our children, will make inferences to the others (Chapter 7), which can be easily evaluated through short social communication queries (Chapter 8) like "Who is Anthony helping learn?" or "How are you helping Anthony learn?". The bad news—more accurately, the hard news—is that we, our children's teachers, have to change enough, so that we can observe, evaluate, and do something about these contingency relationships ourselves—we can't teach that which we don't know.

What happens because of all this social communication is important: Children evolve a *systems picture*, which is an *ideological stance* toward others. It represents the relationships between members that produce the emotional, access, and restructuring consequences for all members (Chapter 7). They learn to see how the contingencies they created contribute to learning some technical behavior (T of VAM-T) and make classroom activities a place to access because of its cohesive contingencies (Chapter 7). They will come to value awareness that observes and evaluates management, as well as management that supports the activity purpose—T of VAM-T. At the same time, they will disvalue those behaviors that don't support learning. Awareness of this value-management-technical-systems picture that children verbalize about involves three component events:

1. They learn to observe, find, and paste together various pieces of contingency-relationship evidence across activities.
2. They learn to evaluate the relationship evidence from the various behaviors during and after an activity.
3. They learn to build plans (predictions), implement them, and evaluate them against the evidence found.

If started in kindergarten or first grade—there is no perfect place to start—the children will come to see themselves as their *first engineering project*. They will see themselves as both the engineer and the engineered product of their behavior. This project is an empirical exploration of how their management behavior and moral values are related and how cohesive management promotes the technical. They will learn, through personal involvement—as scientists and engineers do—the process of controlling the self and others during activities. Social communication makes these relationships overt (observable in-the-moment and after-the-fact) and will help make this systems perspective a reality, a frame of mind, so to speak, for all children.

When teachers or children talk about activities over time, the contingency system becomes a "picture," "representation," "schemata," "cognitive map" that emerges from the array of classroom activities in which children participate. Given that they have participated in it, the evidence should not be classified as "fake news" or "biased."

Being aware is to verbalize about the contingencies created by the self or others during an activity. These are either congruent or not with the classroom's moral rights and duties (Chapter 9). The addition of social communication examples that directly teach (through examples) will help build this picture and children's awareness. The planning and intervening strategies (Chapters 15 and 16) offer several solutions to promote both a systems picture and fair justice within the classroom. For example, during the intervention strategy the main component is to "find a better way" that promotes a match between the management and the morals without the stigma of "blame" on the members involved in the conflict. Essentially, the intervening strategy "slows down" and "reenacts" the conflict. This is critical to learning the key step of an awareness repertoire: to *observe in-the-moment*. Working in-the-moment can create communicative instances that both induce or consequent management behavior interactions that can truncate the need for the intervention strategy.

However, to teach children to become members with *awareness* requires a more detailed analysis. The developmental process requires the separation between the awareness of the self and that of others. In general, children, like adults, can usually observe and classify others' management behavior more accurately than their own. Observing and evaluating their own management is a bit more difficult. It is difficult to become unbiased; Fortunately, children have an advantage. They are more adaptable towards change. Their "picture of themselves" is not cast in stone.

AWARENESS REPERTOIRE CONTENT

The content of an awareness repertoire has eight parts. When children gain awareness, they will be able to:

1. Discriminate (by naming) the morals (rights and duties) required for the classroom activities to begin, continue, and end.
2. Discriminate examples of the management behaviors required for various activities.
3. Discriminate if an example of a management behavior that is or is not congruent with one or more of the classroom's moral values.
4. Discriminate the consequences that result from 3.
5. Discriminate if a management behavior supports other management behavior of the activity.
6. Discriminate if a management behavior supports the technical behavior of the activity.
7. Discriminate in-the-moment if management interactions (3, 5, 6) used by the self or others is cohesive or coercive.
8. Describe in contingency terms, what is named (1-7).

These restate one through seven from the **VAM-T Component Relationships** section above, but indicate what children must be able to do. The first two components provide evidence that children can discriminate (through naming) both the morals or the management behaviors needed for an activity. The third component discriminates if there is a moral-management congruence. The fourth is the management-management congruence. It discriminates if there is congruence between two or more children (interacting members). This is the interaction where most conflicts originate. The fifth discriminates the management-technical relationship congruence. This is the interaction between children and the teacher during the delivery of instruction (T). The fourth and fifth are specific types of moral-management congruence that indicates where the management interaction takes place. The sixth adds the consequent events that result from a congruence or non-congruence from 3, 4, and 5. The seventh adds observing and evaluating congruence or non-congruence in-the-moment. Discriminating the V-M and M-T congruences or non-congruences is the starting point for recognizing the three types of consequences caused by management behavior or technical behavior. The eighth is to verbalize about these components as a contingency, which is usually expressed as an if-then relationship. Based on the awareness evaluation, managers perform a ninth step by:

9. *Engaging in a management strategy that supports activity interactions that are congruent with the group's moral values.*

What management behavior would follow given an awareness evaluation? The answer depends on what the children have learned about the management repertoire. Initially, the teacher performs this management function. Once children begin learning about the intervening strategy, they can participate (Chapter 16).

However, in the beginning, children have no way to talk about management behavior. Therefore, the teacher both verbalizes about what behaviors occurred and performs the needed management behavior to reinforce cohesive or correct coercive behaviors of children. Initially, about all children can say about the management interactions (3, 5, and 6 above) involves words like "helps" and "hurts" members. In other words, their observations result in descriptions and evaluations that are crude at best.

The management behavior that results from the awareness evaluation takes management behavior in one of two directions: 1) it keeps cohesive management behavior going or 2) stops-and-replaces non-congruent management as soon as possible. Social communication (Chapter 8) describes and queries children about these contingency components, and gradually adds more precise contingency language (Chapter 15). The language additions would normally be introduced during direct instruction. Eventually, teachers query children to see the extent to which children can use the language of contingency awareness. A "compact" contingency statement could be the following:

If we cause cohesive contingencies for everyone,
Then we produce effects that bring about our activity,
so that our means and ends fit our moral values.

How we move from a vague language of awareness to a strong language will take a long time. What children get is their first "causal picture" of their home world. They will see patterns and will be able to express them as contingencies. Special emphasis will gradually point to 1) inducing cohesive behavior with a push, 2) the types of consequent events that occur (emotional, access, and restructuring) that pull, 3) at whom 1 and 2 are directed, and 4) observing if the interactions are reciprocated between members at any point during an activity or other activities (Chapter 7).

Building an Awareness Repertoire

We want to give children more than bits and pieces of an awareness repertoire. We want them to have a "system's picture of awareness," so that they can gain control of the futures that we are giving them. With such a picture, children can eventually apply the *language of awareness*, for example, to compare the historical evolution of big ideas like slavery, treatment of indigenous people, colonialization, rights and duties across societies, use of weapons, and the moral consequences of each. These can be followed by children eventually doing research about what to do and why (Chapter 17). Do we want them to "handle" a wider range of real problems before they leave school and select fields of study? Doing so is akin to tuning and practicing with an instrument *before* playing it in public. The heart of awareness is who is doing what to whom and how to talk about this "doing." Management aligns the awareness so activities achieve cohesive means and ends.

Additionally, children learn to see their managership as a *quality* of the group. The teacher is not only teaching individuals, but the group as well. Thus far, unity has been used as a general quality-of-the-group term (Chapter 5), but often we fracture it into qualities like harmony (disharmony), cooperation (competition), and justice (injustice) that are *aspects of unity*. Children will slowly come to see themselves not only as *individual citizens* but as *contributing citizens* as well. This double view balances the "individualist" and "collectivist" views of humanity. Children become the controlling managers by using their management repertoire in-the-moment with others. Some would call the achievement of such qualities as "unifying humanism." Collective managers (as a group) see themselves as part of society and can make decisions that benefit society's members when contingencies require such.[7] Their *social thinking and action* moves beyond their primary group and its activities." They go out into the world attempting to "balance" rights and duties of members. Will this help them avoid cognitive, corporate, and government gridlock and the emotional states such experiences produce for individuals and groups?

The above teaching method of *social communication* and using the intervening strategy are not to be taken as the teaching methodology needed for achieving the above content objectives of awareness—more detail is needed relative to its "unfolding over a time frame." Since, we can't separate values, awareness, and management content, the teaching of all three must be synchronized; thus, all three must be initially taught, expanded, and integrated with great care.

Types of Managers

Children enter the classroom with a range of behaviors. These may or may not support classroom activities. Children are usually not aware of what they are managing. All experienced classroom teachers have witnessed and have had to deal with a wide variety of methods that children use to help or hinder activities.

Our civil and criminal legal systems have defined thousands of coercive manager types and subtypes like murder, vehicular homicide, manslaughter; libel, slander, breach of contract, and property damage. Luckily, young children do not need this range of examples to observe their managing behavior within the classroom. What they do need is knowledge of biased discriminative sub-classes like those based on race, gender, politics, and religion that populate social, legal, and governmental subsystems. These can be part of the example sets used to teach the *awareness repertoire* that exposes the emotional, restructuring, and access consequences produced by such discriminatory (coercive) managing tactics. We can distinguish four classes of managers.

1. **Within group** cohesive managers
2. **Outside of group** cohesive managers
3. **Within group** coercive managers
4. **Outside of group** coercive managers.

These four classes pivot around two variables. The first is the *location of the managers*. They can be from within or from outside a particular classroom activity group. When from the outside, the managers can include

---

[7] This statement is not about a type of government, but about the type of citizens that populate the society and its government. These managers can see beyond themselves when the situation demands it. At the moment, the Covid-19 Pandemic and the Black Lives Matter movement are two examples of how many people are looking beyond their own needs to those that apply to all citizens. The real concern is this: can we teach more children to look beyond themselves without the need for radical social problems and injustices striking them in the face☒

those in another classroom group. They may even be from outside the classroom, as when siblings or parents' model or tell members what to do. Today, we call such outside managers "influencers."

The second variable identifies managers in terms of being either *cohesive* or *coercive*. The cohesive managers *add to* (help, support) the unity and value purpose of the group. The coercive managers *subtract from* (hinder, impede) the unity of the group and the group's value purpose.

In the classroom, there are often several activities or groups working simultaneously. During the beginning, continuing, or ending of these simultaneous activities, a group or an individual can support activity flow for their activity group (1) or support work for another group (2). This support from outside the group may be as simple as modeling the behavior of the activity plan. Also, a group or an individual can stop or slow down activity flow for their activity group (3) or stop or impede another group (4).

Thus, the discriminations that classify a manager are a combination of these two variables, at least initially. Thus, a child can discriminate "cohesive managers," for example, as those who are activity members and who add to an activity. So, after initial teaching, we may ask a child, "What kind of manager is in this example?" The child may say, "A cohesive manager." Then the child is asked, "How do you know the person is a cohesive manager?" Now, the child can provide a single sentence with a two-component answer: "Because the manager was a group member and helped the groups activity continue." The teacher may go on to ask about the specific management behavior that helped the activity continue. Soon, we have children who are aware managers. Such teaching can easily take place during the intervening strategy as Chapter 12 pointed out.

Anyone in the classroom can be a *cohesive* or a *coercive manager*. The problem is that these categories are not black or white, there are degrees of each, as there are in any justice system. The intervening strategy sorts out these degrees (Chapter 16).

A Manager's Control

The third variable that contributes to awareness is the teacher-children and children-children *controlling relationships*. Sociologists talk about the *types of power* such as *legitimate* and *expert power*. These two types of power are usually ascribed within a school to teachers and principals. In social science and politics, power is the capacity of an individual to *influence* the behavior of others.[8] Influence is just a "beautification" replacement for control. How control is achieved (roughly) through either inducing or consequencing behavior (Chapters 6 and 7) that may be further classified as legal or illegal, fair or unfair. Given that each of us are controlling managers to some degree, we can view manager control from a very simplified *control-*

---

[8] https://en.wikipedia.org/wiki/Power_(social_and_political)

theory perspective.[9, 10] In doing so, names like legitimate, expert, political, social, or economic power to influence can be eliminated, up to a point. For the purpose here, five management control relationships suffice. In the following, the standard terms of "positive" and "negative" are replaced with the terms "cohesive" and "coercive."

1. **Full complete control:** Manager(s) can control the starting, continuing, and stopping of an activity. Such managers define both the activity's means and ends.

2. **Full cohesive control:** Managers can induce the starting, continuing, and ending of an activity. But other managers can alter its control with negative (coercive) control.

3. **Full coercive control:** Managers can stop an activity from starting, continuing, or ending. But other managers can attempt to circumvent such coercive control with cohesive control.

4. **Partial cohesive control:** Managers can help or support an activity's starting, continuing, or ending. But other managers may "hinder" its start, continuance, and ending with coercive control.

5. **Partial coercive control:** Managers can restrict or stop an activity's starting, continuing, or ending. But other managers may support it's starting, continuing, and ending with cohesive control.

There is a "tension" between these relationships, especially if we view them from the perspective of "fully-formed" adult behavior, and not from young children's nascent beginnings of awareness about the control being used. The five control relationship classes (types) help children (or teachers) determine who has what kind of control and the tension between them. For example, the bully may seem to have full complete power over the bullied. If such a controlling relationship exists and is observed, how would other group member or members alter their behavior to change this coercive relationship? The answer depends on the moral-values of the group in concert with their management repertoire and how they use it, as a group or as individuals. The intervention strategy (Chapter 16) illustrates how group members can work together to achieve full cohesive control over behavioral interactions that are evaluated as coercive and replace them with those that are cohesive.

Often, those at the top tier of an organization or government are those who have full control over the activities undertaken (at least for a time). But this view moves us well outside the awareness concerns of young children in classrooms. Yet, it is in the classroom where unity is born and strengthened,

---

[9] https://en.wikipedia.org/wiki/Control_theory_(sociology)
[10] https://en.wikipedia.org/wiki/Social_control_theory

and thus provides children the means to achieve some moral-management ends so that classroom activities can be undertaken successfully. Will children's early learning and use of awareness followed by management behavior be enough to start them down a path toward seeking unity in later life activities?

The five types of control relationships require qualifications. Even the dictator's full, complete coercive control (1), may face citizen members that group together and initiate any one of the three main side-effects of coercive management toward dictators: escape, avoidance, or countercontrol (Chapter 4). Dictators with full complete control (1) can be overthrown. Thus, some forms of government try to build in "checks and balances" that monitor their own behavior. They want to avoid "high crimes and misdemeanors" or, at the extreme, "crimes against humanity." This balancing act is what classrooms and schools, as governments, can and need to expose to children. The planning, intervening, and learning strategies supply the "checks and balances." By teaching these three strategies, along with the others, children are given their first system of government and their first system of justice in which they practice checking and balancing themselves during their activities.

But will this learning and practice within classrooms and schools provide children with the management repertoire to coordinate the management-moral relationships that they will need when they govern the planet? Such governance goes beyond the "right to vote" or "speak out." It requires full participation as witnessed through the use of planning, intervening, and learning strategies—as well as time coordination and a time frame required to achieve ends.

For adults, the types of manager control involve politics and its politicking methods. Such methods—usually described as the *agency* of *agents*—are used during planning to make a decision about activities. They require give and take.[11] When the managers making activity decisions are inflexible ideologues, gridlock often stops progress; the planning never "gets off the ground." Means and ends are confused and "minor points" truncate moving forward. We see this in the world today. Governments, for example, often find themselves in what has been described as *political gridlock*.[12] This gridlock results in grave consequences. It fosters the stagnation of social programs, economic instability, infrastructure decay, and environmental pollution. Planning—not just some vague policy—becomes a "great debate" not a social problem-solving tool.

The assumption is that teaching children VAM-T repertoires together truncates the development of inflexible ideologues (Chapter 19). The truncation occurs because children are being confronted by the

---

[11] https://en.wikipedia.org/wiki/Politics
[12] https://en.wikipedia.org/wiki/Gridlock_(politics).

evidence of their management behavior. They learn to observe if their management that is or is not congruent with their moral values. They witness the consequences that result from the behaviors. (How teachers expose individual and group manager tactics in a manner that supports "healthy" learning and group unity is a methodical problem requiring careful exposition.) Again, the most effective method to do so is related to teachers' verbal behavior (social communication methods—Chapter 8) that exposes the VAM-T relationships and links them within and across children and activities. Essentially, they learn to see the contingencies created for each other with their management and technical repertoires.

Politicking, as methods for reaching compromises, can help children become better planners—they can induce and consequent behavior that sends the group toward building plans that benefit all. They come to see what management is at work. These methods of compromise are often called cooperative or non-partisan politics. *They are emergent qualities of the planning group.* The more often they reach compromises, the more they learn how to do so and the more they will do so. Managers may build coalitions of consensus to bring about decisions about means or ends. This is the guts of children's management: the extent to which they support change to the activities on which they are working. And how they carry it out during activity planning, implementation, and evaluation (Chapter 15).

As Chapter 15 indicates, planning establishes its *ends* (ends of production) first, followed by the *means* to achieve those ends (means of production). Relative to values, one or both can be congruent with the moral values of the group. Often, it is not immediately known if the ends or means are congruent with moral values. Only when the emotional, access, and restructuring consequences are exposed through evidence-based evaluation of *manager means* and *moral-value ends* can success be observed. The biggest problem is that the value ends are often well into the future. This is where the risk lies; Where the "limits of our knowledge" (our areas of ignorance) meet the aware, rational, civil "mind." This is where unintended consequences may or may not emerge. These consequences may or may not interfere with means or the ends. A plan, as said, is a prediction—thinking ahead—that may or may not function as expected. Conflicts expose the flaws in a plan (Chapter 16). These conflicts may be in-the-moment or well into the future.

Teaching methods focus on both the *means of production* that reach toward the desired *ends of production*. Both the means and ends are accomplished via the manager's management behavior that either is or is not congruent with the values of the group. They learn that the means are events that can be modified via the evidence data emerging from the activity's implementation and evaluation (Chapter 15). The teaching of the management strategies focuses on children gaining explicit (overt) examples of cohesive manager methods based on the moral-value standards of the classroom. With the interlinked pair, they may just be able to make the world a unity of people, not peoples.

Rules of Managership

Managers, as those who are part of activity contingencies, add to or subtract from an activity's efficiency and effectiveness. Managers add cohesive management to activity contingency plans in order to make them functional. Or they do not. Only by discriminating this managership can teachers, 1) increase their accuracy in describing and querying children about how they are interactively managing each other, and 2) manage themselves with awareness in-the-moment. All this activity behavior induces or consequents children's management behavior, as the means and ends of an activity unfold. These are the facts about our managership. They can be expressed as the *rules of managership*.

1. Aware managers establish conditions that induce (push) *only* cohesive management or technical behavior.
2. Aware managers use cohesive consequences *only when* cohesive behaviors occur.
3. Aware managers use corrective consequences *only when* coercive behaviors occur.

All three rules apply to all classroom members: teachers and children. Rule 1 indicates that the elements of an activity's conditions must be congruent with and *induce cohesive behavior*. Effective teaching begins with conditions conducive to learning not only the technical behavior, but managerial and moral value repertoires as well. Together, these three areas of knowledge help children and what many call the "classroom culture" to flourish.

Rule 2 indicates that cohesive consequences (Chapter 4) only follow behavior that matches the conditions. We do not want to reinforce various forms of coercive or "disruptive behavior." For example, when conditions for a reading or science activity have been established, the matching behavior would be the management and technical behavior needed to begin, continue, and end such activities.

Rule 3 stipulates that punishment, in all its various verbal and physical forms, should only be used with great caution regarding behavior that does *not match* conditions. The above *non-matching* behavior would be behaviors like name calling, sleeping, texting, or whispering to others during a reading or science activity. Management's intervening strategy is a procedure that aims to replace the punishment of *non-matching management behavior* with what is called *corrective teaching*. This stops non-matching behavior in its early stages *and* induces and consequents matching behavior. The process is called finding *better ways* that are identified by the members and immediately practiced by those in conflict, which may include all classroom members.

When the rules of managers are broken continually by teachers or other caregivers, their children eventually fill the culture with those who behave in ways that are counterproductive to their and other's emotional, social, physical, and economic development. They produce conditions and consequences that engender a range of effects that are often unpleasant, if not down-right dangerous to all those around them. But if teaching matches the "rules of managership" while teaching the aware, rational, civil citizen content, children begin taking on both their rights and duties. Eventually, they can verbalize about these and employ the management behaviors that bring about the technical behaviors of interest.

Social Communication and Awareness

Observing managers across the range of activities and classifying them in real time is made possible by one fact already stated:

All management instances are examples or non-examples evaluated in relation to moral value statements.

Chapter 9 presented examples of 1) teachers communicating to children their moral-management behavior relationships and 2) children communicating about their moral-management relationships for themselves and others. We do the same in this chapter, but add "language awareness" components to them. As with Chapter 9, we begin with the teacher

Teachers Representing Awareness

Here is example three from Chapter 9:

(3) Marlowe, helping Sharon gave her a chance to finish her assignment on time. She is happy and you give her access to success. You followed the **helping and happiness rules**. Excellent!

Notice that this is a contingency description of the relationship between Marlowe and Sharon. The focus is on two rules. The first thing that can be done is to alter this statement gradually.

(3a) Marlowe, you helped again. This time you gave Jason a change to finish his work. I am glad you are aware of how others need help. **Your awareness helps keep our activities moving forward.**

This example is not meant to directly teach children an awareness language. It is just used to point out that what was done required awareness and that Marlowe's awareness helps keep activities moving forward. After such examples, we can turn to queries.

(3b) Marlowe, what were you aware of today during reading? [CR: That Marissa needed help on her assignment.] **I thank you for being aware, for keeping a sharp eye on what needs to be done for others.** It helps us finish our activities.

The focus on awareness is done through the teacher consequenting Marlowe's presumed awareness: it helped another child and the class activity as well. If Marlow could not answer the query. The teacher could do the following to prompt it:

(3c) Marlowe, what were you aware of today during reading? [CR: I did my work?] Yes, you sure did. **But you should also be aware that helping Marissa was another way to help the group move forward.**

This example can be changed to be a "before-the-behavior" prompt, where the behavior is seen by the teacher and prompts the child to be aware.

(3d) Marlowe, what could you be aware of at this time? [CR: (looks around), I could help Sharon. She is in the get help area.] **Yes, you are aware and looking around you. Your awareness is improving.**

In this example, the teacher realizes that Marlowe could help Sharon. Next, the teacher prompts Marlowe to help and tests to see if the term "aware" is in the working vocabulary of Marlowe. Between 3a, b, c, and d, we gradually build up awareness in-the-moment. At times, the teacher's consequent behavior defines or clarifies the terms and relationships needed. At times, the teacher consequents behavior that is accurate enough for now. At times, the teacher observes and needs to prompt the children to observe, and then consequents that observation. All of these can take place but not necessarily in the order presented. What needs to be done depends on the direct management instruction delivered (Chapters 11-18).

Children Representing Awareness

As in Chapter 9, the child (speaker) is describing his or her M or T behavior (the B following it), with the related moral value (Z), that may induce (Mi) or deliver consequences (Mc) for themselves or others. Where it applies, the speaker's behavior is connected with its function relative to others, which can be an inducing event (B1/S1) or a consequent event (B2/C1). The clearer, more consistent, and patterned the activities, the more quickly the contingencies will be seen and become expressible by children. The following begins with a child describing an activity contingency. It begins with rules of the classroom (moral value statements, Z). The difficulty is that adding awareness requires a query to get it going. Here are some examples that extend those from Chapter 9.

(1) Today I followed the working-with-others rule (Z1) during reading group (S1), by organizing (B1/S2) and taking my turn (B2/S3). My management (B1/B2) helped the group continue (C1) and complete the activity on time (C2), with only one reading error (C3). We all applauded working together (C4/Z1).

We see that this child has expressed a contingency that occurred during reading. But it is not in the language of awareness that brings out the contingency pattern.

(1a) [Teacher: What were you aware of today during reading?] I pushed the group toward following the activity procedure and pulled them by pointing out the consequences that our working together made possible. [Teacher: You have clear awareness of your activity contingencies.]

(1b) [Teacher: What do you need to be aware of during reading?] I must push the group toward performing the activity procedure and pull them though it by pointing out the consequences as they occur. [Teacher: you are aware of the relationships between you and the other members. Let's see what happens.]

If this is done with the group members present, they know what to expect. More importantly, they get a description of the reading contingency that they can imitate. The teachers "shores all this up" with consequences that point to the description as being in the class of awareness.

As children gradually become aware of the contingencies they are establishing, performing, or have performed—inducing events, behaviors, and consequent events—teachers often need to move the children though their description or prediction step-by-step, as in the following.

(1c) [Teacher: Zeno, what is the first thing to be aware of as you supervise reading?] I have to make sure everyone knows the activity procedure. [Teacher: Then what must you be aware of?] I will need to observe that they follow the procedure. [Teacher: what is next?] I will tell them about the consequences they are creating. [Teacher: You know the reading activity contingency. You see how you must behave to get the activity completed.]

Now, let's say that 1c was done just as the activity started and the other group members heard this prediction. How, would the teacher seek out the evidence for this prediction? The answer is in querying the rest of the activity members in a manner similar to the following at the end of the activity.

(1d) [Teacher: Was Zeno's prediction about making you aware of the reading procedure, correct? (Call on a member). He made the procedure clear. [Teacher: did you know what behaviors to perform? (Call on a different member).] Yes, he was helpful by calling on us by name to read. [Teacher: did you observe the consequences he pointed out? (Call on a different member).] He asked us how we felt and that we read with only one error. [Teacher: I see you agree with Zeno's prediction. Moreover, you all observed the evidence which tells you so. You are all becoming aware of the contingencies you create for yourselves. What consequences did you create for Zeno? (Call on a different member.)] He seems emotionally positive, and now his supervising is getting quicker and more accurate.

In example 1c, the teacher induced (pushed) the supervisor to make a prediction about the reading contingency. Essentially, it pushed by prompting for the activity contingency plan. In example 1d the teacher confirms that prediction by querying the other members about each component of the contingency arrangement. This uses members to consequent themselves for their awareness and has them point out the consequences themselves. The group is being used to build their own awareness. Most likely, various members will be aware of parts but by the time such an interaction is complete, the group has the same awareness that any individual can add.

Of course, reaching such "contingency clarity" of 1c and 1d take extensive time to achieve. But they don't take clumps of time. The above statements, even 1d, is only a fraction of a minute long. It only lengthens if teachers jump to far ahead of what strategies have been taught and the terminology used. The language of contingency awareness takes time.

When seeing anything that looks like inappropriate manager behavior—as that which disrupts an activity—members are witnessing an example of what has been named "coercive management." A classroom rule (duty) has been broken. The intervention strategy deals directly with coercive or supportive-coercive management behavior. However, by teaching the management strategy repertoire to children with *well-formed example sets* that have a range of cohesive examples and a few that show their limits (coercive examples), one moves toward preventing coercive manager management behavior.[13] Add strong cohesive consequences that begin with learning T, then you link all the moral-management-technical relationships together.

What is observed are various steps of the various management strategies, be they cohesive and coercive. If spotted early enough, naming the step or asking for a step provides a micro-level teaching tactic (as verbal social communication) that can truncate potential coercive management and reward cohesive management that children have come to master.

---

[13] This assumes that during the teaching of any management strategy, the focus is on examples of cohesive management that facilitate activities and with only a few non-examples that expose the limits of what cohesive management entails.

(Prompt) Zander, what is your next step in organizing? [Zander: I have to arrange myself for the activity to begin.] You have been organizing, keep it up.

If the rest of the group hears this, they also have been prompted. However, a prompt can be used because someone appears to be going "off base" relative to organizing or when you just want to consequent the groups organizing.

Coercive Behavior

When coercive manager behavior is spotted after the fact (or it is just underway), the intervention strategy is implemented. See Graphic 10.1 for some simple verbal examples that indicate that the strategies have not been taught, that they are often expected of children, and not performing them induces conflicts.

When strategy steps are known by all, either the teacher or children can observe whether the step, as an instance of management behavior, can be classified as cohesive or coercive relative to the moral values of the classroom. Thus, anyone in the classroom can nip coercive manager behavior in the bud or reward cohesive management with methods like those in outlined in Chapters 6, 7, and 8.

One can be a planner, organizer, learner, supervisor, helper, sharer, or intervener and be either a cohesive or coercive manager. What most people do is focus on the negative social (coercive management) behavior. This does not directly teach cohesive manager behavior. Teaching the management strategies in combination with moral values directly promotes cohesive management because everyone will eventually discriminate cohesive and coercive instances of manager behavior across all management strategies and activities. Making discriminations at this level of detail prepares children to induce (push) or consequent (pull) manager's in-the-moment.

Perspectives on Manager Development

Initially, children's manager methods are simultaneously controlled by their genetic endowment and social environment. For the rest of their lives, this back-and-forth, interactive, relationship continues. The extent to which individuals gain and remain harmonious with their social environments depends to a great extent on the way this environment teaches them about their managership and how to use it in the various social spheres of family, classroom, friends, and workplace. At the same time the "social environment" must see itself as a "self" that allows behavior to evolve to meet new and demanding situations. The social environment, essentially, has to have a "self" whose perspective includes the two criteria for surviving and adapting to reality:

1. Nothing surges up out of nothing without having antecedents that existed before.
2. Everything is in a perpetual state of transformation, motion, and change.

Such a social environment self is akin to all individuals having a "notch" that links them together so the jigsaw puzzle pieces fit together. It almost like having a common world language with which to communicate.

To achieve "unity" within any context requires a 1) social structure, 2) a moral values repertoire, and 3) an interactive-interdependent management repertoire. Observing and evaluating the relationship between 2 and 3, requires an aware repertoire. This does not mean that the social structure is a rigid bureaucracy. The system can and must have rules, but that does not mean they are *situation* or *activity inflexible*. Without clearly specifying all these components across activities, children explore and learn about their social worlds through happenstance. For most, the contingencies and social structures in which they live are bound to remain invisible. They may see no further than through Me/My optics. Only with direct instruction will they observe through We/Us optics.

Without knowledge of all VAM repertoires, parents and teachers can't with any assurance evolve children who become aware, rational, civil citizens. The physical and social worlds are changing rapidly and simultaneously. Aware, rational, civil behavior may be paramount to children's survival. Yet, the awareness repertoire—as a meta-language—is just one part of a system of behavior that makes up the ARC citizen. Awareness without moral values, management, and technical repertoires will result in nothing more than anarchy—just another social boat without a moral rudder.

11

Organizing Strategy

Organizing is the strategy of efficiency. It gets an activity's resources in the right place at the right time to keep it going. The 2020 pandemic illustrated that many large organizations could not distribute vaccine resources without a great deal of chaos and dissention. Although organizing was only one of the management problems, it most certainly contributed to the difficulties encountered.

The performance of every human activity begins, continues and ends with organizing—they all need resources throughout their duration. In the classroom, once an activity's starting time arrives, organizing is its starting point. It continues, often as a background operation, throughout the activity. Organizing is also the first strategy in teaching children to manage themselves—they need to be in the right place at the right time with the needed resources—themselves, books, pencils, and paper in hand. What could be a better first step in the process of evolving children into rational and civil citizens? It induces the starting behavior of the valued purpose of the activity. Initially, children are managees following a manager, usually their teacher. Gradually, they become able to do it without direction. Next, they learn to contribute to the design of organizing during activity planning (Chapter 15).

At least three profound consequences occur when children can organize themselves. First, organizing reduces the chance of conflict in transitioning from activity to activity. Second, teachers expend less time and energy supervising their organizing behavior and managing the conflicts that often accompany it. Third, the added time allows for more teaching and learning. Teaching can focus on what needs to be learned by both individuals and small groups, which is the first moral value of the profession. This chapter outlines and examines the content of organizing in a way that allows it to be taught to very young children.

Organizing is a Process

Organizing is a process. The child, the adult, and the corporate group use the same process of organizing. It is the complexity of human activities in which organizing takes place that hides its process steps, their complexity, and their relationship. All organizing follows the five steps illustrated in Graphic 11.1. These five steps are used to initially teach organizing. These steps require that six discriminations need to be directly taught. They include: *Organizing, resources, locate, transfer, arrange,* and *return.* For each of these, children learn simple operations to carry them out. Of these, *resource* is the most complex. However, the five steps are the *pattern of organizing.* Step 1 is a pure discrimination (Chapter 2); thus, it is presented as a question, "Is organizing needed?" This discrimination sets organizing in motion. Its answer is based on whether or not a new activity is beginning. A parent may holler, "Time for dinner." A teacher may say, "Let's start our reading activity." or "Please, organize for reading." These induce organizing (Chapter 6) but only if the expected consequences follow—the child gets to eat or gets to read; if not, the children cease to organize with efficiency. They complain.

Like any human strategy, the details of how the steps are carried out depends on the type and complexity of the activity. For example, organizing for a trip to the moon or manufacturing electronic equipment require much more time, effort, and coordination to organize resources than children organizing for lunch or group reading activities. Yet, the process steps are the same, even if the steps are carried out in varying orders or require different resources.

Because young children usually can't read when they enter the social world of the classroom, we teach organizing through a set of examples that show them the range of what is appropriate to each step of the strategy. The initial examples come from activities they already know, be it getting up in the morning, eating a meal, or dressing themselves. But even on the first day of school, these examples are expanded by walking children through the range of classroom activities. Each activity requires slightly different bits of organizing.

When children come to follow the pattern and know how to perform the steps for each activity, one of two things can happen. The first is to teach another strategy. The second is to expand on the discriminations and operations related to more complex organizing. These are not necessarily mutually exclusive events. Often, what direction is perused depends on the children's reading behavior and the extent to which the terminology and use of the strategy is included in what is read.

When the steps are finally known, in the sense that children can repeat them verbally and carryout the steps across activities, then activities move along at a much quicker pace. All the children need to do now is to verbally "walk through" the organizing for an activity. Soon, the verbal walk becomes a thinking walk and, eventually, an automatic walk, at least for known activities. To some, this organizing *pattern of thought* is called a *cognitive*

❖ **ORGANIZING** ❖
1. Is Organizing Needed?
2. Locate Resources
3. Transfer Resources
4. Arrange Resources
5. Return Resources

GRAPHIC 11.1: Organizing's steps.

map. However, it is really just verbal behavior reduced eventually to an almost automatic brain process that controls behavior—children sense the world and behave. It is *becoming aware* that gets organizing and the rest of the management strategies operational. Organizing is the starting point for teaching the management strategies. It begins the process of moving children towards aware, rational, civil behavior that is under their control.

If children learn to organize at a young age, they will continue to do so as their activities gain in complexity. They will do so for two reasons. First, they now have a pattern from which to work, a blueprint so to speak. It induces (sets-the-occasion-for) organizing and, thus, the start of any activity. Second, they will be able to make strong inferences about what organizing is needed because they know the steps to perform and how to perform them. However, their organizing needs to lead to successful activity learning. Without learning the technical behavior (T), organizing or any other management strategy will not become an integrated, unified repertoire of useful procedures. If T is learned, three primary consequent events occur for children: a positive emotional state will emerge, use of the strategy will be connected to this state, to time will be saved, and they will have more time for other desired activities. Thus, all three types of consequences result: emotional, restructuring, and access (Chapter 5). These consequences are simultaneously connected to any management behavior performed.

However, coercive management (as interactions with others) can undermine any of its advantages. One or more of the organizers may, for example, be coercive towards others involved. Children may fight for a seat, run into others, take their sweet time to locate their place in a group, or forget an activity resource. These not only disrupt the activity but indicate that the valued purpose (T) and organizing strategy links have not been established. Usually, children need to verbalize about the steps of organizing until any member can walk the class or a group though the steps as they occur in an activity.

Organizing is a component of a system of management. You can't take it, as a part, out of the whole and expect the system of management to function. But it can be inserted into an existing management plan that involves following the rules (duties) of the classroom (Chapter 9). The outline of the strategy steps in Graphic 11.1 is "true enough" for successful performance, and is a good start to the children's reflection on their first management strategy that sets them on the road to acquiring aware, rational, and civil behavior.

ORGANIZING'S DISCRIMINATIONS & OPERATIONS

When one adds the sub-steps that involve discrimination and operational elements, a detailed "full" strategy emerges. This strategy requires reading behavior, which means that the faster reading is acquired,

❖ ORGANIZING ❖

1. IS ORGANIZING NEEDED?
 a. What resources are needed?
 b. How many or much of each?
 c. What quality of each?

2. LOCATE RESOURCES
 a. How can they be located?
 b. Where are they located?

3. TRANSFER RESOURCES
 a. Where are they needed?
 b. How can they be transferred?
 c. When are they needed?

4. ARRANGE RESOURCES
 a. When are they to be arranged?
 b. How can they be arranged?

5. RETURN RESOURCES
 a. What needs to be returned?
 b. When can they be returned?
 c. How can they be returned?

GRAPHIC 11.2: Organizing's steps and discrimination queries.

the faster children can gain management expertise. Each step of the strategy is "facilitated" by these sub-step *discrimination queries.* They help ensure step success. Graphic 11.2 identifies the sub-step questions children answer for each step. Their answers are tested against the evidence, which essentially entails following the steps without the occurrence of conflicts (Chapter 16). Initial teaching can be done in a "management activity," one devoted to teaching the strategies directly through a set of real-world and classroom-based example sets.

In complex activities, adults move through the steps in a back-and-forth manner across steps, doing a bit of locating, and then a bit of arranging, and so on. For children, organizing is usual done in a lock step—1, 2, 3, 4, 5—fashion.

1. Is Organizing Needed?

The first step in an ongoing stream of behavior is to discriminate if organizing is needed (step 1). The answer pivots on the fact that a new activity is starting. All human activities—be it eating breakfast, going to the lunchroom, reading a book, building an electric motor, discovering how to edit genes, or building a theory—require organizing. Next, children answer the question: What resources are needed (1a). These include people, time, materials, tools, and place. It is important to know how much or how many of each is needed (1b). These are discriminations based on an inductive inference, which is usually past evidence for the same or a similar activity. If the identification of the type and the number of resources is done correctly, the first step toward avoiding delays and conserving resources, as the activity unfolds, is achieved.

Graphic 11.3, Activity Resources, summarizes the basic resource requirements for an activity. Each resource question focuses the organizer on a feature of a particular type of resource. Often when engineers think about the resources, they focus on a sixth resource type, *energy*. However, for young children, they (the people resource) and the tools usually supply the energy requirements. If a bit of science or engineering is being taught, this resources guide can be expanded to include energy as a sixth category. But in general children do not need to classify activity resources until the full strategy is introduced. They just need to name the things that are required for the activity like pencils, paper, books, when to start, and where to go. Reading behavior changes things. The full strategy is an "enhanced" cognitive map. Children can use it to set-the-occasion for organizing and as a consequent event that guides their thinking about resources or "affirms" their prediction about resource needs.

The manager of a complex corporate project sets out the resources in a "resource list" and then attempts to "allocate" and "level" the resources required for the various project activities. The goal is to maximize the use of resources across the time and space devoted to the achievement of the corporate valued purpose. Such complexity is not a part of children's lives. Listening to the teacher, reading in a group, eating lunch, or playing at recess are relatively simple by comparison.

❖ RESOURCES ❖

1. PEOPLE
   a. How many are needed?
   b. What behaviors are needed?
   c. When are they needed?

2. MATERIALS
   a. What types are needed?
   b. How much or how many are needed?
   c. What quality is required?

3. TOOLS
   a. What types are needed?
   b. How many of each are required?
   c. What quality is required?

4. PLACE
   a. How much space?
   b. How much comfort?
   c. How can resources be arranged?

5. TIME
   a. How much time is needed per day?
   b. When do people start and stop?
   c. When are other resources arranged?
   d. When are all resources returned?

SYSTEMS THINKING: If a resource changes, others may change also.

SUCCESS THINKING: If a resource is scarce or critical to success, locate a backup.

GRAPHIC 11.3: Activity resource classes.

Often, teachers do many of the organizing steps for their young managers. This is where they verbalize the operations and discrimination queries of the strategy. Only when the full strategy is taught (Graphic 11.2) are these queries directly taught. However, if neither the teacher or the children have the language of organizing, the activity is far more difficult to begin, continue, and end. When children begin to look confused or ask themselves questions like "What is next?" or "What do I do?", they are indicating that something is missing. When all classroom members know and can follow the steps and think through each step's queries, the probability of success increases. Eventually, everyone will see that organizing is applicable to all their activities, but only if there is success first and foremost with T and then with the M of the activity.

The *systems thinking* and *success thinking* notes, at the bottom of Graphic 11.3, are heuristics. They are maxims. The first reminds organizers when any resource is changed, other resource requirements may need to be altered. The resources for an activity need to be reexamined to ensure that the activity can be completed. The *success thinking* note focuses on the backups or redundancies needed to ensure that the activity can be completed even if a resource fails. The extra pencil, pad of paper, the flashlight, and the spare tire are redundancies for writing and taking a trip. It is at the point where systems and success thinking take place that one begins to see why the strategy of organizing has remained hidden for so long and, thus, has gone untaught or at least not directly taught to children, so that they have a general pattern to follow and a common language with which to talk to each other and their teacher about an organizing question or problem.

2. Locate Resources

Organizing continues with locating the resources (2). This is a step based on two discriminations. The first is, "How can they be located (2a)." The second is, "Where are they located (2b)." The first deals with resources that are not on hand or possibly even known. Two kinds of discriminations give them help: knowing the classes (i.e., categories) into which the needed resources fall and the resources that can help them identify the specifics of such resources. For our young citizens, this is not usually involved in their locating efforts. It is the second question (2b), "Where are they located?" that poses the biggest problem. Parents are children's first example of a resource locator. The child can't find a shoe or a toy. So, they ask a parent or caregiver the "where" question. As they gain background knowledge about the location of resources, the speed and accuracy of locating improves.

Often, children begin this locating by randomly looking. Then, they ask parents or teachers. Later, with various tools and communication devices, they can locate a great deal with precision (2a). Today, many use the Internet with its array of search engines to help classify and narrow the range of possible locations (2b), and finally to pinpoint a location. Once they find what they need, well-organized children (and adults) make a contact list. They learn not to do this element of organizing over and over again if they don't have to. They have what is termed a "supplier." Such organizing is a few years ahead for young children. But along the way, they will learn to hierarchically classify things by way of the technical behaviors they learn. Of course, teaching such classifying can begin when the resource list (Graphic 11.3) is introduced.

All this searching leaves out two important concerns for advanced organizers: the "best" cost and the "right" type (Graphic 11.3). Often children don't know that things "cost" or what particular type of tool, material, or part to use. So, they query other persons to help them make a selection. In doing so, they are using a crude learning strategy. Thus, even during the fairly early stages of organizing, the management strategies intermingle with each other and with other technical repertories. However, at the start, adults are children's guides. They already have knowledge of the best and the useful, at least for the activities in which children are engaged. Moreover, if one doesn't know, all they need to do is "walk through" the learning strategy with them to find out what types are needed. Thus, this is a learning opportunity for all managers-in-training.

Project managers call all this locating "resource identification" and "resource assignment." Children, on the other hand, just want to locate a special tool, a pen, a toy, or a shoe that is misplaced (was not returned to its location—step 5). If the going-to-an-adult behavior happens every few minutes, the value of teaching organizing may strike home. But to directly teach organizing with ease, the language must be clear. First, in terms of its steps and, eventually, about its sub-step discriminations and operations. Only then can teachers model examples, prompt their use, and correct any organizing miss steps. This will allow teachers to stop engaging in any form of "disciplinary procedure" to resolve conflicts based on a lack of organizing behavior.

3. Transfer Resources

Transferring the located resources (3) is an operation based on three discriminations. The more complex the activities, the more important these discriminations become. First, children have to identify where the resources are needed (3a). The activity may take place in one or more locations, with the latter requiring a distribution of resources. The resources of an activity, especially a complex one like performing a science experiment, may require a specific, safe method for transferring resources. Thus, figuring out how to transfer them (3b), a discrimination, is the next discrimination query. Finally, these resources must be in the right location (3a) at the right time (3c). To have them at an earlier time may complicate the activity; having them too late will slow it down. There is no "right order" in which to ask or answer these three transfer-resource discriminations. But for children in the classroom, the operation of transferring resources usually amounts to taking them in hand and moving the resources and themselves to where they are needed (3a).

In the adult world, we often see such transfer behavior in plans for major social activities—as policies and procedures—undertaken by States that end up as what is called "gridlock," "chaos," or even "social discrimination" as when some group members are purposely or accidently excluded or put at the end of the resource-receiving line.

A company's "project manager" will talk in terms of "resource scheduling" and "resource distribution." However, even here, the steps of transferring require considering the same three questions. Again, activity complexity hides the three decision components of this step. Corporations use tools like project management software to guide them in making the needed decisions while organizing.

4. Arrange Resources

Arranging transferred resources (step 4) is an operation that has two important discriminations. The first identifies when they must be arranged within the location (4a). For children drawing a picture with others or undertaking a reading activity, the first question is answered by, "As soon as they are transferred because they are needed there from the start." In building and manufacturing activities, the arrangement within the activity may be ongoing; particular types of resources are arranged in the work area across time.

The second query element asks how they can be arranged in the activity location (4b). The resources are transferred on time but the details of their arranging are not complete. They are unarranged. Children need to figure out how to arrange their resources for use. Often children pay no real attention to this step. Teachers show them how. But the goal is to have children predict the answer. Doing so illustrates that they are thinking ahead (Chapter 15); they are making an inference. The consequent events that come from "being arranged for use," are usually emotional stability across the group and access to the activity T event.

In building and manufacturing, answering the how of arrangement often requires elaborate planning for the reason of ensuring smooth, uninterrupted work flow—even if the resources sit in a corner until the time they need to be arranged. Project managers talk in terms of "organizational structure." Once the manufacturing or "physical plant" organizational arrangement is set, the specifics of arranging resources for use is left to the person performing this management activity. There are terms that apply: "first-in-first-out" and "just-in-time" organizing. The child's activities just don't require such detailed arrangement processes. However, in the later elementary years, they often engage in activities that involve both in class and outside-class elements, or working with others in a different time zone for a science project. Such activities require different resource arrangements and careful planning.

5. RETURN RESOURCES

The returning of resources (5) is usually a simple operation, one based on three discriminations. However, it is one of the most troublesome parts for every organizer, especially young children. This final step of organizing involves returning reusable or unused resources to their "base" location," so that the next time they are needed they can be quickly located. The child puts away the crayons, paper, and drawings. The jacket is hung up and the dirty clothes deposited in the hamper. The science equipment is cleaned and stored and in one place and the materials in another. For children, this element of organizing is often called "picking up after themselves." The consequent events involve the emotional "peace of mind" knowing where things are located, saving time "finding things" and the environment is ready for another activity. These consequences are emotional and access related.

Three discriminations need to be made in returning resources. The first identifies what needs to be returned (5a). The second identifies when various resources need to be returned (5b). Resources are not always returned when the activity is complete. Just watch the organized and competent technician or repair person. Tools and parts are put away as the activity moves forward. Thus, there is less returning at the end of the activity and the activity moves forward at a smooth pace.

The third question, how can they be returned (5c), again requires a mode of transportation. This may require transferring resources back to some other, perhaps, distant location like the stock or equipment rooms. In the office environment, this has more to do with arranging a desk or closet, so that resources are ready for their next use. Children have a simpler world; they just need a place for pencils, crayons, paper, and other resources. The biggest concern—especially for parents and teachers—is that these resources get back into their right place. Forget about alphabetical arrangements or things set out in neat rows. If children would only return them to roughly the appropriate location! Doing so on a fairly regular basis is a first step toward "awareness" of self-in-the-world.

With the returning of resources, the organizing for an activity is complete. If children get stuck answering the organizing process questions during an activity, their organizing strategy behavior is incomplete. If children encounter a "glitch" in their organizing, they may still turn to the teacher for an answer. If they do so and can specify the glitch in terms of the steps or sub-steps of organizing, then everyone should shout for joy. The teaching of organizing has started to take hold; they have started to gain a rational method. It's the first bit of management language that helps them avoid inappropriate behavior, which is moral behavior by another name. As their organizing and knowledge base improve, and they continue to practice and eventually plan their organizing, they will come to answer their own questions. When they do so, they are using the planning strategy to flush-out any problems that they may have with the organizing of an activity. At this point, teachers lead by modeling and prompting planning.

This last situation applies to all the management strategies. Asking relevant questions with the language of management, illustrates that rational behavior is growing. Like walking and talking, once learned, the behavior of the child can't return to its previous methods. These major behavioral steps or changes are sometimes called "cusps" or "developmental milestones." The language cusp is the one focused on here because it is the foundation of awareness, rationality and civility. Reading and writing are the sub-repertoires of language that add permanence to it, allowing our thinking to be reexamined and evaluated in the light of newer evidence—all of which involves language use. We return to this area of thinking in the planning strategy (Chapter 15).

Discriminations & Operations

Organizing, like all the management strategies is a combination of discriminations and operations. With organizing, all but step 1 are operations that rely on two or more discriminations. All of these are keyed to what, when, and where questions. The operations for steps 2, 3, 4, and 5 are operations that most "normally endowed" 5-year-old children can perform within classroom activities. That they will perform them is another question; one that depends on how we teach it.

When added up, all the discriminations of the full strategy come to 14. It is interesting to note that even step 1, a discrimination, has sub-discriminations. Here they deal with the "heart" of step 1, the basis for what is required for all activities: resources. This eventually means teaching the content of Graphic 11.3. In doing so, there is less chance of not including necessary activity resources. The teaching of 'What is an activity?' and 'What is a resource?' are easily taught.[1]

1. Activities are just things that one needs or wants to do. Is eating breakfast an activity? [Reply: Yes.] How do I know? [Reply: It is something we need or want to do?] Your turn.
2. Resources are needed for every activity. Is food needed for a breakfast activity? [Reply: Yes.] How do I know? [Reply: food is what you eat.] Your turn.

---

[1] These examples do not imply that what is presented is all there is to do. The "example set" technology has been carefully laid out by Siegfried Engelmann and Douglas Carnine in *Theory of instruction: Principles and practices*, New York, NY: Irvington Publishers, 1982. Follow link for a PDF.

We could elaborate on each of these. First by modeling a few examples and non-examples before we ask them to reply make the discriminations. Such teaching is just using sets of examples to initially mark the range and limits of a discrimination. Second, we can ask them to name some activities they participate in. After resources are taught, we can ask them to name some of the resources for the activities that they have named previously. Eventually, it can become a game that can be much like a spelling bee. By the age of five or six years, children have many activity and resource names from with to draw. Each day of each activity, they should be able to name the activity and its resources.

You can directly instruct children in such discriminations or teach them by some "discovery" teaching method. However, the children must be able to make inferences about their future or upcoming activities. The two most important are identifying 1) the activity itself and 2) what resources are required for it. Time is saved by directly teaching the discrimination and through a history of activities to gradually get the children to make the activity and resource predictions that represent inductive inferences. For children this induction is almost always by enumeration—It was like this in the past, so it will be like this next time.

The Consequences of Organizing

When children, after learning to organize and the development of reading-writing-speaking repertoires, something new can happen. If they can—through their writing, speaking, and interactive behavior—demonstrate that they know the steps and sub-steps of organizing, some consequent event should happen. As the appendices illustrate, there are several evaluative elements to determine the criterion for their organizing prowess (evidence) like filling out the advanced strategy forms and flowcharts besides their consistent demonstration of organizing. The consequence of doing so can be their first "management" or "citizenship" badge. It may be accompanied by a certificate of accomplishment. Some of these "certificates" are exampled in the appendices at the end of the book. With the development of their reading-writing-speaking behavior, learning the strategies becomes easier, as does our interlinking of moral value, awareness, and management behaviors. This progress for children is repeated for all strategies, including using the management strategies as a "system of strategies" (Chapter 18). With their knowledge and use of the organizing strategy, they have successfully begun their journey towards becoming aware, rational, civil citizens

A Brief Side Note on Teaching

Although this text is not about teaching, it will help to get the "gist" of how organizing and the other strategies are taught. There is a direct instruction method that is very similar across the teaching of all management strategies. It can be divided into approximately nine steps.

1. The strategy is initially taught as a T of a "management activity." They can participate in the modeling with peers that sets the stage for imitation of the strategy wording and its performance.

2. At the start of classroom activities, examples of the steps are pointed out and named as children perform them. This can be done throughout the activity until a strategy's steps are performed. (Social Communication method.)

3. As (2) is progressing, start to query children about what steps they are performing or need to perform as activities unfold. These queries confirm that they have remembered the language and operations involved. (It also confirms that they are aware of their management behavior in real time.)

4. During steps 2 and 3 above, point out the consequent events that result from strategy use.

5. Children are prompted when needed to keep on track. This helps avoid conflicts. Most of the of the prompts are queries about what strategy step to perform next.

6. Turn the analysis of the strategy over to children. They name the steps, identify the consequences that resulted for themselves and others—emotional, access, and restructuring. This can be done before, during, or after any activity. (It builds their awareness of who is doing what for whom.)

7. Once children can read, a large posting of the strategy can be placed on the wall or a small one pasted to their desk or table tops. This prompts learning, remembering, and strategy teaching.

8. The above steps can be repeated when the "full" strategy is introduced (Graphic 11. 2). This is where postings of the strategies are very helpful. (They would be called "knowledge systems," "cognitive maps," or "strategy posting" by various researchers.)

9. They redesign a strategy needed for activities or design new activities that use one or more strategies. (This is an introduction to the planning strategy.)

There are other elements that enter into management teaching. But the pattern above will be used for nearly all strategy teaching. There are essentially two elements. First, the operations are learned. Second, the discrimination queries are added. However, what is key is the language facility and awareness that comes with learning each strategy. Once the basic steps of the seven strategies are learned and reading is developing, the strategy system posting (Chapter 1, Graphic 1.2; Chapter 18) can be displayed and used as an overall guide to helping children reflect on what strategy to use and why they should use it.

12

Helping Strategy

If we tried to capture the original American Spirit in a dozen words, helping would be among them. America, for example, evolved from the Atlantic to the Pacific with neighbors and community members who gave a "helping hand." Helping citizens enable people to complete their activities, leads to informal teaching and learning, and helps build unifying relationships. These are powerful social consequences.

Yet, providing a helping hand to those around us seems to be disappearing. It may be because of crime and violence. It may be because we hire experts to build and repair everything we use. It may be because we don't understand how helping fits into the complexities of modern life. It may be because citizens have gone down an evolutionary path that focuses on Me/My group thinking. No matter what the reasons, our heritage and language indicate the importance of helping. Yet, it has remained something that we are just supposed to do; something that should emerge naturally in all of us. We can continue to leave this emergence up to happenstance. However, another option is to carefully examine its forms and directly teach them; to instill them in all of us, from childhood onward.

Because helping is so important, a family of related words has evolved to identify its various forms. *Aiding* suggests that helpers take a necessary role in the activity of another. The activity cannot be completed without them. *Assisting* denotes a subordinate role by the helpers, one that may make the activity much easier, more efficient, or more fun. *Supporting* indicates anything from "not interfering with concentration" when someone is working hard on an activity to "cheering others on" to maintain their focus to keep trying their best.

Helping is related to *working together*, were the aiding, assisting, and supporting involves *participating, collaborating,* or *cooperating* within or across activities. When members help to ensure that individual and group activities are successful, they are promoting working together. Helping is one of the first places children's management tactics can be identified.

Helping Processes

A close look at helping reveals that it is a set of four related subprocesses. All are special forms of organizing where the helper is a resource that is "recruited" into an activity that has been stalled, difficult, or dangerous. As a result, helping may well need to incorporate all the steps of organizing to use the human resource most effectively.

The four subprocesses are illustrated in Graphic 12.1. There are two initiated by the *helper* (left hand side) and two by the *helpee* (right hand side), with each having *acceptance* and *rejection* forms. When we place these four processes together, their similarities and differences are exposed by examining the steps of each.

Either the *helper*, the citizen who gives help, or *helpee*, the citizen who receives the help, first discriminate *Is helping needed?* (Step 1 of all 4 subprocesses). The discrimination requires observing if the activity would offer one or more of the following benefits to the helper or helpee: 1) the activity may be hard, 2) it may be dangerous, 3) it may offer a chance to learn something, 4) it may offer a chance to form a new relationship or build a stronger one. These four possible "causes" are *inducers* at this point in the helping process, be it asking or offering. These inducers have an element of moral values. Just by suggesting these four possible "causes" for engaging in helping indicates a moral choice relative to *who is doing what for whom.*

Once the need to help is identified, step 2 follows for the subprocesses. Either the helper *offers to help* (step 2 for the left side of Graphic 12.1) or the helpee *asks for help* (step 2 of the right side). If the offer or asking are accepted (a discrimination), the helping proceeds (step 3 of the top two subprocesses). When this helping is done, the helpee thanks the helper (step 4 in the top two) and the helper accepts thanks given by the helpee (step 5 of the top two subprocesses). However, if the offer or asking are rejected (step 3 of the bottom two subprocesses), helping does not occur and the helper or the helpee accept the rejection (step 4 of the bottom two subprocesses).

The helper's offer to help is often very simple, "Zelda, do you need help?" The helpee's request is equally simple, "Martha, can I get your help?" The rejection of a request to share can take a variety of forms, "No," to "Not now, perhaps later." The rejection of an offer has similar variety, "No." to "Thanks, but I like doing it myself." The rest of the helping steps are equally simple. Yet, often they are done in ways that corrupt the helping adventure and create negative emotional states. The stinging rejection and just being ignored when one requests help are two culprits that stop helping in the short or long term. Again, such behavior produces negative emotional states as consequences (Chapter 5).

These different forms of helping are important. We all have known dysfunctional helpees. They can't ask for help or accept it when offered. The macho father and the super mom often fall into these categories, as does the politician who says, "We want to do our own thing." They are independent Me/My citizens, ones who may be willing to help at times but can't seek it out or accept it. The consequences include the burden of excessive caregiver responsibility and children don't learn both sides of the helping coin,

❖ FOUR FORMS OF HELPING ❖

❖ OFFER & ACCEPT ❖

1. Helper: Is Helping Needed?
2. Helper Offers to Help.
3. If Offer Accepted, Help Is Given.
4. Helpee Thanks the Helper.
5. Helper Accepts Helpee's Thanks.

❖ OFFER & REJECT ❖

1. Helper Asks: Is Helping Needed?
2. Helper Offers to Help.
3. Offer is Rejected.
4. Helper Accepts Rejection.

❖ ASK & ACCEPT ❖

1. Helpee: Is Helping Needed?
2. Helpee Asks for Help.
3. If Asking Accepted, Help Is Given.
4. Helpee Thanks the Helper.
5. Helper Accepts Helpee's Thanks.

❖ ASK & REJECT ❖

1. Helpee Asks: Is Helping Needed?
2. Helpee Asks for Help.
3. Helper Rejects the Request.
4. Helpee Accepts the Rejection.

GRAPHIC 12.1: Four Forms of Helping.

There are also those who can't accept a rejection of an offer to help or when asking; they feel that the rejection is a rejection of themselves. This is where teaching often requires carefully exposing the potential emotions for both participants.

Bringing all four subprocesses out into the open represents the first step toward making helping a smooth, rhythmic part of everyday life, without creating negative emotional states in either the helper or the helpee.

Helping's Discriminations & Operations

From the above analysis, a number of discriminations prompt the simple operations of helping. These are outlined for the helper and helpee in Table 12.1.

Question one involves the same discrimination for both the helper and helpee. It is based on observing any of the four "causes" that induce (set in motion) helping. Seeing that an activity is dangerous or hard, offers a chance for learning or building a relationship between participants. For the helper especially, this discrimination is an inductive inference. Moreover, the cause of offering or asking can be different for the helper and helpee. This inductive inference may be wrong, but it may be right for one or more reasons. But rational and civil behavior begins at this inference point.

	TABLE 12.1: Helper and Helpee Questions	
	Helper Questions	Helpee Questions
1.	When is helping needed?	When is helping needed?
2.	How can one offer to help?	How can one ask for help?
3.	When would one give help without an offer or an ask?	When would one accept help without an offer or an ask?
4.	How can one coordinate help?	How can one coordinate help?
5.	How can one reject a request to help?	How can one reject an offer to help?
6.	How can one accept a rejection?	How can one accept a rejection?
7.	When would one thank a helpee after giving help?	How can one thank a helper for giving help?

Question two is a discrimination that induces a very simple operation. The helper's offer is usually just a question: "Zelda, do you need a hand?" or "George, how can I help?" The helpee's request is about equal: "Martha, can you give me a hand with this?" or "Can you help me relocate this big thing?" If the helpee needs knowledge about how to do something, this will often be embedded in the asking: "Martha, can you help me with this? I am a not sure how." A similar situation can arise from the helper's viewpoint: "Zelda, I know about that, can I help?" Within the classroom, an offer or a request for help is often related to M or T of VAM-T repertoires.

Question three deals with the recognition (discrimination) of danger on the part of the helper. We are all risk averse. Giving help in such situations is most likely built into our biology as is caring for an infant. We grab the arm of someone walking in front of a moving vehicle or someone who is about to walk into a wall. In the age where cell phones are attached to our ears, helping has become obvious. Often our "situational awareness" is reduced to a single, focused input. We are usually thankful to those who have all their sensory systems on line. If no one has such awareness, helping could not occur.

Question four involves discriminating of who shall take the lead. In almost all helping situations, someone takes the lead. Usually, this is determined by a helper and helpee interaction. In fact, the way that one offers or asks for help (question 2) will often indicate how each party will participate in the activity. The helpee may say, "Can you help, I am not sure how to do this." The helper may say, "I am not sure what to do but can I help." Now, the supervision of the activity has been decided (Chapter 10). Of course, there are times when both parties have to think about how to do the activity. They "think or consult together" to find a rational path to completion.

Question five deals with discriminating a rejection that is immediately followed by an operation. The helper or the helpee may not accept an offer or an ask for various reasons, which are often unknown. But with direct instruction, they will learn a few "polite" possibilities. This all that is needed. These "canned replies," allow children to quickly make a polite reply. The potential helper may say something like, "I can't right now, my teacher is waiting for me. Perhaps another time." The potential helpee may say, "I like doing this alone. It relaxes me. But thanks for the offer." The glaze of politeness has been added, but we all know that by the third or so offer or ask has been rejected, we cease to offer or ask such people.

Question six deals with discriminating an operation that controls the emotional state that for the helper/helpee may arise from a rejection. This emotion is often controlled by two manager events. First, the helper or helpee "explains" why the offer or ask is rejected. This is, at least, partially exposed in the rejection statements in question five. By explaining these states, the helper and helpee can usually truncate any possible emotional upheaval from a rejection. Yet, the real key is that discriminating a rejection induces a bit of thinking like "the rejection of helping is due to the rejector, not the rejected." This is an important "lesson" for young children who are sensitive to any form of social rejection.

Question seven is different for the helper and helpee. For the helper, the discrimination is usually based one of the reasons that prompted the offering to help. It is usually related to learning something new. For the helpee, it is a norm, an expectancy, that applies to the helpee, no matter what the cause of the helping. If there was a potential danger, the helpee may say, "You saved my bacon. Much thanks." Such behavior on the part of the helpee appears to be universal across cultures. With direct teaching, both the helper and helpee will have some canned responses that keep helping evolving into the future.

In all the above questions, the goal is to build helper and helpee situational awareness. The teaching example sets are used to evolve their active in-the-moment managership. Situational awareness is at the heart of all managing—it is objectivity applied to our human behavior in a particular context. All management strategy teaching aims to build this situational awareness.

Combining the Helping Subprocesses

The four strategies of helping can be combined by using "IF" and "OR" statements as illustrated in Graphic 12.2 (see Appendices for an intermediate form). Similar to the organizing strategy, there are discrimination and operation sub-questions for the helper and helpee. Table 12.1 listed the discriminations and operations. With only slight rewording, they are built into the strategy with "IF" and "OR" statements. These are questions related to each strategy step which the helper and helpee will need to answer until the strategy becomes an automatic part of their answers. They are also prompts to guide children, usually in the form of queries, that keep early helping moving forward. Children can ask and answer such queries themselves as a review of a helping instance or as a prediction. In the context of the combined strategy, the questions require some elaboration.

Questions 1a, b, and c are essentially the discriminations that induce helping (question 1 of Table 12.1). First and foremost, helping reduces the chance of risk. After that, the offer or ask can reduce hard work to something manageable, provide a learning opportunity, and possibly engender a new friendship. If helping moves forward without mishap, usually positive emotional states are created in both the helper and helpee.

Question 2a, b, and c apply to how one offers or asks. They are, as the questions above indicate, simple operations based on knowledge of examples that fit the limits of how to offer or ask. However, 2a is an animal of a different sort. It applies when there is danger or risk and there is no time for offering or asking. Here the helper just halts them physically or says "stop" in a "command voice" if the former can't be done. We feel better stopping a potential hazardous accident than witnessing one. We are, as said above, living in the age of focused attention to the devices attached to our hips, ears, and eyes.

Question 3a and b are a replacement for question 4 in Table 12.1. Through a verbal interaction or by way of question 2, the supervision of the activity is decided. Those involved come to see their part in a particular helping context. As said, often it may require both parties to participate in solving a problem that has arisen as helping proceeds. Step 3 may require a

❖ HELPING ❖

▶ Helper and Helpee Steps ◀

1. Is Helping Needed?
   a. Does the activity look hard or dangerous?
   b. Might something be learned?
   c. Might a relationship be made?
2. Offer to OR Ask for Help.
   a. When would help be given without offering or asking?
   b. How can one offer?
   c. How can one ask?
3. IF Offer OR Asking is Accepted, Work Together.
   a. How can one help?
   b. How can one be helped?
4. IF Offer OR Asking is Rejected, Accept Rejection.
   a. How can one accept a rejection?
   b. How can one give a rejection?
   c. How should one feel about a rejection?
5. When Helping is Done, Thank OR Accept Thanks.
   a. How can one give thanks?
   b. How can one accept thanks?

GRAPHIC 12.2: Combined forms of helping.

bit of supervising on the part of the participants. However, in the helping situation, this need usually requires no formal supervisory experience. Usually, the helper and helpee work out who is doing what during helping. It just requires a little social communication to move forward with the activity. It's all in the offering or asking.

Questions 4a, b, and c relate to questions five and six in Table 8.1. They are more about simple "polite" methods of rejection, as well as the helper and helpee having knowledge about who is responsible for the rejection. Essentially, the helper will fall into one of the categories of *aiding*, *assisting*, or *supporting* the activity. During teaching, the example set used will include examples of each sub-type of helper.

Questions 5a and b are related to question 7 in Table 12.1. These are simple operations that are given as the activity is completed. The helper may thank because they learned something, as well as accept thanks. The helpee will give thanks automatically. Even with helping, the activity may not be completed. Here, the helpee would still be obliged to say something like, "That didn't work, but I sure appreciated your help. You helped me stay calm in the attempt." The means and ends have been expressed in a polite manner. That is all that is required. If one lives in a culturally diverse area, politeness can vary across groups. Again, a range of examples must be employed. It is here that children can be sent home to ask their caregivers questions about what they would consider appropriate. This is just one common way to get caregivers to participate in children's homework, as well as to help caregivers see what their children are learning. Again, the example set will illustrate a range of polite to non-polite rejections from helpees.

Consequences of Helping

As can be gleamed from the above, helping has wonderful consequences for children (and adults). First and foremost, it provides them with unique learning opportunities. In the home, they can learn the "ins-and-outs" of family life by learning to cook, launder, clean, and even to manage the family budget. If done with equity in the classroom and school, the same is true. Children start this learning by helping with these activities and, eventually, being able to do them themselves. The classroom is no different: it prepares them for the larger social world. Much of helping is about all sorts of informal learning. Helping should evolve from the classroom to transfer to the school setting and beyond. It supports, as said earlier, the building of strong, unifying relationships. There is reciprocity at work here; especially when children work together in pairs or larger groups. All that is needed is to observe and feel the consequences of mutual helping and the emotional satisfaction of activities completed together with efficiency and effectiveness (Chapter 7). Strong emotional bonds are the foundation of unity. Teaching promotes unity by using statements and, later, questioning techniques, so that children come to observe and recognize what helping is needed and what it accomplishes for them and those around them. All three types of consequences emerge: emotional, restructuring, and access (Chapter 7). During instruction, the consequences of both the means of helping and its ends need to be pointed out. Again, either the means or ends of an activity may be coercive or cohesive. Both may deliver emotional, access, or restructuring consequences.

Opportunities for Helping?

We teach helping in the classroom, but do we employ methods that extend it to all possible activities (contexts)? Asking children for helping examples for how to ask or reject help from caregivers is a start. But, are they asked not only for how they help in their various classroom activities, but how they help at home, their emotional state when doing so, and the consequences for themselves and their caregivers? Do they have such opportunities in school as well? If the opportunities to help are numerous, then teaching occurs with only a few short "management activities" that set out the examples that apply to the four helping processes.

The example sets used to teach, as said, should include children as modelers. Simply start by asking them, "Who knows how to help?" Children will give replies, some crude and others more sophisticated, but all will be clarified by walking the children through examples that identify the range and limits of helping. Usually start with the positive subprocesses and then move to the ones with negative replies. The more they know about helping and the more they practice, the better they will be at helping during moments when another child needs it. This is where students who possess the academic, T, of an activity can be the helpers for others.

Establishing group-based activities induces helping. During the design of classroom activities (planning strategy), the valued purpose is to anticipate where helping may be needed or prepare children by asking before the activity, "Who can help if it is needed?" Once the teaching of one or more of the four subprocesses of helping is underway, such questions are all that are needed to prompt the helping, which increases the probability of activity success, especially in terms of the means used to achieve the activities technical behavior end, its valued purpose. However, one must set up the classroom activities, so that they provide opportunities for helping.

Like all the management strategies, the earlier helping is taught, the better the chance of instilling its methods. Observing its positive consequences from that point on may assist the strategy in emerging on the world stage, even before the children learn to read. They may show-and-tell about what helping they have done or that they have witnessed in everyday life. The "What management?" game is a great mechanism to provide a context for expanding this or any management strategy. The game is outlined in the Appendices.

Like all the management, awareness, and moral-value content in this book, helping isn't something that can be "dumped" on children when they are older or during a semester course. It actually starts when, as infants, they open their mouths to be fed. In the classroom, it starts when they enter the room.

13

Sharing Strategy

Sharing, like helping, is a social strategy; it can't be done alone. Sharing involves both a sharer or sharee in a special form of organizing. The sharer usually provides the sharee with a resource for some activity or some part of an activity. Thus, they may both be involved in the same activity, but the sharer often does not use the resource while it is shared. Exceptions include things like sharing crayons while drawing, a scale to weigh objects, or a ruler to measure them. Sharing often requires that all the steps of organizing may need to be considered. Of special importance is clearly specifying the condition in which the resource is returned.

In everyday life, the sharer provides the sharee with a resource needed to continue their activity. Generally, sharing occurs during times of natural or human-made disasters. Yet, our emerging world-wide communication networks illustrate just how extensive the need is and how much more could be done through sharing resources to wipeout the vast inequalities and hardships that exist across individuals, communities, and nation states. Many spend their entire time engaged in securing water, food, shelter, and healthcare for their families. If we want to promote a world where individuals and groups have access, without excessive labor, for these basics, then teaching young children to share is an important strategy to begin wiping out existing inequalities. This is a moral-values view that steps outside the classroom, but it is in the classroom where such sharing can be given birth.

The advantages of sharing have their first impact on family and classroom systems. In both, it conserves resources, enables members to keep activities moving forward, and promotes unity. When we share knowledge, both teaching and learning can occur. Such activities build strong relationships; we observe and feel our membership, our unity in making life a bit better for ourselves and others. Like all activities that unify, emotional states become positive and compatible. Thus, sharing can engender all three consequent types (emotional, access, and restructuring) for both sharer and sharee.

We see the importance of sharing through its language markers. For example, *lending* is a synonym for sharing. We let someone use our resources (Chapter 11) for a period of time. *Borrowing* is sharee-initiated sharing. *Reciprocal sharing* implies having access to each other's individually held resources. To work, reciprocal sharing often requires a plan covering who, what, when, and where resource use occurs. *Joint ownership* is the sharing of mutually held resources by a group. Here, we often talk in terms of "cooperatives." Such ownership is again based on a carefully planned activity. The existence of "grocery cooperatives" and "buying groups" are just two examples. *Giving* defines the boundary for sharing. We give part of our resource wealth to others in need. Often, this involves indirect giving through charities. With giving, the sharer relinquishes ownership of resources. Yet, when we *help,* we give our time; another resource. When we *share knowledge* about something, we are giving something we can't take back, but we have not lost it. Sharing knowledge is *almost* synonymous with teaching.

The above indicates helping and sharing are linked and have much in common. Yet, there is one profound, less tangible feature that makes helping and sharing distinctly different: at minimum, the sharer must "trust" the sharee or at least have some knowledge of their past sharing behavior. As in science, this trust has social and historical roots. Usually in everyday life, trust is lost when resources are not returned or returned in a non-working condition.

In the end, there are four primary managing tactics (small operational behaviors) that corrupt sharing's trust requirement. These include:

1. The stinging rejection when offering or asking.
2. Returning a resource in a dysfunctional state.
3. The failure to return a resource.
4. The lack of thanks.

All these have the power to halt the evolution of sharing. In the adult world, the lack of appropriate sharing leads everyone to thinking they need to own their own resources. As a result, consumption of resources increases. The above coercive managing tactics may arise because children are not directly taught sharing. Thus, potentially useful sharing events go unnoticed or avoided. Offering and asking do not occur.

Bringing all four sub-processes of sharing out into the open represents the first step toward making sharing a smooth, rhythmic part of everyday life, without creating negative emotional states in either the sharer or the sharee. After that, all we need to do is induce sharing and, then, pointing out the means and end consequent events of doing so in real time. The teacher is not the *alone arranger* and all classroom members can contribute to both sides of sharing: 1) inducing and 2) consequencing it in the context of any activity contingency.

Sharing Processes

Like helping, sharing has four sub-processes. Graphic 13.1 indicates that sharing can be initiated by the *sharer* (two forms on the left side of Graphic 13.1) or by the *sharee* (two forms on the right side). Each of these have an *acceptance* (top row) or a *rejection form* (bottom row). When we place these four sub-processes together, their similarities and differences are exposed.

❖ FOUR FORMS OF SHARING ❖

❖ OFFER & ACCEPT ❖

1. Sharer Asks: Is Sharing Needed?
2. Sharer Offers to Share.
3. If Offer Accepted, Share.
4. Sharee Thanks the Sharer.
5. Sharer Accepts Sharee's Thanks.

❖ OFFER & REJECT ❖

1. Sharer Asks: Is Sharing Needed?
2. Sharer Offers to Share.
3. Sharee Rejects Offer.
4. Sharer Accepts Rejection.

❖ ASK & ACCEPT ❖

1. Sharee Asks: Is Sharing Needed?
2. Sharee Asks to Share.
3. If Asking Accepted, Share.
4. Sharee Thanks the Sharer.
5. Sharer Accepts Sharee's Thanks.

❖ ASK & REJECT ❖

1. Sharee Asks: Is Sharing Needed?
2. Sharee Asks to Share.
3. Sharer Rejects the Request.
4. Sharee Accepts the Rejection.

GRAPHIC 13.1: Four Forms of Sharing.

Either the sharer (the resource holding manager) or the sharee (the resource receiving manager) can identify if sharing is needed (step 1 of all 4 forms). Once the need to share is identified, either the sharer offers to share or the sharee asks the sharer to share (step 1 of all 4 forms). This depends on who discriminates the need to share.

If the offer or asking are accepted, the sharing proceeds (step 3 of the top two forms). If the offer or asking is rejected (step 3 of the bottom two forms), then there is no sharing, but a negative emotional state, as a consequence, may emerge. Thus, step 4 of the bottom two forms is needed. The emotional-thinking state from a rejection may be positive, negative, or neutral. No human being, especially a young child, enjoys rejection. Thus, it is important to teach two emotion-controlling events. First, the sharer or sharee should know how to "politely" reject an offer or an asking (step 3 of bottom two forms). Second, the two rejected managers must know emotion-controlling thinking that lets them stay at least in a neutral emotional state (step 4 of the bottom forms). This state will help these "rejected" managers to continue to offer or ask to share when it is needed (step 1). Initial teaching begins with offer and accept.

Although dealing with rejection is important, as it is in helping, there is an even more difficult situation to deal with. This is the return of a resource that has been abused or broken. What should happen here? What should both the sharer and sharee do? Should the latter get the resource cleaned, repaired, or replaced? Should he or she just apologize? What should the sharer do? Should the sharer's behavior be dependent on the sharee's response relative to the condition of the resource returned? There are no "right" answers to these questions. But their consideration can be built into the full sharing strategy. In general, the sharing of "critical" or "limited" resources requires a "sharing-a-resource plan," so that all parties know how the sharing will proceed and end.

Sharing's Discriminations & Operations

From the above, a number of discriminations and their following operations are important. These are outlined for the sharer and sharee in Table 13.1.

Table 13.1: Sharer and Sharee Questions	
Sharer Questions	Sharee Questions
1.	Is sharing needed?	Is sharing needed?
2.	How can one offer to share?	How can one ask to share?
3.	How can one reject an asking?	How can one reject an offer?
4.	How can one accept a rejection?	How can one accept a rejection?
5.	How should the resource be returned?	How should the resource be returned?
6.	How could the sharer accept thanks from the sharee?	How could the sharee thank the sharer?

Question one involves a discrimination for both sharer and sharee. It is based on observing if an activity appears to be unable to start or appears stalled because of a missing resource. This inductive inference may be wrong, but it may be right. Thus, it may be better to err on the side of offering or asking to share.

Question two is a discrimination that induces an operation that is often profoundly simple. The sharer's offer is usually a question: "Zelda, do you need a pencil?" or "George, what do you need?" The sharee's request is about equal: "Martha, can I use the red crayon?" or "Can you share your ruler?" (If the sharee needs knowledge about something, most of the time, it is a request for help on an M or T behavior.)

Question three deals with a rejection that is a discrimination immediately followed by an operation. The sharer won't usually offer to share if the resource is critical, scarce, or in use. The sharee who knows that the resource is critical, scarce, or in use, will not usually ask to share. They will seek other resource securing alternatives. These three resource states are usually what guide the sharer's operation for accepting a request to share: "Wonda, I will be done with my ruler soon, then you can use it." or "Sorry, but I will need it for my next activity."

Question four deals with accepting a rejection. This is an emotional operation that is often controlled by two sharing events. First, the sharer or sharee "explains" why asking to share is rejected. For the sharer, this explaining is usually related to the critical-scarce-in-use discrimination. For the sharee, rejection usually comes because what often looks like the need for a resource is often related to decisions about performing the activity that makes it look like one is stuck because of a resource need (question 1). By explaining these states, the sharer or sharee can usually truncate any possible emotional upheaval from a rejection.

Question five, is a norm, an expectancy that applies to both the sharer and sharee. If the resource is critical, scarce, or in use, then there may need to be a clear expression of when and what to expect upon return of the resource. Either the sharer or sharee can initiate this expectancy. It usually ends in a "promise" of when to return the resource "in good condition" by the sharee. Adults may even sign a contract, as when one borrows from an equipment rental firm.

Question six is an operation based on the answer to question five, how should the resource be returned? If the resource is returned on time and in good working order, the sharee will usually thank the sharer; she may even briefly mention or point out the condition of the resource along with the thanks: "Thanks for letting me use it. It is ready for its next use." or "Thanks, it let me do my work and it is all cleaned up." Of course, there will be a conflict if a shared item is not returned in the condition promised. If this situation arises, the intervening strategy (Chapter 12) can apply. It is for this reason that sharing by adults often leads to small-claims court. They have not been taught to make needed sharing discriminations up front.

Combining the Sharing Strategies

The above discriminations and operations can be combined into a full sharing strategy that is applicable to both the sharer and sharee. Like helping, the four sub-processes of the sharing strategy can be combined by using "IF" and "OR" statements as indicated in Graphic 13.2. Like helping, there are a subset of thinking items for each sharing step that set-the-occasion for the various sharing operations to proceed. These are important during the teaching of the full strategy. Initially, the questions can be incorporated into the modeling of sharing, with children being the modelers.

❖ SHARING ❖

▶ Sharer and Sharee Steps ◀

1. **Is Sharing Needed?**
   a. Who needs a resource?
   b. What resource is needed?
2. **Offer to OR Ask to Share.**
   a. How can one offer to share?
   b. How can one ask to share?
3. **IF Offer OR Asking is Accepted, Share Resource.**
   a. How can resource use be organized?
   b. In what condition should resources be return?
4. **IF Offer OR Asking is Rejected, Accept Rejection.**
   a. How should one feel about a rejection?
   b. How can one reject an offer?
   c. How can one reject an ask?
5. **When Sharing is Done, Return and Thank OR Accept Thanks.**
   a. Is the resource returned as talked about (3b)?
   b. if no to 5a, how can sharing end?
   c. If yes to 5a, how can thanks be given and accepted.

GRAPHIC 13.2: The combined forms of sharing.

Questions 1a and 1b are clarifications once sharing appears to be needed (step 1). These two questions parallel those asked in the organizing strategy, but they involve looking beyond one's own activity or, at least, to someone else in an activity group. The answers for 1, 1a, and 1b are inductive inferences based on evidence of what is needed for an activity to proceed. In everyday life, observing the need to share involves, like all the management strategies, "situational awareness."

Questions 2a and 2b are just reminders of the range and limits of offering or asking. It can include who, when, and where to ask. Quiet, relaxed times for the sharer would perhaps induce him or her to share. For the sharee, planning ahead of time may make one more flexible to when sharing is needed. Combining 2a and 2b can further ensure that the offer of asking is accepted. All that can be done here, is to cover the range of civil examples of asking. Yet, as some have shown, we have a toolbox full of ways that induce the sharer to agree to share.[1]

Questions 3a and 3b are the critical points in advanced sharing given that acceptance has occurred. One does almost all the steps of organizing (Chapter 11) in complex situations. Although children will need to eventually see that sharing is a special form of organizing, they do not need this view early on. First, the four forms of sharing are taught to young children one form at a time.

This teaching should be carefully done. We do not want the sharee to feel that he or she is receiving charity, nor do we want the sharer to feel pressure. Thus, a bit of diplomacy is required in our approach to offering or asking to share. We observe nations who want to do it by themselves with "no strings attached." Often sharing is rejected because of what is termed "ideological differences" between sharer and sharee. Even a "reciprocal trade agreement" can be seen as sharing different resources that various nations need. But here we observe the "winner-loser mindset" of agents at work. "Win-win" for all agents (managers) gets lost. Ultimately step 3 is taken care of when there is a reciprocal history of sharing: the needed "trust" is established that reciprocal sharing will occur in the long run. We see the delicacy of sharing within the United Nations and its international sub-organizations like United Nations Children's Fund (UNICEF) and United Nations Educational, Scientific and Cultural Organization (UNESCO).

Question 4a is a norm-based discrimination. If we want sharing to continue, the feeling that emerges from a rejection should not be "harsh" or "negatively" expressed. When the norm can be discriminated, 4b and 4c can be exampled through simple operations that are based on what is taught for 4a—the norm. For example, "I am sorry but I am going to use it in a few minutes." or "I appreciate the offer, but I have what I need for now." The norm for many is often called being "socially polite" so the rejection does not "sting."

Step 4 involves making sharers or sharees see that the rejection of offering or an asking to share is not a rejection of their resource, and by extension, a rejection of themselves. It is the rejector that has a problem, as long as the offer or ask is appropriate (Question 2).

Questions 5a is a discrimination that can be established during step 3. If step 3 has not clarified the details of organizing the shared resource, then the answers to 5b and 5c are anyone's guess. If 5c occurs, then the thanks and its acceptance are easy operations. They are nothing more than polite civility. When a shared resource is returned clean or in better condition than it was originally, the added bit of civility toward the sharee by the sharer goes

---

[1] Martin, S. J., Goldstein, N. J., & Cialdini, R. B. (2014). *The small big! Small changes that spark big differences.* London: Profile Books.

something like, "It looks like new. I appreciate that. Thanks." Children don't usually encounter this situation in the classroom, but they will in their community and in later life.

The civility feature of sharing can be made overt in the classroom by first indicating that the classroom resources are the communities, which includes their caregivers, and they will be used by future children. Second, sharees can be rewarded with thanks when their returns are "clean." Third, they can be informed when resources are abused. Within the classroom, abuse can be corrected during the conflict resolution (Chapter 16, Intervening Strategy).

Consequences of Sharing

As can be gleaned from the above, sharing has some wonderful consequences for children (and adults). First, it provides them with unique opportunities to get to know their neighbors—access that can foster positive emotions. Second, it builds relationships, especially if reciprocal sharing gains a history of success. Restructuring through sharing can lead to community relationships that support unity. Third, it can keep the entire class moving forward. Members have a greater chance of finishing their activities in a positive emotional state, which helps avoid conflicts. All three types of consequences occur because, like helping, activities are 1) made easier, 2) more efficient, and 3) increase the probability of success.

Opportunities for Sharing?

Like helping, sharing can only occur if its classroom activities are structured to provide sharing opportunities. The opportunities can occur within and across activities. Sharing between activities need not be done in close physical proximity or close in time. Children can offer or request toys, tools or other resources beforehand. Such sharing can employ an introduction to planning, as can organizing and helping.

To promote sharing, we can have two children do the same activity at the same time. All that is needed is to limit the resources, so that they need to share to complete their activities. After they have shared a few times, see if they share without a request or a prompt to do so.

Teaching sharing begins with the acceptance forms of the strategy. And like all the other management strategies, the earlier sharing begins, the better the chance of instilling all its steps, observing their occurrence, observing and feeling the consequences in real time, and building children's trust in using them. All this learning increases the probability of promoting the emergence of sharing outside the classroom; first in the school, then in the community, and then in the world.

Like helping, sharing isn't something that can be "dumped" on children in a "short course" when they are older—remember the need for trust and how it is built over a history of interactions. Trust is an inductive inference about the managing of other's behavior. It requires time and opportunities to instill. Each instance of appropriate sharing builds on past instances.

Since teachers are always sharing various bits of knowledge, it is helpful to eventually point out the bigger picture of sharing. From the community to teachers and from teachers to children, we are all managers of what will be or was shared and the trust they acquired from being sharing managers. Later, queries can be used to gather evidence (validate) if children can observe sharing and its consequences in real time (see Chapter 5 and 6). If they can do so, they gain another view of their managing in a social system. Again, the most powerful teaching tool is our social communications repertoire (Chapter 8) that describes and queries children about their learning as it occurs before, during, and after activities. As with helping, the consequences of both the means (micro-management) and ends (macro-management) of instances (Chapters 1 and 2) of sharing need to be revealed many times, at first by the teacher and then by children. In the end, sharing is a social activity that requires a flexible social repertoire. It can't be done alone but must be part of a learned inter-human process of mutual concessions and compromises. The group goal in the classroom is to ensure that children have time to practice these mutual interactions.

14

Supervising Strategy

Parents begin supervising their children's activities from birth. Teachers begin from the first moment children enter their classrooms. Both supervising activities are difficult. Parents struggle because there 1) is no way to talk to infants about the activity being performed or what infants need, and 2) the infants have no knowledge of the activity being performed. The infant is on "automatic" to suckle, cry, and squirm when a "basic need for survival" emerges. But by the time most children enter the classroom, they have mastered eating, walking, and talking to some extent.

As teachers, we struggle because 1) there are so many to supervise; 2) children seldom know even the rudiments of working together in large groups; 3) have no knowledge of how to perform the activities required of them; and 4) they are in a dynamic growth timeframe that continually "urges" them to seek out events and perform actions without thought. They just want to do and control the world around them. As a result, teachers require an extensive management repertoire, most of which has not been clearly taught to them. Classically, teachers supervising behavior was called "classroom management." But children need to learn to supervise themselves individually and in groups. If we continually supervise them, they will only learn to supervise themselves and others by happenstance.

This chapter answers the question, "What is the language and process of supervising?" Like the previous management strategy chapters, it only hints at the evolutionary teaching methods required to instill this strategy along with the others.

Supervising in Perspective

Effective supervising is a lifelong learning process. What is presented here goes beyond what young children will or need to achieve by the end of elementary school, but its details may help teachers survive and be successful in the classroom from any early career point.

The supervising strategy—unlike organizing, helping, and sharing—provides the behaviors needed to keep group members working efficiently and effectively throughout any activity. It is based on a clear contingency plan. Organizing, helping, and sharing are the first steps toward promoting We/Us unity by our neophyte citizens. Yet, it is supervising that begins to increase the probability of setting the We/Us unity in "full motion stereo."

The planning and intervening management strategies are the underpinnings of supervising and, thus, the supervisor (Chapters 15 and 6).

Knowing how to supervise keeps activities moving forward, as does organizing, helping, and sharing. However, supervision explicitly aims to guide activity "flow" from beginning to end. One may guide this flow through coercive methods of discipline. But here, supervising is presented as "guidance" that seeks to achieve a "group harmony," a "working together without conflict" among members. Harmony is essentially a feature of group unity. The only places where unity may develop but harmony does not, appears in our struggles against natural and citizen-made disasters, terrorism, and war. The first two require unity that leads to harmony. The latter two never achieve harmony. They are fights between Me/My moral-value groups.

The supervisor "handles" the interactions of a group's members, adjusting to unexpected events like a need to help or to avoid or stop conflicts. It induces and consequents members' behaviors in a continuous, repeating cycle. Moreover, when all children know the supervising strategy, they do not need to wonder about the what, when, where, why, or how of an activity. They will know that supervising is governed by the activity plan and will know what to expect from the supervisor. This "knowing" by both the supervisor and supervisees further induces and adds to the realization of positive consequent events.

The main behavior of the supervisor is to: 1) induce and consequent behavior throughout an activity's means and 2) inform members of the extent to which they are achieving the activity's ends. These inducing and consequent events bring about all three consequent classes: emotional, access, and restructuring (Chapter 5). When children are taught how to supervise themselves individually and in groups, it contributes to making them unified, adaptive, and independent.

However, teachers must know the steps and query elements of supervising if they hope to model and evolve the strategy effectively day-in and day-out. If they can't, some children may learn something about supervising themselves and others. But only direct, step-by-step teaching can ensure that every group member can take over the supervision of activities successfully when necessity requires it.

If supervising is directly taught, it potentially changes the operation of the classroom. First, teachers no longer have to be the "master supervisor" of all their activities. Supervising can be turned over to their fledgling supervising citizens. Second, teachers gain time to ensure that all children learn the curricula—their "prime directive." Third, the language and steps of supervising provide teachers, as a group, with the beginnings of a problem-solving tool. They gain a verbal repertoire to talk about, analyze, and redesign the supervising of activities to avoid or solve problems. Such a *knowledge-sharing process* only happens when everyone has knowledge of the supervising strategy. Fourth, there are extensive emotional benefits as well. When children are observed supervising themselves in appropriate ways, they experience emotions akin to what parents feel when children take their first steps or say their first words. This puts teachers' emotional (X) state in a positive place that further helps teaching. Essentially, the only way for children to learn to supervise their activities efficiently and effectively requires that they practice supervising their activities. This is a very gradual learning process that can begin with children working in pairs.

SUPERVISING AS A PROCESS

Supervising is a process that prompts (induces) and cohesively reinforces (consequents) the performance of those engaged in an activity. It guides carrying out activities by directing the resources involved—people, tools, materials, time, place, and energy—throughout an activity (Chapter 11). The supervisor guides not only organizing, but the members' implementation of the activity's contingency plan (Chapter 15). As a result, the needed behaviors are performed, and the other resources are in the right place and arranged, so that the valued purpose is achieved within the activity's context and timeframe.

It is supervising that sets activities in motion and keeps them going until all resources are returned, which is their end. It is the activity contingency plan that all supervisors use as a guiding "template" for supervising. The plan informs them what they should observe throughout the activity's time-space context. Of course, the better the plan, the better the chances the supervisor has for success. However, even a strong plan will fail without a trained supervisor, and even the strongest, best trained supervisor can't achieve success when a plan is rationally weak, especially in terms of achieving the T of the activity. During a group activity, there is almost always a designated supervisor—but this does not have to be once all the children know and have practiced the supervising strategy, and been both in supervisor and supervisee roles where they learn to see "both sides of the fence."

Rationality and civility are conceived in an activity plan. They are birthed and nourished in supervising. Planning brings into the open an activity's valued purpose; the activity's T. Supervising brings into the open the moral control tactics that do or do not fit the plan's valued purpose. This is the point where the relationship between moral values and management comes to life—where it can be observed and evaluated. Organizing, helping, and sharing begin to bring out a sense of coercive or cohesive tactics (Chapters 11, 12, and 13). But the tactics of the supervisor can support or derail the entire activity by using coercive tactics, which usually lead to conflicts (Chapter 16). Supervisees may also use coercion to disrupt the activity or employ an insidious form of disruption called "apathy" or "I don't give a XXXX." Thus, the effective and efficient supervisors seek not just the control of means to achieve ends, but the creation of group unity (Chapters 4 and 6). When unity is a feature of the group, the member's support the supervisor's supervising and the supervisor supports those supervised. The probability of unity emerging is increased when all group members know the supervisory strategy and have taken on both the roles as supervisee and supervisor across various activities.

Even when working alone, there is also a need to supervise. We all talk to ourselves about how to proceed with activities. We ponder and mediate on what to do next or on the quality of the work so far. This is the "managing self" supervising the "technical self," so to speak. Whether supervising a group or ourselves, supervising consists of five steps.

As said earlier, teaching is a special form of supervising, one where the supervisees do not know much about how to do the activity's valued purpose, T. This fact allows supervising to be modeled and the steps named as teaching proceeds. The steps of supervising are embedded in teaching. Although to model supervising during teaching will initially slow it down, it will accelerate teaching for the reasons listed above.

Graphic 14.1. gives the five steps of supervising. As with the previous strategies, supervising begins with discriminating if supervising is needed (Step 1). Steps 2 through 5 are all operations based on a set of discriminations. The wording has again been selected for young children. Words like talk, direct, look and point out are known to most children. Supervising, plan, progress, and consequences will require separate discrimination teaching events. The initial teaching and expansion of the consequent events that emerge from behavior is an ongoing affair. It takes time and, thus, would be initially taught and expanded from almost the first day of class.

The ways in which these steps are carried out depends on the activity plan and those involved. It is the supervisor's use of these steps and the variations required across activities that will ensure activity success and the development of positive emotions in the participants.

Unlike previous strategies, the steps of supervising never quite unfold one after the other as identified in Graphic 14.1. Step 1 is done at the very start of the activity. It is a pure discrimination based on the supervisees' knowledge of the activity and if anything is new in the plan. Step 2 is based on the Step 1. The supervisor supplies the parts of the plan that may be unknown to the supervisees. Steps 3 and 5 are done frequently during an activity and often summarized at its end. Step 4 is a discrimination based on observational evidence about progress. It seeks to answer two questions: 1) is

❖ SUPERVISING ❖

1. Is Supervising Needed?
2. Talk About the Plan
3. Direct Activity Flow
4. Look for Progress
5. Point Out Consequences

GRAPHIC 14.1: Supervising steps.

the activity moving forward according to the plan. 2) what are the consequences that are occurring, and 3) are the means of the activity being carried out. Thus, step 4 is a set of discriminations that helps the supervisor to control steps 3 and 5.

Step 3 is what is done by the supervisor to ensure that the activity (the activity procedure) is "flowing" along. Usually, one just mentions what is next, if needed. When the activity is flowing, the supervisor can remain quiet or point out (indicate or query) members about the consequences (step 5). When progress towards the valued purpose, T, is being achieved, the supervisor can, again, remain quiet, point out, or query about the access consequences that result from achieving each part of the activity procedure. Step 5 content can involve emotional, access, and restructuring consequences. The tactics in directing activity flow (step 3), thus, depends on the background of the supervisees, the means of the activity, and its ends.

The plan's steps are often a procedure that is repeated throughout the activity. For example, in a reading group, each member may read a sentence or two and then another student takes a turn. This is repeated until the passage is completed. Along the way, the supervisor may ask questions about the reading. During the procedure, the supervisor calls on members randomly. Following the qualities of behavior identified in Chapter 6, if everyone keeps taking their turn without hesitation we have *willingness*, *quickness*, and *efficiency*. If they read correctly for the most part, we have *accuracy*. If the members catch each other's errors and they keep going without member conflict, then we have *persistence* (in the face of failure). They can be evaluated individually or as a group on these features. Both teachers and supervisors describe or query supervisees based on these qualities.

SUPERVISING'S DISCRIMINATIONS & OPERATIONS

Like organizing, each of these five steps are composed of discriminations that prompt operations and make the completion of the strategy steps possible, especially when activities are complex. Graphic 14.2 identifies these discriminations. They are presented as questions as in the previous strategies.

There is a direct relationship between the complexity of the activity and complexity of supervising. This complexity occurs across three dimensions. First, the steps of the process do not follow in a predictable, linear fashion. Second, each step many need further discriminations to be successful. Third, with complexity comes the difficulty in observing the evidence that makes the discriminations possible.

What makes the learning of supervising difficult is that the discriminations are usually private events. The supervisor is often not aware of them or they have fallen out of remembering because they were done in

---

❖ SUPERVISING ❖

1. IS SUPERVISING NEEDED?
   a. What supervising is needed?
2. TALK ABOUT THE PLAN.
   b. What in plan is new or unfirm?
   c. What do members know?
3. DIRECT ACTIVITY FLOW.
   a. What direction is needed?
   b. When is it needed?
   c. How can it be given?
   d. How can conflicts be avoided?
4. LOOK FOR PROGRESS.
   a. What has been done?
   b. What should be done?
   c. Is there progress?
   d. How can members be told?
5. POINT OUT CONSEQUENCES.
   d. What ones are happening?
   e. What ones could happen?

GRAPHIC 14.2: Supervising steps and discriminations.

the distant past. These are most likely the reasons why supervising has not emerged sooner for children. By making supervising a public process, as done in Graphics 14.1 and 14.2, it becomes possible to teach it and to see its variations without losing sight of its commonality and its pattern across activities. The language and pattern (its steps) also make it possible to discover why specific instances of a manager's supervising failed or succeeded. All the wording used in Graphic 14.2 are appropriate for young children with beginning reading skills. Example sets for terms like "progress" and "consequences" will be needed. The simplified strategy with just the five steps—Graphic 14.1—does not require reading. Each step of supervising has from two to four discrimination sub-steps. These are examined below.

1. Is Supervising Needed?

First, the supervisor must decide if supervising is needed (step 1). It is based on 1) the evidence of past supervisee performance, 2) newness of activity procedures, and 3) the size of the group. Just realizing that supervising is needed leads to an almost simultaneous second discrimination (1a): what supervising is needed? This discrimination flushes out the extent to which supervising is needed. However, as supervisors gain more experience with supervising, then they can answer 1a with greater accuracy through knowledge of steps 2 through 5. For example, the supervisor quickly thinks through these steps to determine where directing the flow is needed and how it can be accomplished, the need to foster progress, and the way to point out consequences. These need to be directly modeled by the teacher.

Additionally, supervising has a number of "assistance views" to help the supervisor achieve success. These are called "supervising heuristics." Four of them, illustrated in Graphic 14.3, apply to step 1 of supervising. However, these are not introduced until after the full strategy (Graphic 14.2) has been introduced. The heuristics are essentially the "problem-solving tool" of the strategy when supervisors encounter the need of a little more "expert" assistance that encourages "reflective thinking."

SUPERVISING HEURISTICS

1. Supervise only the activity steps needed.
2. Lead with questions when possible.
3. If the activity can be performed in many ways, let those supervised decide how.
4. Always look for progress.

GRAPHIC 14.3: First supervising heuristics.

The first heuristic essentially directs the supervisor to keep supervising simple. If activity members know the activity, very little supervision is needed. Steps, like talking about the plan, can be skipped or the supervisor may follow heuristic two and lead off with a question or two about the plan that the supervisees are believed to be able to answer.

The second heuristic encourages participation by asking, not telling. There is nothing more discouraging than to listen to something one knows about. Let participants tell what needs to be done, how to do it, and identify the consequences that result. This talking, however it is done, is outlining the contingencies of the activity plan. Also, during an activity, it is very simple to ask what needs to be done next. Moreover, the participants' answers will guide supervising, so that it focuses on the needs of a particular group. Also, group knowledge may add elements to the plan that the planners or the supervisor overlooked. Such questioning adds a participatory element to a supervisor's repertoire, which is a unifying tactic (Chapter 6). Now, the supervisees are learning about supervising and contributing to it in the same breath. As these managees gain in activity variety and management behaviors, questions become more general. The interaction becomes what is called an "open-ended communication" interaction. If teachers model questioning techniques during an activity before teaching supervising, the children will enter the activity (teaching episode) with a "supervisory model" to facilitate learning, which breeds creativity. To some, the supervisor is being "generative."

The third heuristic suggests that supervisors should allow supervisees to decide the way something is done whenever possible. This is especially true when the activity can be done in a multitude of ways. The decision to allow supervisees to decide based on the activity's needed behaviors. But often, by asking about the plan (Heuristic 2), the need for a change to the plan can be suggested. This engenders giving the supervisees a chance to decide for themselves how at least parts of the plan need or can be adjusted. If the needs don't, to some degree, match the supervisees' behavioral background and the time constraints, then heuristic 3 would not be followed. Often, when children decide how, their design decisions follow traditional lines, but they may invent, "on the fly" so to speak, other or more effective methods (operations). This situation is just another method to help the group become unified. Supervisees see themselves as manages of "their plan" and generators or initiators of any success that follows. They gain what some social scientists would call "agent efficacy." Here it is more viable to say, "manager efficacy" or "manager effectiveness."

The fourth heuristic, always look for progress, is just a repeat of step 4, look for progress. Even if the strategy heuristics are eventually reduced, this heuristic needs to be there. Using it, supervisors set in motion a method to engender cooperative supervising, which in turn engenders the quality of unity to the group. Also, looking for progress helps supervisors assess whether the plan is working, which is the second part of planning— implementing and evaluating the plan (Chapter 15). Thus, supervisors may facilitate both the evaluation of a plan and its replanning, as well as helping them to adjust their supervising to supervisees. This is civil inductive behavior towards humans at its best.

Following all four heuristic guidelines can greatly increase the immediate effectiveness of a new, fledgling supervisor who can read. Now, these and the other guiding heuristics can be posted (placed) on desks or on walls. As a result, the probability of activity success across dimensions like work harmony, product quality, individual satisfaction, and speed to completion are amplified.

2. Talk About the Plan

Activity participants need to know the elements of the plan (step 2). First, they must know what is unknown or new to the activity (2a). This may include the resources needed, the management and technical behaviors required, and the consequences for themselves and others in terms of the means used (micro-management) and the ends achieved (macro-management). These are the heart of the plan's contingency. By knowing the range of resource requirements (Chapter 11), the supervisor has a domain of knowledge to guide this step. Next, knowledge of the participants guides their supervising technique (2b). This step is especially important if the performers were not involved in the planning of the activity; thus, they know less about the plan.

By telling or questioning members about the plan, supervisors take a first step towards keeping an activity moving forward. They induce expectations about the consequences of its products or services; as well as about how members should manage themselves. They can have members decide who does what or generate goals that are congruent with the plan or the project the activity seeks to complete.

Often planners leave the details of how a plan unfolds during an activity unspecified. When such instances arise, the supervisor can provide these or the supervisor can let activity members determine how. Just how fast and at what level of quality do they want to work? Again, when supervisees help set out the means, they form a commitment to the activity. They are "invested." When the means are realistic predictions based on evidence like past performance dimensions, then the supervisor can see this as progress relative to past behavior (Chapter 6) and consequent it.

3. Direct Activity Flow

Once an activity is underway, the supervisor keeps it going by directing its flow forward (step 3). This step is essentially verbal communication (Chapters 6 and 8). First, the supervisor discriminates what direction is needed (3a) and when it is needed (3b). These two elements require knowledge of what has been done and what needs to be done next. The difference between the two determines what direction is needed. How that direction can be given (3c) depends on the intersection of three discriminations that the supervisor makes: (1) the members' knowledge of and experience with the activity, (2) their knowledge of the plan, and (3) their tactics of supervising themselves as they perform within the plan.

If the supervisor knows that the member or members are knowledgeable in all three areas, directing activity flow reduces to silence or something as simple as, "This project is progressing towards success. Does anyone need anything?" As the members' knowledge and experience increase, the supervisor moves to questions, and leaves detailed descriptions of the activity only at critical, new points in its execution. The ways in which the supervisor directs activity flow, helps with the final discrimination (3d), avoiding conflicts. The key to avoiding conflicts is essentially performing the behaviors suggested above. This is usually enough to avoid conflicts. This amounts to inducing and, later, consequenting supervisees' behavior in ways that they find emotionally positive. If a conflict does arise and the supervisor could do nothing to avoid it, then the intervention strategy is required (Chapter 16).

4. Look for Progress

As supervisors monitor or direct activity flow (step 3), they look for progress (step 4). From the observations gained, the supervisor can usually answer the discrimination question, "What has been done (4a)?" Answering the discrimination "What should be done (4b)?" requires knowledge of the activity plan or experience with the activity under similar conditions. By comparing *what-has-been-done* (4a) against *what-should-be-done* (4b), the supervisor discriminates (determines) the answer to "Is there progress (4c)?" as an activity unfolds (moves forward). Progress focuses on moving towards the completion of an activity or, at least, the extent to which the valued purpose of the activity is being achieved. The final question about progress, is how to tell members about it (4d). This is a discrimination based on what the supervisees know about the plan's means and its end objective. This telling or querying of supervisees can be done individually or as a group—it depends on the complexity of the activity and how the group is organized in time and space. It is here that a supervisor's tactics spring out into the open. Just how civil was the telling? The two primary methods are through direct telling and questioning members about their progress or lack of it. This is the reason for the supervising heuristic "always look for progress." It is an especially important guide when interacting with young children; they are just learning to observe what their behavior is producing—often in others— as the activity unfolds.

5. Point Out Consequences

Supervisors need knowledge of the types of consequences—emotional, access, and restructuring (Chapter 5)—and be on the lookout for them (5a). What ones could occur (5b) is a discrimination based on the observations that pivot around seeing and stopping potential conflicts (an unwanted group consequence), and seeing any adaptations by members that kept the activity moving forward—the imaginative, in-the-moment behaviors like helping, sharing, or organizing materials in ways that may have been left out of the plan. As with step 4d, indicating progress, these consequences can be pointed out through a variety of statements or queries (5c). But as supervisees gain experience, questioning allows supervisors to evaluate the extent of their knowledge or their attention to the activity.

Consequences occur during and after an activity. Activity behaviors "produce" such consequences continually. So, what are the consequences of an activity that are or could happen (5a, 5b)? To observe and examine them requires the individual and social perspectives on consequences (Chapter 5). They must be directly taught.

Progress focuses on seeing the difference between the plan and the completion of the activity. Activity consequences emerge from both the product (activity ends, macro-management) and the process to achieve them (activity means, micro-management). Perhaps the end for an activity is that all members want to complete the objective of the activity, its T. The means of how they get to this end, is a mix of the supervisor and supervisees behaviors, which is a two-way street. Our focus is on what means the supervisor uses to achieve progress that produces the ends. If the supervisor's tactics (means) result in everyone achieving the end (a restructuring consequence—perhaps they wrote a story) and everyone enjoyed doing so (emotional consequence), then we have a supervisor who has been civil to activity members while "getting the job done." In other words, the supervisor has demonstrated *cohesive micro-management*.

The step of pointing out consequences (5), requires that supervisors "roughly know" what consequences are possible in the short or long term (5a) and then determine which are going to happen (5b). The activity plan should include these. All these discriminations can go down the drain if the supervisor can't find a way to express (point out or ask about) the consequences to activity members (5c). Consequences, as Chapters 4 and 5 pointed out, are powerful: they push (induce) behavior into the future and help cement (consequent) activity conditions to its behavior. In the future the conditions' elements, often as members and other resources, will come to positively induce starting other activities.

The supervisor's practical, real-time tactics for pointing out consequences emerge from the teachers' modeling them when supervising. The first step is to describe the consequences. The second asks children to describe the consequences they are producing. The third asks children to predict their consequences and confirm their predictions. The fourth is to have them plan activities and the supervising methods they will use to produce the planned consequences. Focusing on these consequences adds to the unity of the supervisees, so that when they supervise themselves and others, they will be able to point them out with statements and questions.

Pointing out consequences also involves indicating what behavior brought them about with their set of resources. This points out the contingency of the activity. Few children and adults see the range of consequences their actions produce without being trained to do so. Additionally, the more experienced participant observes different consequences than a novice. Experienced participants have seen and felt them relative to participating across a range of the management strategies and across a range of activities. Thus, they have multiple views of the activity world because they have been supervised and have supervised. Over time, supervisors and supervisees switch places, so that they observe and feel consequent event from both directions.

When children change their supervised or supervisor positions within activities multiple times over the early years of schooling, they observe and feel at least the emotional consequences produced by different types of tactics both of supervisees and supervisors. If we reward cohesive and correct coercive management of both, children will be able to name and describe their and others' management. To do this will require the technical behavior of reading and writing. Combined with the intervention strategy, any coercive management tactics that are developing, may be examined and altered before they become ingrained. This is the specific valued purpose of the intervening strategy (Chapter 16).

Supervising Heuristics

Graphic 14.4 presents nine supervising heuristics, which are applicable to both teachers and children. Relative to quality management, these are "general guiding rules" called *heuristics*,[1] which were first clearly promoted by George Pólya in *How to Solve it,* [2] a book about mathematical problem solving. Graphic 14.4 presents nine supervising heuristics applicable to supervising for both teachers and children.

Nearly all engineers, as well as mathematicians, promote the use of heuristics to facilitate problem solving.[3][4] These heuristics would eventually be taught as part of supervising. If children can read, doing so is easy (see the study cards and flowcharts in the Appendices). The parentheses at the end of each heuristic identifies at least one feature of a group that I think each heuristic helps promote.

Children can learn to supervise many activities without spelling out these heuristics. However, by directly teaching them (there are a number of methods to do so), much is gained. First and foremost, these guidelines are relevant to all day-to-day activities outside the classroom. As a result, they

SUPERVISING HEURISTICS

1. Think about what supervising is needed before an activity begins. *(Strengthen the Chance for Progress)*
2. Reduce supervising as members' knowledge increases. *(Build Future Supervisors)*
3. Supervise only the steps of the activity that require it. *(Increase Participation)*
4. If the activity can be performed in many ways, let those involved decide how. *(Engender Creativity)*
5. If the activity can't be performed, let those involved learn how. *(Foster a Desire to Learn)*
6. Always, look for progress and its consequences. *(Seek Out Quality)*
7. Avoid conflicts by talking about progress and its consequences. *(Build Harmony)*
8. Use questions to point out progress and its consequences. *(Build Rational Citizens)*
9. Connect members' behavior with the values of the group. *(Build Civil Citizens)*

GRAPHIC 14.4: Supervising heuristics.

---

[1] https://en.wikipedia.org/wiki/Heuristic
[2] https://en.wikipedia.org/wiki/How_to_Solve_It
[3] https://en.wikipedia.org/wiki/George_Polya
[4] https://en.wikipedia.org/wiki/TRIZ

will help promote children's successful transfer of supervising when they are out in the world.

When teaching these heuristics, only a few examples of each heuristic will be needed for their basic understanding and use. Most of these examples can be from children's direct experience with being supervised and supervising. From this point, children will be able to continually add examples that are relevant to each heuristic. If they memorize these, they will always have them as their "touch stones" to successful supervising. Heuristics are like "mini-valued purposes" that give direction to both rational and civil problem-solving behavior. Supervising is a strategy with steps, discrimination sub-steps, and heuristic guides that help achieve "success." But the success only happens if supervising is supported by 1) the managees and 2) all the other strategies of management's system of strategies, especially organizing and planning.

Summary

Most classroom plans establish what needs to be done, the resources required, and the technical and management behaviors to carry out an activity. The plan is an expression of a complex contingency, it specifies the structure for functioning and the functioning methods to achieve the value-purpose end. Effective supervisors know each part of the plan. Beyond that, they must assess the participants' experience and what the participants consider important to success. All of this knowledge guides how they supervise. When an activity is ongoing, the continual and iterative application of directing activity flow (3), looking for progress (4), and establishing consequences (5) occur. However, even for the knowledgeable, experienced activity members, this flow is critical to continuing the relevant activity behaviors. Knowing how requires direct instruction.

15

Planning Strategy

Planning is a strategy that guides managers in the design of activities to meet some valued purpose. Within the classroom, the valued purpose to be planned and achieved can become a moral value purpose. At some point in time, nearly all large-scale human activity purposes control, to some extent, how members interact or produces consequences for members in the distant future. Realizing this relationship does not guarantee that planning can predict this change. Three problems exist. First, we can't see the consequences of any purpose-based behavior perfectly; some do not show up until some distant future has arrived. Second, our rationality is bounded by at least our ignorance of both means to our purpose or its achieved ends. Third, carrying out multiple valued purposes can cascade into something totally unexpected. Thus, caution is required.

From a management perspective, planning leads to replanning. Yet, there are those who throw out the plan without digging into the evidence that would help get the plan working with greater efficiency and benefits. This is the adult world where such a "political strategy" has Me/My written all over it. It is often called "power politics," which has nothing to do with creating societal unity, besides disrupting or destroying it.

Teachers, like all engineers, use planning to design or improve a design that in the classroom involves activities that instructs children in some part of some technical repertoire. Planning is itself part of a technical repertoire—a management strategy—that is taught directly to young children, so that they can design and evaluate their own activities (Chapter 1). The present moral-value claim is that teaching planning to young children will help them avoid many of the dangers that will confront them when the world is theirs. They will be able to give their future a higher probability of unity and, thus, a stronger starting point from which to solve the problems the last few generations are leaving them. With a planning repertoire, teachers prepare children to see the risks and at the same time hand them a tool to move forward.

All plans have "degrees of success." We base the degree of success on the evidence gathered during and after the plan's implementation. Planning is abductive reasoning (Chapter 1). Planners embed agreed-on-evidence and the method to gather it within their plans. Planning managers make the evidence for success 1) a public, social contract between members, and 2) any manager or managers should be able to gauge a plan's success during the plan's implementation or post implementation. These two steps in *evidence management* are known as part of what scientists call *"objectivity,"* which is systems-critical to the scientific and technological processes. Evidence management consists of *evidence identification* that is impersonal and *evidence gathering* that is impartial.[1, 2]

There are *risks* inherent in any plan in terms of its means of production and the end consequences that the means produce. When we plan within the scope of available knowledge, the planning behavior is classified as rational. When our rational behavior breaks down—a point where means of production are not those desired or ends of production produce coercive consequences—we replan and replan again, if necessary. This is a *recursive process* because the evidence gathered and the patterns exposed changes the planners and very gradually their planning process. This process represents a *qualitative change* in both planners and planning. With language, we pass these changes on—as scientists, engineers, and artists do—through modern communication methods.

With training, multiple managers should be able to observe—within the *limits of observational precision*—the same data points. With young children, evidence identification and gathering needs to be done with special care. Here, we continue the focus on moral management behavior (VAM interactions) of children and the degree of success in obtaining T (in VAM-T). For the most part, the plans children come to design and then evaluate focus on the impact they have on members of the classroom.

Objectivity is only one of many problems that arise in planning our moral-value selves to live within some social system, some context. It is difficult because everyone becomes both experimenter (manager) and experimentee (managee of the evidence investigation). Part of this difficulty concerns observational bias (Chapter 6), which is part of impartiality. At the same time, all plans have limits-of-application and flaws. But if a plan's consequences are without "major flaws," or "true enough for now" members begin to take the plan and replicate it, perhaps with improvements within the classroom.

What is the "goodness" in finding flaws and the resulting redesign work? It builds what all humans need. Some call it "resilience," some "endurance," and some "fortitude." Chapter 7 called it "persistence." No matter what it is called, it helps increase the probability of survival and, perhaps, a "good life."

But on the way to applying the twin peaks of objectivity and replication to our daily lives, something has happened. It may be the result of several

[1] Rescher, Nickolas. (1997). *Objectivity: The obligations of impersonal reason.* Notre Dame, IN: University of Notre Dame Press. Chapter 1 and beyond.
[2] https://en.wikipedia.org/wiki/Objectivity_(science)

events. First, there may be obdurate Me/My moral-value subgroups—that obtrusively insist on focusing on specific means or ends without looking at the evidence. Second, there may be a lack of "trust" of others, be they individuals, corporations, or governments. Third, there may be some that do not believe in the knowledge gained from science and technology's past work. Fourth, some may be ignorant of the methods of science and technology. The controlling reasons, as beliefs, may be one or a combination of these. Would it serve us better to focus on a) the plan as a whole, b) how it can be evolved within the system environment, c) its impact on the larger system, d) a willingness to wait for evidence, or e) understand that redesign is involved in the evolution of any plan? Teaching planning can give children all of these perspectives that contribute to the unity of members.

Every one of these five reasons relates to moral-value conflicts. Science has never been value-free—even though many have claimed so. We see how non-free it is today through the work of bioscience and medical technologies that seek to cure, improve, and redesign ourselves, so that individuals have a chance to survive and live long.[3] Can we give children a planning repertoire that helps to engender a moral-value unity or a planning repertoire that brings about something else?

Although there may be several good plan options to achieve moral-value unity, these are often tackled, in the early stages at least, through research and development. Within the management system of strategies, the learning strategy is applicable (Chapter 17).

Like all of the management strategies, planning is a social technology invented and developed by humans for humans. It is presented from the moral-value viewpoint of members' working together using cohesive management methods in the context of moral values. It is an elaborate form of our newest sociotechnology tool: *social communication* (Chapters 5 and 8). This chapter presents planning as the foundation for achieving unity. In taking this road, the aim is to avoid bias while promoting objectivity and replicability to achieve the means and ends of a plan, which in the classroom is related to achieving the VAM-T repertoire relationships. When groups can do so day-in and day-out, they have achieved an important form of replication: *moral-management replication*. Consistent moral management, as our daily newscasts inform us, is not easily achieved. From persons on the street, scientists across disciplines, leaders within corporations, to presidents and prime ministers of nations, we find examples of inconsistent moral managers. One purpose of a planning repertoire is to spot such inconsistent managers.

---

[3] G. H. von Wright (1993). *The tree of knowledge and other essays.* New York, NY: E. J. Brill. Chapter 10, especially p. 177; however, the whole chapter gives the context.

Planning as Government

In general, the planning strategy is first used to create governments, large or small, that specify how two or more individuals will interact. When governments plan, they generally begin by establishing policies. *Policy planning* focuses on the values of the group. It may state them with more or less rigor and establish the basic social structures needed to carry them out. This is what national governments do in their constitutions. This is what corporations do in mission statements.

Once established, the plans that move a government or corporation forward are about 1) the means to achieve ends and 2) the ends to achieve. They do both within their moral values and the structures thus far established. This is *procedural planning*. Its valued purpose focuses on the design and evaluation of plans that fit within the morals, other values, and social structures established. Policy planning that includes children is addressed briefly in the section on Children and Planning. This chapter focuses on procedural planning.

The extent to which and the ways in which children participate in planning identifies that form of government, just as it does across the Nations of the World. As young children, they begin by participating in other manager's plans. This early form of government is an autocratic regime. It must be so, given their developmental biology.

No matter what governing background children have encountered, when they enter their initial classrooms, at least three facts are clear:

1. Children do not have a language to guide their planning behavior.
2. They do not understand the governing processes between citizen-citizen and citizen-government relationships.)
3. Third, they have no group planning experience.

All three facts point to the need for direct instruction. The first difficult educational decision is what we want them to become. Do we want to give them the social tools to interact as a unified group? Or should we take some other direction, so that they are nothing more than vassals of the oligarchs or dictators, be they benevolent or not? If the latter, there would be no need for this chapter or this book. Since, this chapter exists, the decision is obvious, at least to the author. It is a moral-value decision.

The chapter begins by understanding what planning entails for young children. Teaching planning and the other VAM repertoires go hand-in-hand. In combination, they move children into a participative "frame-of-mind." This teaching is a long-term project, not just another lecture or short-term course. Only as a long-term project can children "internalize" the strategy—instill it. In developing this frame-of-mind, conflicts will emerge.

These new managers are children after all. They are just starting to learn. Nearly everything is new and exciting to them. They behave inductively toward this newness with their nearly boundless energy. They imitate and follow the group in all sorts of ways that may engender conflicts. Conflict resolution techniques will be needed (Chapter 16) as the steps of planning are undertaken over and over again. But with careful modeling and prompting, unified planning behavior will emerge.

Planning's Advantages

Relative to our daily lives, planning helps us meet goals, achieve rewarding and enjoyable consequences, overcome challenges and obstacles, and satisfy our values. The deeper our understanding of planning and the more we integrate it into our family, classroom, school, and work activities, the more we learn to influence the quality of life in the here and now. Thus, it becomes our DNA of tomorrow. The assumption is that nearly everyone wants to influence their quality of life, which is just an extension of the assumption of how humans seek to control the world (Chapter 1). It is taken, here, as an axiom, such as those that begin with "we hold these truths to be self-evident."

By teaching children to plan, even more gains are made. They take another step toward being independent and adaptive rational, civil citizens, who are aware of the control they exert over others. When children can plan, it frees caregivers from doing all the planning. Caregivers gain a "partner" from an early point. This results, as with organizing and supervising, in more time for other things—things that could build even stronger relationships with others, helping to strengthen our social-enterprise. These partnerships illustrate to children that they have membership and the ability to contribute. This inspires what many call "trust" in others and "confidence" in themselves.

Everyone benefits emotionally as well from the resulting partnership. Negative emotions should be radically reduced when facing new problems. The language and process of planning provides everyone with a way to talk about and to begin handling individual and group problems as they arise. The emotional response "What shall we do!" is replaced by "Some planning is needed, let's begin." Thus, rational thought becomes the "first action." It can begin before fear strikes home.

The more deeply rooted the planning strategy, its language, and perceived benefits, the greater the individual's or group's "resistance" to letting the old primitive brain "switch on" aggression and related emotions. Instead, the rational brain switches on and begins going about its problem-solving, fear-reducing, and mayhem-limiting business. However, to make this switch from our flight-fight-freeze methods to this new rational method of control, requires extensive training and practice in using the "preternatural ability" or "prescient understanding" by those in a field of study. Doing so results in avoiding problems like cognitive, social, and governmental gridlock.[4] The reactions that spring from the unknown or past encounters are squelched by the immediate call to action by rationally-trained citizens that think before they leap. Yet, action cannot wait for big problems to occur, our inductive behavior must be primed. It only takes one *trusted* group member with advanced discipline understanding to announce real or potential problems, so that prevention or lowered risk prevail. To some, this is called seeing "problems coming forwward." [5] Within all disciplines, there are such people.

From a teaching perspective, such behavior is the interaction between a person's disciplinary knowledge, a strong repertoire within it, and humans' ability to generalize (make inferences) beyond the "strictly known." We are not usually prescient outside our specialty domain, but with group unification, there comes a "trust" between members and those with prescient understanding. Now, *the group* can set out to make strong inductive inferences about real and potential problems from what most would call "insufficient hard evidence." Within a unified group, it only takes one who sees ahead, to keep the group successfully moving forward. Such individuals help groups avoid catastrophe, but only if we have learned to trust with our eyes wide open—to see a manager's "real" intensions for providing this "future view."

Planning as a Process

Planning is a verbal interaction process (Chapters 4 through 8) that builds plans by minimally or radically modifying one or more existing ones with new or old combinations of ideas. Two main types of plans are relevant to teaching children: 1) those that simply modify an existing plan that has no real effect on the surrounding context and 2) those that are new and require insertion into an existing context, often changing other activities as well. All of today's social and environmental problems are of the latter type. However, teaching planning to children begins with the former.

Planning has five distinct steps that break into two distinct components (Graphic 15.1). The discriminations and operations for five planning steps include: plan, design, select, implement, and evaluate. A total of five words and their action variants—planning, designing, selecting, implementing, and evaluating. Each of these steps require making a set of discriminations to achieve each step. Like all the strategies, planning begins with a discrimination. In this case, "Is planning needed?"

---

[4] Rescher, Nicholas (2005). *Complexity: A philosophical overview.* New Brunswick, NJ: Transaction Publishers. See Chapter 10, sections 3 and 4.

[5] Lewis, M. (2021). *The premonition.* New York, NY, USA: W. W. Norton & Company.

The first three steps involve the identification of the planning problem to be solved, the design of a plan to solve it, and its selection by members. This first component can be called *thinking ahead* for young children. Thinking ahead builds a *prediction argument* that represents the managers' best hypothesis about how to solve a problem. This prediction involves ideas that fit together, are congruent with past knowledge, and the evidence data that planners think will tell them about how well this plan works during implementation and beyond—remembering that day-in and day-out implementation is a form of *replication* that gives evidence of quality control.

The second component, called *thinking behind,* consists of steps four and five. Thinking behind builds an *evaluation argument.* This evaluation argument's conclusion is based on the evidence gathered (the thinking behind premises) and identifies how well the prediction, the thinking ahead, worked. It points to areas of success and the points at which redesign may be required.

The plan is first implemented (step 4). During this time, managers observe and take data (gather evidence) on two fronts. First, they observe if the implementation followed the plan. Second, they observe how well the plan is working once implementation is underway (the plan is "in play") or is completed (the plan's means and ends consequence data has been gathered). When the evidence is gathered, the evaluation of the plan can begin (step 5).

The implementation and evaluation steps, 4 and 5, are not separate. Often, a plan may be functional (macro-management ends are achieved) but its implementation (micro-management means) has problems. At the other extreme, the plan can't be implemented because one or more resources are missing (Chapter 11), be it a tool or the behavior of members. The managers may have to stop the implementation and redesign the plan even before implementation is completed and its consequences assessed. (A variation of the intervening strategy can be used here.) Often a plan fails because the means or ends consequences—emotional, access, or restructuring—may not have been the ones predicted by the plan. These types and degrees of "failure," almost always require redesigning a plan (replanning).

As with the other management strategies, we begin teaching planning to young children at the "step" level of detail (Graphic 15.1). When children can read, they can begin working with a more complex planning process, as the one illustrated in Graphic 15.2. This involves the discriminations that gives each step of the strategy a higher probability of success, just like the other strategies. These discriminations become necessary as activity complexity

❖ **PLANNING** ❖

1. Is Planning Needed?
2. Design New Plan
3. Select New Plan
4. Implement Plan
5. Evaluate Plan

GRAPHIC 15.1: Planning Steps

increases. It is at this point that many, educators and non-educators, have the following belief:

Young children can't learn such a process during the elementary grades.

This is a false belief. It becomes false as soon as one has the needed knowledge base and methodological tools to implement the strategy. These include 1) the direct instruction analysis and design tools that make the abstract and the covert thinking involved in planning overt and 2) the use of children's well known existing activities like eating, walking, brushing teeth, tying shoes as the starting place for learning to plan. These activities are already examples of a plan. Children know the steps and can even verbalize most of them. Others have planned them and helped youngsters implement them. We use this knowledge base and the children as modelers in the context for teaching abstractions like cause and effect (of which a plan is an example), consequences, implement, data, evaluation, and the others that populate Graphic 15.2, as well as the strategy heuristics discussed below.

We see the failure to understand planning as a complex process through the plans made by the World's governments, who for the most part have no idea how to evaluate what they design (or listen to the evaluators), often because the plan is made unduly complex by various partisan Me/My groups. Another reason is that governments are often set up, so that its planners don't have to experience the consequences of what they plan; they are "above the law" citizens. Our children can do better, but only if we teach them.

Planning's Discriminations & Operations

The five steps of planning are expanded in Graphic 15.2. The *discrimination query* sub-steps direct the thinking needed to complete each step with a greater probability of success, fewer flaws, and less risk. What follows goes well beyond what is needed to plan with children, at least for the first three grade levels. The idea is to provide a fairly detailed picture of planning, so that the sub-step discriminations can be made and, later, incorporated into their future adult activities. Although planning can begin with the teacher as a strong guide, the use of the full strategy must wait until the children can read. It helps if the terms used in the planning strategy can be embedded into the reading and spelling curricula.

1. Is Planning Needed?

Planning begins with discriminating that an activity plan has a problem (step 1). This is the sensing of a problem. Its affirmative answer cascades into two other discriminations that focuses this initial recognition or feeling. The first is to clearly identify what activity actually needs changing (1a). This helps avoid changing the wrong activity. Because an activity is not working well does not mean it is the activity that requires changing. The cause can occur because of a related activity or because of an activity at the larger systems level like the school. If the planners think they have identified the activity that needs changing, then they must discriminate why it needs changing (1b). This "why" is not an attempt to "detail the cause" of the plan's dysfunction. It only seeks a general view or idea that the activity plan produces some set of undesirable consequent events relative to its means and ends. Often these events emerge because the plan is unclear about the relationships of "rights" and "duties." New technology can also make past relationships unnecessary and cause tensions between various members at various government levels. Such cases are just another reason for teaching planning: change should not scare citizens, nor should the thought of duties.

However, things are not so abstract when initially teaching planning to young children. For example, the activity plan may work (ends are achieved), but the consequences of its implementation (as its means to achieve its ends) are unsatisfactory. Perhaps everyone is exhausted even though everyone learned the required material or achieved some product like a poem or paper. Or the plan may not work within the time frame, but everyone enjoyed it and learned something.

For young children, most often, a human behavior, as a resource, is missing. The goal is to recognize that this something is or is not needed, which are the *means-or-ends consequences* desired. The two sub-steps of step 1 focus on what activity needs changing and the reasons for making the change.

❖ PLANNING ❖

1. **IS PLANNING NEEDED?**
   a. What activity needs changing?
   b. Why change the activity?
2. **DESIGN NEW PLAN**
   a. What steps need changing?
   b. How can they be designed?
   c. Does anything else change?
   d. Can the steps be followed?
3. **SELECT NEW PLAN**
   a. Does the plan fit the resources?
   b. What are the consequences?
   c. Does the plan fit our morals?
   d. Is everyone willing to try?
4. **IMPLEMENT PLAN**
   a. Is the data being gathered?
   b. Is the plan being followed?
5. **EVALUATE PLAN**
   a. Was the plan followed?
   b. What were the consequences?
   c. Were there problems?
   d. Is change needed?
   e. If yes to 5d, then go to 2a.

GRAPHIC 11.2: Planning steps and discrimination queries.

The better we know our activities, the easier it is to answer the questions of step 1. If we want a class science trip, it may be necessary to alter some other activity or activities to gain time, alter how they are performed, and gather money, or some combination of these. However, we never begin in a vacuum. The difficulty is seeing the relationship between 1) what we want to bring about and 2) what needs to be altered to make it so. Often, we begin with a plan or plans used by others and make alterations that fit the present situation—the context of resources and values. This is exactly what a technical discipline's professionals try to do.

Discriminating what activity plan or plans that need changing (1a) and why change them (1c) help planners avoid the trap of stating solutions before they have identified the problem. The three discriminations questions of Step 1 are usually interactive. The attempt to answer any one of them may change answers to the others. The questions of Step 1 can also undergo change, as Step 2 is undertaken.

2. Design New Plan

When we design new plans (Step 2), we first begin with the plan identified in 1b and, then, ask (2a), "What changes are needed?" This discrimination focuses on the components of the identified plan (1b). We then discriminate further by asking (2b), "How can they be designed?" With children, we provide them with experience in changing planning steps of an existing activity. Since we know the activities that children need to alter, this teaching activity is well within the boundary of our existing activity knowledge of how they can be performed or are usually performed. Even here we (as caregivers and teachers) want to be objective, unbiased, and flexible. And we must do so even when we see the errors in children's changes to a plan or a replanning. Experiencing failure has been important throughout the history of thought and action. Chapter 6 called this "developing persistence."

The discriminations continue with question 2c, "Does anything else change?" This requires looking within and, at times, across activities. As a new plan is being designed, it is important for example to consider development time. If children do not know some of the management behaviors (not necessarily the strategies) required then development time (as learning and practice) will be required during early implementation. If such development is not taken into account, unforeseen conflicts can arise.

Making changes requires the same *systems thinking* perspective identified in the resource guidelines for the organizing strategy (Chapter 11, Graphic 11.3). Thus, teaching organizing before planning, sets the stage for planning. What is required is pointing to the resource list and asking, does anything else change? This simple step initiates dealing with discrimination question 2c, "Does anything else change?" If the children have 1) a history of walking through the classroom's activity plans, 2) have received verbal communications (Chapter 8) as they did so, and 3) have been taught to observe and name the types of consequent events they produce, then their suggestions of what changes to make will often be practical and accurate enough to move forward, even if they prove wrong.

What remains is the interaction across activities. If the pattern of the new activity plan is consistent with other activity patterns, then there is no need to alter other activities. For children, most activities only require behavior-development time, especially if the "special activities" identified in Chapter 2 are in place, so that children can always stay appropriate from activity to activity. But there are times when options need to be added to the existing special activities.

Next, children must answer discrimination query 2d, "Can the steps be followed?" Their answers for the various steps added or changed need not be practical or reasonable from our viewpoint, only theirs (unless real danger is involved). If there is agreement. they can move forward. If not in full agreement, they can always vote or play rock-paper-scissors. If the discussion gets "heated," the intervening strategy applies (Chapter 16).

3. SELECT NEW PLAN

Selecting a new plan (Step 3) is often called a *design-level evaluation*. It "selects" or "approves of" a single plan as the prediction of what will work well enough to get started with the new activity. This is a *frame-of-mind* acceptance. Not all members may agree on means or ends. All they need is an agreement to get started. In adult planning, this step often implies that multiple plans result from Step 2. However, young children do not proceed this way. They initially build one plan bit by bit, changing a step here and a step there as they move forward.

The discriminations of Step 3 begin by asking if the needed resources are available (3a). If they lack resources, then design modifications are required. This necessitates returning to Step 2 and doing some redesign work. If the resources are available, designers next discriminate its potential consequences (3b), which requires knowledge of the types of consequences. This clarifies the design (step 2).

The selection process continues with 3c, "Does the plan fit our morals?" The answer requires that the children can discriminate if the plan follows the rules of the classroom, its moral values. Problems may arise if following the rules have not been seen has helping them learn or has not produced cohesive emotional, access, and restructuring consequences. It helps extensively if the "rules" have been introduced as the "duties" of the classroom (Chapter 9). What has been left out is the linked relationship of the VAM-T repertoires, which is a detailed way to make the 3c discrimination.

When the answers to 3a, b, and c are completed and positive, it is usually just a small inferential leap to answering 3d, "Is everyone willing to try?" If there is a group "yes," they move ahead with step 4. This group willingness to go ahead with a plan is often dependent on what many would call the "trust" of other members. This "trust" does not spring from nothing. It emerges as a function of the three design requirements: 1) histories in carrying out activity plans, 2) social communication that exposed the interrelationships between members, and 3) having been taught to observe and feel the types of consequences they produce by their interactions during activities. Social communication—by both teachers and children—unites the answers to 3a-c. Children see who is doing what for whom and the consequences of doing so. This takes time to achieve, but eventually children will be able to perform the social communication between themselves.

At times, a consensus can only be reached by one of two methods. First, they vote on their willingness to try the plan (3d). Second, teachers can intervene as a mediator (Chapter 16) to facilitate consensus. However, the turning point of consensus depends on the extent to which children have experienced a variety of cohesive consequences from past plans, ones that the teacher has designed. They will learn to "trust" in their plans as they now do for the teachers. With consensus, Step 4 ensues. But first two important issues.

Evidence and Plans

What has been skipped to this point is the need for evidence, the data that supports or rejects the prediction argument. It begins to be considered in Step 2d, and expanded during Step 3. Evidence supports a proposition.[6] It usually takes a declarative form, but in a planning situation a question is more useful because it asks for a *discrimination from data*, not a *discrimination from preference*. The discriminations of Step 3 can be compacted into a general question, "How well will the plan work?" We seek to determine if our prediction argument's conclusion (the plan) has a chance of working as we think it should. Is it such that we think it is "true enough" to move forward?[7] This is a cognitive need, especially in regards to our moral values (3c).

The answers to the questions of Step 3 point directly at the evidence needed to support or reject question 3d. For children, the evidence, as data points, are expressed as answers to four questions.

1. Could the plan be followed?
2. Was the implementation completed?
3. Were the consequences realized?
4. Was the Intervening Strategy used? (Were moral-management relationships broken?)

These are, in fact, the fundamental evaluation questions of any plan, be it by children or governments who design plans dealing with social problems or issues. For children, we help them reason about the relationship between these questions. From this reasoning, they reach a judgement (3d).

---

[6] https://en.wikipedia.org/wiki/Evidence
[7] Elgin, C. (2017). *True enough*. Cambridge, MA: MIT Press. (Very roughly, the phrase "true enough" acknowledge a need to weaken a commitment to "truth" in order to allow our representations and exemplars as a basis for inference and action when our interests are cognitive, as in step 3c, and we want to avoid idiosyncrasy, bias and chance.)
@ https://vdoc.pub/documents/true-enough-3mji8fkfkuog

When step 5 is undertaken, the same questions are used. Step 4 involves the implementation and gathering of data. In the design phase (step 3) these questions are *design-level evaluation questions*. In step 5, they are *implementation-level evaluation questions* that judge the "fitness" of the plan. However, it is never an all or nothing discrimination judgement. It is a continuum of possible judgements from highly positive to highly negative. Usually, the judgement is to replan that adjusts parts of the plan to fit the contextual problems that the implementation exposed. This replanning judgement is another expression of the *frame-of-mind* of planners, implementers, and evaluators.

The more complex the plan, the more difficult it is to make the needed judgement. This is true of social programs that impact human lives and, thus, we recognize that ignorance is not bliss. Notice how scientists and engineers can get to the moon and back, develop and control nuclear reactions, and modify genetic code to cure that which was once thought incurable. They have dug deep into the subject matter, made plans, implemented and evaluated them (even if they have had to fight for the research dollars). They tried and tried again, getting "righter" each time.

Yet there is one key place where the "we got it going and now we will make it better" *frame-of-mind* is not applicable. It is when the consequences of implementation are highly dangerous. When dangerous consequences are probable or exposed, we turn to research and development, and then to small tests before widespread implementation. However, children are not working at this stage and will not be doing so until much later, usually when they are full-fledged scientists and engineers. All of this *activity-to-avoid-danger* seeks out the evidence required to build stronger beliefs about proceeding or to abandon the activities. We return to evidence in Step 5.

From Simple to Advanced Planning

When children reach more advanced planning, Step 2 can be seen in terms of at least three types of planning:

1. A subgroup designs the planning and it is used.
2. Several groups design a plan and one is selected by all, and
3. Several groups design a plan and then a new plan is created from the chosen parts that members select.

Each of these requires "trust" in the planning group or the selected plan. The second requires a "group vote" and "trust" in the selected group and their plan. As the choice of a design is made, the members go through discrimination questions 3a-c, which sets-the-occasion for agreement on question 3d. The third requires "working together" without "gridlock" or "emotional" problems—the intervening strategy is not required. Here, a new question rises, "What parts give the best plan?" This is an unknown even if the members "walk through" questions 3a-c as a group. Again, a vote or mediation is required. For all of these, trust is built up through a history of interactions that verbal communication exposes.

All three types lead to potential problems with answering question 3d, "Does everyone think it will work?" The above types emphasize the evolutionary development of plans and that all three variations should eventually be practiced. We must trust in planners and their plans. If children participate in all the steps of planning, they become experimenter and experimentee managers across a range of planning types. As a result, trust will emerge.

4. Implement the Plan

If the evidence for the plan has been identified and methods to gather it established, then during implementation two discrimination questions need to be asked and answered. Question 4a, is the data being gathered, helps ensure that it is being taken by someone. Interestingly, having one, two, or even three children set about observing the implementation, will precipitate three important changes. First, letting children observe and take the data "empowers" members, they have been the designers and so they are the ones taking "responsibility" for its evaluation. Second, it changes the behavior of the evaluated, they tend to behave more "rigorously" relative to the steps of the plan. Third, they do not fear such evaluations. This is not like a boss critically observing them, but of the group observing their own management. Now, they—especially with explicit social communication (Chapter 8)—see the power of their management from both ends, as managers and managees.

Question 4b, is the plan being followed, is somewhat redundant with the evaluation questions. It is included because all children can easily contribute to its observation (with training) at least within the subgroup in which they are working. If a plan is not followed, then it can't be clearly evaluated. Learning the steps may be needed or following it may not have been possible because of extreme flaws.

5. Evaluate the Plan

Implementation gathered the data. Step 5 lays out the answers to the evaluation questions. In the above section on *Evidence for Plans*, four clear questions were asked. The following illustrates why these are important evidence questions for social plans.

Evidence Question 1, could the plan be followed, was directly addressed in design element 2d, can the steps be followed? The evaluation question 5a, "Was the plan followed?" is its evaluation counterpart—the plan's prediction descendent. By knowing the answer to this question, we observe the "gross" usefulness of the plan. No matter if the answer is more positive than negative, or vice versa, we ask the other evidence questions to observe why the results were so. This question is mostly about the means of the plan.

Evidence Question 2, was the implementation completed, is just an extension of the first evidence question. It adds an important element of any plan: time. If something can't be completed on time, there is a flaw in how the steps come together. Often, this question points out that the plan may be too complex. A little "simplifying" is needed. This means that human and non-human resources did not come together as needed in the time frame allowed. If the plan's implementation is not completed but the plan was "followable," then we know that the plan's resource analysis was faulty to some extent. However, we must be cautious here; as heuristic 8, outlined below, intones, "Give the plan time to work." Usually, the problem, like learning a dance step, takes time to become smooth relative to the rhythm of the music and the context of the dance. It is an important data point and suggests that more data is needed.

Evidence Question 3, were the consequences realized, were they directly addressed in selecting the new plan question 3b, what consequences are desired? This requires, as said, knowledge of the types of consequences and the use of social feedback in other activities to make them observable. If the plan could be followed (evidence question 1), at least some emotional consequences were realized. If the plan was completed (evidence question 2), then more can be said relative to access and restructuring consequences. These consequences relate to both means and ends. Given that most classroom activity plans focus on a technical, T, behavior as an end, the access and restructuring changes focus on what was learned and its potential use. This says a lot about the clarity of the teaching. Usually, if the consequences are not realized, a combination of teaching and the management behavior of children needs to be examined. To help untangle this confounding, the last evidence question is asked.

Evidence Question 4, was the intervening strategy used, is an indicator of design selection question 3c, does the plan fit our values? If the strategy was used, all-things-being-equal, it is an indicator that something is amiss with management or that the plan made it difficult for cohesive management to occur. All-things-being-equal suggests that if the intervening strategy is needed with frequency in other activities, no real conclusions can be drawn from a yes answer to question 4.

The judgement call of accepting, rejecting, or redesigning a new activity is never easy. Help comes in the form of a new plan that is just a small extension of an existing plan that the children have mastered. This untangles much of the confounding that can occur between resources, management, and teaching behaviors.

When children are asked, is change needed (5d)? they initially look at each other and have an expression of "I don't know!" It is here that teachers must take the lead and prompt them towards an answer by leading them down the "line of evidence" road. This is a verbal communications process (Chapter 8) that ensures that the answers to 5a-c and 3c-d are brought together. If we model this "relationship weighing" between questions early on, they will imitate. If they decide that change is needed, then move to 5e, if yes to 5d, then go to 2a. This entails redesign work. Redesign is usually not a time-consuming event; they have spotted the problems within the existing plan, via the evidence gathered.

Even when there are problems, there may be no reason to improve upon the plan (5d). It may just need more time to work. Even a partial solution may be acceptable for now. Giving the plan a chance to work is an important heuristic of planning, both from the perspective of giving children time to learn new behaviors and to see the desired consequences emerge, especially the emotional consequences that often surface fairly quickly from management tactics. If there is a history of negative emotions, it takes a history to eliminate them. As said, one of the most productive ways to build cohesive management is to put all children in various activity management roles. They are planners and implementers of plans, the supervisor and the supervised, the helper and the helpee, the guiders and the guided during the resolution of conflicts (Chapter 16).

Heuristics for Planning

Most groups have not learned to plan, practiced planning from an early age, or understood the general heuristics of planning; especially, 1) give a plan time to work, 2) quality springs from accurate evaluation and replanning, and 3) planning never ends because our world and our notion of quality evolve. These heuristics are "humanistic moral statements." They are planning's moral values because, in the long run, they alter the ways in which planners plan—they yield an impact on the planners, the planning process, and those for which the plan was devised. These heuristics support the evolution of the social structures and their survival. They guide the ways citizens, local governments, and Nations interact during planning and, thus, create emotional, access, and restructuring consequences for members (Chapter 7).

Planning, as a problem-solving method, involves changing ourselves, so that we can observe and operate on ourselves or the world in new ways. Here we focus on changing our social selves—on how we interact with others. The planning strategy starts this process. However, a set of heuristics are applicable. They are just another way to "manipulate" ourselves to keep problem-solving behavior moving forward during the planning process. Graphic 15.3 presents the guides that apply to the "frame-of-mind" of planners.

Heuristic 1 points out that planning is a process that does not require any sort of answer to begin. So, planners should just start by confronting the problem as it is first perceived. The mathematician sits down with pencil and

PLANNING HEURISTICS

1. Plans evolve in the making; so, just start.
   (Use Planning as a Problem-Solving Tool)
2. All planning springs from previous plans.
   (You Never Start Totally in the Dark)
3. Constantly ask, "What needs to be changed or solved?" *(Keep Focused)*
4. Don't evaluate contributions during the design step. *(Increase Contributions)*
5. If stuck during the design step, switch to the learning strategy. *(Build Persistence)*
6. Plans seek to fit the values of the group. *(Promote a Humanitarian World)*
7. If possible, test the plan in a small way before trying a large implementation. *(Reduce Waste)*
8. Give the plan time to work. *(Get Enough Data for an Accurate Evaluation)*
9. Quality springs from accurate evaluation data and replanning. *(Promote Quality)*
10. Planning never ends because our world and our notion of quality evolve. *(There is No Perfect Plan)*

GRAPHIC 15.3: Planning heuristics.

paper, and manipulates the components of the question of interest. An answer may eventually emerge. A problem is solved.

Heuristic 2 tells designers that you never start in the dark. There is always some plan or plans that provide many bits and pieces that can help. Often a plan used in one context can be used in a different one with minor tweaks. Quality management practices give us more than a hint of this.

Heuristic 3 points out that there is always a chance to change the design. So, we keep asking what needs to be changed or solved. Often, a starting direction leads us somewhere other than our original thoughts. This leads to heuristic 7.

Heuristic 4 directs planners to get all the ideas or solution components as possible. It should really read "At each design stage (2a, 2b, and 2c), don't evaluate input until contributions are exhausted." It also applies to any redesign that the evaluation data (5d).

Heuristic 5 suggests that getting stuck while planning can be avoided by switching to other management behaviors—like the learning strategy. We do not want "designers' block." The best way to avoid it is to change the self by learning something new, even if we don't know exactly why or what that newness will entail.

Heuristic 6 reminds designers that they are working within a system even if they are only changing one activity or part of an activity. When a group has existing activities with existing values, this is the context within which they design.

However, there are times when revolution may be required, either within an existing activity or across the group of activities. Often, this need for change arises because new moral values emerge or old moral values are not being fulfilled. Presently, new technologies are requiring changes in our moral values that usually take the form of who should control what for whom. However, if the group "understands" Heuristic 10, then the need for revolution may be peacefully obtained.

Heuristic 7 focuses designers on the need for being cautious and saves bundles of time and emotion during implementation. So, they start small if possible. However, there are events like pandemics and environmental crises that require more than starting small; they require research and development as underpinning that make sure we get the design elements as close to "true enough" as possible. Even when extreme dangers exist, the evolution of an implemented plan will take place. This relates directly to Heuristic 10. We evolve in the doing.

Heuristic 8 reminds the designers and evaluators that a plan takes time to work, as does anything else in the world. So, give it time to work, so that an accurate evaluation can be made. Often if extra time or space are needed, replanning is required.

Heuristics 9 and 10 fit together in that a quality plan needs accurate evaluation data and replanning. But no matter how good designers are at planning, it never ends. Together, these last two heuristics are like a Taoist mantra that aims at making the designers *one-with-the-universe* of values, environment, and citizens. The mantra may foster the emergence of behavior that is akin to compassion, simplicity, selflessness towards the design of activities. Although all ten heuristics are related to cohesive management, the last two are most prominent in this regard.

The Complete Plan

When the process of planning is complete, what things should we see? Heuristic 10 noted that there is no perfect plan. Yet, there are those plans that we look at and know, at least with some high level of confidence, that these plans will create the desired cohesive emotional, access, or restructuring consequences if followed.

Just what are the components of a workable plan? In other words, what "image," "cognitive map," or "frame-of-mind" should we have as we go through the planning process? This image usually emerges after we have designed and evaluated a number of plans. It is essentially the *pattern of a plan*. With this pattern of thought, it is much easier to move forward. It becomes a setting even for planning and for moving through the planning steps. The *complete plan* is not a single image or frame-of-mind. It is an expanding set of images.

1. The planning is a contingency development strategy.
2. The plan attempts to develop a VAM-T arrangement of behavior to solve some problem.
3. The planning arranges the system of management strategies to control the emergence of particular consequent events.

These were all derived and simplified from quality management practices identified in Chapter 1 and now being used by many disciplines.

Think of a planning problem as an empty box. The design of a plan would fill that box, often in a haphazard fashion, until no space is left. Planners fill the box as they carry out the design steps of the planning process. The evaluation tells planners if the design was "true enough." The design of an activity has six distinct parts that are clarified by asking the following eight questions about the plan being designed.

1. What resources are needed? (People, time, place, tools, etc.)
2. What VAM-T behaviors are needed?
3. What are the possible consequences? (The types and who receives them are at the top of the list. They are moral values.)
4. How do 1, 2, and 3 fit together over time? (The activity is carried out with the help of the six other strategies.)
5. What implementation data needs to be gathered? (This is directly related to the contingency components 1-3, and the way they are carried out, 4.)
6. Who will gather the implementation data? (This all depends on question asked but generally involve observations or checklists.)
7. How will the data be evaluated? (Think in terms of who, how, and when the data will be evaluated.)
8. Will the expected data support the group's values?

The first three questions focus on an activity's contingency components—those things needed for any plan. The fourth spells out how the resources fit together and come together over time—a system question. Questions five, six, and seven focus on securing evaluation data. Question eight focuses on one of the most important consequences: how the plan, successful or not, fits with the moral values and the valued purpose to which the planners subscribe. What we often confront here is the relationship between management tactics and moral values, either those of the teacher, children, or both.

The above complete plan pattern-of-questions looks like the general outline for a science project. In essence, it is. Perhaps because life is much like a science experiment, one where all of us are experimenter and experimentee. Every plan has results—good or bad or ugly. The better our "experimental" plan—it is still a prediction about the future—the more likely that VAM success will emerge along with T.

Fortunately, the rigor of children's plans and their answers to the above questions are not the same as those required of scientists. We are not testing hypotheses like scientists do. We are testing *social procedures* much like an engineer tests the design of artifacts. The difference between the scientist and the social engineering of an activity is in the ability to change it so it fits our values and the other consequences desired. These are things on which the theoretical scientist does not focus. However, it is the *pattern*—the moving through contingency design, implementation, evaluation, and back again— that we want to keep in mind as we proceed. The pattern forms a system like the one outlined in Chapter 1—it is a sociotechnical pattern, one invented by humans for humans.

Our goal is to engineer other plans on top of other plans (replanning plans as we move forward in time with new evidence). Heuristics 9 and 10 point out that data is required to gain and maintain quality in an ever-changing world. Following this pattern is something that few who build social plans—policy design and its implementation—at the governmental level ever seem to gather without their ideologies and partisanship getting in the way of both the building or their evaluation. In other words, they do not know how to *think ahead* or *think behind*. Basically, most governments just forget about using data and giving a plan time to work (as both the planning strategy and its heuristics suggest).

ChildreN aNd PlaNNiNg

The key to teaching planning is to guide children in making "micro-plans." These involve taking one part of a plan and changing it. Children, for example, can plan a new way to organize an activity by changing some resource component or who locates, transfers, arranges or returns activity resources. Another, is "how to get help" (as a special activity) during one or more existing activities. The latter is often important when an activity involves working in groups to learn the T of VAM-T.

The plans children build will not dot every "i" or cross every "t," but they need to consider, if not achieve, the fundamentals of a complete plan, eventually. Still, it is critical that their plans be evaluated, but with a gentle hand. When children are in the early elementary grades give them a lot of latitude. The needed perspective towards their plans should be something like the following when things go wrong:

> *Gee-whiz, so you see the plan did not go so well,*
> *but what did you learn for next time?*

This is the *mistakes are no big deal* approach that encourages planning and learning from experience. It tells them that a plan gone wrong can be corrected and that many parts of it were right enough to be reused in replanning. They are learning as teachers are—nearly continuously. In other words, schooling does not teach children, or any of us, everything. However, the better they are at learning and planning, the faster they can meet their needs to survive and live well.

On the other side of the coin, what is done when things go "righter" with each plan or its replanning? A useful perspective may go something like:

This plan is working very well, but what do you think
will make it even better in the future?

Lastly, children can eventually do policy planning. Usually, this can only happen at the school level and when children have demonstrated a history of successful planning. To be a member of a school planning group requires stakeholders to consider participation requirements, both in terms of the range and limits of this participation.

What Blocks Complete Planning?

As said above, ideologies can get in the way. Past methods or thinking must be changeable. Yet, all things begin with ideas. A system of ideas is a theory or an artifact design like a better bottle opener. Yet, theories and artifacts are both tested and retested. This cycle of testing is one of the requirements of any VAM-T contingency (Chapter 3). The goal is not to prove the ideas; they are the axioms on which the theory or design begins. The proof of the theory or design is its functionality: Its "success" at doing something, directly or indirectly, in the real world. It is a pragmatic justification based on evidence. Our world is presently filled with ideologues and partisans, as those who "stick to the party's" agenda no matter what the prediction or evidence suggests. The primary consequence of unmovable ideologues and partisanship is governmental gridlock; The group goes nowhere on the problems that confront them.

There are five areas of ignorance that most ideologies and their partisans have that promotes gridlock. These include:

1. The extent to which or the ways a plan is implemented.
2. The range of consequences that result from a plan.
3. The time it takes for enough data to be gathered during evaluation (our patience while evidence is gathered).
4. Failure to draw conclusions and make changes to the plan based on gathered evaluation evidence.
5. Failure to distinguish between the means and ends of a plan.

The evaluation data being gathered that make up the arguments for the redesign of a plan is not from tradition, texts, the text's interpretation, or precedent.[8] These are types of past evidence. They can be foundations to or

---

[8] Huhn, Wilson. (2002). *The five types of legal arguments*. Durham, NC: Carolina Academic Press.

a guide during the designing of plans. That does not matter. Once the plan is in play, no matter what ideas were foundational, it is the evidence of the here and now, the action of ourselves on ourselves, that move us into the future. It does so in all of technical disciples from art to bioscience. The mishaps are usually of two kinds: Me/My moral-value-purpose perspectives of within discipline managers or, more often than not, the "political" control that enters into the disciplines.

However, the plan's evaluation evidence is about what the planners identified as how "smoothly" the plan was implemented and how "well" it is working.[9] Costs occur. There are implementation and maintenance costs. These costs are more than economic, they involve all types of consequences, including the "values fit" of the plan within the system in which the plan fits.

Gridlock emerges because the ideologues can't separate the ends—as what the plan can achieve—from the means—the steps that get to the ends. The result: Lines are drawn in the sand before planning ever gets off the ground. For example, the United States wanted to eventually give all citizens the right to vote (end). But the methods (means) to make it so was confronted by the Me/My perspective that resulted in Jim Crow laws that were implemented across a number of states. Only lip service was paid to the right to vote. These states—as governments—made sure part of their whole voting community did not have "reasonable" access to voting. We can say the same for most rights and duties around the world. The consequences are, even today, racial, social, economic, political, and sexual discrimination and persecution throughout nearly all, if not all, of the earth's systems of governments. These forms of denial of others' equality arise from the incongruence between their management tactics and their supposed moral-value purposes. Chapters 9 and 10 expanded on moral values, awareness, and their relationship.

Planning as an Adaptive Enterprise

Today, in the adult world, most management conflicts result from Me/My subgroups. What often ensues is counter control (Chapter 4) and gridlock. Thankfully, children are not yet emersed in these ideological-rigid subgroups. The present world of managers has not had a history planning as presented in this chapter.

Now imagine that we teach planning to children that is 1) based on evidence and replanning, 2) they practice this strategy, so that plans lead to cohesive means that induce value purpose ends over and over again, 3) they are aware of the power of the abductive process, 4) have been both planners and plan followers, and 5) have felt the consequences of following the heuristics of planning. What *emergent quality* will we see in both the individual child and the planning group? The prediction is that that they will

---

[9] https://en.wikipedia.org/wiki/Evidence

adapt, they will be flexible, and they will value "true enough" for now and move forward. To them, nothing is cast in stone. Rationality and civility prevail. They will be ideologues but not ones cast in stone. In a very real sense, they will be contextualists—as seeing the need for change when the context changes—and not textualists—as seeing what has been the case must continue to be the case because it is in some text, written some millennia ago.

Summary

The purpose of this chapter was to bring the process of planning out into the open, so that children can partake in its value in daily life and have a chance to make it part of their social repertoires. The end T (of VAM-T) is to give children a system of repertoires, so that they can govern themselves through the range of social, political, economic, and environmental problems we are leaving them. They will avoid moral value and management ignorance that leads to gridlock. They will spot this ignorance in-the-moment because they are aware and adjust their management as needed. If they do so, we should jump for joy because they can, then, be put in the class called *aware, rational, civil citizens*. What remains a concern is how they will transition into an "adult world" where many untrained planners exist in hordes (Chapter 19).

16

Intervening Strategy

Conflicts tear at the fabric of Social Unity. They have been doing so since dawn of human history. War and slavery were the norm. With the Age of Enlightenment, the pattern was altered, at least a bit. However, we are still far from anything like Social Unity. The intervening strategy is designed to reweave or help build that Social Unity within the classroom.

Conflicts may be an inevitable feature of the human condition. But can we reduce their severity and frequency? The answer is unknown at the larger societal level, but within the classroom, the answer is yes. The approach for doing so includes at least the following: 1) start when children are young, 2) provide them with a set of moral value statements—as a rule-based repertoire about how to interact with others, 3) link the moral value statements with the management behavior that represents following the value statements, 4) teach them a specific management strategy to resolve their conflicts when moral-management conflicts arise, and 5) teach the other management strategies to help children manage themselves to avoid conflicts.

Any method to reduce or eliminate conflicts does not stand alone. All the previous management strategies work with it. When we help and share, we make tasks easier. When we organize and supervise, we get activities going and keep them moving forward. When we plan and learn, we know where we are going and have some idea of how to get there. The intervening strategy is just part of a system of repertoires (VAM-T).

The system of management strategies reduces stress and the possibility of non-civil behaviors. The intervening strategy stops and resolves conflicts that occur. At the same time, it provides social communication across classroom members and is designed to promote the evolution of a unified social system.

We all know that natural conflicts, like fires and storms, can have fatal consequences if prompt action is not taken. Even if these events have only a low probability of happening, we establish special activities to deal with their occurrence. By planning and teaching the intervening strategy, we give children a social (management) tool to stop their conflicts and further promote cooperation and harmony—two indicators of Social Unity. With this strategy, children can turn potential hazards into an opportunity to change, so that they see the advantages of conflict avoidance.

Our present methods of resolving conflicts as witnessed by a world of growing prison systems, acts of mass violence, corporate abuse of workers, and governmental gridlock testify to the fact that present societal methods have failed. Attempts to legislate civil (moral) behavior have not worked anywhere. Neither has law enforcement or criminal punishment practices, as increasing crime and recidivism attest. Something else must be done. Here, that something is represented by using a conflict intervention strategy to help instill moral-management behavior from an early age.

Teaching the intervening strategy starts by modeling it with children's limited participation. Gradually, their participation is increased. Unlike going to a courtroom and watching a complex set of interactions that only a few experts really understand, they enter into a conflict resolution procedure that has the key components of a courtroom, but is applied to conflicts they have witnessed or in which they are involved. They become, once again, experimenter and experimentee. At any time, they may be judge, jury, defendant, or prosecutor. This gives them their first practical course in conflict resolution. They practice finding and practicing resolutions that take place in the classroom or school. In the long run, this is a prevention approach that instills a "resolution process" that does not require a fleet of specialists.

Because the history and brutality of conflicts are so pervasive, the end of this chapter deals with what many call noise and bias that often occur in the resolution process. In science and technology, noise and bias would fall under the categories of reliability and validity. This chapter proceeds by laying out the content, their relationship, and the process of conflict resolution.

INTERVENING AS A PROCESS

Intervening is a social process performed by two or more managers. The steps of the process "mirror" the culture's system of justice. Such systems are founded on a set of processes based on the moral values of the culture. In the United States, the process is embodied in such documents as the Constitution of the United States and the legal machinery that has been evolved under it. The present child-based intervening strategy emerges from this social-cultural foundation. However, instead of trying to remediate or punish those who enter into conflicts, the intervening strategy is designed to stop conflicts from an early point, to find appropriate moral values-based management behaviors, and to practice them.

The intervening strategy is a socio-technical tool used from the bottom up, not the top down. It is for the immediate benefit of classroom members. It is not something learned in a day. It is an event applied over and over again across the range conflicts that occur in classrooms and schools. It takes years to fully realize its consequences. How children will eventually modify and use it when the world is theirs is unknown.

It may or may not drastically reduce the need for large special interest groups called judges, lawyers, and enforcement officers. These special groups often input three confoundings into our present system: noise, bias, and non-adjustment to circumstances. These are discussed at the end of this chapter.

The strategy has five steps outlined in Graphic 16.1. First, aware managers must realize there is a conflict. Conflicts are inter-personal behaviors that delay or stop an activity for one or more members. Second, stopping a conflict is only possible when the members have a process to safely stop conflicts and, then, to resolve them. Third, as children learn more about management strategies, they will gradually see a wide range of better ways that can resolve conflicts. These are practiced by those in conflict and observed by all members. Fourth, if a settlement—as a form of payment for damages—is selected, the settlement is carried out. Fifth, the conflict is documented by disputants and the intervention supervisor. Documenting is the "score card" of a classroom's history of conflicts.

The intervening strategy requires the direct teaching of five terms. These include *intervening*, *conflict*, *better way*, *settle*, and *document*. It begins like the other management strategies with a discrimination: *Is there a conflict?* An affirmative answer starts one down the intervening process. As conflicts and activities become more complex, discriminations are added to each of the five steps to strengthen resolutions (Graphic 16.2).

❖ **INTERVENING** ❖
1. Is There a Conflict?
2. Stop the Conflict
3. Find a Better Way
4. Settle the Conflict
5. Document the Conflict

GRAPHIC 16.1: Intervening steps.

One of the first questions usually asked is how can young children carry out such steps? The answer is brutally simple: *They can't.* At least not at first. Only through slow evolutionary teaching will they come to do so.

They learn the steps gradually, just like walking, talking, and reading. First teachers, the adults in the room, must clearly identify and model the steps. This teaching employs social communication to place the steps in plain view; initially by stating and then by asking the students what step is next (Chapter 8). We want to start strategy use as early as possible. (As Chapter 7 indicated, the steps can be practiced and, thus, remembered through music, song, and dance.)

The children start using the process by classifying the event as a conflict, presenting evidence, and finding better ways. Gradually, children gain a larger role in the process. Teachers take an increasing observational role, helping them as little as possible as they negotiate their own resolutions by following the steps of the strategy. This is just a glimpse of the teaching required. From this abbreviated illustration, it should be clear that early teaching involves discriminating conflicts from non-conflicts, evidence from non-evidence, better from non-better ways, and settlements that fit the conflict from those that do not.

Most crucial is the way in which "cause-and-effect" is treated within the strategy. In many classroom conflicts, the "cause" is not clear and the effects may lie well into the future. All these bits of the strategy are required, so that children can make *aware, rational, civil judgements*. It is a slow evolutionary process where children learn an important lesson in civic duty: they are managers of their own behavior and for those with whom they live (Chapter 4). Like the other management strategies, we start teaching with the five basic steps. Again, this adds another "level" of control to evolving the aware, rational, civil self. This addition helps truncate the fight-flight-freeze self. There may be conflict ripples but, hopefully, no tsunamis.

Intervening's Discriminations & Operations

Each step of the full intervening strategy involves a set of discriminations and a few operations that make it a more powerful process to stop and resolve conflicts. Graphic 16.2 presents the sub-steps that are entailed in strengthening the intervening strategy. Like organizing and supervising, intervening is a special kind of planning; one designed to resolve and eliminate conflicts. It is a catch-all strategy that engages when and where the other management strategies have failed. With it, the seven-strategy management system forms an interlocking system to keep activities moving forward with the maximum chance of being successful.

❖ INTERVENING ❖

1. **IS THERE A CONFLICT?**
   a. Who can stop the conflict?
2. **STOP THE CONFLICT**
   a. How can it be stopped?
   b. Is more needed?
3. **FIND A BETTER WAY**
   a. Who can be the guide?
   b. What are some better ways?
   c. Select a better way.
   d. Practice the better way.
4. **SETTLE THE CONFLICT**
   a. Is a settlement needed?
   b. What are some settlements?
   c. What settlement would fit?
   d. Monitor the settlement.
5. **DOCUMENT THE CONFLICT**
   a. Was a better way needed?
      (Card areas 1-6, 9)
   b. Was a settlement needed?
      (Card areas 1-9)

GRAPHIC 16.2: Intervening steps and discrimination queries.

1. Is There a Conflict?

What constitutes a conflict (Step 1)? Primarily, it is interpersonal behavior that stops, delays, or puts activity members in danger. When members exit to the planning or learning strategies, there is no conflict. The activity has not been stopped because of a conflict, but because of some lack of knowledge usually related to the activity. The members may see the possibility of conflicts and, thus, decide to replan an activity; learn something that may help prevent a conflict; or simply to discover how others are doing such an activity. A conflict can be between managers who are engaged in the same or separate activities. Those in conflict may be individuals or groups.

As soon as an activity members identify a conflict, they first decide who can stop it. (1a). Often, it is not the person who sees it. In everyday life, it may be more appropriate to dial 911 or scream out for help. Initially, children need their parents and, then, their teachers to stop the conflict.

However, a conflict is not just about the specific member or members in conflict. It is between the conflictors, other members, and the moral values of the system. This triangular interaction must be observed and made overt (with social feedback) to reduce future conflicts. Conflicts often deny other members their *right* to a learning activity. Stopping and resolving conflicts is a *duty* to participate, which is something akin to being summoned to serve as a juror. From the reverse perspective, members have the *right* to participate in the justice process.

2. Stop the Conflict

Those who stop the conflict first decide how (2a). Auditory and visual signals are recommended. One like standing up, raising the right hand (as when one takes an oath to citizenship), and says something like, "Please stop the conflict" or "We observe a conflict." Given today's technology, the methods of stopping a conflict are almost limitless. It may *not* even be necessary for sub-step 1b to be made public; thus, protecting the person announcing the conflict.

If multiple members observe the conflict, they could, as a group, perform the stopping operation. Such multiple-member action becomes a powerful social cue (an inducing event) that has great power to stop a conflict and the negative emotions that may have given it birth (Chapters 4 and 6). Like a jackhammer, group action pounds a stake into the heart of conflicts—all members see that group coordination has strong consequences (Chapter 5). More directly, multiple-member action informs those in conflict that they are disturbing an activity and announces that the members, as a group, support stopping it. Reaching such a point takes time, during which the teacher models and prompts the strategy. Gradually, children acquire an expanding role as they learn to make sub-step discriminations. When a conflict is stopped, teachers can back up and rehearse various group actions.

Once the guide (1a) has stopped the conflict by deciding how (2a), the guide decides if more is needed (2b). If a conflict is stopped in the very early stages, and those involved begin appropriate behavior, then no more in the way of conflict resolution is needed. All intervening behavior ceases.

(There may be a designated "negotiation table" where those in "potential conflict mode" go to resolve their own conflicts.)

When is a better way or more needed? Graphic 16.3 lists five important conflict discrimination questions. A "yes" answer to any of them indicates the need for further intervention behavior that begins by selecting a guide (3a). This guide may be the person who stopped the conflict but it is often more helpful if another member is engaged. In this way, more children participate.

The extent of the conflict, as indicated by the five questions in Graphic 16.3, outlines a rough estimation of the increasing severity of conflicts. In general, questions one and two require finding a better way and four and five require not only a better way but a settlement for what is normally called "damages." This is a "payment" to one of the conflictors or to the entire activity membership. The latter is often called "community service."

Question three in Graphic 16.3 is a transition point. Here one may transition from simply finding a better way to needing a settlement. Like all legal systems, an intervening process has gray areas. Here a case-by-case judgment is like a "fairness doctrine." But can fairness be learned without a history of being involved in conflict resolution in the context of a value system? It is an assumption here that only a long personal history of being a participant in the resolution process can help in the development of aware, rational and civil children, as well as fair judgments. At this point, the concern for variability, bias, and special conditions comes into play. Hopefully, this history will reduce the severity of conflicts, so that only better ways are required.

Can classrooms and schools provide the experience needed to make such judgments? Both are social systems. They provide children with a chance to practice rational, civil behavior on a moment-by-moment, day-

---

WHEN CONFLICTS OCCUR
▶ Is a Better Way Needed? ◀
▼ Consider ▼

1. Does the same conflict continue during an activity or across activities?
2. Does the conflict interrupt the activities of those NOT involved in the conflict?
3. Do those involved have a history of conflicts?
4. Does the conflict damage property?
5. Does the conflict put someone in danger?

▲ Consider ▲
▶ Is a Settlement Needed? ◀

GRAPHIC 16.3: Conflict judgement guides.

by-day basis, over multiple years. Part of that experience focuses on resolving and eliminating conflicts. Yet, will children, as adults, transfer such behavior into the social system, so that a fair, unbiased, and simpler system of justice emerges?

With advanced complexity, things seldom get simpler. Yet, when members have knowledge of a system's pattern, even greater complexity appears simpler and more manageable. In a sense, they "compress" the complexity into almost automatic behavior. Today, a hint at an answer is seen in the rise of world-wide social communication systems where young citizens are acting in all areas of social justice. Many are fighting for individual, ethnic, gender, congressional, or social equality. Part of this behavior springs from members' biology. Many are appalled by how humans treat humans. Even those seasoned in violent conflicts are nauseated by their outcomes. Never before have children had the tools that allow them to observe such treatment and communicate about it on a daily basis. Hopefully, the intervention strategy, along with their other VAM-T repertoires, will help them in their planning for social justice when the world is theirs. Otherwise, the revolutions they will eventually undertake will just be rudderless anarchy.

3. Find a Better Way

"Find a better way" promotes finding a match between management behavior and the group's morals without the stigma of "blame" on the members involved in the conflict. Essentially, the intervening strategy "slows down" and "reenacts" the conflict. This is a critical step of an awareness repertoire: to *observe in-the-moment*. The strategy helps children 1) *reobserve instances* of management behavior between those in conflict, 2) *compares* their management behavior within the existing set of moral statements (as classroom duties). This evaluation is the extent to which the management behavior is cohesive or coercive. If there is a "clash" between morals and management, the intervening strategy continues. If there is not clash—as in one member helping another—then a "Thank you." may be observed and appropriate. However, to teach children to become members with *awareness* requires a more detailed analysis.

Finding a better way (Step 3) involves finding a guide (3a), which is initially the teacher. Next, the guide leads members in finding any number of better ways (3b) that represent appropriate behavior that could replace conflict behavior. (It is like step 2 of the planning strategy—design a solution.) Children will often find many better ways. They are seeking to replace coercive management behavior that led to the conflict with cohesive management behavior. The next element selects the better way (3c) and then has those in conflict practice it (3d).

Finding better ways is relatively easy when everyone knows that those in conflict could have said or done something toward each other that would have stopped the conflict in the early stages or avoided it altogether. All that needs to be said is something like, "Let's plan some better ways for this interaction." The key to finding better ways is this:

All coercive management behavior can be seen as an instance of failing to employ a management strategy or one of its steps.

However, until children learn these strategies, teachers have to guide them. Children will find better ways even if they can't name the strategy that is applicable. What is done until the strategies are learned is to ask them two questions: "What classroom rule has been broken?" and "How could those in conflict follow it?" When the other management strategies are learned, these two questions can be expanded to include: "What management strategy could have been used? and "How would it be performed?"

It is critical not to confuse the technical behavior (T) being learned from the management behavior (M). There are instances where not being able to perform the technical behavior (T) is the cause of inappropriate management behavior (M). This is why there needs to be a special activity that allows children unable to perform the technical behavior to have a method to access an activity that gives them help.

Going back to the "oldest point in the development of the conflict," there usually emerges an easy interaction that will show itself. For example, Jake and Zelda are peacefully sitting at their desks drawing and, perhaps, sharing crayons. Suddenly, Zelda laughs at Jake's drawing and says, "Red elephants! You fool!" From that point, a "conflict spiral" can begin in any of a number of ways. There are at least four possible better ways. Here they are with commentary on why they are better ways.

1. Jake asks the teacher for help. (Jake senses a conflict and uses the helping strategy. It is appropriate and rational behavior for a young manager.)
2. Jake could ask Zelda what was wrong with red elephants in his drawing. (He alters his emotional state by seeking the cause of Zelda's laughing. This is supervisory behavior that avoids conflicts.)
3. Zelda could have kept quiet. (Zelda is being self-supervisory by way of step 1b of the supervising strategy.)
4. Zelda could have asked Jake a question about his drawing. ("Why did you use red?" This action is again supervisory behavior exhibited by Zelda that can truncate a conflict. We can see this as being diplomatic behavior.)

A group may find all four of these better ways, and others. Once better ways are suggested, those in conflict make a selection (3b). There should be agreement on and a commitment to the better way by those in conflict. If an agreement can't be reached, have each party select a better way and then have them practice both. Again, the social context has a powerful influence on the parties in conflict to come to an agreement. As an alternative, the class can select the better way. This technique represents using group-based (compatible) contingencies as a way to control members (Chapters 5).

Next, the parties decide on when and how to practice the better way (3c). In the early stages of teaching, it is immediate. Like planning, this step ensures that the resources (more appropriate management behaviors) have been located and placed in the immediate need location. The better way is a short interaction that can be practiced three or four times.

Better ways take no more than a few moments to practice. It is important to have appropriate responses from both parties. Here is what the practice of a selected better way might look like for the Jake and Zelda example:

1. Zelda: Why did you color your elephant red?
2. Jake: I made it red because it is pulling a fire truck and red warns people of trouble.
3. Zelda: A red elephant looks strange, but that is a good reason to make it red.

By going over this better way a few times, they not only gain a model, but practice it as well. If it is viewed by the class, imitation by way of observational learning will be at work for everyone. Many better ways are often nothing more than "diplomatic" or "courteous" remarks, questions, or gestures done early on in an interaction.

4. Settle the Conflict

Some conflicts require a settlement. Step four begins with deciding whether a settlement is needed (4a). To make this discrimination, the same conflict guidelines presented above in Graphic 16.3 are used. A settlement is usually needed if Item 4 of the guidelines, does the conflict damage property, or item 5, does the conflict put someone in danger, are answered in the affirmative. The resolution guide can decide if a settlement is needed and involve the entire classroom in making the decision. A discussion and vote can be used to decide if a settlement is needed. However, a settlement occurs after selecting and practicing a better way. Settlements are often longer-term with no in-the-moment need for implementation.

Finding possible settlements (4b) is like finding better ways (3b). The difficult problem with settlements is deciding if the settlement fits the conflict (4c). This is second-tier planning; the process has found a better way and, now, must decide on further consequences. Most of the settlements that apply to the classroom or school involve 1) loss of access to an activity, 2) performing a "chore" activity for others, 3) paying for that which was broken or damaged, 4) being expelled, or 5) some combination of these.

Deciding on the appropriate settlement is one of the hardest decisions in any system of justice—be it family, community, state, nation, or world—

has to make. At times, there is no clear answer or blame (cause). All those involved in the conflict may have to settle relative to the larger system. Often, it is not just one party or the other.

At this point, two facts should be remembered. First, if we teach the management strategies from an early age, fewer conflicts should be experienced, and few that require a settlement. Second, after children have experienced the intervening strategy, they can be involved in using the planning strategy to change the intervening strategy, making decisions on better ways, determining when settlements are needed, and what better ways and settlements fit what conflicts. But until that time has arrived, there is a need to plan for various types of settlements and to decide what conflicts they fit. This often requires a school-level determination; there is a need for consistency across classrooms and years. Eventually, there will be a need for children to control conflicts that may be at the school level.

The last element of step four ensures that the settlement is carried out and evaluated (4d). This may be done by the guide (2c), but another member can be selected. At this point, the guide or someone selected documents the conflict.

5. Document the Conflict

Documenting a conflict (step 5) occurs whenever a better way is needed (step 3). It is a way of keeping track of the severity and frequency of conflicts in a fair and consistent manner. Children often forget previous conflicts. This forgetting needs to be eliminated, at least for a while. Documenting a conflict helps maintain a balanced and realistic picture for all involved, as well as informing all those involved about the extent to which their intervening strategy plan is working. A plan for intervening requires evidence and its evaluation. Complete documentation involves as many as nine categories of information. These include:

1. When the conflict occurred.
2. The member stopping the conflict.
3. The name of the disputants.
4. A short description of the conflict.
5. The better way selected.
6. Indication that the better way was practiced.
7. The settlement option selected (if needed).
8. Indication that a settlement was performed (if needed).
9. Signature of disputants (or acknowledgement by the guide).

Graphic 16. 4 identifies these nine items. They can fit on a 5-by-8 or 6-by-9 note card. It can be called an *intervening document card* or by another name. Besides cards, it can be a document that is part of a computer program. With the latter, a database can be added to quickly summarize and classify a classroom or school's history of conflicts.

```
┌─────────────────────────────────────────────────────┐
│            Intervention Document Card                 │
│ 1.  Date: _____ Time: _____ 2. Stopped By: ____  ___ │
│ 3.  Names: _____  _____  │
│ 4.  Description: _____ │
│ 5.  Better Way: _____ │
│ 6.  Better Way Practiced? YES NO                      │
│ 7.  Settlement: _____ │
│ _____ 8. Finished? YES NO      │
│ 9.  Signed: _____ │
└─────────────────────────────────────────────────────┘
```

GRAPHIC 16.4: Intervention document card.

If only a better way is needed (5a), documenting includes items one through six, and nine. If a better way and a settlement are needed (5b), documenting includes all nine items. If there is doubt about the need for more, documenting can include items one through four. If the *Intervention Docket Procedure*, described below, is used, documentation becomes very easy because the 5-step resolution process is delayed for a later time outside the activity (see below). This is a "special activity" as described in Chapter 2.

Although a computer program will keep the history of conflicts and allow for their analysis, a file box can be used to keep the history of conflicts. This history is critical to evaluating and redesigning the strategy process. Why a file box even if there is a computer program? Simply to let children eventually write in the information (data) and engage directly in-the-moment. Now that projectors are common in some classrooms, the computer program interface can be shown. It makes little difference if they write or type. If a file box or computer is used, it is sectioned into *Unsolved Conflicts, Being Solved*, and *Solved Conflicts*. If disputants begin to find better ways on their own before others see its beginnings, shout for joy; effective teaching has taken place.

Implementing the Strategy

Some preliminary planning is necessary if the strategy is to be used successfully. Six of these were discussed above:

1. What is and is not a conflict (1b)?
2. By whom and how the conflicts will be stopped (2a)?
3. What conflicts require more (2b)?
4. What are some possible better ways (3a)?
5. What types of conflicts require a settlement (4a)?
6. What settlements are just (4b)?

Additionally, a group will have to decide on processes to help them interact to 1) find better ways and settlements, 2) determine how they will document conflicts, and 3) decide how classroom members can play an increasing role in the conflict resolution process. Try to answer them with designs that are simple and straightforward. These answers make the intervention strategy easier to teach, implement, and evaluate. The strategy can be used in two basic ways:

1. Standard Intervention Procedure

The standard procedure is described above. This procedure inserts the entire strategy into an ongoing classroom activity where the conflict occurred. It is classified as an *emergency activity* (Chapter 2). A conflict has occurred and is stopped, then the intervention proceeds with the first four items on the document card filled out. As the intervention proceeds, the next items are filled out as needed. If it is decided that no better way or settlement is needed, then place the card in a resolved section of the conflict document box, as would be done for conflicts that require better ways.

When using the document card, describe the conflict in a sentence or two. This is not a detailed attempt at explaining cause; just describe the instances that were observed (document card item 4). Here are two short descriptions appropriate for the document card about Zelda and Jakes's conflict.

"Zelda laughed at Jake's drawing. Jake scribbled on Zelda's."
"Zelda and Jake had a conflict during picture drawing."

The second is better in that it does not describe details that suggest any causal pattern, as the first does. When it comes to hearing descriptions by those in conflict, the members need only be given one opportunity. Avoid excuses and try to get at better ways as fast as possible. The goal, as well as the focus, is on building appropriate replacement behavior as soon as possible. By immediately continuing the steps of intervening, excuse and frustration (stress) behavior are short-circuited. Children are quickly focused on appropriate replacement behavior. This is the major advantage of the *standard procedure*. The conflict is in-the-moment and the students are to resolve it in-the-moment.

Conflicts evolve and the aim is to help children observe and evaluate their coercive behavior as early as possible and move quickly to cohesive behavior. Eventually, they will come to stop their own conflicts from the very earliest stages and continue the intervening process if needed, or turn to appropriate management behavior before the intervening strategy becomes necessary.

2. Intervention Docket Procedure

The second way to use the intervening strategy is the *intervention docket*. It is a powerful alternative to the standard procedure after the standard procedure has modeled the strategy. First, it can be used when there is no immediate need for a resolution—often children, once stopped, immediately return to their activities with appropriate behavior. Second, it can be used when there is not enough time to implement the entire strategy. Third, it allows for a careful implementation of the strategy without concern for time constraints relative to ongoing activities.

A specific time is usually set aside for the procedure's use. Depending on the extent and number of conflicts, the docket activity can be done at the end of each day, the beginning of each day, or once or twice a week. There is no right way, but there are many satisfactory docket activities to help children evolve their conflict-stopping behavior.

After a conflict occurs, the first four items on the Document Card are filled out. Children are informed that the conflict is on the Intervention Docket. The document card is partially filled by the designated member. Docket Intervention steps are as follows.

1. A guide, initially the teacher, takes out the cards from the unsolved conflicts section of the box.
2. Go through the intervention strategy steps for all the unsolved conflicts.
3. If a better way is required, it is practiced.
4. If a settlement is needed, then a settlement is selected and a monitor is assigned to determine when the settlement is complete.
5. If a settlement is needed, The *Docket Card* identifies the settlement and the monitor, and then is placed in the *Being Solved* section of the document box.
6. If any other cards are in the *Being Solved* section, they are examined and the monitor identifies if the settlement was completed or is being completed.
7. When the steps of the conflict intervention strategy are complete, those in conflict can apologize to the classroom. Perhaps, they pledge to work to manage themselves, so that future activities have a better chance of being completed.
8. When the conflicts are fully resolved, with or without settlements, the cards are transferred to the *Solved Conflicts* section.

The disadvantage of this procedure is that the conflicts that come up during the docket procedure are no longer "fresh" to the children. But if the conflict is re-presented to them correctly—the document card helps here—it is usually enough. The advantage is that the conflictors or other members have time to think of interesting and better ways to behave under the conditions that ignited the conflict. This is the reflective thinking that professionals perform when their activities do not go as planned.

Reminding children of their conflicts is often embarrassing, but by the time the intervention docket process arrives, they may have reflected on some possible better ways. But the desire to avoid embarrassment may also be enough to stop the onset of coercive behavior in the future. It is more than "saving face." It can be an event that only requires a single trial to be learned, similar to touching a hot stove.

During the docket meeting, all classroom members participate in finding better ways and designing settlements. This class-wide participation illustrates to everyone "solutions of avoidance." It dovetails with the planning strategy because those who have experience with the planning strategy will eventually foresee potential conflicts. They may now become better at designing activities that avoid conflicts. Also, if children move from *arbitration* to *negotiation* because of this history, they may fill out the first four items on the document card and place it in the box. If such happens, then the document cards will indicate the *evolution of the strategy* from one controlled by all members to one controlled by those in conflict or who see a potential conflict.

The Docket as a Teaching Opportunity

If the time arrives for the Intervention Docket Activity and there are no conflicts or only one or two minor ones, the time can be devoted to 1) teaching various discriminations related to any management strategy, 2) teaching any of the strategies, or 3) reviewing past conflicts as a method to show classroom members how they have grown socially and are now managing themselves in ways that help them learn. It is their right as fledging citizens and their duty to provide others the opportunity to learn.

If conflicts are documented on a large graphic display, as the number and types (better ways and settlements), it can have powerful group control—this social feedback can change children's behavior just by seeing how they are evolving from day-to-day as a group. Usually, such a graph doesn't need to be explained. Just seeing it filled out is usually enough. Some call this a "group contingency" procedure that rests on the commonality of consequences, be they positive or painful (Chapter 5). In the long term it induces behavior in-the-moment (Chapter 6).

Eventually, conflicts will become few. This demands a celebration. The children may laugh, most likely because they will see how they have grown, are embarrassed by their prior behavior, or both. This is also a sign to expand the entire strategy to the school level. Here again, careful detailing of the procedure and who is involved is required.

Conflicts and Judgements

The above stated that all conflict behavior can be classified as *moral-management incongruence* between members. But realizing what conflicts entail is only the start of the matter. The judgments that result from any social justice system across human history have a number of problems.

These involve variability, bias, and context consideration in reaching a judgment. Much of this arises from the "X component" of an individual's contingency background or present emotional state (Chapter 3). The view taken here is restricted to social justice systems and, more specifically, what the classroom or school system needs to consider in its planning.

The problems of a social justice system can be seen as the inconsistent application of judgments that do not give the same class of "crimes" the same "penalty." Nearly, everything said here has been well documented across disciplines.[1, 2]

1. Variability in Judgments

Variability has two basic forms: intra- and inter-variability. Intra-variability exists when a judge is inconsistent from case to case. A single individual employing the intervening strategy makes the final judgment. On one day, the same class of criminal behavior may be given probation; on another, a year in prison; on another, five years in prison. Often, the cause of this variability is the X state of the judge at the time of sentencing. It may be because of a lack of sleep, a state of hunger, an accident, a family squabble, or the individual is not liked by the judge. Or, maybe it's simply Monday morning at 8 am and no coffee was available. These are on the negative side of judgments, but at times it may be a positive X state; the judge had a good night's sleep, a great breakfast, received a gift from a loved one, or liked that the plaintiff was courteous.

Inter-variability exists when a panel of judges, like the entire classroom, makes the judgment. The cause of this variability is often a mix of X states. However, group judgments have a social feedback factor between members that can lower the probability of variability from case to case. Any one member might say something to keep the group focused and consistent in the application of better ways or penalties.

The *social communication* (Chapter 8) between members is just one powerful operation to control variability. Another is a *review of conflicts* to see who has done what to whom. The group "investigates" its own management behavior in the context of the moral values of the classroom, which begins with the social duties (rules) of the classroom.

Yet another is the content of the *conflict guidelines* (Graphic 16.3) that move the group in classifying the conflict. If variability occurs here, it is often related to guideline 3, the history of conflicts. At what point do we have enough evidence to say that the history only requires a better way or that the

[1] Kahneman, D., Sibory, O., & Sunstein, C. R. (2021). *Noise: A flaw in human judgement*. New York, NY: Penguin Random House. For a synopsis see: https://www.youtube.com/watch?v=OmghBwlYw_Q&t=143s&ab_channel=Little%2CBrownandCompany

[2] https://en.wikipedia.org/wiki/Bias

history requires a settlement also? There is no easy answer here. As children learn about their management repertoire, they will change their requirements. They will also learn to examine the time between conflicts to help them determine wither a settlement is or is not needed.

2. Bias in Judgement

Biased behavior is another way to rend the fabric of Social Unity. By definition, *bias* is a disproportionate weight in favor of or against an idea or thing, usually in a way that is closed to change, often derived from prejudice or just plain unfairness. Biases can be innate or learned.[3] We develop biases for or against an individual, a group, or a belief. In the classroom, bias is often related to various peer groups, those different from one's group, or as a result of what they have observed and heard in their community. Bias can be debilitating to individuals and groups. Bias in the classroom or school relates to human-to-human interactions. It often arises during the intervention strategy, and we see it as a cluster of variability that shows up when we layout the conflict data and witness a set of outlying data points that is specific to an individual or group. Within the classroom and school, statements by members often indicate a bias against an individual or group, it is helpful to consider these statements as conflicts.

To control bias, we can use two special tools. The first is the inducing events (activities) identified in Chapter 6. These deal with the emotional side of the fence. The other is mixed-group activities that lead to academic success (T of VAM-T). If members work together and succeed together, they will unify. They may not become fast friends, but they will have what many call "respect for each other" or "trust in members."

3. Context Consideration in Judgment

The intervening strategy often involves not just the immediate cause of the conflict (e.g., Mary struck Jose; Jose said Mary was stupid) but with the "circumstances" that lead to the cause. What if Mary just lost a loved one? What if Mary's parents are divorcing? What if Mary is scheduled for a big operation? What if Mary missed last night's supper and this morning's breakfast? All of these possibilities require a consideration in determining the type of better way or the settlement. It is important to separate the immediate cause from the prior or background cause. What matters here is the consistency in any considerations being made. The aim is to keep variability and bias minimal, and deal with the background circumstances with consistency and objectivity, which is often put in the class of "fairness."[4]

---

[3] https://en.wikipedia.org/wiki/Bias
[4] Rescher, Nicholas. (2001). *Fairness: Theory and practice of distributive justice*. New Brunswick, USA Transaction Publishers. Ps. ix-x.

All three discriminations—variability, bias, and context—need to be directly taught and continually reflected on during interventions. Additionally, it needs to be remembered that young managers often have a first inclination to be harsh with their judgments. Because of this early "predisposition" towards harsh verdicts, the range and limits of settlements must be set out ahead of time. Thus, teaching "What is a settlement?" occurs, usually, as the intervention strategy is introduced to children. They need careful guidance, so that they learn to observe and avoid variability and bias, as well constantly consider the context during resolution activities. Again, it is important to remember that the strategies form an interlocking system of management designed to help children solve problems, so that activities keep moving forward with the maximum chance of success and benefit.

Conflict Resolution in the Classroom

Often there is a conflict between *what has been the case* and *what could be the case*. In classrooms and schools, there exists a resistance to turning over the governance of conflicts to children. The reasons why are complex and beyond the scope of this text. However, if schooling is considered to be a practicum in aware, rational, and civil behavior, teaching children to resolve their own conflicts is the only way they will gain the fullest possibility of governing themselves and their group. They can only learn so much from textbooks. The rest needs to be instilled by immersing children in direct teaching and practicing what has been taught. They learn by manipulating all the processes involved in managing themselves in the context of the moral values of the system.

Children eventually replace old conflict behavior, like those depicted in Graphic 16.5 with resolution behavior. The table illustrates the wording that often accompanies conflicts. Notice that the conflicts are grouped by management strategies. As said, all conflicts are the result of moral-management incongruence and often it gets "inflamed" by wording like that indicated in Graphic 16.5

❖ CONFLICT INDUCING MANAGEMENT ❖

Organizing:
1. "Why can't you remember your pencil. Organize yourself."
2. "You can never find your shoes. What did you do with them?"
3. "You don't watch where you are going. You ran into me again."
4. "This room is a mess. Clean it up!"
5. "I tripped over your toys again. Can't you put things away."

Helping:
1. "Can't you ask for help. Now, we have a mess."
2. "Can't you see that I need help here. You are so self-centered."
3. "Don't get mad at me for this mess. I offered to help."

Sharing:
1. "Can't you share with your members? You're so selfish."
2. "Don't get mad at me for not being done. I offered to share."
3. "With a little sharing, you would not have done a sloppy job.

Supervising:
1. "Why didn't you ask me how to do that. I am your supervisor."
2. "That's not how you do that. You are useless."
3. "Everybody knows how to use a hammer. Are you that dumb?"
4. "That's not how we planned it. You never follow a plan."

Planning:
1. "If you thought ahead, I would not be in pain."
2. "What were you planning to do? Now you have a mess."
3. "You plan without considering me. You are so self-centered.
4. "If you watched what you are doing, you would not this mess."
5. "You have done this wrong again. You are a slob as a planner."

Intervening:
1. "I told you not to treat others like that. Don't you learn."
2. "There is no excuse for such behavior. You're a delinquent."
3. "You're just a troublemaker. You should know better."

Learning:
1. "If you used a dictionary, you would not misspell everything."
2. "Don't you know how to do that. You have a rock for a brain."
3. "You didn't follow directions. So, you wasted time and effort."

GRAPHIC 16.5: Conflicts begin with or result from coercive management behavior.

17

LEARNING STRATEGY

Initially, children take to learning with joy, wonder, and enthusiasm. When children aren't sleeping, they are learning—first by observing, touching, and moving things, then by asking questions, and later by reading and experimenting. They take to learning because it offers discovery.[1] Gaining knowledge lets children control their environment and themselves emotionally, physically, and intellectually. These consequences combine to propel children to continue learning, to gain further control over themselves and the world in which they live.

Sometime during childhood though, many lose their joy in learning. The causes are often social, unintentional, and unrealized. To prevent this loss and ensure the continued joy of learning, we need to teach children how to learn from the earliest possible age. They should be able to work individually and harmoniously with others who seek to solve problems, as well as prepare them for those who may not have the same joy of learning or learning background. Such preparation requires a strong *socio-technical tool* to guide learning—one that helps them get unstuck or venture down "curiosity's road." If we give them such a tool, they will always have a technique to get unstuck, to keep the momentum going when faced with difficulties or obstacles.

LEARNING AS A PROCESS

To learn is to change, to evolve, so that one can observe and operate in the world in ways not previously considered or thought possible—new management methods are born that result in a new *frame-of-mind* toward systems previously learned. Learning, as a process, guides the gathering and sorting of "knowledge" through methods like observing, questioning, reading, and experimenting. It helps children (or anyone) solve problems, which may begin with events like climbing stairs or saying a new word. Or they may be as complex as uncovering methods of altering DNA. Or as difficult as gaining control over fear. Or as scary as altering a bias toward an individual or group. Only through a process that leads to changing ourselves

---

[1] Rescher, N. (2001). *Cognitive pragmatism: The theory of knowledge in pragmatic perspective.* University of Pittsburg Press. Pittsburg, PA. (He argues: eliminating the unknown sets us on a path of discovery. That it is a survival mechanism that has led to science.)

can we overcome the pain of not understanding the world. Unlike planning and intervening, learning sets out to alter the manager or a group of managers, so that they become more, something different than *what was the case*. How they change alters their future behavior. Like planning and intervening, learning adds to the mix of management processes that keep activity behaviors moving forward.

When an *instance of learning* is "complete," children are changed. The change results in emotional, access, and restructuring in thought and action. They have altered themselves. They can now change the world around them in new ways. Successful learning and its communication breed more learning. It is a recursive process of self and group development. Over history, it has resulted in a world community that is still warring but has achieved a frame-or-mind that recognizes the further need to change its management methods to ensure survival and a better life. Who survives depends on the type of management and moral-value frames-of-mind that guide learning.

To ensure that learning is recursive, joyful, and its consequences realized, we need to divide the learning process into steps, give it a clear language, and teach the strategy until children engage in it whenever they have a question that needs an answer. This is how science started, but now we are applying science to our social selves to reach our full potential. When teachers and children have this process as a firm repertoire, they gain another method of communicating. The language of learning and its accompanying frame-of-mind will keep them discovering together.

The learning process, like the other management strategies, consists of five steps. The strategy is essentially an outline of the scientific method. Graphic 17.1 presents the five steps. The wording of the steps was chosen to assist young children in their learning.

Step 1 discriminates if learning is needed. It sets a learning adventure in motion. Learning is needed when nothing else seems to solve a problem related to anything from moral values, awareness, management, or the classically technical repertoires. This instance of learning may be as simple as being curious about the use of a word or as complex as why moral values are important.

❖ LEARNING ❖

1. Is Learning Needed?
2. Organize Resources
3. Unpack Resources
4. Pack Knowledge Found
5. Return Resources

GRAPHIC 17.1: Learning steps.

Step 2 organizes the resources, and denotes that the organizing strategy is embedded into the learning process, giving another glimpse at how the management strategies form a system of strategies that help children. It continues to use the word "resources" (Chapter 11) and not the word "sources," a term often used when referring to that which is cited.

Step 3 unpacks the resources. It is the process of finding knowledge within the resources.

Step 4 refers to putting together the knowledge found, so that it can be understood and communicated to one's self and to others.

Step 5 uses the word "return." It functions as it did for organizing: it brings closure to an instance of learning.

The strategy introduces a few new terms: *learning, knowledge, unpack, and pack.* Most likely, "unpack" and "pack" are in the vocabulary and action knowledge base of young children—but don't assume it, test it. Only two are slightly difficult, learning and knowledge. These can easily be given placeholders, by using example sets to set the range and limits of both terms for now. Young managers are not working at the margins of psychology or philosophy where questions about what learning is or what knowledge entails—questions that have resulted in some very large books. Arguments over such questions are not in children's purview.

"Learning resources" amounts to an expansion of the existing set of examples that fit into the "tool resource" class identified in Graphic 7.3. "Knowledge" can be considered another subclass of things in the "material resource" class.

The organizing and planning strategies are the foundations of the learning strategy. Because much of learning about something in the elementary classroom takes place in groups, supervision and the remaining strategies become important. This does not mean that learning as a process waits until the other management strategies have been acquired. It just means that the initial five-step process needs to be carefully taught by teachers. The learning process, unlike the planning process, seeks to change those involved in the process, as opposed to designing and evaluating the "outer" world of the classroom, school, or the classically technical-based project activities.

LEARNING'S DISCRIMINATIONS & OPERATIONS

When learning becomes complex, its steps are not enough. Graphic 13.2 outlines the discriminations that give its steps a greater probability of functioning successfully.

1. Is LEARNING NEEDEd?

When confronted with a learning situation, children must first discriminate if it is a learning problem as opposed to another type of management problem (Step 1). The problems of humans are never-ending

❖ LEARNING ❖

1. IS LEARNING NEEDED?
   a. What needs answering?
   b. Why learn it?
2. ORGANIZE RESOURCES
   a. What resources help?
   b. Locate, transfer, and arrange.
3. UNPACK RESOURCES
   a. Where is the knowledge?
   b. What do the resources tell?
   c. Is the knowledge clear?
   d. Does the knowledge help?
4. PACK KNOWLEDGE
   a. How can it be arranged?
   b. When should it be arranged?
   c. What more could be learned?
5. RETURN RESOURCES
   a. What needs to be returned?
   b. When can they be returned?
   c. How can they be returned?

GRAPHIC 17.2: Learning steps and discrimination queries.

because for each instance of learning (that may or may not solve a problem), new questions requiring further learning arise.[2]

Because problems are never-ending, joy in solving them will reduce stress and help in the pursuit of answers. As toddlers, they may ask a question like "What is this?" or "What are these?" that simply seeks a name. Later they explore more difficult questions like "How do spiders spin a web?" Later still, they may explore questions like "Why do we have moral values?" or "Why do we have different moral values?"

Often, they must unpack a complex process full of new names and actions. Each of which entails a learning problem within a learning problem. For young children, most of the problems they tackle can be sorted with the basic comprehension question classification scheme: who, what, where, when, why, and how. Most of the content is about things adults know about. or know where to get the knowledge resources needed. As children grow, however, harder learning problems require a strong background in science, technology, reading, and knowledge manipulation techniques. Even here, we continue to give them knowledge of various resources like encyclopedias and other reference works. As learning problems become harder, teachers need to keep one rule in mind:

Never be embarrassed about NOT knowing,
just engage in the learning strategy.

The learning problem is given context and boundary when children ask themselves what they want to learn about (1a). Often, they are stuck during planning, want to do something different, want to make something more aesthetically pleasing, or are curious about what something is or how it works. All of these are potential reasons for engaging in the learning strategy. This discrimination question (1a), is often not answered clearly. But it is the beginning of the learning adventure.

---

[2] Rescher, Nicholas. (2000). *Inquiry dynamics*. England, UK: Routledge. (ISBN: 9780765800077)

When do children stop a learning adventure? When the "why" of learning is satisfied (1b)—at least within the classroom. If they plan an activity to build a birdhouse or decide what to feed snakes, there is no need to learn all the skills of building and feeding. All learners have an immediate boundary limit, as well as a time limit.

There are times when nothing more than children's curiosity propels them toward learning. They have no problem. This is the space in which many children exist. It is the state of curiosity. We just need to help them learn enough to satisfy their curiosity and strengthen their continuing love of learning. They have changed enough for the moment—they observe, talk, act, and feel differently. These changes are powerfully reinforcing, propelling children into continual learning. They are motivated at a cognitive and emotional level. In a world that is changing at an exponential rate, the continued joy of learning becomes a powerful survival mechanism. While children are fragile, they are plastic. We can strengthen or destroy this love. Thus, our teaching must foster this "cognitive mechanism" of survival, so that it increases and becomes an even bigger joy.

2. Organize Resources

The knowledge needed to solve a learning problem can be found almost anywhere. Quickly, children start to question those around them and eventually experiment on the world. Early on, the focus is on asking others and reading. The first element in step 2, organizing resources, is to decide which resources could help (2a). Within the classroom, the obvious resources are the teacher and other children. Next come ones like dictionaries, encyclopedias, books, or the internet on specific topics. Whatever the learning resources, they next, need to be organized in the sense of being located, transferred, and arranged (2b). This element is not stated as a question because it is essentially the guts of the organizing strategy. It is an operation that they already know.

When a few resources are kept at home, in the classroom, or on the internet, members can engage in learning at every opportunity. However, just going to the library and seeing the smiles on children's faces when they take out books, hints at the joy of holding a book and turning the pages, something that often begins with their parents reading to them. This biologically-based joy is strengthened or weakened by their entire social environment. This "social element" of learning continues even for advanced learners; they attend conferences and communicate around the world with others who have related interests. This is beginning to happen with children around the world through the internet and its network of social applications. All such activities cement the joy of learning and instill the learning process into every fiber of their being and becoming. All it takes is starting them off from an early age by those who are governed by the frame-of-mind that learning should be a joyful experience, even if it is hard work.

3. Unpack Resources

With the needed resources at hand, whether people, books, tools, or some apparatus for an experiment, the unpacking process begins (3). After they have some experience with the learning strategy, children can check where the knowledge is within the source (3a). Early on, this involves anything from asking others to examining tables of contents, indexes, page headings, or using search engine results.

Children continue the unpacking process to determine what the resources tell (3b). Then, they decide if the knowledge that they have found is clear (3c). If it is not clear, they have a learning problem within a learning problem. For example, they may need to go to a resource, like a dictionary, that tells them about a word and its meanings.

The unpacking process does not have to be from reading or observation. An experiment may be needed to discover the answer. Performing the experiment is the unpacking, and an experiment usually requires a teacher or a text to guide it.

Once the knowledge is clear, they discriminate whether the knowledge helps solve the learning problem (3d). This discrimination is based on the relationship between (1a) and (3b). If what needs answering (1a) appears to agree with what the resource tells (3b), then the resource helps (3d). Of course, "What do the resources tell?" (3b) will have had to pass any clarity issues (3c).

The (3b), (3c), (3d) elements will, at some point, require more advanced support behaviors to resolve clarity issues. They may have to compare the "pieces of knowledge" across resources to determine if they contradict each other or know when the pieces are unambiguous. An experiment that gives differing results confronts the agents with a contradiction. Generally, the knowledge resources children use usually don't require them to confront such issues. But eventually, they will. More importantly, it helps them observe the difference between "useful sources" and those that contain "biased sources." As before, the background to the learning strategy is the technical skill called reasoning.

There will be times in the unpacking process when a resource tells something not included in the learning problem that is obviously applicable to what the child wants to learn. It is the knowledge that is helpful in a way not previously realized. By using that knowledge now, they can alter their learning goal, perhaps for the better. It may even help open some areas of learning that the child finds especially fascinating and, thus, induces and consequents more learning. Their reasons for wanting to learn more about something may be unknown. The fascination is observable in their behavior in the form of their persistence, preference, and choice to engage in learning (Chapter 7).

4. Pack Knowledge

The knowledge that was unpacked, even if clear, needs to be packed (step 1), or organized relative to the learning problem. This is just a special instance of arranging resources (step 4 of organizing). For young children, there is almost a one-to-one correspondence between what is learned and the learning problem. One source is consulted, and its knowledge leads to an acceptable answer. The packing amounts to little more than a restatement of the basic question of element (3d), "Can you tell me what you learned?" When what was unpacked is in a usable form, it is arranged well enough (4a).

However, if the problem requires multiple resources or many bits of knowledge, discrimination (4a) becomes more difficult. Here, children are again in need of avoiding vague (unclear), ambiguous, contradictory, or fallacious statements within or across resources. We must teach them to see these fairly quickly. Here text is better than talk. If clarification is needed, another learning problem exists. Other resources need to be consulted. Again, this is a learning problem within a learning problem. Seeing these difficulties in arranging what is known will usually lead to more learning challenges.

For young children, clarity in arranging, like clarity in unpacking (3c), usually is not a problem. The resources like dictionaries, atlases, and encyclopedias are clear. There are no arguments about the knowledge usually presented. However, the clarity problem is relative to children's background knowledge. Their usual problem is not understanding the meaning of the words, phrases, or sentences. This why it is important to ask children questions as they read. But the goal of such questions is not to just test students on their comprehension of a text, but to model question asking and, then, turn the asking and answering over to them. In this way, they learn to see what they know and don't at various text levels (e.g., words, sentences, paragraphs, etc.)

Given the acceptance of the knowledge found, the next packing element (4b) seeks the answer, "When should the knowledge be arranged?" This situation is usually not a problem for children until they reach homework age. Now, they must add the answer to their learning repertoire.

The final discrimination about packing the knowledge found, and what more could be learned (4c), is not often an early learning problem. But its answer or answers can spur further learning and its joy. This situation will eventually require complex thinking skills that have a lot to do with rational thinking and the *patterns in knowledge*. For example, if what, when, or where questions are answered by a bit of text, they should be able to discriminate that how and why questions are not answered. Also, they will need to discriminate the difference between a description, comparison, evaluation, explanation, prediction, or even building or controlling something in the world.

Discriminating what is not known is directly related to inducing emergent behavior (Chapter 4). Once they begin to discriminate these unknowns, they induce themselves—as individuals or groups—to continue learning. They will keep seeing where to go next. By teaching children to make such discriminations, they are learning to behave inductively toward the material in the same way as those engaged in advanced science and technology disciplines do. As a result, questions about the unknown emerge. The "what more" question is not about clarity. It is about the unknown. The better our general metalanguage of knowledge (how to talk about knowledge), the stronger we can make this inductive behavior. (See *Further Thoughts* below.)

Their past learning may also require "reorganizing" or "assimilating" the new with the old. This element of learning is essentially a repacking step. Again, their general metalanguage of knowledge plays a key role. Here the questions lead them to discriminate differences and similarities across sources.

Helping children discriminate (4c) builds curiosity and inquiry skills and helps them see what others are leaving out of their talk or their arguments. Exploring discrimination questions (4c) in a group activity, lets them expand their vision of the possible with each other. Seeing what is not learned or expressed has survival value. The question "What more would you like to learn?" is only a small deviation from "What more could be learned?" Asking it of children prompts them to build their inductive nature and curiosity. It is a starting point.

Initially, children are not confronted by problems that require a great deal of knowledge integration or a search for clarity. They do not have to deal with the labyrinths of theory and argument that surround and direct the physical, biological, and social sciences. However, even if the answer is known, the situation may offer an opportunity to guide children through the learning process. Giving them a specific answer does not help. Giving them a way to find answers does.

5. RETURN RESOURCES

With the packing of knowledge, the learning adventure is essentially complete. However, the problem of returning learning resources is the same as in the last step of the organizing strategy. Element (5a) guides acknowledging what needs to be returned. Element (5b) guides the "when" of the returning. Element (5c) guides the decision of how to return. This brings an instance of a learning activity to a close. However, at times, children will be using resources like teachers or parents. In such cases, step five reduces to a convention called "thank you."

When their learning problem involves the relationships between members (uncivil management), solving it requires a different strategy. It requires a special form of learning: conflict resolution (Chapter 16). Since nearly all human relationship issues are problems between moral values and management behavior, it is best to use a strategy that deals with them directly.

Further Thoughts

The learning strategy's steps and discriminations all rest on its underlying reasoning processes. They add muscle to the strategy. Some of the components of this muscle have been addressed above—What more could be learned? Is the knowledge clear? Are the bits of knowledge contradictory, ambiguous, or vague? Additionally, does the text describe, compare, or explain why or how things work? How can I organize what I just learned with past knowledge? Making the discriminations related to each step of the learning strategy will eventually require this "behind the scenes thinking muscle."

The first bit of thinking is about various types of documents that are learning resources, such as card catalogs, indexes, librarians, and internet search engines. The second, covers the basic knowledge resources that can be unpacked like dictionaries, encyclopedias, and general reference books.

Another concerns the methods of representing knowledge—our concern here. This is the hardest-to-grasp bit of muscle: the *language of knowledge*—a meta language, similar to those of awareness and grammar. (Chapters 1 and 10). It is the way in which a discipline looks at and talks about the elements and relationship of its domain of interest; its subject matter.[3, 4]

For all science, engineering, and art disciplines, knowing its language of knowledge is foundational. Disciplines fracture content and methods in terms of their "elements" and "relationships." This may be why a discipline, if it fractures are even *true enough* to begin with, will never run out of questions or new methods to answer them.[5]

The concern that sparked this section was that literacy comprehension questions and the grammatical approach to knowledge analysis do not align with children's operations within the various technical disciplines. This may be one reason why science and engineering disciplines have trouble communicating with those without at least one strong classical technical background. Can such alignment take place?

Would having a language of knowledge—even if only "true enough"—prepare children sooner for deeper learning within various disciplines? Can

---

[3] National Academies of Sciences, Engineering, and Medicine. 2022. *Ontologies in the Behavioral Sciences: Accelerating Research and the Spread of Knowledge.* Washington, DC: The National Academies Press. https://doi.org/10.17226/26464.
[4] Medland, M. B. (2007). Tools for knowledge analysis, synthesis, and sharing. *Journal of Science Education and Technology*, 16, 119-153. DOI: 10.1007/s10956-006-9019-1 @ https://www.researchgate.net.
[5] Rescher, N. (2000*). Inquiry dynamics.* New Brunswick, NJ: Transaction Publishers.

we teach children from their early "experiences" with language to start observing their world in terms of the relationships between the "talk-text-reality triangle?" This is what scientists and engineers do, even if reality becomes highly abstract in the sense of being represented by a mathematical formula or a complex process graph. What is this *language of knowledge* approach that can "prepare" our young citizens to critically examine scientific knowledge? If found, it will require teaching. However, it may well replace much of what we are already doing during early literacy teaching.

Part of this language, relative to children, is that they "observe" what the presented knowledge (verbal, written, or graphic) is composed of and what work it is doing. Disciplines do this in terms of its content elements that are combined into their actions. These are verbal and physical actions that actually describe, compare, evaluate, predict, explain, control, or build a disciplines conceptual and physical world.

Being able observe what is missing or unknown, especially for young children, requires more than a sprinkling of knowledge from the various science domains as usually given to children in the elementary years. It is something that only those with advanced scientific or engineering histories achieve. At some point, it is embedded in their "thinking" or "cognitive" approach to observing the world and solving an array of problems.

Do children really need such a *learning tool,* this *meta-language of knowledge*? There are four strong reasons outside of the above questions. First, if done from an early point, children will sooner rather than later observe the *patterns within* the content they are learning. How the bits of talk and written material align with reality and each other. Such a language is like an "advanced organizer," "concept map," or "process diagram" of a discipline's content and method. Second, children should gain a higher probability of observing the relationships between various discipline areas. This not only deals with the patterns in what is learned, but the crosscutting abstractions like cause and effect, scale and proportion, structure and function. Third, this organizational tool would help remembering and relating "items" of what they have learned. They ask themselves, "What does this item of text or talk tell me?" and "What work does it do?" Finally, it should help them share knowledge with others, within or outside a domain—children will have an underlying method that will help them clearly communicate with themselves and others.

We must remember that science rose out of the ambiguity of common knowledge and its everyday use of language. Has science learned enough to help "update" our approach to teaching everyday language and literacy? Can we give children such a sociotechnical tool from an early point in their learning? Will such a tool help children transition easily from literacy of everyday life to one of science, art, and technology? Will such a tool help children become aware, rational, and civil citizens? Will such a tool be a fault-catching device to help children deal with the world of fake news, ill-focused political plans, and attack campaigns? Will such a tool help engender a world filled with scientific, artistic, and technologially endowed citizens? Will such a tool promote communication and, thus, foster *social unity*? As Nicholas Rescher reminds us:

> "Knowledge development is a practice that we humans pursue because we have a need for its products.... The discomfort of unknowing is a natural aspect of human sensibility. To be ignorant of what goes on about us is almost physically painful for us.... Homo sapiens is a creature that must feel cognitively at home in the world."[6]

Nearly everyone during the Covid-19 pandemic experienced the pain of the unknown, its dangers, and much more. This *meta-language* may well help us explore ourselves, the rest of the world, and cognitively prepare our children to handle, at least emotionally, the unknown, besides the future we are giving them.

Science and technology emerged from common knowledge.[7] But we also see how science has invaded common knowledge. Who does not believe that the Earth revolves around the sun in an elliptical orbit every 365 days? Can we now flip the coin and ask,

"How can science change our approach to teaching literacy to children, one that is congruent with fracturing knowledge as the sciences do?"

It is possible because of the emerging tools of ontology development. But it is an ontology (as the elements and work language does) not for a single discipline perspective, like the Gene Ontology,[8, 9] but for the way they are taught to observe the text-speaking-reality triangle. Exposing this triangle is what literacy instruction and English grammar do not do.

Should moving forward in giving children such a meta-language tool be a hard sell to schools, designers of curricula, and caregivers? The answer is yes. The reasons are for. First, it requires extensive change on the part of all stakeholders. Second, it will require extensive curricula development because the language of knowledge is in a primitive state. But we are reminded that scientific thinking and understanding are essential for all the world's people.[10] Although, this meta-language is emerging, integrating it into the existing curricula would represent a new "perspective and starting point" for beginning literacy instruction. But such difficultly emerges

---

[6] Rescher, Nicholas (2001). *Cognitive pragmatism: The theory of knowledge in pragmatic perspective*. Pittsburgh, PA: The University of Pittsburgh Press. Ps. 1-2. (ISBN: 0-8229-4153-8)

[7] Bunge, Mario (1989). *Philosophy of science: From problem to theory, Volume 1. Revised edition*. New Brunswick, USA: Transaction Publishers. Pg. 3.

[8] https://en.wikipedia.org/wiki/Gene_Ontology

[9] https://www.ncbi.nlm.nih.gov/pmc/articles/PMC3037419/

[10] National Academies of Sciences, Engineering, and Medicine 2021. *Call to Action for Science Education: Building Opportunity for the Future*. Washington, DC: The National Academies Press. Page 6. https://doi.org/10.17226/26152.

because our present "grammarian" approach to literacy has become embedded in human thought. Third, it will become political. Politicians who seek an unchanging Me/My world will continue to direct laws and funds for their benefit. In the same vein, schools resist change, as do those who govern curriculum development. Fourth, there is the problem of moving from design level planning to project evaluation proof.

The problem of moving from design to proof is far more complex than going to the moon because it involves the entire society to change and to participate. The problem pivots around having a few observable intermediate steps to help buoy its continual implementation, and, thus, maintain forward progress. However, like going to the moon, society will eventually gain a great deal from its teaching. Where does this teaching begin? Should it begin with infants?[11] As the he United States National Academies of Sciences, Engineering, and Medicine remind us, infants come ready to learn.[12, 13]

---

[11] http://www.thinkingbabies.org/downloads.html. Download: *Inventing an Infant Learning Environment (PDF book)*.

[12] Institute of Medicine and National Research Council. 2000. *From Neurons to Neighborhoods: The Science of Early Childhood Development*. Washington, DC: The National Academies Press. P. 139. https://doi.org/10.17226/9824.

[13] National Academies of Sciences, Engineering, and Medicine. 2012. From Neurons to Neighborhoods: An Update: Workshop Summary. Washington, DC: The National Academies Press. https://doi.org/10.17226/13119.

PART 3

BEYOND THE CLASSROOM

Part 1 presented the "underlying" knowledge about human behavior that makes the teaching of the VAM-T repertoires possible. It dealt with both the categories, relationships, mechanisms, and operations that makes it possible for teachers to instruct children in *becoming* ARC citizens.

Part 2 focuses on what it means to be an ARC citizen. Simultaneously, Part 2 explores how caregivers, teachers, and the school system have a hand in evolving children into aware, rational, and civil adults. Part 2 shows how society can assist the fledgling learners in this process.

Part 3 prepares teachers to instruct children, so that they function in the larger world. Children need to leave the classroom, navigate the world and survive. It explores how the Part 2 repertoires fit together as a system of repertoires. This is the objective of Chapter 18.

Yet, children need more. They need to move beyond the "narrow" confines of morals in the classroom to the "broader" concerns of the outside world, to the civilization they will inherit. Chapter 19 explores discovering moral values through the use of the learning strategy.

When children know the system, its moral values, its management behavior, and discern moral-management fit, then they have a chance of "fixing" whatever is amiss. This "fixing" has the objective of building "unity" between members and the system. As teachers empower classroom members, they are also empowering their children's groups. At this point, the "resource tools" in the appendices help children work together and solve any unforeseen problem.

The Appendices that follow Part 3 provide the support tools to help teachers implement instruction and help their children learn the repertoires and the system. They require reading skills. To ensure that ARC enabled children survive in the larger world, these "thinking" (or cognitive) tools must become almost automatic, so that they can truncate their flight-fight-freeze reactions and replace them with a "relaxing awareness" of the world around them. This will enable them to "work together" to solve the multifaceted, open-system complexity that exists in our world.

18

A System of Repertoires

Chapter 1 argued that aware, rational, civil citizens evolve through the development of four interacting repertoires. These include moral values, management, agency, and technical repertoires. Their interaction was modeled as the VAM-T system of repertoires. Where V = moral values, A = agency, M = management, and T = technical. This text only deals with the first three repertoires; the technical are already being taught. To ensure that such citizens evolve requires directly teaching young children the VAM-T repertoires and their relationships.

The text's assumptions reduce to four. First, aware, rational, civil citizens are the goal of social structures like the classroom. Second, the larger social structures seek to survive, evolve, and give its citizens an "equitable life." Third, aware, rational, civil behavior emerges from making explicit the four repertoires: moral values, awareness, management, and technical. Fourth, interlinking (relating) the VAM-T repertoires makes it possible to instill children with aware, rational, and civil behavior. It is the interlinking that instills the repertoires: behaviors get "wired together." When children are so instilled, they can observe, evaluate, and do something about the social behaviors that are either cohesive or coercive toward the group's value-purposes.

The Hidden Content

A *moral values repertoire* was defined as a set of statements that describe the *social interactions* required between members of a group that supports the beginning, continuing or ending of activities in social systems like the classroom. When instances of social interactions—as management behavior—are congruent with the moral value statements, then children and teachers are being civil to themselves and others. The concern with moral values has nothing whatsoever to do with questions like: "Why do we have moral values?" "What is the origin of moral values?" and "Who's moral values?" We are simply looking for what social behaviors are required to make the group function, to move toward its value purpose. The classroom is examined as it exists; the starting point is *now*. We take children from their entry point. Their evolution is planned from this point. Since young children have little, if any, explicit awareness of moral, awareness, management, or technical repertoires, all must be directly taught in one way or another.

The concern, at least at the classroom level, is with the question "What moral behaviors are required, so that all children have an opportunity to learn and evolve?" The simple, negative answer is that without moral (civil) behavior, the evolution of children would not occur; classrooms would be in a constant state of anarchy. The more complex, positive answer pivoted on four points. First, the classroom is a social activity, established by a community with the goal of changing children from *those-who-can't* to *those-who-can*. Second, this goal is a moral value because it is designed to evolve children. Thus, teachers have a *duty-of-evolution*. Third, the teacher's duty-of-evolution requires that children, at minimum, follow a set of social rules (interaction requirements) of the classroom. Fourth, these rules represent the moral duty, the social interactions, required of children, so that all members access their right to the evolution the community deems necessary for them to become fully-fledged citizens. Historically, the focus has been on the T of VAM-T. The argument has been that four repertoires are needed by children to solve the problems that they will face when the world is theirs.

However, the answer is not complete. Teaching children to "obey" or "follow rules" is not the same as teaching them to be aware, rational, civil citizens. To do the latter, the repertoires and the relationships between moral values, awareness, management, and the technical must be directly taught. The text's goal is to clearly define the VAM repertoires, illustrate the VAM-T relationships, and identify the biological, behavioral, and social mechanisms of which these repertoires are a function. These are used, along with a variety of instructional tactics, to control children's evolution. Although the content and relationships are specified, the methods of teaching were only outlined int this text.

The Starting Point for Teachers

Teachers start this teaching process by setting up a classroom structure that allows children to manage themselves, individually and in groups. The structure consists of the range of activities that give children a variety of contexts in which to apply their gradually emerging civil behavior (i.e., management repertoire) and to remain civil even if conflicts (non-civil behaviors) occur.

The *management repertoire* replaces our vague and ambiguous notions of social behaviors. This repertoire is both a set and a system of strategies that included organizing, helping, sharing, supervising, planning, intervening, and learning. Each had five steps that started with a *discrimination query* like "Is organizing needed?" or "Is planning needed?"

If answered in the affirmative, the strategy is set-in-motion. Each strategy step—across all seven strategies--had sub-step *discrimination queries* that help ensure that the steps can handle activities as they become more complex (Chapters 11-17). The management strategies were designed to foster rational behavior through strategy use. The two most direct strategies to promote rational behavior were the planning and intervening (conflict resolution). With both, children learn to follow the evidence, much of which is their own behavior.

Rational behavior entails building arguments that make decisions (as conclusions) that arise out of evidence-based facts (as premises). Within the classroom, these arguments begin with a logical tool called abduction were a predictive argument (thinking ahead) is followed by an evaluation argument (thinking behind) that assesses the predictive argument. "Strong" rational behavior will eventually necessitate teaching a range of logical tools like spotting formal and informal fallacies. This beginning allows children to observe, evaluate, and change themselves to achieve some end. In the classroom, this end is usually a T, the technical behavior being taught. In the long term, children will come to eventually use VAM-T as VAMT repertoires to solve the problems they will face when the world is theirs.

The awareness repertoire, the A in VAM-T, is a meta-language repertoire, like English grammar, that in this case links moral values and management behavior. It is used to describe and evaluate the extent to which management behavior (as taught from rules or as strategies) fit the moral values of the classroom. The management strategies are a "fine-grained" approach that allows one to analyze and synthesize social behavior as activities progress. The language of awareness gives children the tools to discriminate *who is doing what to whom* and operate on this "doing what" and "to whom." Children observe, describe, and evaluate these relationships. The language lays out the contingency relationships between all four repertoires.

Cohesive management behavior is social behavior that promotes an activity. Coercive management behavior is social behavior that does not do so. For the most part, the management strategies are taught from a cohesive perspective: the examples point to a range of what to do to fit the moral values of the classroom. The rules of the classroom are also presented as the needed (positive) social behavior needed for activity success—they are cohesive statements. To correct coercive management behavior, the intervening strategy is employed. The ability to link moral values to management and management to technical behavior gives children verbal awareness of their VAM-T relationships.

Although technical repertoires—as STEM, HASS, or SHAPE—*may give* children rational and civil behavior, they are often discipline dependent. The direct teaching of moral values and management across a range of classroom activities seeks to ensure that rational and civil behavior will emerge when children enter adult life with all its complexities. There are two objectives. The first was to help children manage the stresses in life, much of which takes place in the context of others. The second was to give children a We/Us as opposed to a Me/My perspective about interacting with others and the world. This objective seeks, in the long term, to move children toward an *intergenerational We/Us perspective*. But the goal was NOT to define the larger moral concerns that they will face when the Earth will be theirs (Chapter 9).

The hypothesis is that directly teaching VAM-T repertoires, over the elementary years, will begin to prepare children to "handle" the world we are handing them. Hopefully, they will make the world a cohesive place for all.

Models, Mechanisms, and Operations

Part 1, Chapters 2 through 8, presented a contingency model of the classroom, the mechanisms of which learning and social behavior are dependent, and a small set of operations that teachers can use to bring about ARC endowed children by about the fifth grade. The first step was to realize that children are *becoming citizens;* they are not already so. Overall, the contingency model was designed to give teachers a language and set of perspectives with which to talk about and engineer classroom activities to achieve the value purposes of their activities—the leaning objectives, which are usually some traditional technical repertoire, T of VAM-T. Chapter 2 analyzed a way to talk about "behavior" from a hierarchical point of view. First, there are the momentary, fleeting *instances of behavior* that make up a *class of behavior*. Classes of behavior are combined into complex behaviors. These complex behaviors maybe combined to engender *repertories* of which there are four: VAM-T.

For example, the supervising strategy is made up of five complex classes, one for each step. These include: is supervising needed, talking about the activity plan, directing activity flow, looking for progress, and pointing out consequences. As activities become more complex, we seek out the discriminations and operations that are its components. *Discrimination queries* help discern when, where, what, and why to perform a strategy or strategy step. The operations involve the actions, verbal or movement, that one performs to achieve a step that moves others toward the activity objective.

Classroom Contingency Model

Chapter 3 introduced the classroom model as a complex, open-contingency system. Each child can be described as a contingency that was expressed symbolically as:

$$\text{Push} \rightarrow [\; X: \text{Mi} \rightarrow (\text{M or T}) \leftarrow \text{Mc} \;] \rightarrow \text{Pull}$$

The brackets represent the social structure, the classroom. X represents both the genetic and historical background of children. The genetic mechanism is outside the control of the teacher. The historical component of X, as the emotional-physiological state in which children enter the classroom, is controllable to a limited extent. For example, the emotions of children can be modified by *inducing events* that induce emotions conducive to learning. These include music, song, and dance, along with various social greetings (Chapter 6). Physiological states like hunger and sleep deprivation can only be overcome with food or rest. The inducing event (Mi) represents management behavior that causes other M and also T. T represents the technical. The C (of Mc) represents the consequent events that result from performing T or M. If T is learned, then Mi and Mc gain causal control over time; they come to cause continued cohesive behaviors. When children enter the classroom ready to learn and are supported by cohesive management behavior and direct instruction, then the probability of both M and T will, over time, increase in probability. As the above contingency diagram indicates, management behavior, as Mi and Mc, can function as both setting and consequent events for X, M, or T behavior.

Chapter 4 placed the individual contingency model (above) within a group contingency model. Other children, besides the teacher, are both an *inducing* and *consequent events* for themselves and others. This is *bi-directional control*. In Graphic 17.1, the circled numbers indicate that 1) the setting operations have an effect on the control of consequent event operations and 2) consequent operations have eventual control over the setting event operations. The interactions of members, because of their variety of emotional states and repertoires, make the classroom a complex open system.

Behavioral Mechanisms

Besides the genetic, neurological, and biological mechanisms behind all human behavior, there are two parent classes of mechanisms that control contingency operations that teachers can manipulate. The behavioral is concerned with the mechanisms of learning, which is (roughly) how most animals would learn in an environment without people—under "nature's contingencies" so to speak. These are the respondent and operant mechanisms, which are called the law of association and the law of effect.

On the respondent side, when neutral events are associated with our autonomic behavior, the associated event can come to elicit the autonomic-based behavior as well. Salivation may be elicited by a bell after an association with the food that originally elicited the salivation. There is also autonomic flight-fight-freeze behavior as opposed to relaxation behaviors that can be associated with other children or the classroom. The "context objective" is for the classroom to become a place that elicits "relaxation" or "I like being here" states when children enter. The tools to do so are direct teaching and social communication (Chapter 8). We also know from operant behavior studies that delivering cohesive consequences increase the probability of cohesive management and technical behavior in most contexts. But there are qualifications to what reinforcing consequences entail.

Social Mechanisms

Social mechanisms make it possible to control the behavioral operations. These social mechanisms include 1) imitation of modelers, 2) unity of group members, and 3) social, often verbal, communication. With or without awareness by their users, these mechanisms control classroom behavior, so that the behavioral mechanisms function to promote learning. The teacher's task is to use these mechanisms in three ways: 1) to control learning, 2) to model social communication, and, 3) to show children how to control their own and others learning with their management repertoire. With the second and third, children are given operations to cohesively interact—they learn to observe themselves as *inducing* and *consequent events* for each other. Thus, members can induce and consequent X, M, or T for themselves or others. They do all this by *modeling* their own X, M, or T behavior or with social communication. All of these are present when children applaud others' success, support others when they are trying hard, help or get help when needed, and when an members stop and replace coercive management behavior.

Complexity of Consequences

Chapter 7 set out the complexity of consequences. The control that consequences have over behavior is a function of the genetic, behavioral, and social mechanisms. For example, if we are hugged, our emotional state changes. If we open a door, we have access to that beyond the door. If we fall, we may restructure ourselves with a broken arm. The consequences of behavior also have direction. If one does not look where one is going, we may bump into things that puts us in a new emotional state, restructured with broken bones, and gaining access to medical care.

When the learning and social mechanisms are combined, we see that the social controls (shapes, develops, evolves) members to fit within the group. Yet, individuals contribute to the control of the social. Both types of control are probabilistic because children, teachers, and schools are open systems. One problem is that the time scales for individual and social system change are radically different. However, with instantaneous, world-wide communication, these time scales are gradually converging. We now observe and feel the impact of world events on a daily basis.

There is a required knowledge base about setting and consequent event behavior. Knowledge about the control consequences have over behavior is not only about the classes of consequent events (emotional, access, and restructuring), but their 1) compatibility (the group is consequenting the same classes of X, M, T), 2) commonality (the events that all of us find reinforcing or punishing throughout life like hugs, laughs, and kind words), 3) evolution (most consequences gain or lose control as we change), 4) direction (aimed at self or others), and 6) reciprocity (members consequent each other in the same ways): cohesive behavior begets cohesive behavior, coercive behavior begets coercive behavior, but only if we start young will we instill VAM-T repertoires.

Inducing events for behavior are supported by a history of consistent consequences. Yet, more can be done, especially if unity is an objective. Unity, as a social mechanism, refers to our basic biological need to associate with others. Eventually, everyone sees the importance of unity through its loss and the resulting emotional state called grief from the loss of loved ones.

Social Communications

Chapter 8 examined *social communication*, which is a language-based method to verbally represent contingency elements that are involved in the evolution of VAM-T repertoires. Social communication can point out inducing and consequent event behavior of individuals or groups. It allows for awareness over an extended time frame. If teachers use it, children will imitate it because that is what children do. Unlike imitation and unity, social communication is *not* built into our biology. It is a social artifact, an invention by us, for promoting our own becoming. The more we know about it and practice it, the more effective our social behavior becomes at controlling ourselves, individually and in groups.

However, with social communication behavior, bias may enter. Often unfair comparisons are made. This lessens the chance of unity, the cohesion needed, so that all children are given their opportunity to learn. Comparing children or a group to their own behavior (past, present, or future) is one that avoids bias and helps avoid some its unexpected side effects, as when comparing different members or groups, so that one is seen as "superior" or "inferior." Comparatives can make or break children's spirit to try or to learn.

Qualities of VAM-T Behaviors

Chapter 7 pointed out six qualities (or features) of VAM-T behavior that help teachers and children evaluate the success of their activities. These were 1) willingness to perform, 2) quickness in starting to perform, 3) accuracy of performance, 4) efficiency of performance (reduced time to do an activity), 5) persistence at performing, and 6) preference for performing a class of behavior. The first four apply to all classes of behavior.

Although this text is not about teaching methods, the chapters of Part 1 illustrate, to some extent, how the above knowledge base contributes to the components of teaching. For example, social communication can illustrate success across all VAM-T repertoires and their relationships. It can be used as a description of children's behavior or to query children to see if they are able to observe and evaluate the evolution of their VAM-T behaviors and the surrounding contingencies.

Management Repertoire

Part 2 of the text, presented the contents of VAM repertoires. Chapters 11-17 detailed the management repertoire strategies. When children can read and have a grasp of the majority of management repertoire, it can be introduced as a system. This introduction helps them further control their interactions with others, as well as determine what a plan and its evaluation will entail. Chapter 1 described this system of management strategies. It is shown again in Graphic 18.1.

When displayed prominently, members can examine it to 1) decide what management is immediately needed, 2) to reflect on an activity's plan and where it was "sufficient" and where it was not, and 3) identify and correct specific management strategy behavior as needed. Once specifics are identified, children can turn to the detailed strategies to decide on how to act *in-the-moment*, so that their management fits their moral values.

The detailed strategies do not tell them specifically what to do.

Discrimination queries guide the behavioral specifics of each step. These questions are "inductive prompts" that keep management behavior moving forward towards completing a strategy step. In a sense, the queries are guides that help avoid conflicts. When stuck on an activity, like organizing, children can turn to each other and ask about how to go about answering these discrimination queries. However, when activities become complex, children can turn to others or to the heuristic guides to

GRAPHIC 18.1: Management as a system of strategies.

manipulate their behavior. Then employing the learning strategy, the goal is to change the self or the group, so that they can solve the problem that engaged them. Then learning is complete, they can observe and operate in ways that were not previously possible. This is where our management behavior meets our creative, imaginative side.

Awareness Repertoire

Chapter 10 dealt with children's awareness repertoire. As a meta-language, it observes, describes or evaluates the relationship between moral values and management behavior. An awareness repertoire consists of five classes of behavior.

1. Name and give examples of agency tactics.
2. Discriminate what tactics are being used by them and on them in-the-moment.
3. Classify if (2) is cohesive or coercive agency.
4. Identify the short-term and long-term consequences of management behavior that is cohesive or coercive agency.
5. If an agency tactic is coercive, discriminate what "better ways" (as social behavior) would make it cohesive.

These classes of behavior are based on the four classes of awareness: cohesive, coercive, cohesive support, and coercive support management behavior. Supporting management behavior is from other groups, inside or outside the classroom, that has some degree of control over an individual or group. The same relationships hold for coercive and coercive support management. Each aware manager has more or less control over the behavior of the self or others. This control ranges, usually for children, as partial cohesive (positive) control to partial coercive (negative) control. However, if group unity is established, the control of any agent over the group usually increases. Often, it only takes one member to keep a group on track, push the group off track, or pull it back on track. With unity, the group has more control to create an environment that achieves the group's valued purpose in a moral way. The consequences of unity are positive emotional states, access to success, and restructuring of the "knowledge state" of members.

Moral-Values Repertoire

Chapter 9 dealt with the final piece of the VAM puzzle, the moral values of the group. The argument was that educating children is a moral value designed to change their behavior. The classroom, as a method of educating, implements this moral value. But at the classroom level, the moral values are initially represented by its rules of social interaction, which were described in terms of rights and duties of members.

These rules illustrate how members must interact to achieve classroom activity value purposes. Moral values have two sides: rights and duties. Teachers have the right 1) to resources and 2) to have children who support their efforts to teach all members. They, also, have a duty to deliver the best possible instruction. Children have the right to the best possible instruction and the duties to help the teacher deliver it and to receive it. Yet, knowing rights and duties does not entail that aware, rational, civil citizens will emerge. Direct instruction is required so *situational* and *shared awareness* emerge and control rational and civil behavior.

Chapter 19 provides a wider view of moral values as they have been evolving. Even if children learn to identify and design their own moral values, awareness, and management behaviors within their classrooms, when they go out into the world things change. The VAM-T of the classroom is expanded to "VAMT-?". The T becomes part of the system of behavior and the question mark indicates the unknown future that will require all repertoires, which children will eventually use to control their future.

Since the mid-twentieth century, the world appears to be moving towards a "unity." However, at the moment, that direction appears extremely tenuous. International organizations, like the United Nations, are gaining greater control over the social-political problems they seek to solve. The Antarctic Treaty System is one example of how nations negotiated a treaty that has strongly stated duties for all of its 54 participants.[1] This early 1960s treaty is the first of its kind. As the treaty has evolved, it has increased the "level of duty," so that those who use the environment leave it undamaged. The Antarctic is the only continent on Earth that essentially has a zero-impact regulation with detailed plans on how to make it and keep it so. However, the Antarctic is part of Earth's open system and recently plastic particles have been found embedded in its snow.

An Engineering Project

To make the four repertoires an integrated, functional reality, the classroom becomes a project where children are the engineers of their own becoming. They learn a greater degree of control over themselves as their repertoires emerge and expand. Their moral values are the guides, management behaviors are methods to follow the guide, and awareness helps them describe and evaluate the moral values and management fit. As their project evolves, they begin to plan activities with their newly emerging management repertoire. To evaluate their project plans, they gather evidence that identifies if their activity uses *means* and achieves *ends* that fit their moral values. If there is a values-management nonmatch, they intervene to find better ways, as needed. These better ways are just forms of

---

[1] https://en.wikipedia.org/wiki/Antarctic_Treaty_System

replanning. With a large management system posting (Graphic 18.1), teachers can guide the emergence of children's use of means to accomplish their intended ends.

As children learn to manage themselves and plan activities, they will eventually define a set of moral values that vary from the original set of classroom value statements (as rules of social interaction). Usually, the changes are not extensive. Often, they are just variations of the existing theme of moral values. It is the process of changing them that helps them see the "reality of their behavior," its extensive level of control. They learn the extent to which a well-defined social environment with its moral value rules leads to activity success. They make the inductive leap: morals help them control both their management behavior and the value purpose of their activities. As they get older, they can be introduced to history, for example, in a manner that investigates the moral values used throughout history to see who-is-doing-what-for-whom. Observation, description, and evaluation awareness places them *in history*, not outside of it. This is a unifying move from classroom-level to world-level moral values. It is here that they will begin to invent their system of moral values. Beyond giving them "rock bottom" moral values for successful behavior with in the narrow confines of the classroom system, their moral values are left up to them as their guide to problem solving within their future social context.

When management behavior "breaks" a moral value in the classroom, children will usually over-correct it. Often these "punishments" are not "better ways" but are "remnants" of what they have observed or experienced in the past. In imitating these past events, their inductive behavior often takes their application "out of bounds." Also, their group behavior, as the seeking of unity with others, causes them to fail to add various suggestions from which better ways can emerge or that makes a settlement just. Three actions help control these out-of-bounds judgements. The first is the conflict guidelines (Chapter 16). The second is establishing better-way and settlement limits. The third is for teachers to maintain some degree of control over the conflict resolution until the first two have taken effect and conflicts are mostly "within bounds" of school and community expectations. As their *conflict resolution* behavior becomes stable, children can become part of a school-level conflict-resolution process. which solves conflicts that occur outside the classroom or can't be resolved in the classroom.

When VAM-T repertoires become inter-linked, several perspectives can arise. The first is called *distributive justice*, which is concerned with the "socially just" allocation of both the good and the bad resources.[2] The second is development of a *trust threshold*, which is an overt evaluation of

---

[2] https://en.wikipedia.org/wiki/Distributive_justice

others from inductive evidence.[3] The threshold's inductive evidence is promoted through a history of social communication and the range consequences that emerge because of their interactive (consequent event) behavior. Third, *intergenerational We/Us thinking* emerges because many consequences take place during future generations and many past management consequent events were coercive toward some subgroups. Children come to see that all their products or services will eventually impact their moral values—they will at least impact the environment in some way that effects the lives of others. Fourth, they will gain an *open-system probabilistic model*, which is knowledge about what social strata— Individual, state, Nation—contributes to controlling the system and, thus, their behavior. The model is deterministic if not strictly causal.[4][5] This will help them demarcate the rights and duties of each social strata. All four perspective can arise through direct teaching of the four repertoires over a period of years.

Perhaps the final question that young builders of a social system will ask is "What social structure or structures fit with the development of aware, rational, civil citizens?" As Chapter 19 illustrates, all social structures from the past to the present exhibit a vast array of conflicts. What could replace or repair them? Part of the answer is related to the "assignment" of rights and duties across all levels of social structures—who does what for whom? Again, without clear, unambiguous content and relationships, the interactions will be as haphazard as they are in most of Earth's constitutions. There is no one right way, but many satisfactory ways if we write such documents from the ground up and the top down.

Children's Future

Obviously, the moral values, awareness, and management repertoires as illustrated in this text do not guarantee that children will become ARC citizens. What it does do is build the initial repertoires upon which more advanced ARC behaviors will be founded. Technical behaviors like spotting faulty formal (deductive) and informal (inductive) arguments are part of the key, as are STEM and SHAPE repertoires. Advanced management repertoires like those taught to scientists and engineers need to be added. Finally, children must learn to use these during planning and its evaluation. As these behaviors become part of their repertoires, they need to observe, describe, and evaluate them in-the-moment, be it during planning or

---

[3] https://en.wikipedia.org/wiki/Trust_(social_science)

[4] https://en.wikipedia.org/wiki/Open_system_(systems_theory)

[5] Bunge, Mario. (1979). *Causality and modern science, third revised edition.* New York: Dover Publications. Pgs. 17-19. @ https://vdoc.pub/documents/causality-and-modern-science-third-revised-edition-1t97jptr55q8

ongoing social behavior. Only then can they move forward with less risk of missing the truly cohesive or the truly coercive.

What happens if children become aware, rational, and civil in the elementary classroom? Will their repertoires "transfer" or "emerge" in everyday life? Will they still be aware of their interactions and their values?

Will they see how they treat others and how others treat them? How will they "turn out" in the sense of entering into and fostering relationships with others, including during their teenage years? One way to help this turning out is to use the *What Management? Game,* as illustrated in the appendix. It can be used like "show and tell" time. Children describe and evaluate the management behavior of others that they observe outside the classroom, in the school, home, and locations they visit.

19

Discovering Moral Values

This chapter takes a wider perspective on moral values than the "minimalist view" required for classrooms and young children (Chapter 9). However, for teachers of our future citizens, it may be helpful to view moral values from a perspective that goes beyond the classroom. Our classroom and educational moral values are a subset of our moral-value system. Where is the world's system of moral values headed? This is a research problem that requires the application of the learning strategy (Chapter 17). The following moves through the steps and sub-steps of the learning strategy to deal with this research problem. Notice that the question is not a hypothesis, we are not taking one side or the other, but seek to represent a "world picture" of where humanity is moving toward a moral value framework.

Step 1: Is Learning Needed?

Throughout this text, the perspective has been that only through a combination and interrelationship of moral values, awareness, management, and technical repertoires will a social system have the cohesive human resources to move "toward a more perfect union." As children enter more advanced education, teachers will need to move beyond the classroom's rules to give children projects that relate to how they would guide the world once it is theirs. This implies developing an awareness of how the world nations manage themselves individually and collectively and the moral values needed to help guide themselves. Ideas like "world moral values" and "intergenerational thinking."[1,2] give us starting points for thinking about moral values from a wider perspective.

1a. What Needs Answering?

Questions like "What world moral values are emerging?" or "Where are the world's moral values headed?" These questions are a starting point for examining moral values beyond the classroom. Again, we are still not concerned with the deep questions such as: "Why do moral values exist?"

---

[1] Heacox, Kim. (27 August, 2021). Why America needs a Department of the Future. *New York Times.*
[2] Bjornerud, Marcia. (2018). *Timefulness: How thinking like a geologist can help save the world.* Princeton, NJ: Princeton University Press.

"Why should we follow them?" Moral values exist and some agents follow them even if many-most-some do not know why they are following them. It appears that both top-down and the bottom-up approaches are required. Classroom rules, as rights and duties, are the bottom up; they are minimalistic; they can't be further broken down, but they can always be changed or exampled with increased clarity. They have an unambiguous purpose—to keep activities moving forward without unintended interruptions.

1b. Why Learn Moral Values?

There are multiple reasons for learning about moral values. First, whatever comes to light from this research may help teachers when our young children become adolescents, teenagers, and adults building their futures beyond what is established in elementary classrooms. Clear moral values are a part of our system of behavior. Although the other repertories need to be advanced as well, moral values are the starting point that guides the application of members' other repertories (Chapter 1, Graphic 1.3). Given that our research ends with a set of moral values, the problem becomes one of planning a social structure or structures that allow morals to become an observable reality in everyday life.

Second, at all levels of social interaction—between individuals, communities, and nations of the world—we are witnessing conflicts. There are conflicts because of drug addiction, racial and gender discrimination, family abuse, organized crime, terrorism, corporate corruption, and governmental mismanagement and gridlock. There are also environmental conflicts over what to do about pollution, global warming, and infrastructure decay. There are conflicts that arise when the disadvantaged observe inequities in the distribution of healthcare, housing, employment, and more.

The picture is actually far more complex. With nearly instantaneous, worldwide communication networks, all of us—not only those disenfranchised by the local inequities between people, organizations, and governments—are finding enormous emotional discontent or brewing rage that appears to be the cause of demonstrations and other vastly more intense conflicts across the globe. These inequalities are exacerbated by witnessing them in-the-moment; they are piled on top of the rage and fear felt by many groups who have a history of being persecuted. Disentangling the causes is not the concern at this point; that is and will be the activity of historians.

When dealing with moral values, we are on a war-time footing to defeat our enemies: our own ignorance and the nauseating fear of ourselves, of others, and of change. At every level of social interaction, gridlock tells us that there are deep problems across all the world's social structures. What this text has tried to point out is that instilling moral values, along with the rest of the VAM-T repertoires, may be far more important the arguing about what social structure is "best." Without simultaneously instilling moral values and the management behavior to achieve unity, as well as planning, evaluating, and redesigning structures to meet some set of moral values, there will be no way to resolve human discontent.

If our children are to survive, we may well have to tighten our belts and make sacrifices for their future by giving them repertoires that will avoid cognitive, social, and governmental gridlock,[3] which is a hope depleting state that renders many with panic attacks, depression, and anger—all are symptoms of PTSD. The assumption here is that gridlock, as one form of human conflict, can only be overcome and avoided by grappling with our moral values head on. This activity is, at most, a necessary but not a sufficient condition for moving forward. It starts us toward making decisions about how to help young children move into their future. They will be the ones who change or adapt existing social structures to achieve their moral-value purposes, whatever they come to be.

Before the emergence of rational, civil behavior, there was war and slavery between groups. The victors became the masters, the controllers, and the defeated became the slaves, the controllees. It appears that humanity has started to turn the corner away from this dichotomy. But by how much and with what replacements? The "Unity of the World" is only a distant ideal believed by a few, at last at the moment. The possibility of dystopian worlds, as disparate as those in *Brave New World* or *1984*, still exist.

STEP 2: ORGANIZE RESOURCES

2A. WHAT RESOURCES HELP?

Our moral values spring from everywhere, past to present to future. Both historic and futuristic tomes can add to what we may see as encompassing "right" and "wrong" interactive social behavior. No matter what documents, knowledge, or beliefs help build a clear moral-value system of statements for our children, we are doing it for them, not for ourselves. Thus, when thinking about children, we are doing *intergenerational We/Us thinking* and not *in-the-moment Me/My thinking*.

Today, there are over 190 constitutions for the world's nation-states.[4] For many of these nation-states, there have been multiple iterations of their constitutions. France has had fourteen iterations since 1791. China went through eight iterations from 1908 to 1982, with five major revisions since 1982. The United States of America has had two constitutions, with the second adding 26 amendments. All of the world's constitutions make more-or-less clear (vague to non-vague, ambiguous to unambiguous) statements about citizens' rights and duties. All these constitutions do establish social

---

[3] Rescher, Nicholas. (1998). *Complexity: A philosophical overview*. New Brunswick, NJ: Transaction Publishers. ISBN: 1-56000-377-4. Chapter 10, sec. 3 & 4, and especially page 183.
[4] https://en.wikipedia.org/wiki/List_of_national_constitutions

structures to implement their moral right-duty statements. But the analyses of these constitutions leave a great many questions about what form they could take and how they should be implemented, evaluated, and redesigned as they evolve into the future.[5]

Presently, 166 nation-states (of the United Nations members) have unitary structures where the central government is ultimately supreme. Others have Federations or Republics where the central government and sub-national units like states, provinces, or regions share consent in order to make constitutional changes.[6] It is within these governmental structures that rights and duties are or are not achieved. As important as these constitutions are, many of them rest on ontologies (as the things we know about and their relationships) and epistemologies (as how we come to know about the things and control them) that are about two and one-half centuries old. The world was a different place at the start of the industrial revolution. Each person is now part of the world, not just a member of a nation state that traveled by horse and buggy, had little medical knowledge, or sanitation technologies. No nation, even as little as 100 years ago, envisioned that we would create a world environment on the verge of extinguishing the human species. This is what our children will inherit. This is our intergenerational gift to them.

While it is nearly impossible to analyze and integrate all the rights and duties expressed in the over 190-plus constitutions, there are other documents that many may want to use to uncover moral-value statements, investigate how they can be implemented in some set of social structures, and observe the management behaviors needed. Thus, another method of searching was sought.

Because we are living in an interdependent world and nearly all the world's nation-states are members of the United Nations, its documents are a good starting point. They are interesting because they illustrate the evolution of human thought toward ourselves and our environment. Documents by the emerging international organizations and international non-governmental organizations illuminate this human evolution. They are enlightening in terms the values expressed and the methods used to make them so.

Step 3: Unpack the Resources

3a. Where is the Knowledge?

Knowledge-related moral values are embedded in nearly all the documents of the United Nations and other international organizations. Many of these organizations working to improve the human condition

---

[5] https://comparativeconstitutionsproject.org/ccp-rankings/
[6] https://en.wikipedia.org/wiki/Unitary_state. The page's graphic, "*The pathway to regional integration or separation,*" illustrates the diversity of governmental structures.

express their over-arching moral values in their preambles, but more digging is required because nearly everything they express directly impacts other humans directly or indirectly.

3b. What Do the Sources Tell?

It is not hard to see how the United Nations and other international organizations are an outgrowth of the founding thoughts like those that surfaced during the Enlightenment, in English common law, and those in the American and French Constitutions. As much as anything, the United Nations arose out of the emotions and fears created by the events of World War II. Even nations, that had no direct connection to earlier historical events, have at least paid attention to the rights and duties of their citizens.

The Charter of the United Nations may well have sprung from the above earlier documents, but it went beyond them from the start. It made adjustments and additions to deal with our rapidly expanding world of evidence-based knowledge, international integration of economies, and the chance that our own behavior could extinguish the species. At the start, "All men are created equal." was scratched and replaced with "All people are created equal."

Yet, this *world perspective* is very young. With the United Nations, moral-values behavior moved onto the world stage for the first time, less than 75 years ago. Our civility, as moral behavior, perhaps, began with the Enlightenment of the 18th century. But it only started to emerge globally with the end of World War I and the birth of the League of Nations with its moral value mandate "to promote international cooperation and to achieve peace and security." Before then, there were very few international non-governmental organizations (INGOs). There were exceptions like the Universal Postal Union of 1874 and the Save the Children Fund of 1919. As of 2013, about 40,000 INGOs provided goods or services for those in need or advocated for various groups and their needs.[7] Can this rise in INGOs mean that a greater proportion of the world's population sees that human life has value and deserve a "good life?" Has the view of humans that emerged with the Age of Enlightenment gained a firm enough hold to continue to grow and guide how the future unfolds?

With the demise of the League of Nations and the founding of the United Nations came a focus not only on nations cooperating but on individuals as well. It was quickly followed by the United Nations Educational, Scientific, and Cultural Organization (UNESCO, 1946), the United Nations Children's Fund (UNICEF, 1946), and the World Health Organization (WHO, 1948). All these international government organizations (IGO) help in tackling the needs of citizens around the world.

---

[7] https://en.wikipedia.org/wiki/International_non-governmental_organization

These needs were seen initially as human rights. The hopeful may ask, "Is a world without borders in the works?"

One of the United Nation's first major value-based documents, of which there are now over 30, was The Universal Declaration of Human Rights. It has been signed, if not ratified, by all but one of the world's states, Saudi Arabia. However, not all signatories fully subscribe to the Declaration. Some object because they feel the rights do not go far enough. Others object because they do not hold to the separation of church and state. For example, the signers of the Cairo Declaration on Human Rights in Islam see the Declaration of Human Rights as having a Western-oriented bias that trespasses on Islamic law; thus, causing citizens of Islamic States to violate Sharia law.[8] Within the United States of America, where the government can't regulate or infringe on religious practices via the First Amendment, there exists extensive infringement by religious groups on the government's interpretation of constitutional freedoms, law making, and taxation. All of the United Nation's documents are directly or indirectly concerned with moral values. Table 19.1 identifies the majority of these documents.[9]

The United Nations gradually moved to include individual duties. The first place it did so was in the 1966 Preamble to the International Covenant on Civil and Political Rights (ICCPR), which says, "Realizing that the individual, having duties to other individuals and to the community to which he belongs, is under a responsibility to strive for the promotion and observance of the rights recognized in the present Covenant."

In 1998, after 50 years of working towards human rights, the United Nations established a "companion" to the 1948 *Declaration of Human Rights* called *The Declaration of Human Duties and Responsibilities*. This document illustrates moral values at the international level. Here, *duty* means a moral obligation, with *responsibility* being a moral obligation that is legally binding under existing international law.[10] This document clearly calls for the two sides of the moral value coin: rights and duties. The Declaration enumerates the rights and duties of all the world's states into eleven categories.

There are also other international conventions that overlap with the above but are stated from a narrower perspective. The Geneva Conventions of 1864, 1906, 1929, and 1949 dealt with the treatment of prisoners of war. The International Labour Organization's Forced Labour Convention of 1930 dealt with use of forced labor of nearly any form, irrespective of the nature of the work or the sector of activity in which it may be performed. The latter became the United Nation's first agency in 1949.[11]

---

[8] https://en.wikipedia.org/wiki/Cairo_Declaration_on_Human_Rights_in_Islam
[9] https://en.wikipedia.org/wiki/List_of_treaties_by_number_of_parties.
[10] https://en.wikipedia.org/wiki/Declaration_of_Human_Duties_and_Responsibilities
[11] There are now about 17 agencies of the United Nations. See the distinction between UN agencies and programs @ http://ask.un.org/faq/140935

There are also other international conventions that overlap with the above but are stated from a narrower perspective. The Geneva Conventions of 1864, 1906, 1929, and 1949 dealt with the treatment of prisoners of war. The International Labour Organization's Forced Labour Convention of 1930 dealt with use of forced labor of nearly any form, irrespective of the nature of the work or the sector of activity in which it may be performed. The latter became the United Nation's first agency in 1949.[12]

Not all these conventions and protocols have been signed and ratified by all member states. But all have been signed by the vast majority of members. However, ratification is a far more difficult process because the representatives who sign do not have full management control (Chapter 10) because their governmental structure requires sub-governments to collectively do the ratifying. The United States of America fits into this class of social structure.

Table 19.1: United Nations Moral Value Documents	
1.	International Bill of Human Rights (1948)
	• Universal Declaration of Human Rights (1948)
	• International Covenant on Civil and Political Rights (1966))
	• International Covenant on Economic, Social and Cultural Rights (1966)
	• Declaration of Human Duties and Responsibilities (1998)
2.	Equal Remuneration Convention (1951)
3.	Abolition of Forced Labour Convention (1957)
4.	Discrimination (Employment and Occupation) Convention (1958)
5.	International Convention on the Elimination of All Forms of Racial Discrimination (1969)
6.	Convention on the Elimination of All Forms of Discrimination against Women (1979)
7.	Convention on the Rights of the Child (1989)
8.	Worst Forms of Child Labour Convention (1999)
9.	Optional Protocol to the Convention on the Rights of the Child on the Sale of Children, Child Prostitution, Child Pornography (2000)
10.	Protocol to Prevent, Suppress and Punish Trafficking of Persons, especially Women and Children (2000)
11.	Convention on the Rights of Persons with Disabilities (2006)

Not all these conventions and protocols have been signed and ratified by all member states. But all have been signed by the vast majority of members. However, ratification is a far more difficult process because the representatives who sign do not have full management control (Chapter 10)

---

[12] There are now about 17 agencies of the United Nations. See the distinction between UN agencies and programs @ http://ask.un.org/faq/140935

because their governmental structure requires sub-governments to collectively do the ratifying. The United States of America fits into this class of social structure.

Also, there are many more international non-governmental organizations to examine. They include, for example: Amnesty International, Children's Defense Fund, Human Rights Action Center, Human Rights Watch, Human Rights Without Frontiers, and United for Human Rights.[13] Each focus on rights, with the United for Human Rights naming nearly all of those noted in the United Nations Declaration of Human Duties and Responsibilities.[14] (See Table 19.2.)

Why are the above organizations all about rights? It could be because they view these as common nation-state violations and it goes unsaid that the duty to provide the rights falls on these states, as indicated in *The Declaration of Human Duties and Responsibilities*. Many states advocate these moral rights, but the behavioral reality, as their agency, is not harmonious with their moral value statements to which they are signatories.

Table 19.2: Human Rights by United for Human Rights.		
1. We Are All Born Free & Equal.	2 Your Human Rights Are Protected by Law	3. Human Rights Can't be Taken Away
4. No Slavery	5. No Torture	6. The Right to Life
7. All Equal Before the Law	8. Don't Discriminate	9. No Unfair Detainment
10. The Right to Trial	11. Innocent till Proven Guilty	12. The Right to Privacy
13. The Freedom to Move	14. The Right to Asylum	15. Right to a Nationality
16. Marriage & Family	17. The Right to Ownership	18. Freedom of Thought
19. Freedom of Expression	20. The Right to Public Assembly	21. The Right to Democracy
22. Social Security	23. Workers' Rights	24. The Right to Play
25. Food & Shelter for All	26. The Right to Education	27. Copyright
28. A Fair & Free World	29. Responsibility	30. Your Rights Go Where You Go

Unpacking this knowledge continues with the environmental documents that have arisen in recent decades. They point to a human-environment-human interaction cycle. Is to maintain ourselves in our environment our duty?

---

[13] See https://www.humanrights.com/voices-for-human-rights/human-rights-organizations/non-governmental.html for a fuller list.
[14] See full descriptions at: https://www.humanrights.com/what-are-human-rights/videos/born-free-and-equal.html

The means (methods) used by organizations and states to promote human survival are moral directives; they impact others. For example, nearly all the world's states have *tragedy-of-the-commons problems*, which is the misuse of the public natural environment and its resources by citizens.[15] As a result, these organizations and states are avoiding their duties and, simultaneously, denying individuals of rights like clean air and water and other basic survival needs. The United Nations recognizes environmental interdependence on many levels and, thus, has established a number of environmental conventions.[16] Table 19.3 identifies the majority of these.

Table 19.3: United Nations Environmental Conventions	
1.	International Plant Protection Convention (1951)
2.	Statute of the International Atomic Energy Agency (1956)
3.	Convention on Psychotropic Substances (1971, Drug Control)
4.	Convention on Wetlands of International Importance (1971)
5.	Vienna Convention for the Protection of the Ozone Layer (1985)
6.	Montreal Protocol (1987, Climate Change)
7.	Framework Convention on Climate Change (1992)
8.	Convention on Biological Diversity (1992)
	• Cartagena Protocol (2003, Biosafety protocol)
	• Nagoya Protocol (2010, Sharing of Genetic and Diversity Data)
9.	Basel Convention (1992, Hazardous Waste Disposal)
10.	Convention to Combat Desertification (1994, Maintain Forests)
11..	Kyoto Protocol (1997, Climate Change)
12.	Stockholm Convention on Persistent Organic Pollutants (2001)
13.	World Health Organization's Framework Convention on Tobacco Control (2003)
14.	Paris Agreement (2015, Climate Change)

3c. Is the Knowledge Clear?

There are at least five problems with the above documents. These problems apply to our understanding of them and, thus, the problem of teaching their content to children. Here is the list:

1. The grammatical complexity and language of these documents are incomprehensible to young children and most adults.
2. They focus on highly abstract (very inclusive) classes that can't be pointed out or exampled in the everyday lives of children or adults.

---

[15] https://en.wikipedia.org/wiki/Tragedy_of_the_commons. See the section about Elinor Ostrom who has illustrated how some local communities have solved their commons problems without top-down regulations or privatization.
[16] https://en.wikipedia.org/wiki/List_of_treaties_by_number_of_parties

3. They weave around and through negative (inaction) and positive (action) rights, which only some lawyers can untangle.
4. They fail to focus on the duties of the individual. Duties are described clearly only to nation states, the documents' signatories.
5. The values are not written to expose the relationships between children's activities and their rights and duties as citizens.

As a result of the above, children can't look from the instances of their agency to see if they fit these internationally oriented moral-value statements to determine their moral-management alignment. If we want children to learn abstract concepts like moral values, they must be grounded in the observable action examples between children and the others in their lives. This includes how they talk to each other about their interactions. This is their awareness, which a meta language that observes, describes, and evaluates their moral-management behavior fitness.

If we want to directly teach *rights* and *duties* relative to interactive behavior within the classroom, we can begin by breaking down the complex language as illustrated by the above five problems and re-configure them from a *design perspective*. Consider the following:

1. Word the values in terms of the lives of children.
2. Avoid the use of highly abstract classes by using example sets to define them, so that they can be pointed out in everyday life.
3. Frame the values in a positive way—identify what to do.
4. Focus equally on duties of individuals and their rights.

Following these points in the design of teaching. Help children look up from their instances of behavior to the moral value statements or look down from the moral values to the instances of their behavior. This allows teachers and children to observe and carry out activities that have an impact on the world. Do we want children to be able to manage the world and themselves in a more cohesive and equitable manner than we have done?

The above points are often hard to visualize or imagine. Consider, for illustration's sake, Isaac Asimov's Laws of Robotics.[17][18] These are interesting for at least three reasons. First, they are all stated as duties with a negative orientation. Second, inaction relative to duties is not allowed. Third, they are hierarchical, with the most abstract being the zeroth law. Only the first two are analyzed here in order to see the thinking involved in applying the above four design points.

Zeroth Law: A robot may not harm humanity, or, by inaction, allow humanity to come to harm.

---

[17] https://en.wikipedia.org/wiki/Three_Laws_of_Robotics.
[18] https://en.wikipedia.org/wiki/Laws_of_robotics

First Law: A robot may not harm a human being, or, through inaction, allow a human being to come to harm.
Second Law: A robot must obey the orders given it by human beings, except where such orders would conflict with the First Law.
Third Law: A robot must protect its own existence as long as such protection does not conflict with the First or Second Laws.

Comprehending the Zeroth Law can begin by replacing the word "robot" with "person." From there, it is possible to define a person is a human being and that all human beings make up what we call humanity. Thus, all the children in the classroom make up a part of humanity. To some extent, we have dealt with the second of the four design points: bringing the abstract into the child's world. The behavior of harming is also understood by most children. "humanity" is an inclusive abstraction class, but it is one that can be brought out into the open. What is required is to overtize the abstractions, often renaming them, and working with examples from children's lives.

Comprehending the First Law, as written, requires the same word replacement and examples used with the Zeroth Law, ones that all children have experienced. We can make it easier by rewriting the first law as, "A person may not harm a person." Now we can rewrite it in a positive form, "A person gives health to other persons." To make "health" comprehensible requires another example set. Now, we have exited the negative and promoted the positive though the swapping of terms and, thus, follow design step three. Now, we can try to employ design change four: employing the idea of 1) the right to health and 2) the duty to provide health—or perhaps "health care," which is something most children have received and can comprehend through simulated examples with children and verbal accompaniment during class. This will lead, most likely, to seeking examples of what children have experienced in terms of healthcare; in other words, about medicines, doctors, and hospitals. Thus, nearly all children can comprehend, with a few examples, "the right to receive" and "the duty to provide," be it health or health care. This is what is described as a right in Article 25(1) of the Universal Declaration of Human Rights.[19,20]

The United Nations documents started by enumerating human rights, but they now clearly show that rights and duties are related—they are reciprocals, if not balanced ones.

Anything we have a right to,
we have a duty to provide others.

---

[19] https://www.un.org/en/about-us/universal-declaration-of-human-rights
[20] https://en.wikipedia.org/wiki/Universal_Declaration_of_Human_Rights

The thinking goes like this: All rights have an origin—someone or some group must take on the duty of dispensing them. Young children can't dispense them to themselves to any degree. We can ask, who should undertake dispensing duties? Who has the duty for whom? The possibilities involve nation states, organizations, individuals or some combination of these. At the start of life, duties are mostly carried out by parents and, when needed, healthcare system professionals. These are essentially our *doers-of-duty*. Today, many international agencies—be they an INGO or an IGO—are populated with doers-of-duty who are attempting to make the world a survivable, healthy, and secure place for all.

Consider ensuring a sustainable environment. The state sets up environmental policy that leads to local implementations. These state and local doers-of-duty have seen the moral problem and responded to it. Now what can the grassroots citizens do to help out? They can, for example, reduce, reuse, repair, and recycle resources to help achieve a sustainable environment. These citizens may know that over 30% of the world's food is wasted somewhere along the food chain[21] and over 70% of its plastic recyclables don't get recycled,[22] which together would just about feed the world's starving and clean up the world's oceans. If this were done, everyone would receive more health and help in achieving a cleaner, sustainable environment. To value healthcare and a sustainable environment are two values that fit together, giving our future citizens a chance at survival and wellbeing. Yet, it appears from the conflicts within and between nations that "mandating" values makes the process political. "Instilling" values makes the process individual, social, and systemic.

Both mandating and instilling values appear required to help individuals achieve the four design criteria for moral values.

3d. Does the Knowledge Help?

While analyzing the various documents, one may realize that we are the creators of our conflicts. Our children will be the ones who inherit them and will have to solve them. Working through the above types of documents may also leave one with the belief that moral values are an important part of the package that makes one an aware, rational, civil citizen. One at least has the pieces of the puzzle to work out a set of moral-value statements.

Step 4: Pack the Knowledge Found

Notice that there has been no talk about what form of government these rights and duties *should* exist within. The range of our governing social structures is enormous. Yet, all these social structures, as forms of

---

[21] http://www.fao.org/in-action/seeking-end-to-loss-and-waste-of-food-along-production-chain/en/
[22] http://www.fao.org/fao-stories/article/en/c/1196346/

governments, are riddled with human-human, human-social structure, social structure-social structure, and human-environment conflicts. The social structure may contribute, but most assuredly more is at play. Here, the more has focused on explicating moral-value statements.

4a. How Can the Knowledge be Arranged?

What set of moral values emerges and how they can be arranged will depend on a learning strategy exploration as done above. The following arrangement took about six months of fairly extensive part-time work to achieve a working draft. Since the earliest draft, they have been reworded for consistency to make them fit together into something that could be called a system of moral values. Why should something so basic take so long? I have no answer to that question, except that it proved challenging to analyze and synthesize the many documents read into a shortlist. Trying to clarify the vague and ambiguous language with which we crouch human behavior was one of the biggest challenges. Separating social structures from moral values proved almost as difficult.

The moral values presented are titled a *code of conduct* but many other titles could apply. This code consists of eight moral-value statements, each focusing on behavior taking place in the context of activities with others. It is presented here—with a small amount of explanation—only because everyone needs a model, for better or worse, with which to start moving forward.

What should be realized, relative to teaching values, is that you do not start with such a document. You build children's moral-values repertoire like any other human repertoire, bit by bit. It has been suggested that one start with a set of rule statements, expressed as duties and illustrate them with examples that cover a range of classroom type events.

The moral values are worded by separating out the dual role of *rights receiver* and *duty provider*. As individuals, we take the ***duties perspective*** when we ask:

> **How do my behaviors help others access the rights**
> **identified in the moral-value statements?**

We take the ***rights perspective*** when we ask:

> **What are others doing that allows me access to the rights**
> **indicated in the moral-value statements?**

Thus, the document begins with:

> **All Members have the RIGHT to Receive**
> **and the DUTY to Provide.**

Equality is built-in by saying *All Members*. Thus, it is not restated in each moral item. The document continues with the enumeration of the eight moral value statements. These are not written for the very young, but they can be simplified for later use. Only after they were written did their profound shortcoming expose itself.

1. **Wellbeing.** Access to activities that provide physical, emotional, and intellectual healthcare needs.

The promotion of our general wellbeing starts with being in physical health, which depends on our knowledge in areas of medicine, nutrition, exercise, and stress management. Promoting emotional and intellectual health has a lot to do with how we feel about ourselves and our knowledge of how capable we are at learning about, managing, and performing the activities we face. In other words, our emotional and intellectual health is often dependent on our management behavior, not just our technical behavior. If we are sick, injured, or can't complete our activities, our emotional health can be impaired. The three forms of health are interdependent. During the discussion of the system of behavior, this was viewed as the current circumstances of children as they enter the classroom. Essentially, this value is a condensation of the World Health Organization's values presented in its Preamble.[23] The main difference is that there is no mention of social wellbeing in the present statement. I believe that is parceled between values two and three, and, perhaps four.

2. **Membership.** Participation in group activities during which members receive the cooperation of other members and systems.

The principle of membership gives a person the right to the support of other group members for any activity that doesn't violate any of the other values. They also have a duty to do so. This value does not address activities outside of the immediate group of concern (classrooms, schools, or families) that the individual may undertake. Helping and sharing, two management strategies, are ways of participating and cooperating.

3. **Justice.** Access to impartial judgments designed to resolve conflicts between members and systems.

When members have different ideas or uncontrolled behavior, conflicts often arise. The *justice value* points to the need for a process that ensures that all can have access to resolving their conflicts, so that they can keep moving forward with their activities. By teaching ourselves to intervene in our own conflicts—a management strategy—we increase our chances of representation and justice. Although the term *justice* implies a group activity, the explicitness of the intervening strategy, as conflict resolution, gives the term "process" or "procedural" clarity. Each individual in the conflict has a set of steps to follow to arrive at an equitable, fair resolution within the system of values.

---

[23] https://www.who.int/governance/eb/who_constitution_en.pdf.

4. **Representation.** Opportunities to speak out about the design and operation of group activities.

Representation denotes that members have the right to speak out, as well as the duty to try to ensure that everyone has been heard from. This encompasses freedom of speech and how the individual contributes to making it so. Today, when people represent themselves, we praise their assertiveness. When managers promote representation, we admire their commitment to shared leadership or participative management. When people speak out, they do so about some activity and its contingency components. Speaking out is always about human behavior in the context of some activity contingency. However, to engage in "opportunities," as in all human affairs, requires two elements: 1) the "motivation" to engage in the opportunity and 2) the behavior repertoires to engage in the opportunities.

5. **Quality.** Opportunities for individuals and groups to perform their activities at a level of excellence.

When the service or product of an activity creates consequences that the members desire, quality has been achieved. These consequences may be aesthetic as well as functional. It is implied that excellence does not spring from nothing. To promote quality, the members have the duty to provide the necessary resources and training and to understand that the definition of quality changes over time. The criteria used to assess children's performance in achieving excellence are not the same as they are for an adult. The problem of "misplaced precision" is common in parenting and teaching.

6. **Adaptation.** Opportunities to handle a wider range of activities.

Adaptation is an extension of quality and membership. Members should have the right to and the duty to promote functional competence, as management and technical behavior, across the widest possible range of activities. This value, like quality, implies opportunities to access more educational training. As an outcome, any member, during times of need or crisis, will be able to take over the activities of others. This value adds "flexibility" to the group and moves toward eliminating discrimination. Overall, members will have fewer expectations about who should perform what types of activities; thus, moving the group towards eliminating various forms of discrimination or categorization of people.

7. **Evolution.** Opportunities to discover new activities and systems.

As the world surrounding a group evolves, the group—be it family, classroom, or school—must also evolve and change. Evolution focuses on ensuring adaptation to a changing world through invention and discovery. The adaptation and evolution of values can create tension. To adapt to existing activities may require conformity to tradition, and to evolve may require a break from it. But to work toward all the Group Values will often counter potential conflicts between these two principles and, perhaps help participants to see their values as a changing system.

> 8. **Resourcing.** Opportunities to distribute, use, and invent resources, so that present and future members and systems have an increased possibility to flourish.

Intergenerational concerns are overtly acknowledged in this set of moral values. Resourcing reminds us that systems are not alone. We have an obligation or duty to future generations and to the planet itself not to waste or over-consume our limited resources. Resourcing goes beyond the four Rs of reducing, reusing, repairing, and recycling as basic environmental duties. Resourcing is about people, materials, tools, processes, time, and energy use. The principle is about our system of resources, including ourselves, from beginning to recycling, so that we can begin again. In a sense, the principle of resourcing is an umbrella principle; it encompasses all the other values. It's like saying: We the people, in order to form a more perfect Unity, must value our resources in the most imaginative ways possible, so that present and future generations have an increased chance to flourish.

This moral value of resourcing focuses on what the United Nations Environment Programme (UNEP) calls sustainable development: "development that meets the needs of the present without compromising the ability of future generations to meet their own needs." Recently, the phrase "circular economy" has been used. The UNEP goes on to define what is called intergenerational equality as "the right of future generations to enjoy a fair level of the common patrimony" and intragenerational equity as "the right of all people within the current generation to fair access to the current generation's entitlement to the earth's natural resource." Environmental equity is seen in terms of a duty to account for long-term impacts of activities, and to act to sustain the global environment and resource base for future generations.[24, 25] Any list of moral values can easily fit on a wall chart for reference, as in Graphic 16.1.

4b. When Should the Knowledge be Arranged?

The arrangement of moral values has no time demand. It is not a classroom project activity, although it could be after the first 4 or so years of school. This text has advocated teaching moral values from the beginning of the school years. Yet, children are learning moral values from birth. Thus, in terms of "when" they are needed by parents and teachers, the answer is as soon as any form of teaching begins.

The classroom is the type of complex social environment that consists of a variety of activities where children interact with others and, thus, they

---

[24] https://en.wikipedia.org/wiki/Sustainable_development
[25] https://en.wikipedia.org/wiki/Environmental_law.

CODE OF CONDUCT

All People have a RIGHT to Receive
and a DUTY to Provide:

1. **Wellbeing.** Access to emotional, intellectual, and physical health care.

2. **Membership.** Participation in group activities during which members receive the cooperation of other members.

3. **Justice.** Access to impartial judgments designed to resolve conflicts between members and systems.

4. **Representation.** Opportunities to speak out about the design and operation of group activities.

5. **Quality.** Opportunities to perform activities at a level of excellence.

6. **Adaptation.** Opportunities to handle a wider range of activities.

7. **Evolution.** Opportunities to discover new activities and systems.

8. **Resourcing.** Opportunities to distribute, use, and invent resources, so that present and future people and systems have an increased chance to florish.

GRAPHIC 19.1: Example of a moral-value system.

must begin to follow the moral values required to carry out these activities. If social feedback is employed and children take both sides of the agency fence—as agent and agentee—through group activities (Chapter 14), a strong possibility exists that the moral values presented to them will be instilled and not just followed under the threat of punishment exercised by authority. The setting out of more complex moral values than classroom rules will help prepare children for the more complex world they will inhabit as adults.

4c. What More Could be Learned?

The profound shortcoming in the above moral-value statements is that there is no way to write them without ambiguity. Each and every one requires a set of examples to model what they encompass. This was illustrated in Chapter 9 on the awareness repertoire. However, when working out the above code of conduct, this ambiguity was not realized. The example sets in the initial teaching of moral values, along with the social interaction communication (Chapter 8) given children in-the-moment, flush out the ambiguity.

Moral values fit within a social structure, be it unitary, federal, or some sort of hybrid. The difficulty is to sort out the details of how these structures operate and what rights and duties are outlined in them.[26, 27]When our children take over the adult world, they will participate in that structure. In doing so, they must decide how moral values take a "living form" in the relationships between individuals and the various governing entities.

This "living form" is the problem of *distributive justice*: how do the social structures distribute resources and how does it redress the claims for past grievances of various sub-groups.[28, 29] There are groups that have been persecuted in the sense of being denied a range of various resources and social interactions. We see these persecutions in literally every single Nation State in the World, no matter what their constitutions imply.

Our children will have to plan how to distribute resources concerned with the common good—like those of clean air and water, food, health care, fire protection, and transportation safety. But they will also have to plan relative to "correcting" past claims—such as enslavements, persecutions, and denials—and "prepare for" future generational needs. How do we deal with past and future claims? How can future generations have claims? Our great, great-grandchildren may or may not have claims relative to the quality of life they are given by past generations. Just how do they make such claims? Perhaps by evolving the moral and social structures internally. Perhaps by evolving them externally through revolution.

Their plans will have to draw lines in the sand of human society relative to who gets what and when. When they inherit a *system of social structures* and begin evolving them into some form of *a more perfect union*, they will most likely find that there is no "right way," no perfect social structure and no perfect distribution relative to equality, equity, need, or fairness at any one moment in history. It is right here that instilled moral values and rationality take hold. Some groups always sacrifice something. The questions are many. Here are three: "Who should this be?" "When should it be?" "How painful (coercive) does it have to be for whom?"

Everything said in this text argues for instilling moral values, agency, management, and technical repertoires. If such is not done, it will make little difference to the social structure and any distribution plan established. Without the needed repertoires, will the world continue on its apparent path? Will today's gridlock remain? Not doing so will bring about institutional decay. As a result, there will be no social evolution that strives toward a more perfect union.

When the world is theirs, our children will have to "invent" and "evolve" social structures that take up the challenge. They will have to plan, implement, evaluate, and update their social structures. They will have to

---

[26] https://www.comparativeconstitutionsproject.org/
[27] https://www.comparativeconstitutionsproject.org/files/RightsIndex.pdf?6c8912
[28] https://iep.utm.edu/dist-jus/#SH2c
[29] https://plato.stanford.edu/entries/justice-distributive/

deal with the changes and consequences that the natural world and the "artifacts built by humans for humans" produce.

To what extent will social structures "oversee" or have "regulation" or "oversight" of its moral values and the plans required to bring them into being? Should the state, for example, fund healthcare and environmental protection activities in the sense of what must be done to sustain research, development, and the programs themselves? The individuals that oversee these activities, these *doers-of-duty*, often have the passion, technical expertise, and the moral where-with-all to carry out these moral-value duties that control the lives of citizens. Does there need to be *grassroots* behavior that is synchronized with these doers-of-duty who set up and manage these moral-based activities? Must these grassroots individual citizens hold the same moral values or is it enough that they be aware, rational, civil citizens holding out for the evidence of progress, fairness, and civility in the long run, while the social structure evolves and the resources in the world redistributes? What is known is that the means to achieve moral-value ends takes time within any social structure.

Means and Ends of Activities

When the values of the group are established, there remains the means to achieve the moral-value ends. This is where *moral-management conflicts* occur. For example, say a group has a desire to provide healthcare to all citizens. However, how do we put this moral value for healthcare into practice? Some citizens want to define healthcare that gives all members a choice of what healthcare they need or want within the limits of medical knowledge. Others want to define healthcare in a narrower sense that discriminates along some moral line. They may not allow women a choice to have an abortion or use contraception. Pro-choice and pro-life agents meet head-to-head about the moral value of providing healthcare to all. What usually happens is, again, individual, group, and political gridlock. Power struggles ensue. Demonstrations erupt. We have these same moral-management conflicts in all areas of human interaction, be they racial, ethnic, religious, economic, political, or gender discrimination. All are about moral-values that conflict with the means of controlling some end. Are such conflicts reason enough to clarify our moral- values?

Ideas, Ideologies, and Ideologues

All rational action springs from ideas. When ideas are put together or systematized, they are ideologies (Chapter 10). All human societies are ideologies, as are all the sciences, technologies, and religions. These ideologies are social technologies because they involve the interaction of citizens that were invented by us for us. We just have to invent better ones. Ones that don't "break" the fundamental behavior and social mechanisms instilled in humans. As the sciences and engineering disciplines are illustrating every day, we may well be on the verge of even changing these.

When citizens become "cast-in-stone" ideologues, there is no clear way to stop moral-management conflicts. However, not all ideologues are bad. We can argue that Elenore Roosevelt and her fervent work on the Declaration of Human Rights or Ida B. Wells and her fight for civil rights and woman's suffrage put both women in the class of ideologues. At the same time, nearly everyone thinks of Adolf Hitler as an ideologue. However, there is a difference. Roosevelt and Wells promoted equality for all. Hitler promoted his Fascist-identified inequalities. The difference is between evidence-based ideologues and those who eschew evidence for their own ends. These are the Me/My groups. Yet:

We are all ideologues. We move forward on some arrangement of assumptions and facts about ourselves, the world, and the universe.

If children are brought up seeing how evidence brings about learning and wellbeing for themselves and others, would they eschew evidence? Or would they work towards finding it and be willing to wait until it emerges?

Children and Ideologues

We are lucky. Children have not yet become ideologues. If we teach them to plan within their moral values, they will not, under most circumstances, become "cast-in-stone" ideologues. They will see that their values and their activity implementations are two different behavioral classes. The building of moral values is based on whatever documents they select. They are making a prediction about what moral values to follow and how to follow them. The evaluation of their plans is based, first, on these moral values and, second, on the function or utility of their activities. Will they come to be aware and, thus, see and feel the difference between moral values and the variety of means (methods) that can achieve them? Will they ever come to be aware and, thus, see and feel that long-term consequences that result from the product or service provided may result in coercive effects on others and the planet?

The assumption is that teaching children the repertoires that make them aware, rational, and civil citizens will truncate the development of *cast-in-stone ideologues*. The truncation occurs because children are being confronted by the evidence of their behavior from an early age. It is evidence that the children, themselves, uncover as they undertake activities. Will they simultaneously be aware of themselves from an individual and a group perspective? They have been the managed and the managers in the same skin, over and over again. They are being instilled with a *general methodology for interacting with others*. Will this *method for interacting* carry across the levels of their social structures?

However, from a wider perspective, there is a need for social structures to set out the relationship between its human components. Graphic 19.2 illustrates a simplified three-component structure that includes individuals (I), states (provinces, regions) (S), and a nation or world (N). In most nation

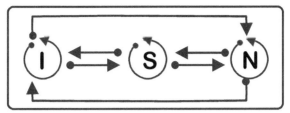

GRAPHIC 19.2: The relationships between individuals, states (provinces), and nations.

states, there are often several local government levels. The aim is to expose the interactive control between these levels. If these relationships are not clearly defined, then there will be conflict. The first step is to realize the moral values; the second is to clearly decide where the decisions lie relative to each class of moral agency—Individuals, states (local municipalities), and nation. The first four questions are:

1. What do individuals have control over relative to states and the nation.
2. What do states have control over relative to individuals and nations?
3. What does the nation have control over relative to individuals and states?
4. Is there a "balance of control" between these social structures?

These are questions about our awareness: who does what for whom and to whom? We will not find answers to these questions in any of the world's constitutions. Take for example, the Constitution of the United States. Article 1, section 8 lays out the federal powers (management control). The tenth amendment acknowledges that the states have powers not enumerated in the Articles of the Constitution. The ninth amendment acknowledges that individuals have powers. However, the moral values, the relationships between the levels of social organization, and who controls what for whom are not addressed. Some later amendments do parcel out some rights. Like the right to vote and what constitutes a citizen.

Additionally, who does what for whom is greatly dependent on technological advances like those for birth control, gender preference, and what constitutes death. From the perspective of rights, we see that the right to "possess a weapon" was written when there were only muskets that would fire about 1 round a minute, when the majority of people hunted for at least some of their food supply, and there was no standing army. Such is not the case today. From the perspectives of duties, nothing has been spelled out for individuals, states, and the nation. This is a duty, a responsibility, we are leaving for our children. Just how inflexible and ambiguous do we want to leave the social structure they are soon to be handed?

What Remains

The learning strategy journey has ended. Although it is new, the world view of moral values as the relationship between rights and duties has started to emerge. Our children are left with the next learning journey: distributive justice, which examines the burdens and benefits of social cooperation,[30, 31] which usually includes the relationships between ideas like equality, need, and equity.[32] Recently, the notion of interactional justice has arisen. Here interpersonal and informational encounters, as daily events, play a role in our notions of what justice entails.[33, 34] This approach looks at morals from the bottom up. It is a form of social communication as advocated for in Chapter 8. In the classroom, teachers and, eventually, children expose the interactions between members and prompt them to be aware of their interactions with others during moment-by-moment exchanges during classroom activities.

The assumption is that instilling the four repertoires of human behavior—morals, management, awareness, and technical—will give our children a useful set of repertoires with which to take them successfully into their futures. Will they plan, implement, and evaluate distributive justice operations that considers everyone or just for some subgroup? Hopefully, they will make for themselves a future with fewer conflicts than we are exhibiting. However, if everyone is not included in a distributed justice plan, then conflicts will continue. We will continue to see the classic forms of coercion: escape, avoidance, and counter control against those managers who are denying them their rights and duties. Hopefully, our children will obtain a world where humanity is moving toward a moral value framework for all.

Final Note: The difficulty with moral values is that they are 1) hierarchical, 2) universal, 3) require wording that exposes their hierarchical and universal complexity, and 4) need context clarity.[35] The eight moral values (p. 299) are second-tier on the hierarchy and are based on our 1) human duty to foster/promote/save life and 2) a human right to life— a first-teir expression that exposes their universality. The eight morals unpack this first tier in terms of eight subgroups, after that context is critical. This is where distributive justice enters.

---

[30] Kaufman, A. (2012). *Theories of Distributive Justice*. In R. Chadwick (ed. In chief). Encyclopedia of Applied Ethics (second ed.). P. 842-850. ISBN 9780123736321.

[31] https://en.wikipedia.org/wiki/Distributive_justice

[32] Wright, S. C., & Boese G. D. (2015). *Meritocracy and Tokenism*. In J. D. Wright (ed.) International Encyclopedia of Social & Behavioral Sciences (Second Ed.). Amsterdam: Elsevier. P. 239-245. ISBN: 9780080970868

[33] Kazemi, A., Tornblom, K., & Mukula, G. (2015). *Justice: Social Psychological Perspectives*. In J. D. Wright (ed.) International Encyclopedia of Social & Behavioral Sciences (Second Ed.). Amsterdam: Elsevier. P. 949-955. ISBN: 9780080970868

[34] https://en.wikipedia.org/wiki/Interactional_justice

[35] Rescher, Nicholas. (1997). *On rules and principles: A philosophical study of their nature and function*. New Jersey, USA: Transaction books.

Appendices

These teaching aids can be found on **ManagingOurselves.Org**. They come in many forms, large and small, and in various formats.

1. Management Strategies: Study Cards

Each of the management study cards has a front and back side. Like most study cards, they are 2½ by 3½ inches in size. The back side relates to the background knowledge that helps induce the use of the strategy, so that it moves forward. As a study device, they can induce strategy behavior or consequent knowledge of or use of the strategy. Both support remembering. These were presented in Chapters 11-17.

2. Thinking Ahead and Behind

This is a graphic that will help planners or anyone who may need to think ahead about what they are doing and then think behind to confirm or evaluate if something does or does not work. It can apply to any part of any plan, be it organizing, planning, intervening, as well as to any strategy in use.

3. Management Buttons

These are buttons can be used as "achievement awards" for members who reach your criteria for gaining knowledge about and use of the management strategies. They can be used to make badges as well.

4. Management Flow Charts

There are seven flow charts, one for each strategy. Only one is included here. They are designed to give children another perspective on the strategies. They illustrate a systematic design method.

5. What Management? Game

The What Management? Game is designed to expand children's application of various management strategies. Within the classroom, the game is like show-and-tell time. It focuses on the management observed outside the classroom. If played outside the classroom, it promotes observation and awareness.

❖ ORGANIZING ❖

1. **IS ORGANIZING NEEDED**
   a. What resources are needed?
   b. How many and much of each?
   c. What quality for each?

2. **LOCATE RESOURCES**
   a. How can they be located?
   b. Where are they located?

3. **TRANSFER RESOURCES**
   a. Where are they needed?
   b. When are they needed?
   c. How can they be transferred?

4. **ARRANGE RESOURCES**
   a. When are they to be arranged?
   b. How can they be arranged?

5. **RETURN RESOURCES**
   a. What needs to be returned?
   b. When can they be returned?
   c. How can they be returned?

❖ PLANNING ❖

1. **IS PLANNING NEEDED?**
   a. What plan needs changing?
   b. Why change the plan?

2. **DESIGN NEW PLAN**
   a. What changes are needed?
   b. How can they be designed?
   c. Does anything else change?
   d. Are all the steps clear?

3. **SELECT NEW PLAN**
   a. Does the plan fit the resources?
   b. What are the consequences
   c. Is everyone willing to try it?

4. **IMPLEMENT PLAN**
   a. Is the data being gathered?
   b. Is the plan being followed?
   c. Is there progress at each step?
   d. What are the consequences?

5. **EVALUATE PLAN**
   a. Was the plan followed?
   b. Were there problems?
   c. Is change needed?
   d. Make changes as needed.

★ THINKING ABOUT
DESIGNING PLANS ★

1. **Designing Activity**
   a. What resources are needed?
   b. What new behaviors are needed?
   c. What consequences are desired?
   d. Do the design fit the group's moral values?

2. **Implementing Activity**
   a. How will the new behaviors be learned?
   b. How will the resources and new behaviors come together?
   c. What evaluation data will be needed?
   d. How will the data be obtained?

3. **Design Activity's Evaluation**
   a. How will you know if the plan's implementation was followed?
   b. How will you know if the plan's activity steps were followed?
   c. How will you know what consequences occurred?
   d. How will the data be presented?

★ THINKING ABOUT
RESOURCES ★

1. **People**
   a. How many are needed?
   b. What behaviors are needed?
   c. When are they needed?

2. **Materials**
   a. What types are needed?
   b. How much or how many are needed?
   c. What quality is required?

3. **Tools**
   a. What types are needed?
   b. How many of each are required?
   c. What quality is required?

4. **Place**
   a. How much space?
   b. How much comfort?
   c. How can resources be arranged?

5. **Time**
   a. How much time is needed per day?
   b. When do the people start and stop?
   c. When are the resources to be arranged?

Systems Thinking: If a resource changes, other resources may change also.

Success Thinking: If any resource is scarce or critical to success, locate a backup.

❖ SHARING ❖

▼ SHARER STRATEGY ▲

1. Is Sharing Needed?
2. Offer to Share
3. IF Offer is Accepted, Share Resource
4. IF Offer is rejected, Accept Rejection
5. When Sharing is Done, Accept Thanks

▼ SHAREE STRATEGY ▲

1. Is Sharing Needed?
2. Ask to Share
3. IF Asking is Accepted, Thank and Use Resource
4. IF Asking is Rejected, Accept Rejection
5. When Sharing is Done, Return Resource and Thank Sharer

❖ HELPING ❖

▼ HELPER STRATEGY ▲

1. Is Helping Needed?
2. Offer to Help
3. IF Offer is Accepted, Work Together
4. IF Offer is Rejected, Accept Rejection
5. When Helping is Done, Accept Thanks

▼ HELPEE STRATEGY ▲

1. Is Helping Needed?
2. Ask for Help
3. IF Asking is Accepted, Thank and Work Together
4. IF Offer is Rejected, Accept Rejection
5. When Helping is Done, Thank Helper

★ THINKING ABOUT
★ HELPING ★

▲ HELPER THINKING ▼

1. When is helping needed?
2. How can one offer to help?
3. How can one accept a rejection when offering help?
4. How can one reject a request for help?
5. When would one help without offering?
6. When would one thank a helpee after giving help?

▲ HELPEE THINKING ▼

1. When is helping needed?
2. How can one ask for help?
3. How can one accept a rejection when asking for help?
4. How can one reject an offer to help?
5. How can one thank a helper after being helped?
6. When would one accept help without asking?

★ THINKING ABOUT
★ SHARING ★

▲ SHARER THINKING ▼

1. When is sharing needed?
2. How can one offer to share?
3. How can one accept a rejection?
4. How can one reject a request for sharing?
5. How can one accept thanks for sharing?
6. When would one share without offering?
7. When would one thank a sharee after sharing a resource?

▲ SHAREE THINKING ▼

1. When is sharing needed?
2. How can one ask for sharing?
3. How can one accept a rejection when asking to share?
4. How can one reject an offer to share?
5. How can one thank a sharer after sharing a resource?
6. When would one accept sharing without asking?
7. In what condition is a resource returned?

❖ SUPERVISING ❖

1. IS SUPERVISING NEEDED?
a. Is activity new or complex?
b. What supervision is needed?

2. TELL ABOUT PLAN
a. What parts are new or unknown?
b. How can members be told?
c. What consequences are needed?

3. DIRECT ACTIVITY FLOW
a. What direction is needed?
b. How can direction be given?
c. How can problems be avoided?

4. LOOK FOR PROGRESS
a. What has been done?
b. What should be done?
c. Is there progress?
d. How can the members be told?

5. POINT OUT CONSEQUENCES
a. What ones are happening?
b. What ones could happen?
c. How can they be pointed out?

❖ INTERVENING ❖

1. IS INTERVENING NEEDED?
a. Who can stop the conflict?

2. STOP CONFLICT
a. How can the conflict be stopped?
b. Is more needed?
c. Who should be the guide?

3. FIND A BETTER WAY
a. What are some better ways?
b. Select a better way.
c. Practice the better way.

4. SETTLE CONFLICT
a. Is a settlement needed?
b. What settlements would fit?
c. Select a settlement?
d. Monitor the settlement.

5. DOCUMENT CONFLICT
a. Was a better way needed? (1-6, 9)
b. Was a settlement needed? (1-9)

THINKING ABOUT ★
★ SUPERVISING ★

1. Think about what supervising is needed before an activity begins.
   (Step Toward Success By Thinking Ahead)

2. Supervise only the steps of the activity that require it. *(Increase Motivation)*

3. New and complex activities require careful supervising. *(Promote Motivation & Success)*

4. If the activity can be performed in many ways, let those involved decide how.
   (Engender Creativity)

5. If the activity can't be performed with present behavior, let those involved learn.
   (Foster the Desire to Learn)

6. Always, look for progress and its consequences. *(Seek Out Quality)*

7. Avoid conflicts by pointing out progress and its consequences. *(Build Harmony)*

8. Use questions to point out progress and its consequences. *(Foster Rational Citizens)*

9. Connect members' behavior with the values of the group. *(Foster Civil Citizens)*

THINKING ABOUT ★
★ CONFLICTS ★

▼ Is More Needed? ▼
CONSIDER ▼

1. Does the same conflict continue during an activity or across activities?

2. Does the conflict interrupt the activities of those not involved in the conflict?

3. Do those involved have a history of conflicts?

4. Does the conflict damage property?

5. Does the conflict put someone in danger?

▲ CONSIDER ▲
Is a Settlement Needed? ▲

Thinking Guidelines ▼

1. If 1 or 2, then a better way is usually required.

2. If 4 or 5, then a settlement is usually required.

3. If 3, then look carefully at the history of conflicts.

4. If a settlement is needed, then the selected better way is practiced first.

5. To make decisions, review the history and types of conflicts as often as possible.

❖ LEARNING ❖

1. **IS LEARNING NEEDED?**
   a. What needs to be learned?
   b. Why learn it?

2. **ORGANIZE RESOURCES**
   a. What resources help?
   b. Locate, transfer, and arrange.

3. **UNPACK RESOURCES**
   a. Where is the knowledge?
   b. What do the resources tell?
   c. Is the knowledge clear?
   d. Does the knowledge help?

4. **PACK KNOWLEDGE**
   a. How can it be arranged?
   b. When are it be arranged?
   c. What more could be learned?

5. **RETURN RESOURCES**
   a. What needs to be returned?
   b. When can they be returned?
   c. How can they be returned?

❖ GROUP VALUES ❖

All Members have the RIGHT-To-Receive and the DUTY-To-Provide:

1. **HEALTH:** Equal access to emotional, intellectual, and physical health care.

2. **JUSTICE:** Equal access to impartial judgments designed to resolve conflicts between members and systems.

3. **MEMBERSHIP:** Participation in group activities during which members receive the cooperation of other members and systems.

4. **REPRESENTATION:** Opportunities to speak out about the design and operation of group activities.

5. **QUALITY:** Opportunities to perform activities at a level of excellence.

6. **ADAPTATION:** Opportunities to handle a wider range of activities.

7. **EVOLUTION:** Opportunities to discover new activities and systems.

8. **RESOURCING:** Opportunities to invent, distribute, and use resources so that present and future members and systems have an increased chance to flourish.

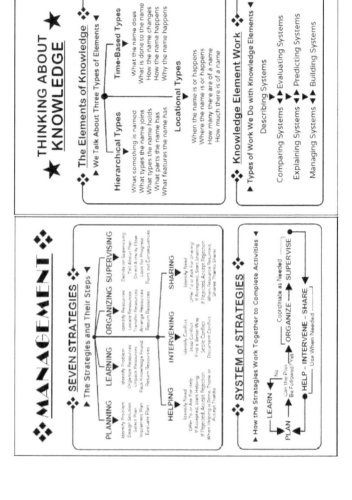

THINKING ABOUT KNOWLEDGE

The Elements of Knowledge
▶ We Talk About Three Types of Elements ▼

Hierarchical Types
▶
What something is named
What types the name joins
What parts the name holds
What features the name has

Time-Based Types
▶
What the name does
What is done to the name
How the name changes
How the name happens
Why the name happens

Locational Types
▶
When the name is or happens
Where the name is or happens
How many there are of a name
How much there is of a name

Knowledge Element Work
▶ Types of Work We Do with Knowledge Elements ▼

Describing Systems
Comparing Systems ▶ Evaluating Systems
Explaining Systems ▶ Predicting Systems
Managing Systems ▶ Building Systems

MANAGEMENT

SEVEN STRATEGIES
▶ The Strategies and Their Steps ▼

PLANNING
Identify Problem
Design Solution
Select Plan
Implement Plan
Evaluate Plan

LEARNING
Identify Problem
Organize Resources
Unpack Resources
Pack Knowledge Found
Return Resources

ORGANIZING
Identify Resources
Locate Resources
Transfer Resources
Arrange Resources
Return Resources

SUPERVISING
Decide on Supervising
Tell About Plan
Direct Activity Flow
Look for Progress
Point out Consequences

HELPING
Identify Need
Offer To or Ask For Help
If Accepted, Start Helping
If Rejected, Accept Rejection
When Helping is Done, Thank or
Accept Thanks

INTERVENING
Identify Conflict
Stop Conflict
Find a Better Way
Settle Conflict
Document Conflict

SHARING
Identify Need
Offer To or Ask For Sharing
If Accepted, Start Sharing
If Rejected, Accept Rejection
When Resource Returned,
Shared Thanks Shared

SYSTEM of STRATEGIES
▶ How the Strategies Work Together to Complete Activities ▼

LEARN → No
Can the Plan
Be Followed? Yes
PLAN → Coordinate as Needed
ORGANIZE → SUPERVISE
HELP – INTERVENE – SHARE
Use When Needed

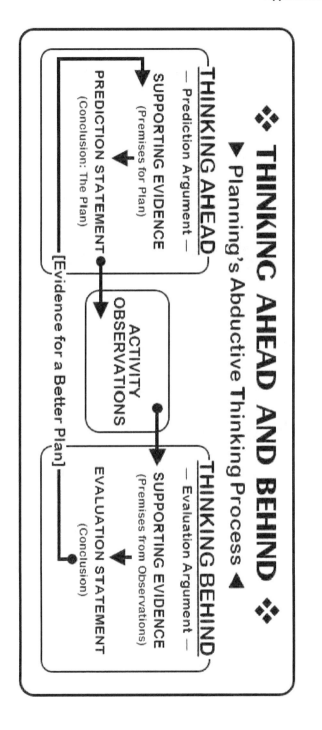

❖ THINKING AHEAD AND BEHIND ❖
▼ Planning's Abductive Thinking Process ▲

THINKING AHEAD
— Prediction Argument —

SUPPORTING EVIDENCE
(Premises for Plan)

PREDICTION STATEMENT
(Conclusion: The Plan)

ACTIVITY
OBSERVATIONS

THINKING BEHIND
— Evaluation Argument —

SUPPORTING EVIDENCE
(Premises from Observations)

EVALUATION STATEMENT
(Conclusion)

[Evidence for a Better Plan]

Management Achievement Buttons

These are colorful: See www.managingourselves.org

They come in various sizes for buttons or badges.

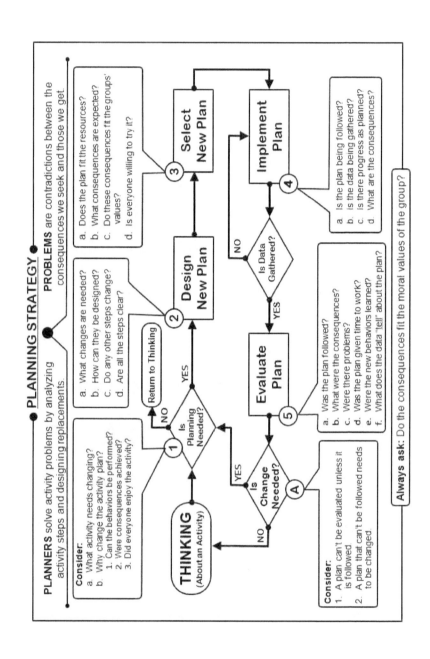

● PLANNING STRATEGY ●

PLANNERS solve activity problems by analyzing activity steps and designing replacements.

PROBLEMS are contradictions between the consequences we seek and those we get.

Consider:
a. What activity needs changing?
b. Why change the activity plan?
   1. Can the behaviors be performed?
   2. Were consequences achieved?
   3. Did everyone enjoy the activity?

THINKING
(About an Activity)

① Is Planning Needed?

a. What changes are needed?
b. How can they be designed?
c. Do any other steps change?
d. Are all the steps clear?

Return to Thinking

NO / YES

② Design New Plan

a. Does the plan fit the resources?
b. What consequences are expected?
c. Do these consequences fit the groups' values?
d. Is everyone willing to try it?

③ Select New Plan

Is Data Gathered? NO / YES

④ Implement Plan

a. Is the plan being followed?
b. Is the data being gathered?
c. Is there progress as planned?
d. What are the consequences?

⑤ Evaluate Plan

a. Was the plan followed?
b. What were the consequences?
c. Were there problems?
d. Was the plan given time to work?
e. Were the new behaviors learned?
f. What does the data "tell" about the plan?

Ⓐ Is Change Needed? YES / NO

Consider:
1. A plan can't be evaluated unless it is followed
2. A plan that can't be followed needs to be changed

Always ask: Do the consequences fit the moral values of the group?

What Management? Game

Preparing to Play the Game

Before playing the What Management? Game, children know or can do the following.

1. Children know that it is okay to use the strategies elsewhere.
2. Are firm on a specific strategy's steps.
3. Children can identify what strategy is being used in-the-moment.

The first is a direct social communication, a request, to children. The second ensures that the students can apply the strategy. The third that children are aware of who is doing what for whom with a range of classroom activities. It is at this point, the What Managment? Game can begin.

The What Management? Game is very similar to that venerable activity that occurs in all classrooms "Show and Tell." However, instead of children describing what they have done or built, the game focuses on them observing *who is doing what for whom* outside the classroom, be it in the school, home, or community. The major questions of the game cover:

1. What strategy or strategy step was being performed,
2. What strategy or strategy step could be performed, and
3. How the strategy or strategy step could be performed.

The first focuses on *who was doing what for whom*. They are gaining awareness. The second focuses on various ways a management strategy could be performed. This involves agreeing or not agreeing with what is performed and what alternatives are available. Because there are often conflicts in the world seeing alternatives is important. If they can spot a conflict or identify a different way to perform a strategy or strategy step, as replacements, the children are learning to observe the strategies in the world and as something that is not necessarily right or wrong. They are learning that human interactions are not cast in stone, there is no perfect way. It is also a key element to designing and adapting plans. The third question, focuses on illustrating how the alternatives could be performed. This can be a practice time for reviewing, expanding, and practicing various strategies. Thus, the game is the first step towards building successful management behavior outside of the children's immediate range of classroom activities.

Preparing to Play the Game

The game can begin after the organizing and intervening strategies have been taught. This is not a firm rule.

By exposing these differences (as well as sameness) through the manner of thinking that the Game demands, the parties can become unambiguously aware of the wide variety of their social behavior. This helps them establish values and a sense of competence. As the game progresses, it helps to develop a "communication channel" through quick back and forth questioning. Moreover, for children, playing the game gives them a wider view of the variability in human behavior, something akin to the eye-opening view when visiting a new culture. From another perspective, it gives children a bit of "insulation" against the diverse, often chaotic and inappropriate influences that the larger social world thrusts upon them.

When and Where the Game is Played

The game can be played in any location that children, parents and child, or teachers and children are together. Here are some of the most obvious locations: home, store, playground, restaurant, library, and while watching TV. Even an individual child can play this game while out and about. This often requires taking notes for later show-and-tell conversations.

Diversity of Game Questions

The What Management? Game is based the above three questions, but as the children's learning increases, more detail can be added. More and more specific management strategy questions can be asked. These include for example:

1. What strategy is that?
2. What strategy step is that?
3. How would you do that step?
4. What step is next?
5. What strategy could be next?
6. Was the management cohesive or coercive

The entire class may participate. At any point the "How do you know?" or "Why do you think that?" can be asked by the teacher or, eventually, the children with regards to other's answers.

Usually, the child telling will identify the strategy. If not start with the first question and from there skip around, doing all or just a couple of the questions. After the game becomes familiar, the order of asking questions disappears.

What Strategy Step is That?

After each new strategy that is initially taught, isolate the strategy with the question, "What [Strategy] step is that?" Tell children to look for management in the store, restaurant, traveling, or watching television. These are what they bring to class. Often the teacher will have to give a few examples. Here is one:

Teacher: Let's play What Management? My turn. I am in the store and see a person putting food can on the shelf. What strategy is that person performing? [Calls on a child.]

Child: Organizing.

Teacher: Who knows what step of organizing is being done? [Calls on a child.]

Child: Arranging.

Teacher: Raise your hand if you think that is the step the person is doing? [Teacher calls on a child.] Why do you think so?

Child: The person is putting things where they are needed.

Teacher: Raise your hand if you think that answer is correct? [Children raise hands.]

Teacher: [Consequence] I think so, too. It looks to me as if we are all getting to know organizing's steps.

Here is a continuation example of what a child may have observed in a store but at the checkout counter.

Teacher: Let's play What Management? My turn. I am in the store and see a person putting food in a bag for a customer. What strategy is that person performing? [Calls on a child.]

Child: Organizing.

Teacher: Who knows what step of organizing is being done? [Calls on a child.]

Child: Transferring.

Teacher: Raise your hand if you think that is the step the person is doing? [Teacher calls on a child.] Why do you think so?

Child: The person is putting things where they are needed.

Teacher: Raise your hand if you think that answer is correct? [Children raise hands.] [Techer call on a child.]

Teacher: Why don't you think it is transferring?

Child: They are arranging the food in a bag.

Teacher: [Consequence] I think you are both correct because the person is transferring them to the bag and arranging them in the bag at the same time. The two steps are done together. It all depends on from where you start looking. [consequence.] You are all getting to know the details of organizing.

[Later, at the end of the day.]

Teacher: [prompt] Keep looking for strategies. We will play *What Management?* again tomorrow.

If a wrong answer occurs, correct with the right answer or let others, as done above, disagree, and then work it out like in the last example.

As children become firm on a strategy's steps, it is helpful to prompt them to look for specific strategies. For example, you may want to focus on the intervening strategy. Thus, the teacher can ask them to spot conflicts and what was done to manage them—remembering that you would not make this request without have gone over what a conflict is within the classroom and employed the intervention strategy a few times in class. This is a good one to observe from watching television.

Testing

How to test the success of the What Management? There are four indicators of success. Each tells something a little different about the extent of the success in teaching children to play the game and learn from it.

The first indicator is that children continue with any instance of the game by playing their part. This indicator reveals that children are enjoying playing the game. They sense positive consequences from the game, including their interaction with their teammates. They may not ask about management, but they respond to questions. Thus, the assumption is that the teaching has been positive and that some learning is taking place.

The second indicator is children's contributions to the game once started. They not only answer questions but they ask them as well without prompting. These self-initiated contributions reveal the extent to which children's skill at observing and identifying management behavior is improving and they find asking questions about the world of management positive. Very seldom will children actively play a game at which they don't feel successful or don't value the relationship it establishes. A level of management comfort has been reached if they continue the game by taking turns without hesitation.

The third, if children's answers are correct more often than not. This reveals that their management skills are gaining in quality. They are seeing management happening all around them. If they can answer the "How do you know?" question more often than not, a substantial benefit from playing the game has occurred. More than just acquiring knowledge of the management strategies has occurred, a highly positive relationship between players has emerged.

Finally, if children initiate the game, their motivation has reached the "choice" stage. They are finding value in what they are learning and who they are learning it with. Scream for joy! Playing the game has been successful on all fronts.

WHEN DOES THE GAME END?

The What Management? Game can be played for years. It will drop out at the point at which the observations of others management behavior offer no more challenge, assuming that the interaction of players is positive. This evolution is similar to the carrying, feeding, or reading to children. When children are proficient at a replacement behavior, the need for the old one disappears. However, the What Management? Game is more like Monopoly or cribbage. Its playing may never end because the world is always changing, as are the players. The nightly news or the daily news stories provide a great deal of wonderfully and bizarrely interesting management behavior to analyze. And when they can provide cohesive management to replace coercive management, children are well on their way to becoming ARC citizens.

Index

Name Index

)

CPSIA information can be obtained
at www.ICGtesting.com
Printed in the USA
LVHW080134291022
731827LV00001B/46